The Cambridge Companion to Old English Literature

CAMBRIDGE COMPANIONS TO LITERATURE

The Cambridge Companion to
Old English Literature

Edited by
MALCOLM GODDEN AND MICHAEL LAPIDGE

CAMBRIDGE
UNIVERSITY PRESS

Published by the Press Syndicate of the University of Cambridge
The Pitt Building, Trumpington Street, Cambridge CB2 1RP
40 West 20th Street, New York, NY 10011–4211, USA
10 Stamford Road, Oakleigh, Melbourne 3166, Australia

First published 1991
Reprinted, 1992, 1993, 1994, 1998

Printed in Great Britain by the University Printing House, Cambridge

British Library cataloguing in publication data

The Cambridge companion to Old English Literature.
1. Old English Literature – Critical studies
I. Godden, Malcolm   II. Lapidge, Michael
829.09

Library of Congress cataloguing in publication data

The Cambridge Companion to Old English Literature / edited by Malcolm
Godden and Michael Lapidge.
    p.   cm.
Includes bibliographical references.
Includes index.
ISBN 0 521 37438 3 (hardback). – ISBN 0 521 37794 3(paperback)
1. English Literature – Old English, ca. 450–1100 – History and criticism.   2.
England – Civilization – To 1066.   3. Civilization, Anglo-Saxon.   I. Godden,
Malcolm. II. Lapidge, Michael.
PR173.C36   1991
829'.09–dc20   90–2673   CIP

ISBN 0 521 37794 3 paperback

CE

Contents

Contributors

JANET BATELY, University of London

CHRISTINE FELL, University of Nottingham

ROBERTA FRANK, University of Toronto

MILTON McC. GATCH, Union Theological Seminary, New York

HELMUT GNEUSS, University of Munich

MALCOLM GODDEN, University of Oxford

MICHAEL LAPIDGE, University of Cambridge

PATRIZIA LENDINARA, University of Palermo

JOHN D. NILES, University of California at Berkeley

KATHERINE O'BRIEN O'KEEFFE, Texas A&M University

BARBARA C. RAW, University of Keele

FRED C. ROBINSON, Yale University

DONALD G. SCRAGG, University of Manchester

JOSEPH B. TRAHERN, JR, University of Tennessee

PATRICK WORMALD, University of Oxford

Preface

O N 26 November 1882 Gerard Manley Hopkins wrote to his fellow-poet and friend Robert Bridges: 'I am learning Anglo-Saxon and it is a vastly superior thing to what we have now.' W. H. Auden too was inspired by his first experience of Old English literature: 'I was spellbound. This poetry, I knew, was going to be my dish . . . I learned enough to read it, and Anglo-Saxon and Middle English poetry have been one of my strongest, most lasting influences.' The list of modern poets who have been influenced by Old English literature (that term is now generally preferred to 'Anglo-Saxon' when referring to the language and vernacular writings of pre-Conquest England) could be extended to include Pound, Graves, Wilbur and many others. One does not have to agree with Hopkins's belief in the superiority of Old English as a medium for poetry to accept the importance of the writings of the Anglo-Saxons for an understanding of the cultural roots of the English-speaking world. The practice of looking back to their writings and their social organization in order to comprehend the present has continued ever since the sixteenth century, when the Elizabethans turned to them in support of their religious and political polemic.

It scarcely needs emphasizing that literature is the record of a particular culture; what Old English literature offers us is not only a mode of poetic expression which startled Hopkins and Auden but a window into a different world of beliefs, myths, anxieties, perspectives. The Anglo-Saxons were at the meeting-point of two major cultural traditions. From their barbarian origins, continually enriched by renewed contact with Scandinavian invaders and continental trade and political relations, they brought a Germanic inheritance of legend, poetic technique, law, pagan beliefs and tribal sympathies. From their contact with the representatives and books of Christianity, they absorbed much of the Latin, and a little of the Greek, tradition of history, religion, science and rhetoric. They were also at a chronological meeting-place. Late Anglo-Saxon England was a sophisticated and advanced country in politics, economic organization and vernacular literature; her peoples looked back, sometimes critically, often nostalgically, to a past when they were barbarians and Rome was dominant. Looking forward, they saw themselves approaching a time of crisis, the imminent end of the world that they knew, and as that anticipated end drew near, they were increasingly inclined to see the Viking raids as signs of apocalypse. Their writings reflect at times the nostalgic brooding on the past, at times the excitement of newly acquired knowledge or the sophisticated possibilities of writing, and at times the urgency of a period of crisis.

In choosing the subjects to be considered in this book, we have been particularly concerned to show the range of writing in Old English and the ways in which that writing draws on the cultural and social preoccupations of the time. The small group of poems which have come to be recognized as the heart of the literary canon are discussed fairly extensively in the relevant chapters: *The Dream of the Rood* in ch. 13, *The Battle of Maldon* in ch. 6, the so-called elegies including *The Wanderer* and *The Seafarer* in ch. 10, and *Beowulf* has a chapter to itself (ch. 8). The collection aims to provide orientation and guidance for those approaching the study of Old English literature for the first time. The contributors have thus been asked by the editors to emphasize established understandings rather than new and more speculative ideas; but, perhaps fortunately, not all have followed the editors' request, and some indication of the many areas of uncertainty, the problems still to be resolved or the traditional views that need to be challenged will emerge, we hope, from the book as a whole.

MALCOLM GODDEN
MICHAEL LAPIDGE

June 1990

Note on the text

Old English poetry, including *Beowulf*, is quoted throughout from ASPR. Prose texts are quoted from the relevant standard editions, and are signalled by editor's name (e.g. *Pastoral Care*, ed. Sweet, p. 10); full bibliographical details of the editions in question are to be found in 'Further reading', below, pp. 282–91.

Abbreviations

ASE   *Anglo-Saxon England*

ASPR   The Anglo-Saxon Poetic Records, ed. G. P. Krapp and E. V. K. Dobbie, 6 vols. (New York, 1931–42)

EETS   Early English Text Society

EHD   *English Historical Documents, I: c. 500–1042*, ed. D. Whitelock, 2nd ed. (London, 1979); cited by page number

HE   Bede's *Historia ecclesiastica gentis Anglorum* or *Ecclesiastical History*, ed. and trans. B. Colgrave and R. A. B. Mynors (Oxford, 1969); also trans. L. Sherley-Price (Harmondsworth, 1955)

Chronological table of the Anglo-Saxon period

from *c.* 400	Germanic peoples settle in Britain
c. 540	Gildas in *De excidio Britanniae* laments the effects of the Germanic settlements on the supine Britons
597	St Augustine arrives in Kent to convert the English
616	death of Æthelberht, king of Kent
c. 625	ship-burial at Sutton Hoo (mound 1)
633	death of Edwin, king of Northumbria
635	Bishop Aidan established in Lindisfarne
642	death of Oswald, king of Northumbria
664	Synod of Whitby
669	Archbishop Theodore and Abbot Hadrian arrive in Canterbury
674	monastery of Monkwearmouth founded
682	monastery of Jarrow founded
687	death of St Cuthbert
689	death of Cædwalla, king of Wessex
690	death of Archbishop Theodore
c. 700	'Lindisfarne Gospels' written and decorated
709	deaths of Bishops Wilfrid and Aldhelm
716–57	Æthelbald king of Mercia
731	Bede completes his *Ecclesiastical History*
735	death of Bede
754	death of St Boniface, Anglo-Saxon missionary in Germany
757–96	Offa king of Mercia
781	Alcuin of York meets Charlemagne in Parma and thereafter leaves York for the Continent
793	Vikings attack Lindisfarne
802–39	Ecgberht king of Wessex
804	death of Alcuin
839–56	Æthelwulf king of Wessex
869	Vikings defeat and kill Edmund, king of East Anglia
871–99	Alfred the Great king of Wessex

878	Alfred defeats the Viking army at the battle of Edington, and the Vikings settle in East Anglia (879–80)
899–924	Edward the Elder king of Wessex
924–39	Athelstan king of Wessex and first king of all England
937	battle of *Brunanburh*: Athelstan defeats an alliance of Scots and Scandinavians
957–75	Edgar king of England
959–88	Dunstan archbishop at Canterbury
963–84	Æthelwold bishop at Winchester
964	secular clerics expelled from the Old Minster, Winchester, and replaced by monks
971–92	Oswald archbishop at York
973	King Edgar crowned at Bath
978–1016	Æthelred 'the Unready' king of England
985–7	Abbo of Fleury at Ramsey
991	battle of Maldon: the Vikings defeat an English army led by Byrhtnoth
c. 1010	death of Ælfric, abbot of Eynsham
1011	Byrhtferth's *Enchiridion*
1013	the English submit to Swein, king of Denmark
1016–35	Cnut king of England
1023	death of Wulfstan, archbishop of York
1042–66	Edward the Confessor king of England
1066	battle of Hastings: the English army led by Harold is defeated by the Norman army led by William the Conqueror

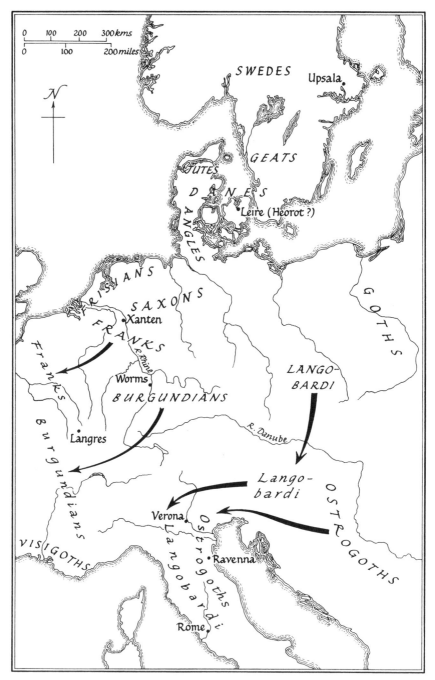

Fig. 1 Germanic peoples of the Migration Age (*c.* 400–600 AD)

Fig. 2 Anglo-Saxon England

PATRICK WORMALD

1 Anglo-Saxon society and its literature

THE country in which this book was conceived, and the literary language in which it is written, are both more than a thousand years old. The 'kingdom of England' was created by Anglo-Saxon politicians, soldiers and churchmen in the ninth and tenth centuries. They and their subjects have left us a significant literature in their own language. Readers may be tempted to take both facts for granted. Yet each is not only exceptional but also extraordinary. No other European state has existed within approximately its modern boundaries for anything like so long. Few other current European literatures have specimens anything like so old. France, Spain and Italy reached roughly today's political shape before England, Germany at much the same time. But all were to be broken up by external conquest or internal collapse. Their 'resurrection' belongs to later-medieval, early-modern or nineteenth-century history. England itself, notoriously, was overrun by the Normans in 1066, but it did not break up. Among sub-Roman successor-states, at least one other had a vernacular literature for a time. The great Frankish king and western emperor, Charlemagne (768–814), had a collection made of 'barbarian and most ancient songs, in which . . . wars of kings of old were sung'. Little or none of it is extant. What does survive on the Continent is, by English standards, limited in quantity and restricted in theme. Literary vernaculars, whether Romance or Germanic, Icelandic or Provençal, flowered only from the twelfth century. Conditions in England after its conquest by French-speakers were in no way conducive to the preservation of native literature. The fact that relatively so much survives is probably because relatively more was written. The first priority of a historical introduction to Old English literature must be to describe the politically precocious society from which it emerged. But a second, hardly less pressing priority, is to explain how it came to be.[1]

Most textbooks on Anglo-Saxon England treat its long history, from the fifth to the eleventh century, as one period. It ought to be divided into two (at least). The best of many reasons is that a single kingdom of England came to exist only after, and up to a point as a result of, the Viking invasions in the ninth century. Even to think of England as a unit

1

before then is to give an impression that it was somehow programmed to develop in a way which other European countries took up to a millennium to follow. That in turn devalues the statecraft of its founders.

Little can be known of the period between 407 and 597, when most of what had been Roman 'Britannia' was settled by Germanic-speakers whom it is convenient to call Anglo-Saxons – though the Angles and Saxons, from the neck of the Jutland peninsula in Denmark and the north German coast (see Fig. 1), were certainly accompanied by others from the Low Countries and perhaps Scandinavia. Most of the sources that purport to tell this story were assembled at a much later date from suitably adjusted oral tradition, myth and imaginative fiction. What can be said for sure is that, by the time we have serviceable records, the leading language of lowland Britain was a variety of Germanic most closely resembling that spoken on the opposite side of the North Sea. Archaeology gives some support to the impression of colonization from that general area. It also testifies to a sharp economic decline in the quality of life once sustained by the Roman province; and, by the sixth century, to the emergence of a warrior culture, whose men were buried with weapons of war, and women with rich jewellery that illustrated its profits.[2]

The picture perceptibly clarifies from 597, because Pope Gregory the Great in that year sent a mission to the people that he called the 'Angles'. Christianity, a 'religion of the Book', brought literacy on a wholly different scale from whatever forms of written communication pagans may have used. Before long, it brought written history. The story of the conversion of the Anglo-Saxons to Christianity was told by Bede in his *Ecclesiastical History of the English People*, finished in 731, perhaps the most eloquent historical work of the European Middle Ages. The political pattern revealed by Bede comprises a dozen or more kingdoms c. 600, varying in size from the Isle of Wight to Deira (roughly modern Yorkshire, between the rivers Tees and Humber: see Fig. 2). The trend of the seventh and eighth centuries was for pike to swallow minnows. The predatory metaphor is apt. King Cædwalla of Wessex, which covered all south-western Britain (except for Cornwall) by the 680s, graciously conceded baptism to two young princes of Wight, so that when he beheaded them as part of a plan to 'exterminate all natives', they could go at once to heaven (*HE* IV.16). The process of elimination left just four kingdoms by c. 800: Northumbria (Deira plus Bernicia, the region extending north to the Firth of Forth); East Anglia (modern Norfolk and Suffolk, whose names witness its own bipartite origins); Wessex; and Mercia, occupying the whole Midland area between the other three. In the later eighth century, Mercia was certainly the most powerful of these realms. Its greatest king, Offa (757–96), overran the kingdoms of Sussex, Kent and East Anglia. But there is no clear sign that this process would eventually have left just one monster in the pond. East Anglia and Kent regained independence when Offa died. Both were again engulfed by his successor, but East Anglia had its own kings once more for the forty years before its conquest by the Vikings in 869.

Historians have nonetheless been encouraged to see a foreshadowed unity in a famous passage of Bede's *History*. He says that all kingdoms south of the Humber submitted periodically to the 'empire' (*imperium*) of one ruler (*HE* II.5). For much of the seventh century, when the alleged overlord was one of the three Northumbrian kings, Edwin (617–33), Oswald (634–42) and Oswiu (642–70), this 'empire' would have dominated most of England, and some of Scotland and Wales. Documentary evidence shows that the status was claimed by the Mercian king, Æthelbald (716–57). The *Anglo-Saxon Chronicle*, a source compiled in Wessex in the reign of King Alfred (871–99), enrols his grandfather, Ecgberht (802–39), in the series. Both sources imply that those who held this status were hailed as rulers of Britain (Latin: *rex Britanniae*, OE: *Bretwalda*). Yet it is equally clear that, whatever the origins or meaning of such overlordship, it was resented and resisted by subject peoples. The bones of Oswald, whom Bede saw as a saint, were at first denied burial in a monastery of the kingdom of Lindsey (Lincolnshire), because its people 'pursued him even when dead with their ancient hatred, since he had once conquered them' (*HE* III.11). There was no foundation here for an emerging sense of common identity.

The fragmentation of *Britannia* relates in an important way to the emergence of a literary vernacular. The Anglo-Saxon settlements were only one of many 'Barbarian Invasions' of the Roman Empire. Elsewhere, there was surprisingly little violence, and notably few signs of antipathy to *Romanitas*, or Roman civilization. 'Barbarian' culture in fact succumbed to the indigenous cultures of the West, as witnessed by the rapid conversion of most barbarians to Christianity, and their ultimate adoption of Romance speech. Decisive in this respect was the survival of a provincial aristocracy, in government service and more obviously in the church, that was prepared to accommodate its new masters. This provincial aristocracy's collective memory of Roman arrangements was a crucial reason why Gaul, Spain and Italy became unitary kingdoms soon after the empire's fall. But in Britain, the Celtic aristocracy lost what Latin veneer it once had: Welsh, unlike French, is not a Romance language, but a Celtic one. The largely retrospective traditions of both the native Britons and the Anglo-Saxons bespoke intense mutual hostility. They are borne out by the paucity of Celtic loanwords in English. Bede was sure that Britons had done nothing to convert his people. Christianity, undeniably, made much less progress in the sixth century among Anglo-Saxons than elsewhere. Vigorous competition for Britain between the military aristocracies of

Celt and Saxon destroyed the *Romanitas* that each might otherwise have absorbed. The balkanization of *Britannia* was a function of the degree of discontinuity between its Roman and post-Roman experience. By the same token, however, Germanic culture in Britain was spared the sort of pressure that today induces ex-colonies, however proud of their own traditions, to write European poetry, wear European suits, erect European buildings and aspire to European constitutions. Liturgical books on the Continent were decorated with designs from the Romano-Christian repertoire, as probably encountered on the wall-hangings of churches and the vestments of churchmen. When gospelbooks appear in England (most famously, the Lindisfarne Gospels of *c.* 700), their decoration reproduces the motifs hitherto used by smiths to adorn the weapons and jewellery of a warrior elite. It is a useful metaphor of what happened to literary language. The Laws of Æthelberht of Kent (d. 616) and the Frankish law code, the *Lex Salica*, both date from the immediate post-conversion period. Each is almost wholly 'Germanic' in content. But *Lex Salica* is in Latin whereas Æthelberht's laws are in English. Barbarian culture on the Continent was suffocated by the civilization it tried to emulate. In Britain it had room to breathe.

As told by Bede, the conversion of the Anglo-Saxons was a tale of two missions.[3] One was led from Rome by Gregory's disciple, Augustine. It was at first effective with Æthelberht of Kent (*HE* I.25–6), with other south-eastern kings and also with Edwin of Northumbria (*HE* II.9–14). But when its royal patrons died (or were killed, like Edwin), it nearly lost its base at Canterbury and became quiescent. The initiative passed to Iona, the abbey founded by the Irish prince Columba (d. 597). Oswald, Edwin's Northumbrian successor, had been baptized when exiled among the Irish, who had adopted Christianity in the fifth century. To re-establish Christianity among his people, he invited missionaries from Iona, and Aidan founded the abbey and bishopric of Lindisfarne in 635 (*HE* III.2–6). Partly because of the political power wielded by Oswald and Oswiu, the Irish mission made a more pronounced impact than the Roman. Its converts included lapsed kingdoms like Northumbria, and those like Mercia as yet pagan. And whereas those evangelized by other missions invariably lapsed at least once, apostasy was almost unknown among the disciples of Irishmen. However, Roman and Irish churchmen differed on several issues, above all the way to calculate the date of the movable feast of Easter. At the Synod of Whitby (664), the matter was decided in favour of Roman methods (*HE* III.25–6). Some Irishmen based at Lindisfarne withdrew. The way lay clear for organization of the English church by Archbishop Theodore (669–90), the papal nominee for Canterbury (*HE* IV.1–3).

In reading Bede's compelling account of the origin of the English church, we must remember that he is not only an excellent source but also a superb historian who, like any other master of the craft, used his own perspective and intelligence to give events a pattern. That pattern has certain idiosyncrasies, and needs modification from other viewpoints. Thus, Bede was an expert on Christian chronology in general, and Easter reckoning in particular. He very probably gave the Easter controversy more significance for contemporaries than it really had. This left an impression of conflict between 'Roman' and 'Celtic' churches that was of course amplified by the confessional bias of later ages, and which is quite false: the Irishmen who were Aidan's counterparts on the Continent showed unusual devotion to Rome. Again, Bede was a Northumbrian. He might be expected to place special emphasis on Iona's mission. He was also a monk from the twin monasteries of Monkwearmouth and Jarrow, which had been founded by Benedict Biscop (d. 690). Biscop had escorted Theodore from Rome, had been briefly abbot at Canterbury, and had used contacts made on his continental travels to build monasteries 'in Roman style' (Bede's proud claim has been fully borne out by site excavation of, among much else, window-glass unparalleled at that time in quantity and quality). Thus, it may also be anticipated that Bede would put still more stress on Rome. Yet his own work implies a key role for Frankish Gaul in the conversion of East Anglia and Wessex (*HE* II.15, III.7 and 18–19), while Biscop's glaziers and masons, as well as some of his books, came from Gaul. The likelihood is that Christianity's advent among the Anglo-Saxons was altogether less neat than pre-supposed by Bede's pattern or any other. Early English Christian culture was startlingly eclectic. Its liturgy and art reveal a range of influences extending beyond Rome, Ireland and Gaul to the Levant, southern Italy, North Africa, Spain and Pictland.[4]

Equally striking is the sheer depth of religious scholarship in parts of the early English church. The Monkwearmouth/Jarrow library collected on Biscop's European travels enabled Bede to read almost all there was to read of the Christian learning of Latin late Antiquity (he also knew some Greek). His experience was not unique. His older West Saxon contemporary, Aldhelm (d. 709), was hardly less learned. Later, the Northumbrian Alcuin (d. 804) described journeys by his own teacher, and listed the books available to York that made him a scholar sought out by Charlemagne himself. Yet if not unique, it must again be stressed that Bede was not typical. Welcome as is the modern quest for *recherché* learning in Anglo-Saxon religious poetry, few monastic libraries can have been as rich as Monkwearmouth/Jarrow's. Bede excused his scissors-and-paste approach to scriptural commentary precisely on the grounds that the major Church Fathers were beyond the material, and indeed intellectual, means of his fellow-countrymen.[5]

Another feature of Bede's account of Anglo-Saxon conversion that raises doubts is the impression given of its smooth, almost automatic, progress. He notes, typically, 'At this time, the [. . .] people received the Faith from the holy Bishop [. . .] under the rule of King [. . .].' Bede wrote with an urgent didactic purpose. A letter of the last year of his life shows that he was seriously worried by the state of the church. He aimed to recall contemporaries to the example of their Christian evangelists. It was no part of his plan to describe the paganism from which they had been rescued. There is thus a temptation to quarry the evidence for traces of 'pagan survival'. But it is much better to stress how very scarce they are (cf. below, pp. 126–41). Compared to Irish, still more to Norse, literature, the Anglo-Saxon corpus is without clear evidence of pagan belief (just as early Anglo-Saxon stone sculpture has a resolutely Romano-Christian iconography, where later Viking crosses are unashamedly syncretist). Archaeology shows pagan cemeteries and burial customs being replaced during the seventh and eighth centuries by near-unfurnished inhumation, first in east-west rows, then in churchyards. Religious change *en masse* is as difficult a thing as historians ever have to explain. No progress is made by denying that there was any real change at all.

All the same, it is reasonable, assessing the conversion of the Anglo-Saxons, to reckon with what was not lost, as well as with what was gained. Inasmuch as Bede does offer a solution, he hints at the appeal of a system of consolation to a world far from sure of its destiny after death. His famous story of the debate on conversion held at Edwin's court has a nobleman compare human life with a sparrow's flight through a warm and well-lit hall in the depths of winter, where king and warriors feast, like those in the heroic poem, *Beowulf*: 'what follows or what went before, we do not know at all; if this new doctrine brings any more certainty, it seems right to follow it' (*HE* II.13). The story has an interesting echo in the *Life of St Guthlac*: this late seventh-century Mercian prince left a warrior's life of rapine for a hermit's spiritual warfare, after contemplating 'the miserable deaths . . . of the ancient kings of his line'.[6] That 'the wages of heroism is death' was just the impression that *Beowulf* itself made on J. R. R. Tolkien. Bede, by contrast, stressed the immortal fame won by Oswald as a Christian martyr (*HE* III.9–13), when his victorious reign ended in defeat and brutal dismemberment by the pagan Penda in 642. Positive considerations apart, the Church had by 597 acquired some expertise in mission techniques. As is well known, Gregory proposed the conversion of pagan shrines into churches (a policy adopted by his papal relative in Rome itself a century before), and that Christian feasts coincide with pagan festivals, as Christmas had been fixed at the Roman Winter Solstice on 25th December (*HE* I.30). Another old move put to new use in England was to accept that pagan gods existed, but to assert that they were no more than deified heroes: Bede thus had no difficulty in giving Woden his traditional place in royal genealogies (*HE* I.15). In this connection, there is a possible Irish contribution too. Mainstream theology discouraged speculation about the afterlife of the unbaptized, and forbade prayers for them. But a persistent theme in Irish Christianity was a refusal to see good pagans as damned. The problem of the Antipodes (featuring in a hymn ascribed to Columba) worried Irishmen, because it raised the issue of those with no chance to hear Christ's word. Ancestors matter to most aristocracies: an eighth-century continental king preferred feasting with his forebears in hell to dining alone in heaven. Hence, a relative optimism about the spiritual fate of ancestors could well explain why Irish conversions 'stuck', whereas those by continentals wavered. But perhaps most important of all is that the Old Testament was the story of another tribal people with a special relationship to the God of Battles. That the spread of Christianity has not spread 'peace on earth' is a truism. Some kings went Guthlac's way, among them Cædwalla, the ferocious conqueror of Wight who abdicated to go on pilgrimage to Rome (*HE* V.7); but not many. Nor was it demanded of them. The Bible itself gave Anglo-Saxons a warrant for a sincere change in their faith without a revolution in their society.

One aspect of Bede's *History* was certainly at odds with reality, but nonetheless had the most momentous consequences. In hindsight, it is easy to forget how strange it is that he wrote the history of the English as if they were a single people (*gens*). The unique power of Bede's historical vision did more than anything else to establish a united 'England' as an ideal invoked by ambitious kings in later ages. But there was no such thing in Bede's time, politically speaking. The conundrum is dissolved by appreciating that this is an *ecclesiastical* history. From his Canterbury contacts (he acknowledged that much of his information came from there, and even implied that it had inspired the whole enterprise), Bede inherited the notion of 'the Angles' as a single people before God, which had inspired Gregory to send his mission, and Augustine to found 'the Church of the English' at Canterbury. Gregory had envisaged two archbishoprics in England and the second was ultimately established at York in 735. But Canterbury never forgot that for two generations after Theodore's arrival in 669, it ruled the whole English church, and it habitually saw its responsibility in such terms. Theodore's first Council, at Hertford (672), was clearly wider-ranging and better-attended than Whitby (though recorded by Bede as a set of minutes (*HE* IV.5–6), whereas he made Whitby an impassioned debate). Among its canons was a proposal for all the bishops of the province to meet annually. By the end of the eighth century, if not before, something like this regularity was achieved, and frequent synods must have fostered a sense of ecclesiastical unity. A council of 747 ordered celebration of the feasts of Gregory 'our father' and Augustine his emissary. By the early eighth century, Bishop Aldhelm at Sherborne and Bishop John of York (d. 721) had been pupils at Canterbury and had doubtless absorbed its way of thinking about church and people (*HE* IV.23 and V.3). Thus, although Bede's was the most powerful voice to speak of the English as a single *gens*, it was not alone. The same note is sounded by the biographer of Gregory the Great writing at Whitby (where Bishop John had been an *alumnus*); by the West Saxon, Boniface (d. 754), who sought to carry the faith over to his people's 'blood and bone' in continental Saxony, and who did so in the closest contact with Rome; and by Alcuin.[7] Much more than grandiloquent claims to *imperium* or 'rule of Britain', the self-styled 'Church of the English' laid ideological foundations for what would come later. It is worth adding that, because councils of the church in the later eighth and early ninth centuries were usually attended by the king and magnates of the dominant Mercian kingdom, they may have furthered notions of some common destiny between secular and ecclesiastical establishments.

The special circumstances of Anglo-Saxon conversion had important implications for the development of a vernacular literature. The role of Canterbury in fostering a sense of English unity may be paralleled by the particular interest of Archbishop Theodore in the possibilities of the English language. Granted the vernacular's early debut in the laws of Æthelberht, it is still necessary to explain how Anglo-Saxons, almost alone among heirs to Christian Latin culture, used their poetry and prose to celebrate its wonders. Theodore was a Greek (from St Paul's home town of Tarsus, a point not lost on grateful English disciples). The eastern church always approved the use of native vernaculars more than the aggressively Latin west, from the days of Ulfila, apostle of the Goths and author of the Gothic Bible, to those of the Eskimos in nineteenth-century Kamchatka. It is thus interesting that Bede should go out of his way to describe how a pupil of Theodore was proficient in *his own language* as well as Latin and Greek (*HE* V.8); hardly a remarkable fact if he merely spoke it. And Theodore's school at Canterbury has recently been shown to have spawned a family of glosses which have frequent recourse to vernacular translation, and which are the oldest glosses of this type in Europe.[8] It may therefore be no coincidence that, according to Bede, the first Anglo-Saxon to compose Christian poetry in his own language, Cædmon, was a cowherd at the abbey of Whitby (*HE* IV.24): Whitby's links with Theodore, through Bishop John and others, were noted above. Nor is it likely to be accident that the bulk of vernacular literature from ninth-century Germany, the only real continental counterpart to Anglo-Saxon output, was variously connected with the abbey of Fulda, founded by the English Boniface; or that the Old Saxon *Heliand* clearly refers to the

Cædmon story in its preface: what marked out English Christian culture as exceptional was also to be found where Anglo-Saxons could pass it on. If the fact that the English church was put in order by a Greek archbishop may help to explain a development of religious verse with no real parallel in Germanic Europe, it cannot account for the corpus of secular 'heroic' poetry; poetry which deals primarily with the ideals and exploits of a warrior society, poetry whose major representative is *Beowulf*. (Current *Beowulf* scholarship has gone far to discredit previous belief in the poem's early date, but has not yet proved that it was late; and it is appropriate to discuss problems of heroic poetry here, because even a late *Beowulf* must have drawn on earlier tradition.) Although the *Beowulf*-poet knew only the Judaeo-Christian God, he also knew that his heroes were pagan: they cremated their dead, a rite never acceptable to the church. The western church officially disapproved of celebrating pagan heroes, for the reason already given: they were (probably) damned. 'What has Ingeld to do with Christ?', demanded Alcuin (referring to a hero who does appear in *Beowulf*) in a famous letter to an English audience: 'the eternal king reigns in Heaven, the lost pagan laments in hell'.[9] Suspicion of the Latin classics did not of course prevent the intensive study without which few of them would have come through the 'Dark Ages'. But that point actually exposes the basic contrast between the two literatures. Nearly all Old English poems survive only in single manuscripts, but heroic verse is extant in mere fragments, apart from *Beowulf* itself, preserved (it seems) because it is about outlandish monsters, like most of the other texts in the manuscript. The sole continental example of heroic verse, the *Hildebrandslied*, may also be a fragment; and, in view of what has just been said, it is perhaps significant that this single truncated specimen comes from Fulda. There must have been something dubious about such material to explain its tenuous survival. However, the Irish did not share the pessimistic view of ancestral prospects; their learned elite ensured that Ireland's was the one early medieval culture, other than England's, with rich vernacular ingredients, including a large body of secular literature about a pre-Christian heroic past. Anglo-Saxons had no learned caste of the Irish type, but many of them were converted by Irishmen, who had found a place for pagans in a Christian cosmos. There is a strong temptation to connect the major Irish role in Anglo-Saxon evangelization with the fact that Ireland and England were the only two parts of the West to celebrate ancestral heroes in their own tongue.

On another view, it might be argued that there is no need to invoke the Anglo-Saxon church in order to explain the existence of Anglo-Saxon heroic poetry. Substantial written composition must be the work of Christians, because the runes used by pagans were not (so far as is known) deployed at length. But why should *Beowulf* not have been written by a layman? There is very little evidence for Anglo-Saxon lay literacy in the early period, and in any case nothing had much chance to survive unless it was eventually copied and kept in a church library. Title-deeds of property or privilege, for example, called 'charters' by Anglo-Saxon historians, were often given to laymen, but all those that are extant had found their way at some point to ecclesiastical archives. Writings intended for entertainment presumably had less chance of survival than legal documents. But if we must conclude that *Beowulf* was ultimately copied by clerical scribes, then clerical hostility to it had clearly to that extent been suspended; so that the main reason to argue its original composition by a layman vanishes. Besides, the ample evidence that churchmen *should not* have bothered with such texts is often evidence that in fact they *did*, and it shows why. Alcuin's letter is mainly an attack on an extravagantly worldly clerical way of life. The council of 747 mentioned above, and a letter of Boniface that partly prompted it, likewise condemn the drinking, feasting, hunting and dragon-decked clothes of the clergy; and these upper-class habits are significantly linked with the patronage of harpists, and liturgical chanting 'in the manner of secular poets'. As the English church became 'established', it tended, as church establishments have (to the anger of Christian enthusiasts, from Christianity's founder onwards), to be identified with society's ruling class. The personnel of the early medieval western church was dominated by the aristocracy. To sing, or to write, of its warrior prototypes came as naturally to them as to live in the style to which, as noblemen, they were accustomed.

The aristocratic ambience of Anglo-Saxon Christianity is crucial. External inspiration may be a necessary condition for the existence of vernacular literature, but it is by no means sufficient. Aristocratic infiltration of the church meant that the idioms of heroic poetry passed into the medium of religious verse. That is not to say that all poems in this style were written by or for noblemen, merely that aristocratic literature set its tone. The cowherd, Cædmon, was obviously not an aristocrat, but the few lines ascribed to him exploit epic vocabulary. 'Dryhten', here and elsewhere the poetic word for the Lord God, meant 'lord of a warband' in *Beowulf* and the early Kentish laws. Nor does it deny the real theological sophistication of some poetry to say that its images of warfare, endurance or 'lordlessness' often come from the young warrior's world. Much of the creative impulse in early English Christianity derives from an aristocratic ethos, whether in literature or in the artistic achievement made possible by aristocratic wealth, and inspired by the love of display that was wealth's normal outlet.

Secular heroic poetry seems to reflect the lifestyle and values of warriors themselves. Protagonists are called *eorl*, the term for 'nobleman' in Kentish law. Their normal weaponry (mailcoat, helmet, sword) is rare enough in burials to imply that it was elite equipment.[10] Older scholars spoke of a 'heroic code', prompting a reaction in the later twentieth century, when Wagnerian images have acquired unhappy connotations. The phrase is unhelpful insofar as it turns social ethic into legal prescription. The aristocratic warband's values were neither more nor less binding than those of a 'gentleman' in a later age: they lose reality as soon as they are precisely defined; they were certainly honoured in breach as much as observance; but they did express the behaviour that a socially dominant class thought proper. The fundamental principle was that the warrior owed loyalty (in theory to the point of death) in return for his lord's generous reward (see also below, pp. 109–11). The ethic is the same as that of 'feudalism', which was simply the period in the history of European lordship when landed reward was central to the relationship instead of just one (usually the last) of the lord's gifts. A recurrent crux of saga is the conflict between loyalties to kindred and lord, memorably epitomized in the *Anglo-Saxon Chronicle*'s story of Cynewulf and Cyneheard: the former's warriors 'said that no kinsman was dearer to them than their lord, and they would never serve his slayer'. Lordship loyalty usually prevails in such tales, but this is not evidence that it was replacing older kinship ties: literature has a predilection for tension that is dramatic because *untypical*, and a warrior society's literature naturally favoured the bond that cemented it.

If heroic poetry is a mirror of a warrior aristocracy, society is also to be viewed from other angles. The major alternative source for early social relationships are law-codes: three seventh-century codes were issued by Kentish kings, and that of King Ine of Wessex (*c.* 690) is preserved as an appendix to the laws of Alfred. These texts show a stratified society, where nobles and slaves both feature prominently, but whose central figure is simply 'free'. Noble or free status was inherited, and expressed by a '*wergeld* (man-money)', payable to one's kin in the event of violent death by the killer(s). Noble blood cost proportionately more than a free man's: up to six times more in Ine's Wessex. A slave had no wergeld as such, but his owner was compensated if he was harmed. Æthelberht's and Alfred's codes both give elaborate lists of bodily injuries, with the payment appropriate to each: 'if a big toe is cut off, let one pay 10/20 shillings'. The point of such a stress on compensation is that early Anglo-Saxon 'law and order' derived from blood-feud. The prospect of vengeance by victim or kin was what deterred aggressors, and the price of blood allowed it to be bought off. Those unable to pay faced a choice of enslavement by an injured party, or exile out of reach of its revenge. The feuds and exiles that bedeck heroic poetry were to this extent part of everyday life.[11]

Impressions of society drawn from legal sources are not, after all, so difficult to reconcile with the literature. Lordship was already making its weight felt in Ine's laws: freemen could be enslaved for working on Sunday, 'unless at a lord's command'. Assessment in hides, units of land originally reflecting the annual needs of a free man and his family, was used to provide king or lord with heavy food-renders. Landlordship and aristocracy tend to go together. Overall, it is from the warrior aristocracy revealed in the literature that the dynamic of change in early Anglo-Saxon society and politics seems to come. The emergent kingdoms of *c.* 600 probably formed around the nucleus of the warrior communities buried in the last phase of pagan cemeteries. The successful seventh-century kings were those whose open frontiers to the north or west gave them access to the loot and lands that would buy the loyalty of warriors, not to mention their specialist wargear. Seventh-century historical narratives offer several examples of young adventurers like Guthlac, their services available to a high bidder, and of exiles who sometimes, like Cædwalla of Wessex, returned to rule. The resentment and rebellion that cut across any putative 'road to English unity' are just what the unquenchable feuds of heroic tradition would lead us to expect. In the best account of heroic society, H. M. Chadwick observed that military nobilities are a cosmopolitan crew, without an inherent loyalty to kings or heroes of their own people, and with a propensity to find 'role-models' throughout the world where they traded their support.[12] It is a warning not to think in terms of automatic national solidarities. And it is a reminder that, as exponents of a late dating for *Beowulf* rightly stress, not all Anglo-Saxon noblemen would see the Danish *Scyldingas* of its opening lines as their natural enemies.

The first of the changes that distinguish Britain under Anglo-Saxons from Anglo-Saxon England was economic. It began back in the seventh century with a revival, or perhaps an unprecedented growth, of trade across the Channel and the North Sea. This stimulated, and was itself stimulated by, replacement of a monometallic gold currency with lower value silver coins better suited to everyday market business. A result was the reappearance of what can be called towns on the English coast, like *Hamwih*, planned in an orderly way for dense population, and more than twice the size of its successor, medieval Southampton. Trade was now based not on the local exchange of necessities and long-distance transfer of luxuries that humanity has practised since hunter-gatherer days, but on low-value commodities transported in bulk. A famous letter of Charlemagne to Offa reveals an exchange of English cloth for continental lava used to make querns. It is part of the evidence that kings protected merchants at the price of levying tolls on their transactions. Offa, like Frankish kings, established a monopoly for coins issued in his name, and must have profited from it. In the long run, the economic expansion that accelerated again from the later ninth century was of course a major determinant of social change. By 1066, one Anglo-Saxon in ten lived in what one can call a town, a ratio that stayed roughly the same until the Industrial Revolution. A law-tract by Archbishop Wulfstan of York (1002–23) looked with significant nostalgia back to times when social ranks were stable, while conceding that a trader who thrice crossed the sea at his own expense earned the rank of 'thegn' (the usual late term for nobleman). His famous 'Sermon to the English' more hysterically complained that slaves had become their owners' masters. Social mobility was never excluded in *wergeld*-based society, but it can only have been boosted by urban and commercial growth. In the shorter term, the enhanced power of a king like Offa may have been based on the ability to cash in on economic change; if so, it foreshadowed that of Alfred and his successors. But, in the short term too, the commercial vortex in the Channel and North Sea sucked in the Scandinavian pirates known to themselves as Vikings.

The ninth-century Viking invasions mark the obvious watershed between the first and second phases of Anglo-Saxon history. English sources perhaps exaggerated the scale and destructiveness of Viking activity, but this should not obscure its impact, especially after 865 when raiding gave way to invasion in considerable force. An undoubted consequence was the elimination of two of the four remaining kingdoms, Northumbria (866–7), then East Anglia (869), whose king, Edmund, was killed in a way which suggests ritual sacrifice to some scholars, and which made him a culted martyr like Oswald. A third kingdom, Mercia, was reduced to a rump ruled by the fourth, Wessex (874–7). Much of north-east England was settled by Scandinavian-speakers; intensively so, to judge from their linguistic effect on English generally, and on the area's place-names. The same area lacked bishops for seventy-five years or more, and its pre-Viking records have almost all vanished, arguing wide-scale disruption and destruction. The tale of how King Alfred (871–99) burned the cakes because he was distractedly brooding on the low ebb of his political fortunes, shows that Wessex itself very nearly succumbed (878). But Alfred rallied, and kept out later attacks in the 890s by an effective scheme of defensive fortification, planned in an extant administrative document, the *Burghal Hidage*, and itself a stimulant to urbanization. Alfred could thus pose as the one remaining champion of *Angelcynn*; he was the first king whose titles claimed rule over all the English (*rex Angulsaxonum/Anglorum Saxonum*).[13]

The opportunity was seized by his able children, Edward the Elder (899–924) and Æthelflæd 'Lady of the Mercians' (d. 918), and his no less gifted grandsons, Athelstan (924–39), Edmund (939–46) and Eadred (946–55). East Anglia and north-east Mercia were overrun (912–19), then Northumbria (927–54). Athelstan's great victory over a coalition of Scots, Welsh and Dublin-based descendants of Northumbria's Viking conquerors at *Brunanburh* (937), was seen by his family as their finest hour. Scottish and Welsh kings were invited (or obliged) to attend the royal court. The apogee of English kingship (as one can now say) was the reign of Edmund's son, Edgar (957–75). He was crowned at Bath in imperial style, then was rowed on the Dee at Chester by eight northern or western kings (973). But when he died, things began to go wrong. His son, Æthelred (978–1016), gained his sobriquet 'the Unready' (a pun to the effect that 'noble counsel', *Æthel-ræd*, had 'no counsel', *Un-ræd*) from a resurgence of Scandinavian assault in his reign, as described with jaundiced genius in the *Anglo-Saxon Chronicle*. A highlight in the catalogue of Anglo-Saxon defeats was the Battle of Maldon (991), when Ealdorman Byrhtnoth of Essex and his warriors were defeated and killed. The raids and invasions from Scandinavia culminated in the Danish King Cnut establishing himself as king of the English after Æthelred's death in 1016. He and his sons ruled until 1042, when the old line was restored by Æthelred's son, Edward 'the Confessor'. The latter's childless death in 1066 led to the succession of his brother-in-law, Harold, and so to catastrophe at Hastings, compared to which the Maldon disaster was a mere skirmish.

The inability of the new kingdom of England to resist conquest raises the possibility that its structure was flawed. The brilliant campaigns of Alfred's children Edward and Æthelflæd are known as 'the Reconquest of the Danelaw', which is a tribute to West Saxon image-building. It was in fact a *conquest* of land that no southern king had ever ruled before. There is evidence that it was resisted by Englishmen as well as Danes, especially in Northumbria, where the final defeat of the Viking claim with the death of Eric Bloodaxe (954) led to the imprisonment of the English archbishop of York. The north-east of England came to be known as the 'Danelaw', reflecting the development of an Anglo-Scandinavian culture on which Viking language and custom left an ineradicable mark ('law' is one of innumerable Scandinavian contributions to standard English vocabulary). The conquest of Cnut may have begun as an effort to take control of an overseas colony, like those that Norwegian kings made in the North Atlantic at this time. England in the eleventh century was divided into four earldoms, which corresponded to the kingdoms of the ninth, and must have reflected their lingering political significance. Mercian and West Saxon nobilities tended throughout the period to back different claimants to the throne. The last act of Anglo-Saxon history began with a major Northumbrian revolt (1065), aiming to put a Mercian earl (grandson of Lady Godiva, the second most famous Anglo-Saxon) in place of Tostig, another brother-in-law of King Edward. The kingdom of England did not fuse spontaneously; it had to be welded by the mixture of force, cajolery and propaganda that is the stuff of statecraft in any age. Nonetheless, the English kingdom was a reality by the eleventh century. There is evidence that speakers of what we call Old English were willing to call themselves 'English', when few if any of their eastern neighbours thought themselves 'German'. The earldoms cannot be seen as heritable or semi-independent principalities, like the French Duchy of Normandy. All successful early medieval hegemonies were founded, like that of the kings of Wessex, on their makers' ability to pose as a people's champion against the common enemies of their faith as well as their property. But Alfred and his family began with an asset that Charlemagne's Carolingians in Francia and Germany's Ottonian dynasty lacked: they could build on the sense of ideological identity that the English had been given by Bede. Chadwick made the striking point that the two heroic poems that certainly were written after 900, on the Battles of *Brunanburh* and Maldon, express precisely the note of authentic 'patriotism' that is absent in the others.

The real political weakness of the English kingdom was a dynastic instability such as was fatal to many early medieval monarchies. The Norman Conquest was the climax in a series of disputed successions, whose drastic consequences arose from the determination of William the Conqueror's followers to share the spoils of his victory. In that context, it is arguable that an efficiently run kingdom was *easier* to conquer. The evidence is that late Anglo-Saxon government was highly efficient. Its main instrument, the shire under its 'sheriff (shire-reeve)', stayed largely intact for a millennium, the envy of the *Ancien Régime*. Coinage was controlled to a degree that is credible only because proven by coin-finds. Vast sums were raised in *Danegeld*, monies used to buy off the Danes, for Kipling the badge of Anglo-Saxon shame, but a resource that Norman kings would labour in vain to levy so profitably. Anglo-Saxon society still consisted of a military nobility, like 'feudal' Normandy or most of the rest of eleventh-century northern Europe. It even had its own badge: the significance of the moustaches worn by most heavily-armed English in the 'Bayeux Tapestry', is shown by the fact that Harold's martial chaplain 'wore his moustaches during his priesthood', and though he shaved on becoming bishop of Hereford, he still contrived to be killed fighting the Welsh in 1056 (the virtue of moustaches was of course that they were emblems of virility but did not, like beards, give useful leverage to an enemy in close combat). As elsewhere, this nobility was sustained by the labour of peasants, and the social trend was for free status to be eroded by the spread of rural serfdom. Yet if the warrior aristocracy sounds the *leitmotif* of the earlier period, the keynote of the later has become the making of an English state.[14]

The charter of the new state was King Alfred's law-code.[15] The preface began by quoting three and a half chapters of the Mosaic Law from the biblical Exodus, then went on to put the codes of Æthelberht, Ine and Offa into the tradition of Christian law-giving beginning with the Council of Jerusalem in the New Testament (Acts XV). The Old Testament, which may once have reconciled Anglo-Saxon warriors to a new faith, now imposed radical obligations. Old Testament logic, for example as deployed in the psalms, was incisive and unmissable. God's justice rewarded a virtuous people and punished one that sinned. Englishmen could see that they had very nearly lost their island, like the Britons before, so naturally thought that they had sinned as, according to Bede, the Britons had. Their exhilarating success as nation builders proved that virtue was indeed rewarded. Subsequent defeats merely showed that it was insufficient. As in ancient Israel, God's favour was to be won only by a holy society. A king's business was to ensure that society was indeed holy. Alfred's first law may have initiated the oath that was certainly enforced by Cnut's time (and indeed far into the Middle Ages, when its significance had long been forgotten). It was taken at the age of twelve, and covered not just political loyalty but also all law-worthy behaviour. Theft was a breach of this oath, punished as what was later called 'felony' (i.e. breach of faith), by death, forfeiture of property and denial of Christian burial. Law and order, clearly, was now a responsibility of the 'state'. And bloodfeud, which had once underpinned it, was now so far as possible restricted in the name of 'promoting Christianity'.

One of the state-building models of the first kings of England was the 'Christian Empire' of the Carolingians. (The choice of Bath for Edgar's imperial coronation is explained if its hot springs were meant to recall those which induced Charlemagne to found his palace at Aachen.) Carolingian influence is probably also behind the monastic 'Reformation' of Edgar's reign, led by Bishop Æthelwold of Winchester (d. 984), with Archbishops Dunstan (d. 988) and Oswald (d. 992).[16] Part of the aim was to stop 'secular encroachment' on monasteries, in effect the aristocratic values that angered eighth-century reformers: when Æthelwold replaced 'gluttonous and lascivious clerks' at Winchester by true monks, he may have been inspired by one of Bede's own proposals. Another objective was an enforcement of the *Rule of St Benedict* over all the abbeys of 'one country'. Though the *Rule* was well-known to early Anglo-Saxon churchmen, it had no monopoly of monastic observance; Bede, who never mentioned any other by name, says that Biscop's *Rule* was blended from a total of seventeen known to him. Pursuit of monastic uniformity was a Carolingian theme, and expressed the ideology that a 'Christian Empire' could only have 'one law'. Half a dozen manuscripts of the edict establishing uniform customs in Francia are extant from later Anglo-Saxon England. It is very likely that the reformers were consciously imitating an aspect of Carolingian ideology. Yet, if the English pursuit of a holy society was the same as the Carolingian, some of their means to this end were different. The 'Carolingian Renaissance', as its name implies, sought to re-establish sound Latinity as the vehicle of religious reform; the vernacular had its place, but it was limited. By contrast, the Anglo-Saxons set out the awesome obligations of a holy society in vernacular literature and legislation which at this time has no European parallel.

Use of the vernacular was seen as the only way to bring home their spiritual responsibilities to people at large. To this end King Alfred launched his educational programme in the famous preface to his *Pastoral Care*. He intended that his people should gain 'wisdom' through access to 'what is most necessary for all men to know'. It was lack of wisdom that had brought down 'punishments in this world', by which he must have meant pagan attack. 'Wealth and wisdom' had both been lost through neglect of the latter, so revived wisdom would logically result in renewed wealth. According to Asser's *Life of Alfred*, the king identified with Solomon, and it was Solomonic 'wisdom' (*sapientia*) that he expected from his churchmen and judges. An insertion in Alfred's translation of Boethius's *Consolation of Philosophy* could be straight from the Book of Kings: 'Therefore learn wisdom . . . without any doubt, you may thus achieve power, though you do not desire it.' Wisdom was a spiritual virtue, yet not other-worldly: the God of Abraham, Isaac and Jacob was not an other-worldly deity.[17]

The same concern with using the vernacular is evident a century later in the work of Ælfric, abbot of Eynsham (died *c.* 1010). In range of learning and grasp of theological niceties, Ælfric was on a par with all but the top Carolingian scholars. Yet his life's work was homiletic exposition of scripture and of saintly life written in English, and at a level intelligible to all. Latin remained the appropriate medium for the truly learned; if too much were made accessible, 'the pearls of Christ [might] be held in disrespect'. But there is no reason, for once, to see protestations of 'simple style' as a rhetorical device. Ælfric sought to address the simple, because in his own youth he had been confronted by a priest unable to account for the fact that Jacob had four wives; such things, he felt, must never recur.[18] Archbishop Wulfstan (1002–23), Ælfric's contemporary, directed vernacular homily yet more explicitly at promoting holiness for a society in crisis. His denunciations of sin, crime and social dislocation spilled over into the legal texts he wrote for Æthelred, Cnut and his own clergy at York and Worcester. Those laws have earned the contempt of legal historians because they are often indistinguishable from homily; the two are indeed mixed together in Wulfstan manuscripts.[19]

Alfred's *Pastoral Care* had been predicated on the fact that 'learning of Latin had declined . . . yet many could read English writing (*arædan*

Englisc gewrit)'. This ought to mean that the Anglo-Saxons were the first, and for several centuries the only, medieval Europeans to find a way of teaching people to read their own language without at the same time teaching them Latin. It is an attractive possibility that a function of one or more of the *codices* of Anglo-Saxon poetry was to teach reading in English: Asser says that Alfred in his youth pored over 'English poems', and ensured that Edward and Æthelflæd 'learned the psalms, and books in English, and especially English poems'. This prized part of the Old English literary heritage may owe its survival to the vernacular's special importance for England's creators. In any event, the availability of vernacular education once more raises the question of lay literacy. Alfred's preface to his *Pastoral Care* expressed the intention that 'all the youth that are English freemen, those that have the means . . . should be committed to learning . . . until they can read English writing well; one can then teach Latin speech to those who wish to learn further and to go on to higher orders'. He set an example in his court school, with his own children being taught along with those of 'nobles and the basely born'. By early medieval standards, it was an amazingly ambitious project. The effects remain difficult to assess, because the evidence is sparse, as before, and as before, it is also blurred. Kings, even members of the royal family, may have been special cases, so that one should not make too much of Ealdorman Æthelweard, who was Ælfric's patron and translated the *Anglo-Saxon Chronicle* into Latin. On the other hand, clerics could be as hard to distinguish from laity as in earlier times. A 'mass-priest', Ælfwine, who could conceivably be the same as a 'scribe' granted land thirty years before, was given an inlaid sword and a harnessed horse in the will of Athelstan, son of Æthelred the 'Unready'.

In the circumstances, the important point regarding use of the vernacular is perhaps that one person with the ability to read from parchment could then read aloud to many. Charters of Æthelwold's foundations at Ely and Winchester, one almost certainly written by Ælfric, say that 'our speech' 'resounds in the ears of the populace', and leaves the layman unable to plead ignorance 'when it is read in his presence'. Ælfric actually addressed more of his works to laymen (mere 'gentry', apart from Æthelweard and his son) than to clergy. They may not, in the modern sense, have *read* them. Equally, it splits hairs to insist that they could not: they still wished to own his books. Again, a passage in one of Ælfric's homilies talks of the way that one 'hears' and 'looks at' the king's writ. From Edward the Confessor's time, probably from before, government was articulated by writs, short vernacular documents whose authenticity was proved by a royal seal.[20] Laymen may not, in the light of Ælfric's remarks, have read them *physically*. But it is futile to labour the point: the fact remains that a king's written word could get through to his subjects as

Latinate administration could not. It is surely arguable that the English kingdom was ultimately the most successful 'Dark Age' state, because it alone effectively harnessed native speech.

The Norman Conquest was the most drastic political upheaval in Europe's post-Roman history. The entire ruling elite was displaced by men that, literally, spoke another language: an ironic symbol of the transformation is that the home of *Beowulf* also produced the oldest manuscript of the great Old French epic, the *Song of Roland*. Eadmer of Canterbury, who greatly admired Lanfranc (1070–89), the first post-Conquest archbishop, and was the devoted biographer of the second, Anselm (1093–1109), professed himself unable to write about what had happened to his class. History has few more poignant spectacles than the men found in Cambridgeshire giving sworn evidence to the Domesday Survey (1086) as to their ownership twenty years earlier of lands which they had now lost. Against this background of cataclysm, the bookishness of the Old English gentry, and its familiarity with administrative documentation, was of immense historical importance.

The extraordinary thing is that English survived the Conquest at all. For two and a half centuries after 1066, the cultural trend was wholly in favour of French: almost the entire vocabulary of English Common Law is French, from 'crime' and 'court' onwards (with 'gallows' an interesting exception). Yet it seems as certain as anything unprovable can be that the knightly Rogers and Godfreys of medieval England spoke English in their off-duty hours. A good indication is that Scotland's language is a species of English, when the 'Normans' invited by Scottish kings to give their kingdom the desired European gloss should have been importing French. One would not think 'Master Nicholas of Guildford' English, if there were not a case that he wrote *The Owl and the Nightingale*. The persistence of English speech and literature is more than a metaphor of Anglo-Saxon law and institutions that Norman and Angevin kings made their own. As is shown by the 1086 jurors of Cambridgeshire, it is a crucial reason why local structures continued to operate. 'Anglo-Saxon' had been anchored by the literate vernacular's role in society and culture. The gentlemen and businessmen who ran medieval shires and boroughs were the figurative, in many cases presumably the actual, descendants of Ælfric's patrons and Edward's sheriffs. Like the Latin speakers of the Roman Empire on the Continent, but unlike the Britons, the Anglo-Saxons transmitted their language to their conquerors. This is very probably because English had itself become a language of literature and government. There is an indirect, yet also a real, connection between the two facts that England is the world's oldest continuously functioning state, and that English is now its most widely spoken language.

1 For Charlemagne's collection of songs, see L. Thorpe, *Two Lives of Charle-magne* (Harmondsworth, 1969), p. 82. In what follows, historical references are given (where possible) to *EHD*. For general orientation in Anglo-Saxon history, see the bibliography listed below, pp. 282–3. I should like to express my gratitude to Dr Jenny Wormald for sensitive supervision during the preparation of this essay.

2 For the wealth revealed by one well-known burial site, see R. Bruce-Mitford, *The Sutton Hoo Ship Burial: a Handbook*, 3rd ed. (London, 1978). A good introduction to linguistic change as reflected in place-names is M. Gelling, *Signposts to the Past* (London, 1978).

3 Much the best account of the conversion of the Anglo-Saxons is H. Mayr-Harting, *The Coming of Christianity to Anglo-Saxon England*, 3rd ed. (London, 1990).

4 On Biscop and his monasteries, see Bede's *Lives of the Abbots of Wearmouth and Jarrow*, chs. 1–14, trans. D. H. Farmer and J. F. Webb, *The Age of Bede* (Harmondsworth, 1983), pp. 185–200; for the archaeology, see R. Cramp, 'Excavations at the Saxon Monastic Sites of Wearmouth and Jarrow: an Interim Report', *Medieval Archaeology* 13 (1969), 21–66, updated by 'Monk-wearmouth and Jarrow', in *Famulus Christi: Essays in Commemoration of the Thirteenth Centenary of the Birth of Bede*, ed. G. Bonner (London, 1976), pp. 5–18. For Bede's imposition of pattern on diverse reality, see (further to Mayr-Harting, *The Coming of Christianity*), two very important papers of J. Campbell, 'Bede', and 'The First Century of Christianity in England', in his *Essays in Anglo-Saxon History* (London, 1986), pp. 1–27 and 49–67.

5 Bede, *In Genesim*, ed. C. W. Jones, Corpus Christianorum Series Latina 118 (Turnhout, 1967), 1. Biscop's library is explored through Bede's output by M. L. W. Laistner, 'The Library of the Venerable Bede', in *Bede, his Life, Times and Writings: Essays in Commemoration of the Twelfth Centenary of his Death*, ed. A. Hamilton Thompson (Oxford, 1935), pp. 237–66. For Aldhelm, see M. Lapidge and M. Herren, *Aldhelm: the Prose Works* (Cambridge, 1979), and M. Lapidge and J. L. Rosier, *Aldhelm: the Poetic Works* (Cambridge, 1985). For Alcuin, see *Alcuin: the Bishops, Kings and Saints of York*, ed. and trans. P. Godman (Oxford, 1982), esp. pp. 114–17 and 120–7.

6 Felix's *Life of St Guthlac*, chs. 16–18, ed. and trans. B. Colgrave (Cambridge, 1956), pp. 80–3. See also P. Wormald, 'Bede, *Beowulf* and the Conversion of the Anglo-Saxon Aristocracy', in *Bede and Anglo-Saxon England*, ed. R. T. Farrell, British Archaeological Reports, British Series 46 (Oxford, 1978), 32–95.

7 For the 747 council, see *Councils and Ecclesiastical Documents relating to Great Britain and Ireland*, ed. A. W. Haddan and W. Stubbs, 3 vols. (Oxford, 1869–71) III, 368. For the Whitby biographer of Gregory, see *The Earliest Life of Gregory the Great*, ed. and trans. B. Colgrave (Lawrence, KA, 1968), pp. 82–3 and 90–7. Boniface's letter on the continental mission is in *EHD*, pp. 812–13; see also pp. 850 and 854 for sample letters of Alcuin.

8 M. Lapidge, 'The School of Theodore and Hadrian', *ASE* 15 (1986), 45–72, at 53–62.

9 Alcuin's letter is partially trans. S. Allott, *Alcuin of York* (York, 1974), pp. 165–6; it should be noted that D. Bullough, in a study forthcoming in *ASE*, will show that this letter was addressed *not* to Bishop Hygebald of Lindisfarne but to an unidentified clerical community, probably in Mercia.

10 For the weaponry in question, see D. Wilson, *The Anglo-Saxons*, 2nd ed. (Harmondsworth, 1971), pp. 108–26, and L. Alcock, 'Quantity and Quality: the Anglian Graves of Bernicia', in *Angles, Saxons and Jutes: Essays presented to J. N. L. Myres*, ed. V. I. Evison (Oxford, 1981), pp. 168–86.

11 For texts of the laws in translation, see *EHD*, pp. 391–478, as well as *The Laws of the Earliest English Kings*, ed. and trans. F. L. Attenborough (Cambridge, 1922), and *The Laws of the Kings of England from Edmund to Henry I*, ed. and trans. A. J. Robertson (Cambridge, 1925).

12 H. M. Chadwick, *The Heroic Age* (Cambridge, 1912), esp. pp. 30–40 and 329–37.

13 The course of Viking raids is plotted clearly in D. Hill, *An Atlas of Anglo-Saxon England* (Oxford, 1981), pp. 32–54; see also pp. 85–6 for the *Burghal Hidage*. A useful collection of translated sources for King Alfred is S. Keynes and M. Lapidge, *Alfred the Great* (Harmondsworth, 1983).

14 For laws of Edgar organizing Hundred and Shire courts, see *EHD*, pp. 429–33; maps of hundreds and shires in 1086 are provided in each of the county volumes of *Domesday Book*, ed. J. Morris *et al.* (Chichester, 1975–86). For the coinage and more evidence of strong administration, see Campbell, 'Observations on English Government from the Tenth to the Twelfth Century', in his *Essays in Anglo-Saxon History*, pp. 155–70. On the Danegeld, see M. K. Lawson, 'The Collection of Danegeld and Heregeld in the Reigns of Æthelred II and Cnut', *English Historical Review* 99 (1984), 721–38. Finally, the mustachioed English soldiery at the Battle of Hastings is illustrated in D. Wilson, *The Bayeux Tapestry* (London, 1985).

15 For Alfred's laws, see *EHD*, pp. 407–16, with excerpts from the preface at pp. 408–9. Full text and English translation of Alfred's lawbook is to be read only in B. Thorpe, *Ancient Laws and Institutes of England* (London, 1840), pp. 20–65; better (but with German translation) is F. Liebermann, *Die Gesetze der Angelsachsen*, 3 vols. (Halle, 1903–16) I, 16–123.

16 See *EHD*, pp. 897–917 for lives of the reformers, and pp. 920–3 for Æthelwold's own account of the reform. For Æthelwold in particular, see *Wulfstan of Winchester: the Life of St Æthelwold*, ed. and trans. M. Lapidge and M. Winterbottom (Oxford, 1991), which contains (at pp. li–lx) an account of the Carolingian texts which influenced tenth-century English monasticism, concerning which the principal document is *The Regularis Concordia*, ed. and trans. T. Symons (London, 1953).

17 For Alfred's preface to the *Pastoral Care*, see *EHD*, pp. 887–90, and Keynes and Lapidge, *Alfred the Great*, pp. 124–7 (and pp. 75, 92 and 109–10 for Asser's remarks on Alfred, his judges and 'wisdom'); cf. W. J. Sedgefield, *King Alfred's Old English Version of Boethius De Consolatione Philosophiae* (Oxford, 1899), p. 35.

18 See Ælfric's *Lives of Saints*, ed. and trans. W. W. Skeat, EETS os 76, 82, 94 and 114 (London, 1881–1900) I, 2–3 (Christ's pearls) and *The Old English*

Version of the Heptateuch, Ælfric's Treatise on the Old and New Testament and his Preface to Genesis, ed. and trans. S. J. Crawford, EETS os 160 (London, 1922), 76–7 (the ignorant priest).

19 Wulfstan's legal texts are: 'The Peace of Edward and Guthrum', V–X Æthelred, I–II Cnut, and Cnut 1020; see *EHD*, pp. 442–76, Attenborough, *The Laws of the Earliest English Kings*, pp. 102–9, and Robertson, *The Laws of the Kings of England*, pp. 78–145 and 154–219. For the Wulfstan corpus, see D. Bethurum, 'Wulfstan', in *Continuations and Beginnings*, ed. E. G. Stanley (London, 1966), pp. 210–46.

20 For the charter, see J. C. Pope, 'Ælfric and the Old English Version of the Ely Privilege', in *England before the Conquest: Studies in Primary Sources presented to Dorothy Whitelock* (Cambridge, 1971), pp. 85–113. The passage from the homilies is found in *The Homilies of Ælfric: a Supplementary Collection*, ed. J. C. Pope, 2 vols., EETS os 259 and 260 (London, 1967–8) II, 659. For late Anglo-Saxon writs, see F. Harmer, *Anglo-Saxon Writs*, 2nd ed. (London, 1989), with discussion by S. Keynes, 'Royal Government and the Written Word in Late Anglo-Saxon England', in *The Uses of Literacy in Early Mediaeval Europe*, ed. R. McKitterick (Cambridge, 1990), pp. 226–57.

2 The Old English language

MOST Old English poetry and a considerable amount of Old English prose is now accessible through Modern English translations. But in order to understand fully and appreciate the literature of the Anglo-Saxon period – its style, verse structure and content – it is necessary to read the texts in their original language. The following chapter is intended as an introduction to Old English, with emphasis on those characteristics and developments that distinguish this older stage of the language from Modern English. The chapter is not, however, meant as a grammar or work of reference, particularly since some simplification of the complex linguistic facts has been unavoidable. Some standard works on Old English language are listed below (Further reading, pp. 284–5).

For the speaker and reader of Modern English who is beginning to study Old English, texts written in that language may at first appear strange and somewhat difficult. This is due mainly to the momentous changes that English has undergone during the last nine hundred years of its development, particularly during the Middle English period (c. 1100–1500), when the structure of English changed from that of an inflected language to one with hardly any inflexional endings, when sound changes affected the pronunciation and spelling of most of the vocabulary, and when this vocabulary became subject to almost revolutionary changes owing to the loss of a large number of older, native words and to the large-scale borrowing of words from other languages, especially French and Latin.

On the other hand, English has to this day retained characteristic elements of its earliest recorded period: first, a 'basic' vocabulary of native origin, including most of the pronouns, conjunctions and prepositions, the auxiliary verbs and the verbs *to have* and *to be* as well as a large number of nouns, adjectives and verbs used in all types of speech; and secondly, certain grammatical features nowadays often labelled 'irregular', like the surviving strong verbs (*sing–sang–sung*) and plural forms like *foot–feet, ox–oxen, sheep–sheep*. A knowledge of Old English therefore is not only a prerequisite to a proper study of Anglo-Saxon prose and poetry; it also gives the student an insight into the historical background of the lexical and morphological structure of present-day English.[1]

The prehistory of Old English

Old English (or Anglo-Saxon, as it is sometimes called with the term commonly used until the early twentieth century) is the language spoken by native Anglo-Saxon speakers from the time of the earliest settlements in Britain, in the fifth century, until the late eleventh century, when the character of the language began to change rapidly.

Since the science of comparative philology was established in the nineteenth century it has become possible to trace the prehistory of Old English and its relationship to other languages. As early as the twelfth century, scholars had observed certain similarities in the vocabulary of several European languages, similarities that apparently were not due to borrowing, but only in the nineteenth century did scholars like Jacob Grimm (1785–1863) develop reliable methods for determining the genetic relationship of languages, and attempts could then be made even to reconstruct unrecorded, early stages of a language.

As a result, we now have the concept of the Indo-European family of languages, languages that are so closely related, especially in their earliest recorded stages, that they must be assumed to be derived from a common ancestor, 'Indo-European', which does not survive, but whose phonology and morphology have been tentatively reconstructed, while its original home remains uncertain. The more important languages or language groups that go back to Indo-European are Indic, Iranian, Armenian, Greek, Italic (with Latin as the best-known dialect), Celtic, Germanic, Baltic, Slavic and Albanian. The criteria that enable us to prove the genetic relationship of these languages are: a common basic vocabulary, and a large number of lexical correspondences among all or at least some of the languages; a common inflexional system, evidenced by close agreements in morphology and grammatical categories; and phonological correspondences that obey strict rules, or 'sound laws'. As an example, we can take the regular correspondence – formulated in 'Grimm's law' – between the voiceless stops p, t, k in languages like Greek and Latin, and the voiceless spirants f, $þ$ (as in ModE *thin*) and χ (as in German *ach*, *ich*) in the Germanic languages:

Latin	Old English	
piscis	fisc	'fish'
tū	þū	'thou'
cor, cordis	heorte (with $\chi>$h)	'heart'

Old English is one of the Germanic languages which derive from a prehistoric Common Germanic originally spoken in Southern Scandinavia and the northernmost parts of Germany, from where it spread in the course of the migration during the early centuries of the first millennium after Christ. Again, phonological, morphological and lexical evidence enables us to distinguish between specific language groups and individual languages that developed out of Common Germanic under various historical, political and geographical conditions. Those for which written records have been preserved are:

1 *East Germanic*:   the only language in this group for which we have written evidence is Gothic; a translation of parts of the Old and New Testaments made by Bishop Ulfila in the second half of the fourth century survives and, being so early, is of great value for the reconstruction of Common Germanic.

2 *North Germanic*:   from which the Scandinavian languages derive. A number of runic inscriptions go back as far as the third century AD, but extensive written texts, from Iceland and Norway, are only preserved from the twelfth century onwards.

3 *West Germanic*:   the languages of this group, for which there is no written evidence before the eighth century, are Old High German (spoken in the Central West and in the South of Germany), Old Saxon or Low German (spoken in Northern Germany), Old Frisian (spoken in areas along the southern coast of the North Sea, and not recorded before the thirteenth century), and Old English. Linguistically, Old English and Old Frisian are closely related, but there are also significant affinities between Old English and Old Saxon.

This classification of the Germanic languages, as well as the assumption of a Common Germanic language (often called Proto-Germanic, or Primitive Germanic) is again based on precise linguistic criteria. Thus, all the Germanic languages – and therefore Common Germanic – are marked by a number of significant innovations: the accent is always on the first syllable of a word; every adjective can be inflected in two different ways (see below, pp. 31–2); and a new type of forming the past tense and past participle of verbs by means of a dental suffix is introduced with the so-called 'weak' verbs (corresponding to the so-called 'regular' verbs in Modern English: *love–loved*, as opposed to the older type *sing–sang–sung*). Similarly, Old English is clearly differentiated from the other Germanic and West Germanic languages by developments in its inflexional system and a number of regular early sound changes (some even going back to the pre-Insular period). The development of the diphthong *ai* of Common Germanic to OE *ā* may serve as an example:[2]

Old Gothic	Old Norse	Old High German	Old Saxon	Old English	
stains	steinn	stein	stēn	stān	'stone'
taikn	teikn	zeihhan	tēkan	tācen	'token'
hailags	heilagr	heilig	hēlag	hālig	'holy'

The transmission of Old English

Apart from a few inscriptions, our Old English texts are preserved in manuscripts which were nearly all written between the late ninth century and the twelfth, and which show, with few exceptions, the dialectal forms of West Saxon. The fact that our grammars and dictionaries are largely based on such texts is apt to create an impression of a relatively stable and uniform language. It is important to remember, however, that such an impression is wholly misleading. Our textual transmission, which is late and predominantly in a south-western dialectal form, tends to obscure the wide range of dialectal variation that must have obtained in a language reaching from the Channel to the Firth of Forth; it also tends to obscure the developments in sounds, inflexions, syntax and vocabulary between the period of the early settlements and the Norman Conquest. There cannot have been any written record of Old English until the Anglo-Saxons (and then only a few of them) learned to read and to write in the seventh century; from the eighth and earlier ninth centuries we only have a few glosses and two glossaries, as well as a few lines of Old English poetry, including Cædmon's famous hymn. No English prose text can be said with certainty to have been written down before the later ninth century. Some of the poetic compositions preserved in manuscripts of the late tenth or early eleventh centuries may well be modernized copies of much earlier exemplars, but it is impossible to date and localize exactly, or even to reconstitute, the original texts in these exemplars. While it seems sensible, then, that our grammars and handbooks should describe as the 'regular' forms of Old English the Early West Saxon ones of the period of King Alfred, and the slightly different ones of the time of Ælfric and Wulfstan, we must always keep in mind that our written texts provide us with a mere fraction of what was once a living language, spoken all over England for more than six centuries.

Once this has become clear, however, it seems safe to say that Old English, as compared with other contemporary languages, has been extremely well preserved. Leaving aside single-leaf documents, we still have about a thousand manuscript books, or fragments of such books, written or owned in Anglo-Saxon England between the late seventh and the late eleventh centuries. More than a third of them, and a considerable number of twelfth-century manuscripts, are written wholly or partly in Old English, or contain at least short texts or glosses in that language. Within the limits outlined above we can thus form a very clear and detailed picture of what the structure and characteristics of Old English were like.[3]

Script, spelling and pronunciation

When the Anglo-Saxons came to Britain, they brought with them the knowledge of runes. The origin of the runic alphabet is obscure; it appears to have been derived from a Roman alphabet, perhaps in the first or second century AD, and to have spread to the various tribes of the Germanic world. Runes, however, normally were used only for short inscriptions and not for literary purposes. The runic inscription on the eighth-century Ruthwell Cross, an early version of part of the Old English poem *The Dream of the Rood*, is a notable exception.[4]

During the course of the seventh century, Anglo-Saxons in religious institutions throughout the country must have learned to write. Presumably they would at first write Latin texts, but it would very soon have been necessary to record English personal and local names in writing, to supply Old English glosses, explaining Latin words here and there, and finally to write Old English texts in prose or verse. In order to do so, the Latin alphabet had to be adapted so as to represent the English speech sounds. The type of handwriting used for the purpose was the same as that employed for most Latin texts (except in de luxe manuscripts) at the time in England, namely Insular minuscule, which in various forms remained the script of all English texts until the early twelfth century.[5]

Adapting the Latin alphabet to English speech was not overly difficult. Most of the vowels and consonants in English corresponded to those in Latin, at least as long as certain niceties of articulation and pronunciation were disregarded. For some Old English speech sounds (a term here employed in the sense of the linguist's 'phoneme'; Anglo-Saxon writing can be said to have been phonemic, with few exceptions) there were no Latin equivalents, and the alphabet was therefore supplemented by the vowel *æ*, by combinations of vowels for the Old English diphthongs (*ea, eo*), and by newly introduced symbols for two English consonantal sounds: *ð* and *þ* (the latter being a runic symbol), used interchangeably for the sounds corresponding to ModE *th* in *thin* and *rather*, and *ƿ*, another runic symbol, for a bilabial semi-vowel, as *w* in ModE *win*. In modern editions of Old English texts, the spelling is usually that of the Anglo-Saxon scribe, though *ƿ* has nearly always been replaced by *w*. Some editions unnecessarily reproduce the Insular letter *ʒ* for *g*.

The speaker of Modern English who wants to read Old English texts aloud needs to observe the following points:

1   In accordance with the principles of Germanic accentuation, all words are stressed on the first syllable, except for words formed with a number of unstressed prefixes, especially *ge-, a-, be-, for-*, as in *gewínnan* 'conquer', *forléosan* 'lose', etc.

2   As opposed to Modern English and Modern French, Old English has no 'silent' letters; every written letter, including word-final *-e* and the initial consonants in OE *cnāwan* 'to know' or *wrītan* 'to write', has to be pronounced.

3   The phonetic value of a letter is not always that of Modern English; it is always that of Latin and therefore often that of other modern languages (Italian, French, German). This is particularly important for the pronunciation of the vowels, which is explained in the following table:

a   as in English *father*, but shortened
ā   as in English *father*
æ   as in English *cat*
ǣ   as (approximately) in English *mare*
e   as in English *let*
ē   as the first element of the diphthong in English *lane*
ea   as *æ* followed by *a*
ēa   as *ǣ* followed by *a*
eo   as *e* followed by *o*
ēo   as *ē* followed by *o*
i   as in English *pin*
ī   as in English *see*
o   as in English *got*
ō   as in French *côte* or in German *rot*
u   as in English *put*
ū   as in English *mood*
y   as in French *tu* or in German *Sünde*
ȳ   as in French *rue* or in German *Süden*

Long and short vowels must be kept distinct because they are 'phonemic', that is, they distinguish different words, as OE *god* 'God' and *gōd* 'good'. Most text editions for beginners indicate vowel length by means of a superscript macron, although no such convention was followed systematically by Anglo-Saxon scribes. Diphthongs are usually stressed on their first element.

The pronunciation of most of the consonants corresponds to that of Modern English. Exceptions are:
(a) the spirants *f, ð/þ* and *s*, which are voiceless initially and finally, as in

ModE *foot/thief, thin/cloth, sin/grass*, and voiced internally between vowels or voiced consonants, as in ModE *drive* (OE *drīfan*), *bathe* and *rose*;
(b) *h*, which is a breathing initially, as in Modern English, but finally and internally is a voiceless spirant as in German *ach* or *ich*;
(c) *c*, *g* and *sc*, and also *cc* and *cg*. For the somewhat complex rules affecting the pronunciation of these letters, a grammar should be consulted. As a general rule – to which, however, there are exceptions – it may be said that *c* is always a stop (as in ModE *can*) if followed or preceded by a 'dark' vowel (*a, o, u*), or if followed by a consonant, but often represents an affricate (as in ModE *chin*) if followed by *æ, e, i*, or preceded by *i*, while *g* – in early Old English actually a velar spirant – should be pronounced as a stop (as in ModE *go*) if followed or preceded by 'dark' vowels or if followed by a consonant; otherwise it is frequently a spirant to be pronounced like the initial sound in ModE *yell*.

Inflexional morphology

The structural development of English is often characterized as a gradual change from a 'synthetic' to an 'analytic' language. Synthetic languages indicate grammatical categories and syntactic functions by means of inflexional endings; analytic languages, in order to mark such categories and functions, employ other means instead of endings: fixed word-order, and elements like prepositions (for case-endings), adverbs (for the comparison of adjectives), auxiliary verbs (for moods and tenses of verbs), personal pronouns (instead of verbal inflexion).

This development had its beginnings in Common Germanic when the word-accent was shifted to and fixed on the initial syllable. As a consequence of this, and as the word-initial accent obviously had a strong, 'dynamic' character, there was an increasing tendency to weaken and reduce the final syllables, carrying the inflexional endings, in all the Germanic languages. This tendency developed into a regular process which can be described in terms of rules or 'laws', with these results for Old English:

1 Old English is no longer a fully inflected or purely 'synthetic' language. Noun endings, for example, no longer clearly differentiate cases and even declensions. Thus the endings *-e* or *-an* occur in several declensions and with several functions (indicating different cases, in singular and plural of masculine, feminine and neuter words); very often, case, gender and number of a noun in a particular context have to be ascertained from an accompanying pronoun (article) or adjective.
2 The original morphological structure of the language has been

obscured. In Common Germanic (as in Latin and other Indo-European languages), the forms of most nouns were combinations of three elements (cf. Latin *mens–a–m*): the root, carrying the lexical meaning; a thematic element, e.g. a vowel, indicating the inflexional class of the word and so, for nouns, the declension; and the inflexional ending, differing according to case and number; this may coalesce with the thematic element. Most verbal forms, by the way, were based on the same principle.

Comparison and reconstruction have made it possible for the grammarians of Old English to classify the nouns (and other word classes) according to this structural principle, but for those consulting the grammars it is not always immediately obvious why a word belongs (say) in what is called the *a*-declension. Here, by way of explanation, is an example taken from the declension of masculine *a*-nouns, the most frequent class of nouns in Old English, to which about 35 per cent of all nouns belong. The Common Germanic forms (reconstructed and therefore marked with an asterisk), particularly in the singular, can give us a fairly clear idea of the morphology of this declension, and where its designation comes from, while the Old English forms show us the results of the process of weakening in unstressed syllables, with endings that are no longer all unambiguous. This process continued, and there is evidence that in spoken late Old English *e, a, o* and *u* in unaccented position had all coalesced into a 'neutral' vowel like that in the final syllable of ModE *token*. The Modern English plural in *-s*, incidentally, derives from the nominative and accusative plural forms of this class:

		Common Germanic	*Old English*	
Sg.	Nom.	*stainaz	stān	'stone'
	Gen.	*stainasa	stānes	
	Dat.	*stainai	stāne	
	Acc.	*stainam	stān	
Pl.	Nom.	*stainōs	stānas	
	Gen.	*stainōm	stāna	
	Dat.	*stainumiz	stānum	
	Acc.	*stainans	stānas	

Four other Old English noun classes are frequent; their paradigms may illustrate what has previously been said about morphological developments in Old English, as may also the fact that some of the less frequent classes tend to adopt forms from the *a*- and *ō*-declensions.

Class	neuter ă	feminine ō	weak masculine -n	weak feminine -n
Approximate percentage of OE nouns	25	25	9	5
Sg. Nom.	scip 'ship'	giefu 'gift'	guma 'man'	tunge 'tongue'
Gen.	scipes	giefe	guman	tungan
Dat.	scipe	giefe	guman	tungan
Acc.	scip	giefe	guman	tungan
Pl. Nom.	scipu	giefa	guman	tungan
Gen.	scipa	giefa	gumena	tungena
Dat.	scipum	giefum	gumum	tungum
Acc.	scipu	giefa	guman	tungan

Please note that the preceding table is a highly simplified representation of the four noun classes, disregarding various subclasses and other special developments.

It will have become clear that the grammatical categories which determine the forms of Old English nouns are case, number and gender. In view of the recent extension of the meaning of ModE *gender* it seems appropriate to remind the reader that the word here is a purely grammatical term: in Old English as in the other Indo-European languages, *every* noun, no matter whether it denoted a living being or not, belonged to one of the three genders, while the various declensions could be restricted to one of the three genders, or could comprise subtypes for two or even three genders. Personal nouns in Old English are usually masculine or feminine, in accordance with their meaning, but even here we have exceptions like *wīf* 'woman, wife', or *mægden* 'girl, young woman', which are neuter.

Adjectives in Old English are inflected like substantives, but with one important difference: for every adjective there are two types of inflexion.

1 the 'strong' inflexion, in most cases a type related to the *a-* and *ō*-declensions of nouns, but with some special endings. The forms of this inflexional type are used whenever the adjective is predicative, or when it modifies a noun referring to something indefinite and not previously introduced, especially when a demonstrative pronoun does not precede the adjective.
2 the 'weak' inflexion, which follows the paradigm of the *n*-declension. This form is used when the adjective modifies a noun previously referred to or specified; a demonstrative or possessive pronoun usually precedes the adjective.

The following example will demonstrate the difference:

Hī sendon þā sōna þām gesǽlig*an* cyninge sumne ārwurðne bisceop, Aidan gehāten.

They then at once sent to the blessed king [referred to previously in the context] a venerable bishop called Aidan [not as yet referred to].

Here are the two paradigms for an adjective (*gōd* 'good'):

		Strong			*Weak*		
		masc.	*fem.*	*neuter*	*masc.*	*fem.*	*neuter*
Sg.	Nom.	gōd	gōd	gōd	gōda	gōde	gōde
	Gen.	gōdes	gōdre	gōdes	gōdan	gōdan	gōdan
	Dat.	gōdum	gōdre	gōdum	gōdan	gōdan	gōdan
	Acc.	gōdne	gōde	gōd	gōdan	gōdan	gōde
Pl.	Nom.	gōde	gōda	gōd	gōdan	gōdan	gōdan
	Gen.	gōdra	gōdra	gōdra	gōdra	gōdra	gōdra
	Dat.	gōdum	gōdum	gōdum	gōdum	gōdum	gōdum
	Acc.	gōde	gōda	gōd	gōdan	gōdan	gōdan

The forms of the *demonstrative pronoun* – which serves as the definite article (ModE *the*) and, as mentioned above, often provides a means of identifying case, number and gender of the noun it precedes – are as follows:

	Singular			*Plural*
	masc.	*fem.*	*neuter*	*all genders*
Nom.	sē	sēo	þæt	þā
Gen.	þæs	þǽre	þæs	þāra
Dat.	þǽm	þǽre	þǽm	þǽm
Acc.	þone	þā	þæt	þā
Instr.	þȳ	þǽre	þȳ	þǽm

The fifth case, an instrumental, is only here preserved as a clearly distinguishable masculine and neuter form.

In the *personal pronoun* there are still separate forms for the second person singular and plural; the second person plural is never used – as in Middle English, where it is a polite form of address – for the singular. The dual forms ('we two', 'you two') are a remarkable survival from a system in which *all* inflected words had three numbers, singular, dual and plural.

		First Person	*Second Person*	*Third Person*		
				masc.	*fem.*	*neuter*
Sg.	Nom.	ic	þū	hē	hēo	hit
	Gen.	mīn	þīn	his	hire	his

		me	þē	him	hire	him
	Dat.	mē	þē	him	hire	him
	Acc.	mē	þē	hine	hī	hit
Dual	Nom.	wit	git	–	–	–
	Gen.	uncer	incer	–	–	–
	Dat.	unc	inc	–	–	–
	Acc.	unc	inc	–	–	–

all genders

				all genders
Pl.	Nom.	wē	gē	hī
	Gen.	ūre	ēower	hira, heora
	Dat.	ūs	ēow	him
	Acc.	ūs	ēow	hī

Old English *verbs* have only two formally distinguished tenses: present and past; the distinction between the forms of the indicative mood and the subjunctive mood inherited from Common Germanic has been largely preserved. For the use of these forms, see below, pp. 36–7.

The majority of the verbs belongs to one of two inflexional types: 'strong' and 'weak'. Strong verbs form their past by means of a change of the vowel in the verbal root (cf. ModE *sing–sang–sung*); weak verbs do not change the vowel, but add a dental suffix (*-d-*, *-t-*) in the past forms (cf. ModE *love–loved, keep–kept*). The following paradigms can do no more than illustrate this principle with examples from the three most common inflexional classes of Old English verbs. A thorough knowledge of the verbal system, which is essential for reading Old English texts, must be acquired from a grammar. Note that plural forms in Old English verbs are identical for all three persons.

		Strong 'to sing'	Weak Class I 'to hear'	Weak Class II 'to love'
Present				
Indicative	Sg. 1	singe	hīere	lufige
	2	singst	hīerst	lufast
	3	singð	hīerð	lufað
	Pl.	singað	hīerað	lufiað
Subjunctive	Sg. 1 ⎫			
	2 ⎬	singe	hīere	lufige
	3 ⎭			
	Pl.	singen	hīeren	lufigen
Past				
Indicative	Sg. 1	sang	hīerde	lufode
	2	sunge	hīerdest	lufodest

		3	sang	hīerde	lufode
		Pl.	sungon	hīerdon	lufodon
Subjunctive		Sg. 1			
		2	sunge	hīerde	lufode
		3			
		Pl.	sungen	hīerden	lufoden
Present Imperative		Sg. 2	sing	hīer	lufa
		Pl.	singað	hīerað	lufiað
Infinitive			singan	hīeran	lufian
Present participle			singende	hīerende	lufiende
Past participle			gesungen	gehīered	gelufod

The strong verbs are divided into seven classes according to the root vowels of the verbs in the various forms. The weak verbs are divided into three classes, depending on different vocalic suffixes which are no longer clearly distinguishable; only four verbs remain in the third class: *habban*, *libban*, *secgan*, *hycgan* ('have, live, say, think').

A third type of verbal inflexion besides strong and weak verbs is represented by the so-called preterite-present verbs (with a strong present and a weak past); they include the frequently used auxiliaries *can*, *sceal*, *mōt* and *mæg* ('can', 'shall', 'must' and 'may'). A fourth type of 'anomalous' verbs comprises *willan*, *dōn*, *gān* and *bēon* ('will', 'do', 'go' and 'be').

Syntax

The sentence structure of Old English is in no way 'primitive'. Authors, particularly of Old English prose, are well capable of constructing complex sentences, making use of coordination and subordination, and of employing grammatical forms and syntactic devices for stylistic purposes, although there are some translations – like that of Bede's *Historia ecclesiastica* (cf. below, p. 82) – which appear clumsy or unidiomatic in places, and although there is some early prose – like the episode of Cynewulf and Cyneheard in the *Anglo-Saxon Chronicle* (under the year 755) – in which syntactic relationships are not always clearly expressed.

The following examples are meant to illustrate the most important points in which Old and Modern English syntactic usage differ markedly:

1   Besides coordination and subordination, we frequently find *correlative structures*, in which two (or more) clauses are introduced by the same adverbial element, like *þā . . . þā . . . ; þonne . . . þonne . . . ; þǣr . . . þǣr . . .* ; in such sentences, we tend to translate one element as a conjunction, the other as an adverb (or not at all).

þā hē ðā þās andsware onfēng, þā ongon hē sōna singan.

When he received this answer, (then) he immediately began to sing.

2   *Word-order* in Old English is not as strictly regulated as in Modern English. But, as has been pointed out above, Old English is no longer a fully inflected language; thus, about 60 per cent of all Old English nouns have the same form for nominative and accusative in the singular, and all nouns have the same form for these two cases in the plural. As a result – if we consider only sentences with the three elements S(ubject), V(erb) and O(bject) – we see that the dominant type of word-order in Old English prose is S–V–O, just as in Modern English; in Ælfric's *Catholic Homilies*, 73 per cent of all main clauses show this order. In subordinate clauses, however, a different, older type of order is still frequent: S–O–V.

And se Ceadwalla slōh and tō sceame
tūcode þā Norðhymbran lēode æfter   } · *main clause*
heora hlāfordes fylle,

oð þæt Ōswold se ēadiga his yfelnysse } *subordinate clause*
ādwæscte.

And this Ceadwalla slew and shamefully ill-treated the Northumbrian people after their lord's fall, until Oswald the blessed extinguished his wickedness.

Of the four other possible types of word-order, V–S–O is usual in interrogative sentences (where the Modern English periphrasis with *do* is unknown) and in sentences introduced by an adverbial 'head':

Gehȳrst þū, sælida?   'Do you hear, sailor?'
Þā ridon hīe þider.   'Then they rode there.'

The remaining types of word-order are much less frequent, but all do occur.

3   In an inflected language like Old English, *concord* has to be observed; nouns, adjectives and pronouns have to agree in number, case and gender (and similarly subject and verb in number and person), thus indicating syntactic relationships:

Hī sendon þā sōna *þām* ges*æ*lig*an* cyninge [dative] sum*ne* ārwurð*ne* bisceop [accusative].

They then at once sent to the blessed king a venerable bishop.

4   The use of the *oblique cases*, genitive, dative and accusative of nouns and pronouns as objects is determined by the preceding verb, adjective or preposition:

Hwæt, ðā Ōswold cyning *his* cym*es* [genitive] fægnode.

King Oswald rejoiced at his coming.

þā flotan stōdon gearowe, wī*ges* [genitive] georne.

The vikings stood ready, eager for the fight.

þā sende se cyning sōna þām þearfum [dative] þone sylfrenan disc [accusative].

Then the king immediately sent to the poor the silver dish. [As þearfum in this example, adjectives can generally be used in the function of nouns.]

Sum man fēoll on īse [dative].

A man slipped on the ice.

5 For the use of *weak and strong adjective forms*, see above (p. 31).

6 The Old English verb has only two formally distinguished *tenses*, present and past: *ic singe, ic sang*. The future may be expressed by the present or, occasionally, with the help of the auxiliaries *sculan* or *willan*, as in Modern English, though these two verbs no doubt always retained something of their original modal force.

The past has to serve for what in Modern English (and Latin) is the past, the perfect and the pluperfect; cf.

Æfter ðan ðe Augustīnus tō Engla lande becōm, wæs sum æðele cyning, Ōswald gehāten, on Norðhymbra lande.

After Augustine *had come* to England, there was a noble king named Oswald in the land of the Northumbrians.

But complex forms with *habban* 'to have' as auxiliary (or *wesan*, 'to be', with intransitive verbs) are beginning to appear in Old English, as in:

Hē fulworhte on Eferwīc þæt ǣnlice mynster þe his mǣg Ēadwine ǣr begunnen hæfde.

He completed in York the noble minster that his kinsman Eadwine had previously begun.

7 Most Old English verb forms can still be distinguished according to their *moods*, and although the use of indicative and subjunctive cannot be as rigorously defined as in Latin, it is possible to give hard and fast rules for their employment. Indicative forms are used in most main and subordinate clauses, whereas the subjunctive appears in main clauses expressing a wish or command, in object and adverbial clauses expressing negation, uncertainty or futurity, and especially in concessive and final clauses, as well as in conditional clauses where the condition is hypothetical or unreal. Compare:

Ōswold hine [i.e. Aidan] ārwurðlīce underfēng his folce tō ðearfe, þæt heora gelēafa wurde [*indicative*: wearð] awend eft tō Gode.

Oswald honourably received him, as a benefit to his people, in order that their faith should be turned again to God.

Gif þū sīe [*indicative*: eart] Godes sunu, cweþ þæt þā stānas tō hlāfum geweorþan [*indicative*: geweorþað].

If you are God's son, command that the stones become loaves (of bread).

Word-formation

In Old English, as well as in the Common Germanic language from which it developed, new words could be freely formed from existing words and elements by means of the three following processes:

1 *Compounding*: two (or more) independent words – most frequently nouns and adjectives – are combined so as to form a new word, as in ModE *teapot* or *loanword*. As for the semantics of such formations, we can say that the meaning of the second element is usually determined or modified by the first: a *mynster-mann* is a man who lives in a *mynster* (monastery), hence a monk; a *dōm-bōc* is a book that has to do with *dōm*, laws and judgement, hence a law-book or law-code; *stæf-cræft* is the skill or science of letters (*stæf*) and writing, hence grammar; and *wīd-cūþ* is something that is known (*cūþ*) widely.

Other types of compounds are less frequent, such as combinations of adjective + substantive like *bærfōt* 'bare-footed' or *heard-heort* 'hard-hearted', which are used as adjectives. It has also to be remembered that, just as in Modern English, the meaning of a compound cannot always be deduced from its component parts. Thus OE *godspell* is not just any 'good narrative' or 'good tidings' (*gōd* + *spell*), but the gospel, while *godspellbōc* (an example in which more than two elements are combined) is the book containing the gospels and nothing else.

Morphologically, the second element of the compound is inflected like the simplex word. The first element remains unchanged. Most often it appears to be in the form of the nominative singular, as in *dæg-rēd* 'dawn', but originally this element stood in the uninflected form of the stem (i.e. root + thematic element), as can be seen in examples like *hild-e-wīsa* 'leader in the fight'. In a number of compounds, the first element is found in the genitive singular (cf. ModE *craftsman*), as in *sunnan-dæg* 'Sunday', *dæges-ēage* 'daisy'.

2 *Prefixation*: This could be considered as a special type of compounding. An element that cannot occur independently or, using 'prefix' in a wider sense, a local particle is prefixed to an independent word (noun, adjective or verb) whose meaning it modifies. Old English had a considerable number of such prefixes, many of which were lost or became unproductive in later times.

Prefixes may have several functions or meanings, like *be-*, with the sense 'over, around', or with intensifying or privative force: *be-gān* 'to traverse', 'to surround'; *be-lūcan* 'to lock up'; *be-niman* 'to take away'. Other frequently employed prefixes include *ā-*, *æfter-*, *for-*, *fore-*, *forð-*, *in-*, *of-*, *ofer-*, *on-*, *tō-*, *þurh-*, *under-*, *up-*, *ūt-*, *wið-*, *ymb-*. The common prefix *ge-* may give a verb perfective sense, stressing the result of an action: *winnan* 'to labour', 'to fight'; *gewinnan* 'to gain', 'to conquer'. The prefix *un-* is used, as in Modern English, in order to indicate the negation or opposite of the word (mostly adjectives and adverbs) it modifies.

3   *Suffixation or Derivation*: An independent word is combined with a suffix, an element that does not (or no longer) occur by itself. Old English had a wide range of such suffixes with which new nouns, adjectives and verbs could be formed. Compare *beorht* and *beorht-nes* 'brightness'; *scyppan* and *scypp-end* 'creator'; *bodian* and *bod-ung* 'preaching'; *mōd* and *mōd-ig* 'proud'; *frēond* and *frēond-līc* 'friendly'; *fisc* and *fisc-ian* 'to fish', *fisc-ere* 'fisher'.

In word-formation, we must distinguish between types that are productive during a certain period, and types that have become unproductive. Thus we have in Old English numerous new formations of abstract nouns in *-nes*, or of agent nouns in *-end*. On the other hand, there are types of word-formation that are no longer employed; they may also have become obscured by sound-changes, as in *cyme* 'arrival' from *cuman* 'come' (masculine noun, *i*-declension, derived from a verb); *dēman* 'to judge' from *dōm* 'judgement' (weak verb class I, derived from a noun); *settan* 'to set' from *sittan* 'to sit' (a causative verb, 'to cause to sit', in the weak verb class I, derived from a strong verb).

A knowledge of the principles of Old English word-formation[6] is important for the student of literature for two reasons:

1   Compounds are extremely frequent in Old English poetry. Anglo-Saxon poets employed – and often coined – them in order to satisfy the requirements of verse structure and alliteration, and also as devices of style. A special kind of device is the 'kenning', a peculiar metaphorical expression usually – but not always – in the form of a compound word, like *hwæl-weg* 'the way of the whale' = the sea; *sæ-mearh* 'the horse of the sea' = the ship; *mere-hrægl* 'the dress of the sea' = the sail.
2   As will have become clear, Old English had a highly developed system of word-formation; compounds and formations with prefixes and suffixes in other languages, particularly in Latin, could therefore be reproduced without difficulty by combining native elements. This is what we find in the numerous Old English loan-translations to be discussed in the section on borrowing below. Compare *trinitas* with *þrī-ness* 'trinity';

salvator with *neri-end* and *hæl-end* 'saviour'; *evangelizare* with *godspell-ian* 'to preach the gospel'; and *crucifigere* with *rōd-fæstnian* 'to crucify'.

Vocabulary: words and meanings

The modern reader who has become conversant with the essentials of Old English morphology and syntax will want to acquire a sound command of the vocabulary. In spite of the limitations of our written transmission (see above, pp. 26–7), it seems fair to say that our knowledge of the Anglo-Saxon lexicon, based on about thirty thousand recorded words, or lexical units (with a total of about three million occurrences), is quite comprehensive, although there must be gaps, and although uncertainties remain as to the meaning and use of not a few words. Some specific difficulties that a modern reader has to face in this field of study may conveniently be mentioned.

In the course of the Middle English period, a not inconsiderable number of vernacular, inherited words died out. Many, but not all, of them were replaced by loanwords of French or Scandinavian origin. Some of the lost words denoted concepts or institutions that had disappeared, like *scop*, 'a court poet and singer' (reintroduced as a technical term by historians in the nineteenth century), or *gesīð*, 'a member of the nobility, a retainer'. But the majority of the losses is found among 'common' words: verbs like *fōn* 'to seize, to catch', *hātan* 'to command, to name', *niman* 'to take', *weorpan* 'to throw', *weorðan* 'to become'; nouns like *rǣd* 'counsel', *ðēod* 'people'; adjectives like *ēadig* 'wealthy, happy, blessed', *earm* 'poor'; and adverbs like *swīþe* 'very'.

Most of the Old English words that survived into Modern English have been affected by changes of sounds and spellings. In many cases such words will be recognized easily in an Old English text (more easily still if the reader has some knowledge of the phonological history of English), as e.g. OE *stān* – *stone*, OE *strǣt* – *street*, OE *hūs* – *house*, but with others the relationship is less obvious, and some words have changed almost beyond recognition; compare OE *āgen* with ModE *own*, OE *fēowertig* with *forty*, OE *hēafod* with *head*, OE *munuc* with *monk*, OE *hlǣfdige* ('the kneader of bread') with *lady*, and so on. Morphological developments also have to be taken into account: a number of Old English strong verbs became 'regular' or 'weak' in Modern English, so that their past is then formed on a different basis (cf. above, pp. 33–4), as in ModE *laughed*, OE *hlōh* (1st and 3rd person sg.), or ModE *helped*, OE *hulpon* (plural); similarly, OE *bōc* 'book' had nom. and acc. pl. *bēc*, but later changed into the 'regular' Modern English declension with *books* as its plural form.

More important than these formal points are differences in the signification of a word in Old and Modern English. Change of meaning is a ubiquitous process in the history of language, and whenever an Old English word is being translated we must make sure whether its Modern English etymological successor actually retains its original sense or senses. Thus, to give only a few examples, OE *fugol* survives as ModE *fowl*, but its meaning in Old English is 'bird', not 'farmyard bird'; OE *wīf* denotes 'woman, married or unmarried'; OE *ceorl* is preserved as ModE *churl*, but is completely different in sense: it is used for 'man' and 'husband' and, in the Anglo-Saxon laws, for a freeborn man who is not, however, a member of the Anglo-Saxon nobility; OE *eorl* is continued by ModE *earl*, but signifies a man, warrior, also a man of noble rank in early law codes; only from the eleventh century onwards does it replace OE *ealdorman* in the sense 'governor of a shire' and then refers to a genuine office and so is not a mere title as in later centuries.[7]

Semantic change may operate on words with a far more complex range of meanings. An example is OE *mōd*, ModE *mood*. The *Oxford English Dictionary* records three basic meanings for the word: (1) 'mind, heart, thought, feeling'; (2) 'fierce courage; spirit, stoutness, pride'; and (3) 'a frame of mind or state of feelings; one's humour, temper, or disposition at a particular time'. It notes further that sense (3) is not always distinguishable from sense (1) in early use. What matters here is that OE *mōd* is found with all these meanings, whereas in Modern English only sense (3) remains. Thus when it is said in *Beowulf* (line 1167) of Unferth (a somewhat doubtful character) *þæt he hæfde mōd micel* – 'that he had great courage' – a translation based on the modern sense of the word would be quite misleading. A look at one of the glossaries or dictionaries of Old English will help us in such cases, while for a more thorough analysis of the meaning of an Old English word it may even be useful to examine its semantic field by considering all words with closely related or overlapping senses, and all etymologically related words.[8] In our case, OE *mōdig*, an adjective derived from *mōd*, is also instructive: in Old English, its meaning is either 'brave, bold, courageous, high-spirited', or 'proud, arrogant, stubborn', whereas the only sense of *moody* today (not recorded before the late sixteenth century!) is quite different: 'characterized by gloomy moods, by frequent changes of mood'. The matter is even more complex in the case of compounds: see, for example, discussion of the word *ofer-mod* (below, pp. 119–21).

Language contact and borrowing

While the morphology and the syntax of Old English may be said to be essentially that of a Germanic language, this is not so with the vocabulary. Before as well as after their migration to Britain, the Anglo-Saxons were in no way isolated from other peoples, cultures and languages. The result of this can be seen in their knowledge of foreign languages, and especially in those elements of Old English that were acquired through borrowing. Etymological research has enabled us to identify lexical elements, loanwords, borrowed directly from a foreign language, but it should not be forgotten that practically any element of one language can be taken over into another language under certain conditions: sounds, inflexional endings, prefixes and suffixes, types of word-formation, syntactic constructions, idioms.

In Old English, we have mainly to do with lexical borrowing, but it seems clear that there was also Latin influence on the syntax. Absolute participles in Old English are usually explained as due to syntactic borrowing. Compare the Old English version of Matt. VI.6:

þū sōþlīce, þonne þū þē gebidde, gang intō þīnum bedclyfan, and þīnre dura belocenre [= Latin *clauso ostio tuo*], bide þīnne fæder on dīglum.

You, however, when you pray, go into your chamber and, with the door closed, pray to your father in secret.

In order fully to appreciate the significance of the Old English stock of loanwords,[9] it would be necessary to deal in some detail with the political and cultural history of the Anglo-Saxons, which is impossible within the compass of this chapter (see, however, ch. 1, above). Among the languages known to some Anglo-Saxons, at least, must have been Celtic British and Irish, Latin, Greek, Old Norse, Old Saxon and French. If we disregard place-names, it seems remarkable how few British words found their way into Old English: words like *binn* 'basket', *brocc* 'badger', *cumb* 'valley', *torr* 'projecting rock, peak', are among the few exceptions. As the activities of the Irish mission in the north were not allowed to last very long, it is not surprising that only a small number of loanwords can be traced back to that influence, among them OE *ancor* 'anchorite' and *cross*.

Latin is of paramount importance. Hundreds if not thousands of Anglo-Saxon monks and clerics – and even laymen – will have had a more or less perfect knowledge of this great international language, but long before the Insular period, the Germanic tribes along the southern coasts of the North Sea must have been in touch with the language and the civilization of the later Roman empire when Roman merchants reached them, or when Germanic tribes further south transmitted to them the new words and concepts. Borrowing from Latin must therefore have been going on for nearly a thousand years. Philologists and historians have developed criteria for approximately dating the reception of Latin loanwords; thus it has become clear that such words in the continental and early Insular periods were taken over in their Vulgar Latin forms and then shared the sound developments of native English words. Also, early loanwords are often common to the West Germanic languages. OE *pund*, ModE *pound*, from Latin *pondo* is an example; it is recorded in Old High German, Old Saxon, Old Frisian (and even in Gothic).

Among the earliest Latin loanwords, borrowed mainly in the continental period, are terms from the spheres of war, state and trade, building, agriculture and household, of which quite a few have survived into present-day English. Examples are *camp* 'battle' (and the derived *cempa* 'warrior'), *cāsere* 'emperor', *cēap* 'goods, purchase' (cf. ModE *cheap*), *pund* 'pound', *mīl* 'mile', *strǣt* 'street', *weall* 'wall', *tigle* 'tile, brick', *mylen* 'mill', *plante* 'plant', *wīn* 'wine', *cycene* 'kitchen', *disc* 'dish', *cīese* 'cheese', and many others, including numerous names of plants.[10]

Latin loanwords of the early Insular period cannot so easily be distinguished from those already borrowed on the Continent, but it is clear that the introduction of Christianity from the end of the sixth century onwards must have necessitated the creation of an English vocabulary for the tenets and practice of the new religion. It is thought that a few of these words will have been in use even before the Christianization, among them *cirice* 'church' and *bisceop* 'bishop'. The bulk of the new words, however, must be borrowings of the seventh and possibly eighth centuries, when terms like *abbod* 'abbot', *alter* 'altar', *mæsse* 'mass', *munuc* 'monk', *mynster* 'monastery', *prēost* 'priest', *sealm* 'psalm', and many others were taken over. This is also the time when words from the sphere of learning and education (to mention only one field in which the church was active) first came into English, like *scōl* 'school' and *glēsan* 'to gloss'.

Many more Latin words became loanwords in the time of the Benedictine Reform of the tenth century, and afterwards. As opposed to the earlier loans, these were always adopted from written Latin, and often retain their original form and sometimes, in the case of nouns, even their inflexional endings; examples are *altāre* 'altar', *corōna* 'crown', *prophēta* 'prophet'.

Loanwords do not constitute the only form of lexical borrowing. New and foreign concepts may also be expressed by means of utilizing the resources of the native vocabulary, and this practice was of utmost importance in Old English, as can be seen in its religious vocabulary or – to give just one more example – in the grammatical terminology devised by Ælfric for his *Grammar*, one of the standard handbooks in late Anglo-Saxon libraries. Apart from loanwords, there are two basic types of lexical borrowing: semantic loans and loan formations.

A semantic loan is created when a native word is employed with the specific meaning of a foreign word, a meaning which is usually somehow related to the range of senses of the native word. Examples are: OE *syn* – originally 'crime, guilt, hostility' – is used in the sense of Latin *peccatum* 'an offence against the laws of God and the Church'; OE *giefu* – 'gift' – translates Latin *gratia* '(God's) grace'; OE *ēadig* and *gesǣlig* – originally both mean 'happy, wealthy' – render Latin *beatus* 'blessed'; OE *dǣl* 'part, portion' is also employed in the sense 'part of speech, word class', translating Latin *pars* (*orationis*).

Loan formations are more or less exact copies of foreign compounds or derivatives, whose elements ('morphemes') are reproduced by means of semantically corresponding native elements. Where this correspondence is sufficiently close, we speak of loan translations, as in OE *þrīness* ('three-ness') = Latin *trinitas* (the 'Trinity') and the examples given above in the section on word formation. We may speak of a loan rendition when not all the morphemes in the translation word correspond exactly to its model; thus OE *mildheortness* is a skilful rendering of Latin *misericordia* ('mercy'), but *mild* is not precisely equivalent to Latin *miser* 'miserable'.

Apart from a few who had been taught in the school of Archbishop Theodore and Abbot Hadrian at Canterbury in the later seventh century, Anglo-Saxons had no knowledge of Greek; the literate among them may have been familiar, however, with Greek words occurring in Latin texts or in glossaries. Greek loanwords in Old English must, almost without exception, have come there by way of Latin. This applies to early loans like *engel* 'angel', *bisceop* 'bishop', and *dēofol* 'devil', as well as to later ones, like *antefn* 'antiphon' or *martir* 'martyr'. An exception is the West Germanic word for the church, OE *cyrice*, German *Kirche*, which is from Greek *kyriakón* 'pertaining to the Lord', a word not used in Latin.

Most of the loanwords from Latin are expressions for new concepts and technical terms. The hundreds of Scandinavian loanwords that survive into Modern English and English dialects have a wholly different character; they are mostly words of everyday life and are thus witnesses of the linguistic situation that must have prevailed in the areas of the Scandinavian settlements in the north and east of England since the late ninth century. Language contact between Anglo-Saxons and Scandinavians was certainly very close, but we know very little about the process of mutual borrowing; tenth and eleventh-century Anglo-Saxon authors and scribes working mainly in the south or the West Midlands were unlikely to use loanwords that had become current in eastern or northern dialects. The bulk of the Norse loanwords appears for the first time in Middle English texts of the twelfth century, by which time the Scandinavian language in Britain was largely extinct. A small number of Scandinavian words do, however, occur in late Old English texts, and it is interesting to see that the concepts they stand for are such as must have been of particular concern for the Anglo-Saxons then: there are words for different types of ships; words like *dreng* 'young man, warrior'; *griþ* 'truce, peace'; and especially terms characteristic of the administrative system and social conditions in the Danelaw: *hūsbonda* 'householder'; *hold* 'freeholder'; *wǣpentæc* 'wapentake', a subdivision of a shire, corresponding to the Anglo-Saxon *hundred*; *hūsting* 'court, tribunal'; *ūtlaga* 'outlaw'; and even *lagu* 'law'.

The Germanic dialect which the Anglo-Saxons certainly understood very well is not – as is sometimes claimed – Old Norse, however, but Old Saxon. There were contacts of various kinds with the speakers of this dialect; the Old Saxon biblical epic *Heliand* was copied and read in England, and the Old English *Later Genesis*, interpolated into the older epic *Genesis*, has been shown to be an adaptation of an Old Saxon poem. Whether words from Old Saxon were actually borrowed is doubtful and difficult to prove, but OE *hearra* 'lord' may be considered as a genuine loan from Old Saxon.

There had always been close relations between Anglo-Saxon England and France, but only a very few loanwords from French (since this had become a language in its own right) are found in English texts before the Norman Conquest, among them those that eventually replaced the Old English words for the sin of pride, late OE *prūd* 'proud' and *prȳde* 'pride'.

Dialects and Standard Old English

In his *Historia ecclesiastica* (I.15), Bede reports that the early Anglo-Saxon warriors and settlers came from three powerful Germanic tribes, the Saxons, Angles and Jutes. This tribal division was no doubt the basis for the dialects of Old English. Grammarians distinguish four such dialects:

Northumbrian – spoken north of the Humber
Mercian – covering roughly the area between Humber and Thames, except for what is now Essex, which must have been settled by Saxons
West Saxon – spoken in most of southern England, south of the Thames, with the exception of Cornwall and of the Kentish dialect area
Kentish – the dialect of Kent and Surrey

Northumbrian and Mercian, because of certain common dialect features, are collectively called Anglian. Kentish according to Bede would be the dialect of the Jutes (whose identity and original home are controversial); he points out that these peoples settled not only in south-east England but also on the Isle of Wight and in southern Hampshire. In any event, when we speak of Old English dialects it is important to observe three points:

1   The dialects are not coextensive with the Anglo-Saxon political or modern administrative units that bear the same names. Thus the Anglo-

Saxon kingdom of Mercia for a long time covered only the western part of the area designated as 'Mercian' in dialect studies, while the modern county of Northumberland is only a small part of the Northumbrian dialect area, which extended from the Humber as far north as the Firth of Forth.

2   Because of the limited written evidence, our knowledge of Old English dialects is incomplete or even fragmentary; for some dialects and periods there is no evidence at all, and even for well-documented periods and dialects we cannot say anything definite about the numerous sub-dialects that must have existed. It is impossible, therefore, to produce detailed and reliable dialect maps for the Anglo-Saxon period, like those that can be drawn for Middle and Modern English dialects and dialect features.

Our knowledge of Northumbrian is mainly dependent on a few short eighth-century texts (including the inscriptions on the Ruthwell Cross and the Franks Casket, and the hymn by Cædmon, preserved in early manuscripts of Bede's *Historia ecclesiastica*) and on three Latin manuscripts (one of them the famous Lindisfarne Gospels) extensively glossed in English in the late tenth century.

For Mercian, we have above all two early glossaries, the Epinal Glossary of the late seventh century and the Corpus Glossary of the early ninth century, and two Latin manuscripts with continuous Old English interlinear glosses entered in the ninth (*Vespasian Psalter*) and the later tenth century (part of the *Rushworth Gospels*).

For the Kentish dialect, there is even less written evidence; there are a number of ninth-century charters, and, in a tenth-century manuscript, two Old English religious poems as well as interlinear glosses.

West Saxon is extremely well documented, but not before the late ninth century. It has become usual to distinguish Early West Saxon (late ninth and early tenth centuries) and Late West Saxon (from the later tenth century onwards), which differ in a few respects. For the early period we have three manuscripts of Old English prose that are more or less closely linked with the literary activities of King Alfred; one of these is the earliest copy of his translation of Pope Gregory the Great's *Regula pastoralis*. Texts written in Late West Saxon are abundant; they include – to mention only the most prolific and important author of the period – the works of Ælfric.

3   Although this is not the place for detailed discussion of such matters, it should be mentioned that texts said to be written in a particular dialect do not always represent such a dialect in a pure form. In West Saxon writings, in particular, we often find scattered forms from other dialects, especially Anglian; for example, such forms are not uncommon in works copied in, or going back to, the Alfredian period. Various explanations for such a

mixture of forms are possible; one is certainly that a scribe's dialect was not always identical with that of the text he copied.

Dialectal features may be of various kinds: phonological, morphological, syntactical, lexical. Phonological differences between the Old English dialects appear to be most characteristic, and most easy to detect; they are treated in great detail in our standard grammars. Inflexional endings are less prone to dialectal variation; in any case, conservative spelling habits in the eleventh century may conceal from us the process of the levelling of final syllables operative at the time in all dialects. This process was most rapid and advanced in Northumbrian – perhaps accelerated there by the close language-contact with Scandinavian speakers – and here the decay of the inflexional system is already clearly visible in the interlinear glosses of the tenth century.

Recent research has greatly contributed to our knowledge of the dialect vocabulary of Old English, particularly in Anglian and West Saxon. While the overwhelming majority of Old English words are in common use throughout the country (but see below for the vocabulary of poetry), there is a not inconsiderable number of words that occur only in Anglian writings and thus can even be used as tests in investigations of the provenance of an Old English text. A few examples of such Anglian words are *lēoran* 'to go, depart', *morðor* 'murder, manslaughter', *symbel* 'feast'. In identifying lexical peculiarities in dialects it is of course necessary to consider chronology and meaning. For Latin *superbia* 'pride', Anglian has *oferhygd* or derivations from this, Early West Saxon uses *ofermōd* or derived words, while Late West Saxon in most cases employs *mōdig* and related words. OE *mōdig* also occurs in originally Anglian texts, but never with the negative semantic associations of pride as a sin.[11]

Among the vernacular languages of medieval Europe, Old English stands out as the only one that, as early as the tenth century, has developed a written literary standard. This 'Standard Old English', as it is called, is based on the late West Saxon dialect and is used in writing across most of the country from the latter half of the tenth century onwards. The political importance of the West Saxon royal house and, above all, the Benedictine reform movement will have contributed to this development. The role of the ecclesiastical centres of this movement, particularly Winchester, and the concentration of reformed Benedictine houses in the English south-west and the south-west Midlands must have been decisive, and it is possible to link this rise of an Old English linguistic standard with the endeavours and achievements of a particular school in which – as has now been conclusively shown – the use of a standard vocabulary was taught, and no doubt also the use of regularized forms of spelling, morphology and syntax. This is the school of Æthelwold, bishop of Winchester 963–84, whose outstanding pupil was Ælfric.[12]

Much has been written about the dialect of Old English poetry. Most of it is preserved in the four great poetic manuscripts, copied in the late tenth or early eleventh century. In accordance with what has been said before, their type of language is therefore West Saxon, but Anglian phonological forms and words in them led earlier scholars to believe that Old English poetry, with few exceptions, is Anglian in origin, probably going back to the time when the great religious and cultural centres of Northumbria and Mercia had not yet been wiped out by the Scandinavians. Nearly forty years ago, however, Kenneth Sisam suggested that what we find in this poetry is in fact an artificial and archaic poetic dialect, perhaps with a dialectally mixed vocabulary. More recent research on the Old English dialect vocabulary, however, tends to support the older view and would acknowledge only a few late poems, including *Genesis B* and *The Battle of Maldon*, as genuine southern works.[13]

The language of poetry

Linguistic usage within a speech community may vary widely according to the purpose and subject of a speaker or writer, the situation in which he speaks, his education and the social group to which he belongs. As a result, a language – apart from geographically determinable dialects – can appear in a variety of forms, styles, or 'registers'. Leaving aside such well-documented special fields as legal or medical literature, we know very little about registers in Old English, and it is therefore next to impossible to say, for example, what colloquial Old English must have been like.[14] There is, however, one exception, and that is the language of Anglo-Saxon poetry, of which we are able to form a clear and comprehensive picture.

A great deal about this subject will be said in other chapters of this book, especially about Old English verse and its linguistic basis, and about such stylistic devices as kenning and variation (see below, ch. 3). Some words about the vocabulary and syntax of poetry are appropriate in the present chapter, however.

As is to be expected, authors of Anglo-Saxon prose like Alfred, Ælfric and Wulfstan differ in their styles in general and in their choice of words in particular. There is, however, a more fundamental difference between the vocabularies of Old English prose and poetry. Anglo-Saxon poets make use of a large stock of distinctly poetic words, words that never or very rarely occur in prose, and they employ such words side by side with others that belong to the common vocabulary of Old English. Among the poetic terms are synonyms, especially for concepts like 'prince, leader', 'man, warrior', for weapons and ships, for 'fight, battle', for seafaring and the sea, but also for 'house' or 'hall', and for 'mind, soul'. Thus for 'man' and 'warrior' we have in *Beowulf* the commonly used words *man, wer, gesīð, ceorl* and *eorl*, but also words that are restricted to poetry: *beorn, guma, hæleð, rinc, secg*. For 'fight, battle', *The Battle of Maldon* has eleven expressions, of which only two may also occur in prose: *gewinn* and *wīg*; four are compounds which are not found outside poetry – *beadurǽs, gārrǽs, gūþplega, wīgplega* – and five are simple words (or formations with the prefix *ge-*) that are part of the special vocabulary of poetry: *beadu, gūþ, hild, gemōt, getoht*.

It seems significant that not a few of these poetic words are similarly employed (in their corresponding forms) in Old Saxon, Old High German and Old Norse poetry. There can be no doubt, therefore, that this poetic vocabulary of Old English represents an ancient Germanic tradition, just like the type of verse that is used without exception for all Anglo-Saxon poetry. Also, words like *beorn, beadu, gūþ* and *hild* are frequent as elements of Old English personal names.

It is difficult to say whether the groups of words cited above, as well as other, similar groups, consist of synonyms in the strict sense of the word. While the denotation of the terms within these groups should have been the same, connotations may have differed. It is certain, however, that words that were often used with a specific, 'technical' sense in prose did not carry that sense in poetry. OE *eorl, ceorl, þegn* and *gesīð* were terms denoting certain grades of social status of the person they referred to, especially in legal prose, but in poetry their meaning was usually just as general as that of *guma* or *secg*.

Such a wealth of synonyms no doubt helped to enhance the stylistic qualities of a poem. But, above all, these words served a practical purpose: in order to satisfy the requirements of the alliterative line, the poet needed for his key concepts a fairly wide choice of words, especially nouns, with different initial sounds. Such key concepts, it should be mentioned, came not only from fields like war and seafaring, but also from Christian religion. Anglo-Saxon religious poets adapted the traditional techniques to their purposes and so were able to give expression, for example, to a concept like 'Lord', 'God' by means of differently alliterating words: *dryhten, frēa, god, hlāford, þēoden, wealdend*.

Another characteristic of Old English poetry, already mentioned in the section on word-formation, is the large number of noun compounds. Poets were obviously free to coin such compounds as could best serve their metrical needs and their stylistic intentions. Again, the majority of these compounds are not found outside poetry, and many of them belong in semantic fields connected with fighting and seafaring. The statistics of a well-known poem's vocabulary structure may be of some interest. In *The Battle of Maldon*, a poem of which 325 lines survive, we have a total of 535 lexical units (many of them, of course, occurring more than once). Among these 535 words there are ninety-seven (= 18 per cent) that do not (or not normally, or not with the meaning in the poem) appear in prose. Out of these ninety-seven, forty-one are poetic words, almost all recorded in other Germanic languages; nine words have a sense that they cannot bear in Old English prose. Forty-seven are compounds, of which only three are also found in prose. Sixteen of the compounds only occur in *The Battle of Maldon* and so may well have been created by its author.

The notes on Old English syntax in a previous section of this chapter (above, pp. 34–7) apply to prose as well as poetry. But, as is to be expected, owing to the exigencies of alliterative verse and its rhythm and to stylistic considerations and traditions, the syntax of Old English verse differs in several respects from that of prose. As a general rule, it may be said that sentences are structured more loosely than in prose, and it should never be forgotten that the punctuation in our printed editions is essentially that of the modern editors who may want to impose on their text a grammatical precision that the poet may not have intended. Often enough, our difficulties with a sentence may have to do with the device of 'variation' (on which see below, pp. 64–5). Another characteristic of poetry is the insertion of parenthetic phrases which interrupt the progression of a sentence but allow the poet to place a comment or explanatory remark where he thinks it suitable, as in *Beowulf* 2706–8 (where the dashes were of course supplied by the editors):

> Fēond gefyldan   – ferh ellen wræc –
> ond hī hyne þā bēgen   ābroten hæfdon,
> sibæðelingas.

They felled the enemy (i.e. the dragon) – [their] courage had driven out its life – and they had cut it down, both the noble kinsmen.

The passage just quoted can also illustrate another typical feature of Old English verse syntax. Whereas (as pointed out above) there is an increasing tendency to employ the order S–V–O in Old English main clauses, this is not so in poetry, where word order is handled much more freely; this is one of the reasons why such poetry makes rather more difficult reading than prose. Of other peculiarities of Old English poetry, at least the use of the definite article (originally a demonstrative pronoun) should be mentioned, which is here employed much less frequently than in prose texts.[15]

Names

Names of places and persons are of great interest to the historian as well as to the philologist, who will want to examine their etymology and word-formation, and who may be able to draw important conclusions from them with regard to characteristic dialect features and the distribution of Old English dialects. A great deal of work has been done on Anglo-Saxon names this century, and the student of Old English who is likely to come upon such names every now and then (not only in charters or in *Doomsday Book*, but in literary sources like Bede's *Historia ecclesiastica*, in the *Anglo-Saxon Chronicle* and in the poem *The Battle of Maldon*) should be familiar with a few basic facts of this subject.

English place-names[16] – but not those of Scotland, Wales and Cornwall – now as a thousand years ago are largely of Anglo-Saxon origin. This at any rate is true of the names of villages and hamlets; it certainly has to do with the fact that most English villages were created by Anglo-Saxon settlers. Some characteristic local feature, natural or man-made, may determine the name of such a settlement, as at Oxford (OE *Oxenaford* 'ford for oxen') or Cambridge (OE *Grantebrycg* 'bridge over the Granta'). Place-names containing an element denoting 'homestead' or 'village' are frequent; among the most common of such elements are -*hām* 'village, manor, homestead', -*tūn* 'homestead, village', -*wīc* (an early loanword, from Latin *vicus*) 'farm, dwelling, hamlet, village', and -*burh* 'fortified place, manor, town'; cf. ModE *Waltham* (village by a wood), *Kingston* (the king's manor), *Greenwich* (green village), *Bamborough* (Bebbe's fortified place). Personal names are often part of place-names, such as those in ModE -*ing*, OE -*ingas*: *Barking* (OE *Berecingas*, 'Berica's people'); *Hastings* (OE *Hǣstingas*, 'Hǣsta's people'), and so on.

The names of the larger towns that had already existed in Roman Britain usually remained British (as *London*, *Dover*, *York*), but were often compounded with OE -*ceaster* (from Latin *castra*), as in *Manchester* and *Winchester*. Also, most of the English river-names (but not those of smaller streams) are of British origin, like *Thames*, *Avon*, *Ouse*, *Severn*, *Stour*, *Tees* and *Trent*.

Of the few Latin elements that appear in Anglo-Saxon place-names, *ceaster* and *wīc* have already been mentioned; to these should be added *port* (from Latin *portus* 'harbour'), as in *Portsmouth*. Scandinavian place-names and place-name elements provide the main evidence for our knowledge of where exactly Danish and Norwegian settlements occurred in England from the latter half of the ninth century onwards. In the Danelaw, such names and elements are especially prominent in Yorkshire, Lincolnshire, Leicestershire and Nottinghamshire. Characteristic Norse names or name-elements in these counties (and elsewhere) are -*by* 'village, homestead', -*toft* 'homestead', -*thorp* 'outlying farm', as in *Grimsby*, *Lowestoft* and *Thorpe*.

The Anglo-Saxons continued the Germanic practice of giving personal names.[17] There were no surnames before the Norman Conquest; normally, every man or woman had just one name, which in most cases was formed as a compound whose elements were taken from a limited stock of words that were traditionally used in name-making. Originally, all such compounds may have been meaningful, but in the course of time, elements were combined that cannot always be said to have made sense as a whole. Examples of compound personal names are:

Ēadgār	'rich, happy'	+ 'spear'
Ēadweard	'rich, happy'	+ 'guardian'
Æthelbeorht	'noble'	+ 'bright'
Cūthbeorht	'famous'	+ 'bright'
Dūnstān	'hill'	+ 'stone'
Ōswald	'god'	+ 'power'

And for women:

Æthelburh	'noble'	+ 'fortress'
Æthelthrȳth	'noble'	+ 'strength'
Hildeburh	'battle'	+ 'fortress'

It was a principle of name-giving that the names of close relatives should alliterate or even that a child's name should include one element of its father's (or sometimes mother's) name. Thus Byrhtnoth, the Anglo-Saxon leader in the Battle of Maldon, is the son of Byrhthelm, and King Alfred (Ælfred) was the son of Æthelwulf and the brother of Æthelberht and Æthelred.

As the range of available name-elements was limited, and as there were no surnames, the same name was often borne by different persons, and this has created not a few problems for modern scholarship. It is the reason why, for example, Ælfric the homilist and grammarian was for a long time considered to be the same man as Ælfric, archbishop of Canterbury (995–1005), or to be identical with other contemporaries of the same name. One way of distinguishing bearers of the same Old English name was the occasional practice of adding a byname to the given name; such bynames could refer to the bearer's place of residence, to his father (Ēadbeorht Ēadgāring 'the son of Ēadgār'), or would simply be nick-names, often derived from physical characteristics. In *The Battle of Maldon* (line 273), Ēadweard se langa 'the tall one' may be an example.

Uncompounded personal names were not uncommon among the Anglo-Saxons, especially in the early centuries of their history. In later times, they became rare, at least among the upper classes. Such mono-thematic names could be either shortened forms of dithematic (compounded) ones, like Goda from Godwine or Godgifu, or Hild from compound names with this element. But there was also a large number of original uncompounded names, like Beda, Ida, Penda, Offa, whose etymology is often controversial. It is hardly surprising that there were also names of

British origin from early times on, like *Cædmon* and *Cedd*, while later numerous Scandinavian names, like *Thurstan, Swegen,* and many others became common.

The study of the Old English language has a a long tradition. During the Middle English period, from the thirteenth century onwards, rapid and radical changes in the English language meant that there were few who were able or willing to read Old English texts. But in the later sixteenth century, after the suppression of the monasteries and the dispersal of their libraries, scholars began to collect Anglo-Saxon manuscripts, to print texts and to study the language. That activity has continued to the present: practically all Old English texts are now available in printed editions, and their language has been thoroughly analysed and described. Even so, a great deal of work remains to be done, in order to perfect our understanding of the Old English language.

1 For comprehensive accounts of the history of English, see A. C. Baugh, *A History of the English Language,* 3rd ed., rev. T. Cable (London and Englewood Cliffs, NJ, 1978), and B. M. H. Strang, *A History of English* (London and New York, 1970). A very useful historical grammar is K. Brunner, *Die englische Sprache: ihre geschichtliche Entwicklung,* 2nd ed., 2 vols. (Tübingen, 1960–2). A valuable guide to the field is J. Fisiak, *A Bibliography of Writings for the History of the English Language,* 2nd ed. (Berlin, 1987). For introductory guides to Old English, see the section on grammars in Further Reading (below, p. 284). Note that throughout this article I use OE to refer to Old English and ModE to refer to Modern English.

2 For a more detailed treatment of the prehistory of English, see P. Baldi, *An Introduction to the Indo-European Languages* (Carbondale, IL, 1983), and E. Prokosch, *A Comparative Germanic Grammar* (Baltimore, MD, 1939). Two recent works by Alfred Bammesberger are particularly useful: *English Linguistics* (Heidelberg, 1989), and 'The Place of English in Germanic and Indo-European', in *The Beginnings to 1066,* ed. R. M. Hogg, Cambridge History of the English Language 1 (Cambridge, forthcoming).

3 For the manuscript transmission of Old English texts, see N. R. Ker, *Catalogue of Manuscripts containing Anglo-Saxon* (Oxford, 1957); A. Cameron, 'A List of Old English Texts', in *A Plan for the Dictionary of Old English,* ed. R. Frank and A. Cameron (Toronto, 1973), pp. 25–306; and H. Gneuss, 'A Preliminary List of Manuscripts Written or Owned in England up to 1100', *ASE* 9 (1981), 1–60.

4 For runes and runic monuments in England, see R. I. Page, *An Introduction to English Runes* (London, 1973); R. W. V. Elliott, *Runes: an Introduction,* 2nd ed. (Manchester, 1989); and Cameron, 'A List', pp. 255–61.

5 The indispensable scholarly handbook in the field of palaeography is B.

Bischoff, *Latin Palaeography: Antiquity and the Middle Ages*, trans. D. Ó Cróinín and D. Ganz (Cambridge, 1990); for Insular script, see pp. 83–95, as well as N. Denholm-Young, *Handwriting in England and Wales* (Cardiff, 1964).

6 A handbook of Old English word-formation remains to be written. Ch. 4 in R. Quirk and C. L. Wrenn, *An Old English Grammar*, 2nd ed. (London, 1958), is a good introduction to the subject. The historical sections in H. Marchand, *The Categories and Types of Present-Day English Word-Formation*, 2nd ed. (Munich, 1969), and the treatments of prefixes and suffixes in the *Oxford English Dictionary* (cited below, n. 7) are valuable.

7 Numerous books deal with general questions of meaning and semantic change, but the fullest and most reliable source for our knowledge of the history of English words that have survived the Old English period is still J. A. H. Murray, H. Bradley, W. A. Craigie and C. T. Onions, *The Oxford English Dictionary* (Oxford, 1884–1928; corr. re-issue with Supplement, 1933; a second edition of 1989 includes the Supplement published in 1972–86). Individual studies of Old English words are listed in A. Cameron, A. Kingsmill and A. C. Amos, *Old English Word Studies: a Preliminary Author and Word Index* (Toronto, 1983).

8 For a stimulating and thorough study of the semantic field that includes OE *mōd*, see M. Godden, 'Anglo-Saxons on the Mind', in *Learning and Literature in Anglo-Saxon England: Studies Presented to Peter Clemoes on the Occasion of his Sixty-Fifth Birthday*, ed. M. Lapidge and H. Gneuss (Cambridge, 1985), pp. 271–98.

9 For a detailed treatment of borrowing in Old English, see Baugh, *A History of the English Language*, ch. 4, and for an inventory of loanwords, M. S. Serjeantson, *A History of Foreign Words in English* (London, 1935).

10 See, for example, M. A. D'Aronco, 'The Botanical Lexicon of the Old English *Herbarium*', *ASE* 17 (1988), 15–33.

11 A. Campbell, *Old English Grammar* (Oxford, 1959), pp. 4–11, serves as a good introduction to the Old English dialects. For work on the dialect vocabulary, see the introduction to F. Wenisch, *Spezifisch anglisches Wortgut in den nordhumbrischen Interlinearglossierungen des Lukasevangeliums* (Heidelberg, 1979). The distribution of the Old English words for 'pride' is treated by H. Schabram, *Superbia* (Munich, 1965).

12 For Standard Old English and the Winchester vocabulary, see H. Gneuss, 'The Origin of Standard Old English and Æthelwold's School at Winchester', *ASE* 1 (1972), 63–83, and W. Hofstetter, 'Winchester and the Standardization of Old English Vocabulary', *ASE* 17 (1988), 139–61.

13 See K. Sisam, *Studies in the History of Old English Literature* (Oxford, 1953), pp. 119–39, and Wenisch, *Spezifisch anglisches Wortgut*, p. 328.

14 But see B. von Lindheim, 'Traces of Colloquial Speech in Old English', *Anglia* 70 (1951), 22–42.

15 Among numerous studies of the language of Old English poetry are H. C. Wyld, 'Diction and Imagery in Anglo-Saxon Poetry', *Essays and Studies* 11 (1925), 49–91, and A. G. Brodeur, *The Art of Beowulf* (Berkeley, CA, 1959), pp. 7–38 and 254–71.

16 The best reference work for Old English place-names is E. Ekwall, *The Concise Oxford Dictionary of English Place-Names*, 4th ed. (Oxford, 1960); for individual names, the Publications of the English Place-Name Society (one or more volumes for every county) should be consulted.

17 For Old English personal names we have specialized studies, but no general treatment. Ch. 6 in P. H. Reaney, *The Origin of English Surnames* (London, 1967), and H. Ström, *Old English Personal Names in Bede's History*, Lund Studies in English 8 (Lund, 1939), xxxiv–xliii, may serve as useful introductions. H. Voitl has provided a review of research in *Archiv für das Studium der neueren Sprachen und Literaturen* 199 (1963), 161–7, and 213 (1976), 50–2.

3   The nature of Old English verse

The verse form used for vernacular poetry throughout the Anglo-Saxon period was that common to all the Germanic peoples, and was carried to England by the migrating tribes of the fifth century. It is therefore rooted in an oral tradition of poems composed, performed and passed on without benefit of writing. Some signs of the ways in which this poetry was created and transmitted can be gleaned from occasional references in vernacular and Latin literature. Heroic poetry in Old English tells of the professional minstrel at the court of kings, singing traditional legends from the Germanic past, and occasionally adding Christian stories to his repertoire, familiar tales made delightful to his audience by his skill in developing and embellishing them. In Latin works we learn something of the transmission of poems in more humble surroundings: William of Malmesbury, in the twelfth-century *Gesta pontificum*, reports King Alfred's story of Abbot Aldhelm (d. 709) reciting secular poetry at the bridge in Malmesbury to attract an audience for his preaching, and Bede, in the *Ecclesiastical History*, suggests that it was normal in the seventh century for men of the lowest social classes when attending festive gatherings to recite poems that they had learnt by heart. Bede tells this in relation to the cowman Cædmon of Whitby who was graced, late in life, with a miraculous gift of song, in a manner reminiscent of other divine visitations of the early Middle Ages, and who thereby became the first to convert the inherited Germanic metre to Christian use. Many others, Bede goes on, did so after him, but none so well (*HE* IV.24).

By the end of the period, there are signs of a fully articulated written tradition. Amongst the poems surviving in manuscripts are four by a man called Cynewulf, who signed his name in an acrostic of runes which presumably would have to be seen rather than heard to make their impact. But the poetry which has come down to us in manuscript owes much to its oral background. Some of the surviving poems may themselves have been transmitted orally, perhaps across many generations, before they were committed to writing, and even those which were composed in writing use techniques and rhetorical devices which were developed in an oral tradition and reflect the needs of that tradition, such as the repetition of sentence elements or the frequent use of mnemonic formulae.

Poems in Old English are untitled in the manuscripts in which they survive, the titles by which they are now generally known having been given to them, in the main, by their nineteenth-century editors. They are also for the most part anonymous. Although Bede reports that Cædmon composed poetic paraphrases of Genesis, Exodus and other biblical books, it is likely that only the nine lines composed at his initial inspiration survive. The only other named poet of note from the period is Cynewulf, who signed four poems, *Elene*, *Juliana*, *The Fates of the Apostles* and *Christ II* (the central section, lines 440–866, of the poem *Christ* as edited in the third volume of ASPR), so that those enjoying his poetry might pray for his soul. But beyond his name and his interest in translating Latin hagiographic and homiletic literature into Old English verse, nothing is known of him. Two other prominent Anglo-Saxons who are better known for their prose writings are associated with some surviving verse. Soon after King Alfred translated Boethius's *Consolation of Philosophy* from Latin into Old English prose at the end of the ninth century, someone recast the sections of the work which corresponded to the Latin *metra* into uninspired but metrically passable Old English verse. It is probable, but by no means certain, that Alfred was that someone. And finally, towards the end of the Anglo-Saxon period, Archbishop Wulfstan, a prolific writer of ecclesiastical and civil legislation and well known for his fiery eschatological sermons, is thought by some scholars to have composed the brief poems on King Edgar that appear in the *Anglo-Saxon Chronicle* annals for 959 and 975.

Cædmon's first nine lines of Christian verse are recorded in eighth-century manuscripts; almost all the other surviving examples of Old English poetry are in manuscripts of the tenth and eleventh centuries, the greater part in the four so-called Poetic Codices, all written within the period 975–1025. These four books have little in common with each other except that they all contain verse. Only one, the Exeter Book, is an anthology of poetry (both secular and religious). In two of the others, the Vercelli Book and the *Beowulf* Manuscript, the fact that some items are in verse is perhaps incidental. In the Vercelli Book, six religious poems are scattered in a collection of homiletic prose, the scribe showing no interest in making a distinction between the two mediums. The only convincing explanation of the compilation of the *Beowulf* Manuscript is that it contains a series of 'monster' tales, some in prose, some in verse, the subjects being a mixture of Christian and secular. Finally, the Junius Manuscript contains religious poetry, Old Testament paraphrase and some lyrics on Old and New Testament themes. It is difficult to reconstruct the reasons for the creation of these books. The content and large format of the Junius Manuscript suggest that it may have had some liturgical use. The Exeter Book was probably made for a wealthy patron; by 1072 it belonged to Bishop Leofric of Exeter, for it was amongst the collection of books that he bequeathed to his cathedral church. The variety of manuscript contexts in which the poems survive adds to the difficulty of determining anything of their origin and transmission.

That books of vernacular poetry existed at an earlier period we know from a story told about the boyhood of King Alfred, in Bishop Asser's Life of the king, in which his mother offered to give a book of Saxon poetry to whichever of her sons first learnt it by heart. (Alfred won it, of course.) It is impossible to know if any of the poems that Alfred knew survived into the copies made a century and a half later. We can only speculate on the period of time over which poetry was copied, as we can about the relationship between oral and written composition and transmission. A few clues may be drawn from the very small quantity of verse that survives in more than one copy. A dozen lines from the middle of *The Dream of the Rood* were carved in runes on an eighteen-foot stone preaching cross in Ruthwell, Dumfriesshire, no later than the end of the eighth century, while the whole poem survives in the Vercelli Book, copied in Canterbury towards the end of the tenth. This suggests the freedom with which popular poems might move around the country, and their ability to survive (either orally or in writing) for hundreds of years. On the other hand, the marked differences between two copies of a passage of homiletic verse, *The Soul and Body*, in the Vercelli and Exeter Books (written within a generation of one another) indicate the freedom with which scribes sometimes made alterations to the material they were copying.

There are no sure objective tests by which poetry can be dated, and no means of proving which of the surviving poems were composed orally and which in writing. All Old English poetry is of such uniformity in form and language that it is impossible to establish even relative dating with any certainty. Bede's story of Cædmon suggests that Christian poetry began late in the seventh century, and analysis of the runes on the Ruthwell Cross and of the spelling of Cynewulf's name in the acrostics suggest that some surviving poetry was in existence in some form from early in the ninth century, although the manuscript copies that we have were not made until almost two hundred years later. The dating of secular poetry is extremely problematic, not least because so little survives beyond *Beowulf*, and because the dating of that poem, which is so crucial to the study of Old English metre, is amongst the most vexed questions facing students today. Many critics still hold trenchantly to the generally accepted view of earlier scholars, that the poem was composed in the seventh or eighth centuries, or just possibly in the early ninth, before much of England succumbed to the attacks of the Vikings. But the voices of those who argue for a later date are slowly becoming more assured. Although very few accept the recently argued case for the hand of one of the two scribes responsible for making the only surviving copy of the poem being that of the author himself, many now believe that the poem could have taken the form in which we have it some time between the birth of Alfred in 849 and the accession of his great-great-grandson Æthelred in 978. Poems on historical subjects can be dated with more precision, but offer no useful basis for establishing a comparative chronology. Those recorded in *Anglo-Saxon Chronicle* entries for the tenth century lack inspiration. In *The Battle of Maldon*, composed after the historically documented battle of 991, traditional metrical patterns are very occasionally replaced by couplets linked with assonance or rhyme similar to that found in contemporary Latin verse, and this heralds the change which was to overtake English poetry by the twelfth century. But against this we must set the fact that the majority of lines in *The Battle of Maldon* do satisfy the constraints of traditional metre, and it is therefore necessary to accept that Old English classical verse could still be handled competently after 991.

Anglo-Saxon scribes copied poetry in continuous lines, as they did prose, although some used punctuation to mark metrical units. The manuscripts give no indication about performance. We might draw some inferences from other evidence, for example the fact that writers use the terms *leoð* ('poem') and *sang* ('song') interchangeably, but so do Latin writers of *poema* and *carmen*, and the word 'lyric' in Modern English may also apply to poetry or to song. The Old English translation of Bede's account of Cædmon renders Latin *cantare* (which may mean 'to chant or recite' as well as 'to sing') as *be hearpan singan*, literally 'to sing to the harp', and Old English poems frequently refer to minstrels as performing to the same stringed instrument, which in fact more resembled a lyre if we judge from manuscript illustrations. The fragmentary remains of a stringed instrument, carefully wrapped in a beaver-skin bag, were amongst the treasures laid in the great royal ship-burial at Sutton Hoo, and this bears witness to the fact that patronage of poetry and of the minstrel was considered an important function of the king. But none of this takes us any nearer to an appreciation of how poetry was performed, and whether the minstrel's art was closer to modern ideas of singing or of chant than of recitation.

The basis of Old English metre, as of English verse of later periods, is one of alternating stressed and unstressed syllables. Some 30,000 lines survive, all of them divided into two, roughly equal parts, each containing two strongly stressed syllables (or **lifts**) and a variable number of lightly stressed ones (each group of which is known as a **fall**). The underlying rhythm may be said to be trochaic or dactylic, with the heavy stresses preceding the light ones, as in the nursery rhyme

/ ×   / ×   /   ×   / ×
Mary, Mary, quite contrary

(where / represents a heavy stress and × a light one). This line falls into two sense-units, the repeated name being one, the character-definition the other, and the two-part structure is underscored by the internal rhyme *Mary:contrary*. In Old English too a half-line is frequently a sense-unit, but the dividing-point or caesura is stressed by a change of rhythm, for example the trochaic pattern might become iambic or anapestic, as in *Beowulf* 7:

/   ×   /   ×   × ×   / × × /
feasceaft funden,   he þæs frofre gebad

[Scyld was] found destitute; he lived to see consolation for that

or the 'reversed' pattern might occur first, as in *Beowulf* 32:

× ×   / ×   /   /   ×   / ×
Þær æt hyðe stod   hringedstefna

there at the quay stood the ring-prowed ship

Instead of the internal rhyme linking the two halves of the nursery rhyme line, Old English lines regularly had alliteration of either or both of the stressed syllables in the first half (in my examples, the words beginning *fea-, fund-; hyð-*) with the first stressed syllable in the second half (*frof-; hring-*). Because of the strength of the caesura, editors usually print the poetry with a noticeable gap, as I have done, and metrists scan it in half lines, called verses. The stress patterns are those of speech, emphasis falling on the semantically important part of a word, not on a grammatical element (e.g. as in Modern English *houses* which is stressed / ×). Usually nouns and adjectives carry the stresses, other parts of speech occurring as lifts only when the sense required them to be especially emphasized, and semantically light words such as the article *the* are generally excluded from the poetry altogether. The trochaic or dactylic pattern is known as Type A, such a semantically empty description being useful because classical terms like trochee and dactyl do not take account of the fact that many verses have three or even four light stresses between the heavy ones, and the lifts sometimes consist of two short syllables rather than a single long one. (The two-syllable lift is known as a **resolved** lift, and is marked in the scansion below with a cup-shaped accent ˘ over the short syllables.)

Type A verses are by far the commonest. The reversed pattern, *he þæs frofre gebad*, is Type B. Type C has the two lifts contiguous, with lightly stressed syllables before and after, as in *Beowulf* 4:

$$\times \quad / \quad / \times$$
Oft Scyld Scefing

Frequently Scyld son of Scef . . .

These three are the only patterns which contain variation on the simple alternation between heavily and lightly stressed syllables, but in Old English, as in Modern English, it was possible to distinguish not two but three levels of stress in normal speech. An example in Modern English might be found in the contrasting stress patterns of the phrases *a black bird*, where *black* and *bird* are equally stressed, and *a blackbird*, where *black-* is more heavily stressed than *-bird*, but where *-bird* is nevertheless more heavily stressed than *a*. The half-stress (most usually found in Old English in the second element of compound words) gives rise to further metrical patterns, Types D and E. There are two variants of Type D, depending on the position of the half-stress (marked \), either that represented by *Beowulf* 1409:

$$/ \quad / \quad \backslash \times$$
steap stanhliðo

towering stone-cliffs

or that found in *Beowulf* 1400:

$$/ \quad / \quad \times \quad \backslash$$
wicg wundenfeax

horse with braided mane

Beowulf 50 offers an example of Type E:

$$/ \quad \backslash \quad \times \quad /$$
murnende mod

grieving heart

There are some slight variations upon these patterns; for example, Type D is occasionally found with an extra unstressed syllable between the lifts, and Types A and D are sometimes preceded by one or two unstressed syllables in some way outside the regular pattern of the scansion, but the vast majority of the verses fit the five major types.

Although the basic types are few, Old English poets achieved a remarkably wide range of effects with them. Most lines contain two contrasting metrical types to mark the caesura, but unity is given to the whole line by the binding of the two parts with alliteration. Few verses or lines are syntactically complete, however. Sentences run on over a number of lines to form a verse paragraph, and it is the metrical pattern of the whole paragraph which is often significant to a poet's design. For example, increase in the number of unstressed syllables would quicken the verse in performance, and repeated used of Types A, B and C might give a passage an insistent beat suitable for narrative. Frequent use of Types D and E, on the other hand, would slow the verse down because of the relatively high proportions of weighted syllables, and produce a style suitable for moments of high drama. Two passages from *Beowulf* will illustrate the point. The first, lines 1008–17, introduces the celebratory feast and gift-giving at Heorot after the defeat of Grendel, where the dancing rhythm and intricate and melodious patterning of sounds provide an image of the gaiety of the company. (The right-hand column lists the metrical types. Elided syllables are unmarked in the scansion.)

× × / × / Þa wæs sæl ond mæl	B
× × / × / / \ × / þæt to healle gang Healfdenes sŭnŭ;	B E
× × / / × / × / × wolde self cyning symbel þicgan.	C A
(× ×) / × × / × / × / × Ne gefrægen ic þa mægþe maran wĕorŏde	A A
× × × / / × / × / × ymb hyra sincgyfan sel gebæran.	C A
/ × × / × / / \ × Bŭgŏn þa to bence blædagande,	A D
/ × × / × / × × / × fylle gefægon; fægĕre geþægon	A A
/ × / × / × / × mĕdŏful manig magas þara	A A
/ / \ × × / × / swiðhicgende on sĕlĕ þam hean,	D B
/ × × / × Hroðgar ond Hroþulf (1008–17)	A

Then came the proper and suitable time for the son of Healfdene [i.e. Hrothgar] to make his entrance into the hall; the king himself intended to take part in the banquet. I have never heard of a nation which behaved with greater decorum in so large a company around their lord [literally: giver of treasure] at that time. Then the glorious [Danes] rejoiced at the feast; Hrothgar and Hrothulf, the resolute ones, their kinsmen, drank many a toast courteously in the lofty hall.

The underlying trochaic pattern is strongly emphasized here, with a predominance of Type A verses. Frequent construction of a line with two

A-verses (1011, 1014, 1015) or with C + A (1010, 1012) has the effect of reducing the usual dislocation of the caesura and increasing the overall regularity of pattern. Additional lyrical effects are produced with internal rhyme, *sæl ond mæl* (1008) and *gefægon:gepægon* (1014). Line 1014 has a most intricate design in that within the rhyme *gefægon:gepægon* the sounds of the first rhyme-word are picked up in the intervening word *fægere*, not just in the alliteration on *f* but in the vowel *æ* (long in the rhyme words but short in *fægere*) and in the syllable-final *g*. The three words together offer a remarkable pattern of alliteration, rhyme and assonance which a competent minstrel could put to good use. The melody of the passage is further enhanced by a subtle increase in alliterating consonants beyond that which is functional to the linking of verses within a line. Normally in Old English verse the fourth stressed syllable in a line is the only one which may not alliterate, but there are two exceptions, both illustrated here. Occasionally throughout the surviving poetry, lines are found with two pairs of alliterating syllables involving all four heavy stresses, either in the pattern *abab* or, less frequently, in *abba*. In line 1016 above, alliteration falls on both *s* (*swið-:sele*) and *h* (*-hicg-:hean*). And sometimes the initial sound of the fourth stressed syllable anticipates the alliteration of the following line, as happens in lines 1009–10 *sunu* (cf. *self:symb-*), again in lines 1012–13 (*ge*)*bær*(*an*) (cf. *Bug-, benc-:blæd-*), and yet a third time in lines 1016–17 *hean* (cf. *Hroð-, Hrop-*). Some critics regard this feature as purely accidental, but it is an accident which happens more than 200 times in *Beowulf* alone, and it would be difficult for an audience attuned to the catching up of initial consonant sounds to ignore it. The effect in the quoted instances is to sweep the listener forward across both metrical and syntactic boundaries.

The second illustrative passage, lines 1408–21, occurs after Grendel's mother has savagely attacked the hall in the night following the feast, and carried off Hrothgar's favourite retainer, Æschere. Now Hrothgar and the Danes must lead Beowulf through the bleak landscape filled with unknown horrors that leads to her lair. The music of the poetry here must reflect the dangerous and frightening journey which ends with the horrific discovery that they make at the water's edge, and we find that many lines have the smallest number of syllables that the metre will allow, the performer slowing down his recitation to give his audience plenty of time to absorb the implications of his words. The larger proportion of stressed syllables associated with Types D and E, and the greater disruption of the flow of the underlying alternating stress pattern which those types create, increase the sense of discomfort that the audience feels.

    × × / × /   / \ × /
    Ofereode þa   æþělinga bearn   B E

    /   / \ × / × / ×
    steap stanhliðo, stige nearwe,   D A

/   /   \ ×   /   \   × /
enge anpaðas,   uncuð gelad,   D E

/   ×   /   ×   /   \ ×   /
neowle næssas,   nĭcŏrhusa fĕlă.   A E

×   /   ×   /   ×   /   /   ×
He feara sum   befŏrăn gengde   B C

/   ×   /   ×   /   /   \×
wisra monna   wong sceawian,   A D

×   ×   × /   /   ×   /   ×   /   ×
oþþæt he færinga   fyrgenbeamas   C A

× ×   /   ×   /   / ×   /   ×
ofer harne stan   hlĕonĭan funde,   B A

/   \   ×   /   /   /   ×   \
wynleasne wŭdŭ;   wætĕr under stod   E D

/   ×   ×   ×   / ×   /   /   ×   \
dreorig ond gedrefed.   Dĕnŭm eallum wæs,   A D

/   /   \   ×   /   × ×   /   ×
wĭnŭm Scyldinga,   weorce on mode   D A

×   × /   /   ×   /   ×   /   ×
to geþolĭănne,   ðegne mŏnĕgum,   C A

/   ×   /   × ×   \   ×   ×   /   / ×
oncyð eorla gehwæm,   syðþan Æscheres   D C

×   ×   /   / ×   /   ×   /   ×
on þam holmclife   hăfĕlan metton.   (1408–21)   C A

Then the son of princes set off across towering stone-cliffs, narrow defiles, confined single-paths, unexplored passages, steep headlands, many a lair of water-monsters. He and a few skilful men led the way to reconnoitre the terrain, until he suddenly discovered mountain trees leaning across a bare cliff, a joyless thicket; a pool lay beneath, bloody and turbid. For all the Danes, the friends of the Scyldings, there was the suffering of terrible mental anguish, for many a thegn, for every warrior, there was desolation, when on that cliff beside the mere they discovered Æschere's head.

The pace of the metre during the description of the journey in lines 1408–13 is slow, with Types D and E predominating, and few unstressed syllables, but with *oþþæt* 'until' in line 1414 the retainers (and the audience) reach their destination, and two quicker lines of Types A, B and C urge us into the doom-laden *wynleasne wudu*, which opens line 1416. Here the E + D metre becomes staccato with the contemplation of something dreadful, although we are not to know what it is until five lines later.

In order to understand the full impact of this passage, it is necessary to move from metre to syntax, word-order and vocabulary, for in Old English poetry there are specialized uses of all three. It is clear even from the Modern English translations given above that sentences in Old English verse run on over many lines, and that they involve considerable repetition. In the passage just quoted, for example, there are six phrases which are parallel objects of the verb *ofereode*, each occupying its own verse in lines 1409–11. Repetition of a sentence element is known as **variation**, and is a distinctive feature of Old English poetry, introducing much of its imagery. Here the series of descriptive terms makes clear the hardship of the journey, for it forces the men into single file without tree cover through unknown territory where countless natural enemies abound. The sentence, although it extends over four lines, is not syntactically difficult, for it has a regular word order of verb–subject–object, allowing the audience to dwell on what is said. In the last sentence of the passage, however, lines 1417–21, the poet builds up the tension by making the audience think about what is not said. Here the syntax is difficult, the variation and carefully manipulated word order leading to one of the poem's most powerful moments. The sentence begins with an impersonal construction, with the deep-structure subject, the Danes, in the dative case: *Denum eallum wæs* 'For all the Danes there was'. The only verb carrying semantic weight is an inflected or gerundial infinitive *to geþolianne*; the verb has the primary meaning 'suffer' and use of the gerund implies necessity, 'a need to suffer'. The 'object' of this verb is a noun in the instrumental case *weorce* 'by means of anguish', coupled with the slightly tautological *on mode* 'in their minds'. This complicated syntax forces the audience to attend more closely, and the variation *Denum eallum, winum Scyldinga, ðegne monegum, eorla gehwæm* allows them time to do so, but also holds up the narrative so that the listener or reader has to wait to learn the source of the Danes' distress. The first clue to it comes significantly at the end of a line in the possessive noun *Æscheres*, but what it is of Æschere that has been found we are not told until two verses later. Normally each verse has a certain syntactic completeness, in that words which are very closely linked grammatically, such as a noun with its qualifying adjective, constitute one verse, as in *steap stanhliðo* 'towering stone-cliffs' and *stige nearwe* 'narrow defiles' in line 1409. This is also the regular pattern with a possessive noun (which is syntactically similar to a qualifying adjective); for example, in this passage the genitive (possessive) case nouns *æþelinga*, *nicorhusa*, *Scyldinga* and *eorla* are all in the same verse as the word they are grammatically linked with (respectively *bearn*, *fela*, *winum* and *gehwæm*). But *Æscheres* is deliberately isolated, grammatical completion not being achieved before the alliterative pattern of the next line is established with *holm-*, so that the weight of the metre can fall upon the vital word *hafelan* 'head'. The horror is complete.

Complex syntax that overruns lines is frequent in Old English poetry, and one of the functions of variation may be to improve understanding in oral performance by the repetition of key sentence elements. In what seems to us the best of the surviving poetry, repetition is employed to identify different aspects of what is described. Here, in the four phrases used of the Danes, the poet first identifies them, stressing their unity, 'all the Danes', then uses the term *Scylding* which is both a general patronymic for the tribe and a pointer towards its line of kings, all of whom (including Hroðgar present here) are descended from Scyld. Hence *winum Scyldinga* 'friends of the Scyldings' implies the Danes' amity to one another and their love of their lord. Similarly *ðegne monegum* 'many a thegn' stresses their loyalty and *eorla gehwæm* 'each of the warriors' their individual bravery. This use of parallel phrases supplies one level of imagery in the poem. However, such variation makes great demands on the poet's vocabulary, and consequently the poetry of the period exhibits a specialized diction. In this passage, *oncyð* 'desolation' and *hafelan* are examples of simple words not found in prose. Also, the wide range of synonyms required for variation, the difficulty of satisfying the constraints of alliteration, and the need to reduce unstressed syllables to a minimum, especially in Types D and E, encouraged the use of compound words, many of which were created by the poets to satisfy the demands of particular contexts. One third of the lexicon of *Beowulf* consists of compounds, most of which do not occur outside poetry or even outside the one poem. In this passage alone, the compounds *stanhliðo*, *anpaðas*, *wynleasne* and *holmclife* are words found only in poetry, while *nicorhusa* and *fyrgenbeamas* are both *hapax legomena*, words recorded only once. The frequency of occurrence of such nonce words is no doubt in part the result of the limited survival of early poetry, but it is hard to resist the suggestion that some examples were created by poets for the contexts in which they are uniquely found.

The compression involved in the act of compounding lends depth of meaning to the poetry. Superficially, *anpaðas* is a simple compound formed from the words 'one' and 'paths', but for an Anglo-Saxon audience – or indeed for anyone aware of combat conditions – a path along which only one person may pass at a time has frightening connotations. The adjective *wynleas* has the familiar pattern of a noun negated with the suffix meaning 'lacking', like Modern English *harmless* or *speechless*. What is lacking here is *wynn*, usually translated 'joy, delight, pleasure' although in *Beowulf* the word is used very specifically of human delight, associated with life in the hall and companionship, all of which are lacking in this lonely, comfortless forest. Many poetic compounds are not simple descriptive terms but circumlocutory, incorporating a metaphor, as when Hroðgar in line 1012 is called *sincgyfan* 'giver of treasure', a reference to the pervasive image of the *comitatus* in Old English poetry, that is, a body of men who vow total loyalty to a lord in return for rich gifts. Such descriptive terms, often periphrastic, are known as **kennings**. Compound words lend themselves to adaptation to different metrical and semantic conditions, since one element of the compound can be replaced by a synonym or a word in a related semantic field. For instance, King Beowulf is called *sincgifan* in line 2311 but *goldgyfan* 'giver of gold' in line 2652 where the poet needs to alliterate on a different consonant. However, the *Beowulf* poet also uses the kenning *goldwine*, literally 'gold-friend', of both Kings Hroðgar and Beowulf, because the relationship between lord and retainer was much more complicated than that suggested by the mercenary arrangement of services offered in return for profit. *The Wanderer* expresses very movingly the desolation of a retainer deprived of the love and protection of his *goldwine* (lines 34–44). If *sincgifa* and *goldgyfa* may be said to be literal descriptions, albeit within the convention of the *comitatus*, *goldwine* involves the greater degree of compression found in many kennings.

Often kennings are found as phrases rather than compounds. Hroðgar is called *sinces brytta* 'distributor of treasure' or *beaga brytta* 'distributor of gold rings' to give double alliteration in the first verse of a line. In *Judith* this formula is developed to great effect: in line 30, the poet used the traditional phrase *sinces brytta* with references to the villain of the poem, Holofernus, when he was entertaining his troops at a feast (the usual opportunity for the distribution of treasure), but an adaptation of the term is then employed twice by the heroine as she is about to behead her would-be ravisher, first when she refers to Holofernus as *morðres brytta* 'distributor of murder' (line 90) and immediately afterwards when she invokes God as *tires brytta* 'distributor of glory'. It was this ability to transfer epithets from heroic concepts to religious ones that encouraged the use of the traditional verse form for Christian purposes. Cædmon's nine-line hymn of Creation, cited by Bede as the first Christian poetry to be composed in English, has a number of examples of compounds and phrases which are developed from heroic vocabulary; for example the kennings used for God, *heofonrices weard* 'guardian of heaven's kingdom' and *moncynnes weard* 'guardian of mankind', may be compared with the *Beowulf*-poet's description of Hroðgar as *beahhorda weard* 'guardian of hoards of gold-rings' (line 921) or with the commonly used heroic formula for kings, *folces hyrde* 'guardian of the people'. The success of poets in adapting traditional forms to serve a variety of Christian purposes, from biblical paraphrase to hymns to the Virgin, testifies to the flexibility of poetic diction and imagery.

Kennings abound in Old English poetry, some of the better known being *banhus* 'bone-house = body', *hronrad* 'whale-road = ocean', *hæðstapa* 'heath-walker = stag'. All of these survive in more than one poem, but many more are unique, such as *feorhhus* 'life-house = body' which occurs only in *The Battle of Maldon*. The latter looks like an adaptation of *banhus*, but it is impossible for the modern reader to know when an Anglo-Saxon poet is being original in word- or phrase-formation because of the random survival of texts. The phrases *morðres brytta* and *tires brytta* work well in *Judith*, but the same kennings are found in other poems too. In fact, the use of traditional compounds and phrases, as well as their adaptation, is part of a wider pattern of the extensive use of traditional formulae, only occasionally changed to fit different circumstances or to satisfy artistic demands. The verse *on sele þam hean* quoted above in *Beowulf* line 1016, for example, occurs also in lines 713 and 1984 of the same poem, while the whole of line 1016 has been used by the poet already, with some slight difference of preposition to fit another context, in line 919: *swiðhicgende   to sele þam hean*. The frequency with which formulaic phraseology, including kennings, recurs throughout Old English poetry should not be seen as detrimental to its overall effect. The fact that a verse or kenning is traditional is of less significance than its suitability for the context in which it is found. A useful example may be seen in the epithets by which the *Beowulf* poet reintroduces King Hroðgar on the morning after Grendel has attacked his hall for the first time, killing thirty thegns. Lines 129–30 describe the king as *mære þeoden, / æþeling ærgod* 'famous leader, fine prince', terminology traditionally used of a strong and victorious warlord which here by its ironic reversal underscores his helplessness in the face of the might of the enemy.

The same poet elsewhere shows an ability to create remarkable effects with the simplest of conventional poetic vocabulary. At the beginning of his poem, he wishes to give an impression of the magnificence of the valuable objects buried with Scyld Scefing in his ship funeral. Only once does he mention any specific items laid in the ship:

> ne hyrde ic cymlicor   ceol gegyrwan
> hildewæpnum   ond heaðowædum,
> billum ond byrnum   (38–40)

I have never heard of a ship more splendidly adorned with weapons of war and battle-dress, with swords and mail-coats.

At first sight the lines appear unremarkable. They open with conventional use of the 'I have (not) heard' formula seen above in line 1011, whereby the author gives a sense of immediacy and authenticity to a scene. The two words for swords and corselets in line 40 alliterate so conveniently that it is not surprising to find that this is not the only line in which they appear together. As a variation upon line 39, they do not appear to add any further dimension to the meaning of the passage. But the sentence becomes more interesting when the metre of line 39 is examined more closely. The two compounds are constructed to create a perfect balance: each has as its first element a disyllabic poetic word for 'battle', *hilde* and *heaðo*, alliterating on *h*, and as its second element another disyllabic word, alliterating on *w* and with vowel assonance, *wæpnum* and *wædum*. Yet the metrical pattern is different in the two verses:

$$ / \times / \times \quad \times \quad / \ / \times $$
hildewæpnum   ond hĕaðŏwædum   A C

and there is a subtle shift of meaning, from offensive weapons to defensive armour. The next verse echoes the shift by picking out one example of each of the general terms of line 39, swords for weapons and mailcoats for armour. The metrical ingenuity represents the craftsmanship displayed in the objects, but the poet has used only the most traditional of formulae and the most obvious words from heroic vocabulary to suggest the glory of the passing of his archetypal king.

The caesura, and the marking of it with a change of rhythm, gave many Old English poets the opportunity to create paradox or antithesis within the poetic line. In *The Dream of the Rood*, the author captures the duality of Christ's crucifixion for the Christian, the horror and the joy, in a series of lines, including 22–3, where the dreamer-narrator contemplates the changing aspects of the cross in his vision:

> hwilum hit wæs mid wætan bestemed,
> beswyled mid swates gange,   hwilum mid since gegyrwed

Sometimes it was drenched with moisture, washed with the running of blood, sometimes adorned with treasure.

In line 23 double alliteration (*swat-* with *sinc-*, *gang-* with *-gyr-*) is supported by a syntactic parallel to confirm what the poet himself refers to as *fuse beacen* 'the changing sign'. The *Beowulf* poet similarly plays on the contrastive possibilities of the two-verse structure by creating a metrical reflection of discord amongst men. A group of Danes at the Frisian court of King Finn have been treacherously attacked by Finn's men, and their leader, Hnæf, has been killed. When it is clear that the fight has reached stalemate, Finn offers a truce. But the Danes, from whose point of view the tale is told, are torn between enforced loyalty to Finn and heroic compulsion to avenge Hnæf, while the Frisians have already shown themselves untrustworthy. The tension is admirably displayed in the metre of line 1100 in which Finn assures the Danes of the Frisian good faith:

> þæt ðær ænig mon
> wordum ne worcum   wære ne bræce   (1099–1100)

that no man would break the truce there either by word or by deed

Each verse of line 1100 is a simple Type A, stressing the parallel of the two verses which appears in the patterning of words and the linking alliteration. On the surface, all is harmonious. But the underlying tension of the situation is represented by the assonance of each verse, the *or-um* sequence in the first verse contrasting with the *æ-e* vowels in the two stressed words in the second. The reader of alliterative poetry should be alive to sound patterns beyond the regular catching up of initial consonants.

The verses quoted in the last paragraph from *The Dream of the Rood* clearly do not fall into the system of five major types described above. Anglo-Saxon poets occasionally made use of extended lines, involving what are known as **hypermetric verses**. These consist broadly of one of the five types preceded by a series of 'extra' syllables. If the hypermetric verse is in the first half of a line, it regularly contains one extra alliterative syllable, but if in the second half, it may not. Hence *The Dream of the Rood* line 23 may be scanned:

$$[\times \ / \times \ \ \times] \ \ / \times \ \ / \ \ \times \quad [\times \times \ \ \times] \ / \ \ \times \times / \ \ \times$$
beswyled mid swates gange,   hwilum mid since gegyrwed

Both verses end with regular Type A verses, both have extra syllables before them, all of which are unstressed except *-swyl-* which alliterates with *swat-* and *sinc-*. Occasionally hypermetric verses occur singly but most are found in groups, and some poems, notably *The Dream of the Rood* and *Judith*, have a regular pattern of alternation between lines of hypermetric and of normal verses which give them a stanzaic effect, although it should be stressed that the stanzas thus produced are far from regular. Such alternation may be seen to lay different degrees of emphasis on different parts of the poem. In *The Dream of the Rood* the two longest passages of hypermetric verses surround the nine lines of normal verses which describe Christ's last moments on the cross, when darkness covered the earth and all creation wept (50–9). In *Judith*, the poet's description of the feast at which Holofernus shows himself to be a bad leader by getting his Assyrian followers drunk consists mainly of normal verses, but a shift into hypermetric verse allows for an effective use of the metre to stress a moral point.

> Swa se inwidda   ofer ealne dæg
> dryhtguman sine   drencte mid wine,
> swiðmod sinces brytta,   oðþæt hie on swiman lagon,
> oferdrencte his duguðe ealle,   swylce hie wæron deaðe
>   geslegene,
> agotene goda gehwylces   (28--32)

Thus the evil one drenched his body of retainers with wine throughout the whole day, the resolute distributor of treasure, until they lay in a swoon, he made all his nobility drunk, as if they were struck down by death, drained of every goodness.

Hypermetric verses widen the gap between the alliterating sounds in the two halves of a line. In line 31, the pattern of alliteration is established by the stressed syllables -*drenc*- and *duguð*-, and an audience that delighted in the completion of patterns of alliteration would have its expectations of a word in *d*- raised through the long series of unstressed syllables in *swylce hie wæron*, to be fulfilled dramatically with the whole weight of the metre emphasizing *deað*, the fate that awaited the army at the end of the poem.

The Old English poetry that has survived may give an unduly limited impression of the range that existed. Scraps, such as the forty-eight lines of *The Battle of Finnsburh*, another poem on the treachery of Finn's men which was found on a single parchment leaf in the eighteenth century and then lost again, suggest that styles not evident in the rest of the corpus may have been attempted. This poem has a compression of story-telling, an example of concise direct speech and a certain wry humour which are lacking elsewhere. But we can deduce very little from an imperfect copy of a fragment of a lost poem, which may have been composed late, under external influences such as those of Old Norse. Most Old English poetry is slow-moving, elevated in diction and moral in tone, but enough has been said above to suggest that the best is far from monotonous. The alliterative metre retained its attraction for English speakers long after post-Conquest French influence introduced other patterns, and the so-called alliterative revival of the fourteenth century produced major works of literature in *Sir Gawain and the Green Knight* and *Piers Plowman*. Alliteration continued to play an important part in the metre of dramatic verse in the fifteenth century, and the Germanic alliterative line should be seen as the basis of the blank verse metre of the sixteenth century. But the tradition of 'classical' Old English verse, with a two-part line, a strong caesura, alliteration, variation and heavy reliance on traditional diction and imagery, is lost with the Norman Conquest.

4 The nature of Old English prose

ONE of the most significant literary achievements of the Anglo-Saxons was the establishment of vernacular prose as an acceptable medium both for the dissemination of knowledge on a wide range of subjects and for the provision of moral instruction and entertainment. By the time of the Norman Conquest, English was being used for scientific and medical works, legal documents, historical records and religious instruction of all kinds, thus fulfilling a public and official role in society. Translations and reworkings of Latin texts had made available to educated laymen and clergy alike key works on philosophy and theology, world history and geography, along with travellers' tales and accounts of the east – occasionally even fiction – while for students in the monastic schools there were textbooks on computus (the science of calculating moveable Christian feasts, such as Easter) and on grammar and rhetoric. Even the gospels and a considerable portion of the Old Testament had been rendered into English. Much of the surviving Old English prose corpus is anonymous, and some of it is strictly utilitarian, but the status which it achieved is indicated by the fact that its authors included a king (Alfred), an archbishop (Wulfstan), two bishops (Werferth and Æthelwold) and an abbot (Ælfric).

When vernacular prose first came to be used for extensive recording in Anglo-Saxon England is not known. The law-code of Æthelberht, king of Kent (560–616), is commonly accepted as the first piece of extant prose in English but it is preserved in a unique manuscript that was not written until after the Norman Conquest. Other early law-codes apparently composed in the vernacular have likewise survived only in late copies and revisions. Early non-legal works such as the English version of parts of Isidore's *De natura rerum* attributed to Bede have vanished without trace. It is not until the second half of the ninth century that we have clear and unambiguous evidence of the use of English on any large scale for the writing of prose. Yet if, from this point onwards, the story is one of remarkable achievement in the exploitation of the vernacular as a credible alternative to Latin, with copying and recopying of Old English texts continuing well into the Middle English period, credit must be given to those pioneers whose works have now been lost but who laid down the solid foundations on which later writers were so successfully to build. The person usually held responsible for the establishment of English prose as a proper medium for subjects of all kinds is Alfred, king of Wessex (see above, p. 17). Alfred himself produced five major works: the Laws of Alfred, with a lengthy preface by the king, the Prose Psalms, the Pastoral Care (a translation of Gregory the Great's Regula pastoralis), the Soliloquies (based mainly on the Soliloquies and De videndo Deo of St Augustine) and a rendering of Boethius's Consolation of Philosophy. A second work by Gregory – the Dialogues – was translated for Alfred by Werferth, the Mercian bishop of Worcester, while two anonymous translations dating from this period – a West Saxon version of the history of the world by Paulus Orosius and a Mercian version of Bede's Ecclesiastical History – may well also have been commissioned or instigated by the king as part of an ambitious plan for the restoration of learning in his land. Literary activity in the second half of the ninth century was not, however, restricted to Alfred and his immediate circle. The Old English Martyrology, an anonymous work of Mercian origin, reflecting (like the Dialogues) an interest in the stories of saints, seems to have been composed some years before Alfred himself began to write. Another major text of the period, apparently unconnected with Alfred though used by Asser in his Latin biography of the king, is the first part of what is now known as the Anglo-Saxon Chronicle, a series of annals in the West Saxon dialect. This 'first compilation', which appears to have drawn on older sets of annals in both English and Latin, was continued and updated both at the end of Alfred's reign and on many later occasions.

The tradition continued in the tenth century. There is a major set of annals relating to the reign of Edward the Elder (899–924) in the A-version of the Chronicle (otherwise known as the Parker Chronicle). Other texts seemingly produced before the last decade of the tenth century are anonymous homilies in the Blickling and Vercelli manuscripts and various penitential texts and medical collections, while a translation of the Benedictine Rule by Bishop Æthelwold and his account of Edgar's re-establishment of the monasteries must both have been completed by 984, the year of his death. A case has also been made for a relatively early date of composition for two short narratives whose subject is the orient – the so-called Letter of Alexander to Aristotle and the Wonders of the East. It is in the last decade of the tenth century and the first two decades of the eleventh, however, when Ælfric, Wulfstan and Byrhtferth began to write, that we find a great range of Old English prose texts again. Ælfric (c. 950–c. 1010), abbot of Eynsham and a product of the cultural renaissance resulting from the Benedictine reforms, is best known for his two sets of Catholic Homilies and a collection of saints' lives. However, he also composed a number of other works on a range of subjects – supplementary homilies and occasional pieces, pastoral letters, a treatise known as *De temporibus anni*, a Grammar, Old Testament translations and adaptations, renderings of Latin texts such as St Basil's *Hexameron* (incorporating material drawn from commentaries on Genesis by Bede) and a handbook on Genesis, known as the *Interrogationes Sigewulfi in Genesin*.

The corpus of English writings by Ælfric's contemporary Wulfstan, archbishop of York (d. 1023), is small in comparison, though his influence appears to have been considerable. In addition to some twenty homilies and the prose portions of the Benedictine Office, vernacular compositions for which Wulfstan was responsible include the *Canons of Edgar* (a text aimed at the secular clergy and offering practical and spiritual guidance), the *Institutes of Polity* (a work defining the duties of all classes of men and attempting to clarify the relationship between Church and State) and legal codes issued by the kings Æthelred and Cnut. An entry under the year 959 in the *Anglo-Saxon Chronicle*, manuscripts D and E, relating to the accession of King Edgar is also in Wulfstan's style, and it has been suggested that two texts concerned with the management of a great estate – *Rectitudines* and *Gerefa* – owe their final form to him.

The third major writer of this period, Byrhtferth of Ramsey, was a Benedictine monk and author of the *Enchiridion*, a manual composed *c.* 1011 in both Latin and English, whose primary purpose was to instruct pupils about computus, but which also included discussion of figures of speech and numerology.

Other works which may be dated probably to the late Old English period include legal documents, saints' lives, possibly also a lapidary and a (now incomplete) rendering of the story of Apollonius of Tyre. A major addition to the *Anglo-Saxon Chronicle* was a series of annals centred on the reign of Æthelred the Unready; other entries take the *Chronicle* beyond the Norman Conquest and, in the case of manuscript E (the Peterborough Chronicle), right up to 1140. A considerable amount of homiletic writing was also composed at this time, including a number of 'hybrid' homilies, borrowing freely from older works on similar subjects.

Of the surviving Old English prose corpus a surprisingly large part consists of works written at the request of colleagues and patrons. Alfred commissioned a translation of Gregory's *Dialogues* from his 'friends', for his private reading, in order that he might occasionally 'reflect in his mind upon heavenly things amidst these worldly preoccupations' (ed. Hecht, p. 1). The translations of Bede and Orosius may, as we have seen, similarly have been composed in response to the king's request to his bishops and other scholars to render into English 'those books that are most necessary for all men to know'.[1] Ælfric not only undertook biblical

translations at the request of Ealdorman Æthelweard, but composed his
set of saints' lives for that patron and his son Æthelmær. Other works by
Ælfric were commissioned by members of the land-owning class, such
as Sigeweard, and by senior clerics such as Archbishop Wulfstan and
Bishop Wulfsige. Wulfstan in his turn wrote for two successive kings of
England. At the same time Ælfric and Wulfstan both appear to have had
as one of their major aims the provision of materials that would aid
others in their task of teaching and instructing the people. For both, as
for Alfred before them, vernacular prose was the most practical and effective means of disseminating knowledge, though both could and did also
write in Latin, and Latin was the language of the authorities on whom
they depended.

The range of writing within Old English prose is striking. The *Anglo-
Saxon Chronicle* for instance – a primary source for historians – includes
amongst its anonymous contributors both providers of strictly factual
records and people prepared to express a personal viewpoint. We may
compare the terse reference in annal 592, 'in this year there occurred a
great slaughter at "Woden's barrow" and Ceawlin was driven out', with
the annal for 1011 (MSS C, D and E), which leads into a graphic
description of the murder of Archbishop Ælfheah by his Viking captors
with a complaint about the way the Viking onslaughts were being
handled:

All those disasters befell us through bad policy, in that [the Vikings] were
never offered tribute in time nor fought against; but when they had done
most to our injury, peace and truce were made with them; and for all this
peace and tribute they journeyed nonetheless in bands everywhere and
harried our wretched people and plundered and killed them.

(EHD, p. 244)

Elsewhere, memorable passages range from an account of great multi-
tudes of accursed spirits with shaggy ears and crooked shanks and
shrivelled-up toes, attacking St Guthlac in his fenland home, to a vision of
the northern region of the earth, from whence all waters pass down, and
above the water a hoary stone,

and north of the stone had grown woods very rimy. And there were dark
mists; and under the stone was the dwelling place of monsters and
execrable creatures   *(Blickling Homilies, ed. Morris, p. 209)*

and to a letter by a princess announcing her love for her teacher:

Good king and my dearest father, now that your kindness has given me
permission to choose for myself what husband I wanted, I say to you truly,
I want the shipwrecked man; and if you should wonder that so modest a

woman wrote those words so shamelessly, then know that I have declared
by means of wax, which knows no shame, what I could not for shame say
to you for myself.   (*Apollonius of Tyre*, ed. Goolden, p. 32).

In early and late Anglo-Saxon periods alike the use of Latin models and
a dependence on Latin sources for ideas was commonplace, and a
considerable amount of the Old English prose that has come down to us
either consists of or includes translation. This prose, though 'derivative', is
nonetheless often of considerable literary interest and at its best can be as
'original' as that writing for which no sources are known. Alfred himself is
a good example of this mixture of dependence and originality. In his
preface to the *Pastoral Care*, Alfred first attempts to justify translation
into the vernacular – part of his plan to restore wisdom and learning to the
land – and then describes his methods of translation in that work as
sometimes word for word, sometimes sense for sense. After he had learned
the meaning of the work from his ecclesiastical helpers, he says, he turned
it into English, 'just as I understood it and as I might most intelligibly
render it' (ed. Sweet, p. 7). In the case of the *Pastoral Care* this usually
involved relatively minor changes within the paragraph and a remodelling
at the level of syntax. Given the nature of Gregory's subject-matter, little
was required by way of clarification apart from the occasional expansion
of passages where Gregory's wording was over-concise for the intended
Anglo-Saxon audience, or where he assumed knowledge of incidents in
the Bible which some at least of that audience might not possess: for
instance, the story of David's sparing of Saul is told in some detail and a
description of Jacob's ladder is provided. However, on occasion Alfred
actually modifies and softens the severity of Gregory's pronouncements.
For instance, where Gregory insists that the person who sets a bad
example deserves as many punishments as the number of men he has led
astray, Alfred adds, 'unless he himself ceases and converts as many as he
can'. Where Gregory states uncompromisingly that all sins will be
punished at Doomsday, Alfred's version refers to all those sins that are
unatoned for. Where Gregory concedes that sins committed out of ignorance or folly may be excepted, Alfred adds to the list sins resulting from
instincts of the flesh or from weakness of character or from infirmity of
mind or body. Where Gregory states unequivocally that a sinner goes to
hell, Alfred hastens to add the rider, 'unless he is helped by his repentance
and God's mercy'.[2] For him it is deliberate and willed and unrepented sin
that counts. Similar modifications are made in Alfred's other translations.
In the case of his rendering of the first fifty psalms, for instance, the king's
interpretation of the translator's role permitted both explanatory
comment and on occasion a Christian softening of the Old Testament
severity: part of the 'meaning' of the text for Alfred seems to have lain in

its relevance for a medieval Christian audience. So, for instance, verses
3–6 of Psalm V, which in the Latin text of the Paris Psalter read:

Mane adstabo tibi et uidebo, quoniam non uolens deus iniquitatem tu es.
Non habitat iuxta te malignus neque permanebunt iniusti ante oculos
tuos. Odisti domine omnes qui operantur iniquitatem, perdes eos qui
locuntur mendacium

appear as

I shall stand in the *early* morning before you *at prayer* and see you; *that is,
I shall perceive your will without doubt and also perform it,* for you are
the same God who does not wish any unrighteousness. The malevolent
man will not dwell with you, nor will the unrighteous dwell before your
eyes. You hate all those who perform iniquity *and do not abandon it or
repent of it*; and you will destroy those who *always* speak lies.

(Bright and Ramsay, p. 7).[3]

Similarly in the Boethius an early sixth-century philosopher's stern
morality is tempered to fit the circumstances of a late ninth-century king.
Where Boethius, a former consul now unjustly imprisoned by an emperor,
makes one of his two speakers, the lady Philosophy, attack kingly power
and condemn high office and riches as (amongst other things) false goods
which prevent the possessor from contemplating the highest good, Alfred
inserts qualifications. It is improperly used power that is evil, not power
itself. Indeed in some circumstances power can be a force for good: rulers
who 'have full powers over the people that are under them and also to
some extent over those about them in the neighbourhood can bring low
the wicked and advance the good' (ed. Sedgefield, pp. 124–5).

As for wealth, this is good when it is used properly; indeed for a ruler it
is a necessity. As Alfred makes *Mod* ('Mind') state in an important passage
of independent and surely autobiographical prose:

Ah, Reason, lo, you know that covetousness and ambition for worldly
dominion have never pleased me very much, nor have I all too greatly
desired this earthly authority, but I have desired tools and materials for
the work which was entrusted to me to perform; that was that I worthily
and fittingly might steer and rule the kingdom that was entrusted to me.[4]

(ed. Sedgefield, p. 40).

And he goes on to name the tools and materials required: men of prayer,
soldiers and workers and the resources to feed, clothe and equip them.
Fame and honour too are in Alfred's eyes not to be dismissed out of hand:
'it is clear enough that good report and good fame of any man is better and
more precious than any wealth', he says. And 'those that have striven after
honour in this world and acquired good renown by good deeds and set a

good example to those who came after them now as a result dwell above
the stars in eternal happiness because of their good deeds' (ed. Sedgefield,
pp. 28 and 139). We may compare the *Soliloquies*, where Alfred adds
the adjectives 'excessive' and 'immoderate', when Augustine states that
he has abandoned wealth, honour and luxurious living (ed. Carnicelli,
p. 73).

Alfred's reworking of his Latin sources in the *Boethius* and the
Soliloquies is indeed considerable. At times it seems as though he is using
his Latin texts as no more than a spring-board for his own considered
responses to their contents and his personal interests. (His own fine
extended metaphor, in the preface to the *Soliloquies*, is of the would-be
builder who goes to the forest – that is, the writings of the church fathers –
for materials.) The freedom that he takes with his authorities is too
considerable to be dealt with in detail here. However, by way of
illustration I would cite his rendering of the *Consolation* II, pr. ii, where
Philosophia puts in the mouth of *Fortuna* a comment on her wheel:

Yes, rise up on my wheel if you like, but don't count it an injury when by
the same token you begin to fall, as the rules of the game will require.[5]

In the Old English version this is replaced by a passage in which the
speaker is Wisdom (Alfred's equivalent for *Philosophia*) addressing not
Boethius but *Mod*, 'Mind':

When I travel up with my servants then we look down on this stormy
world just like the eagle, when he travels upwards above the clouds in
stormy weather, so that the storms may not harm him. So I would then,
Mind, that you should journey up to us if you so desire, on condition that
you seek earth with us again for the benefit of good men

(ed. Sedgefield, p. 18).

Alfred then goes on to transform an exemplum of Croesus, cast down on
Fortune's wheel, into an exemplum of Croesus, saved from death by
heavenly intervention.

Great freedom is also exercised by the anonymous translator of
Orosius's history of the world, the *Historiae adversum paganos*, who
demonstrates impressive classical knowledge as well as considerable
literary flair in expanding brief allusions in his source. An example of the
latter is the moving speech by Leoniða (Leonidas) which embellishes the
account of the battle of Marathon in bk 2, ch. 5:

Now we know without any shadow of doubt that we must lose our own
lives because of the very great enmity that our persecutors have towards
us. Let us nonetheless consider how we may this night overcome by
stratagem the greatest number of them and achieve for ourselves the best
and longest-enduring reputation at our end.   (ed. Bately, p. 47)

And instead of a couple of brief references to the rape of the Sabines, we have in bk 2, ch. 2 the whole story, briefly but effectively told, and concluding with a vivid word-picture of the wives of the Romans, 'running with their children between the fighters and falling at the feet of their fathers, and imploring them for love of the children to put some end to the fight' (ed. Bately, p. 39).

Orosius's book was a history told from a Christian standpoint, the primary aim of the early fifth-century cleric being to answer the charge of some of his contemporaries that the times in which they lived were unusually beset with calamities, and that this was due to the abandonment of pagan gods and the general adoption of Christianity. Accordingly his was a Christian reinterpretation of world history with a message of some relevance to a ninth-century Christian England troubled by the attacks of the pagan Vikings. The author of the Old English version at once exploits this relevance and through careful selection and modification changes the emphasis of his source. Christ's birth becomes a watershed, separating a past of unrelieved misery from a present characterized by universal manifestations of mercy and peace and an undeniable improvement in man's lot. Calamities are shown to be largely deserved, but tempered by God's mercy: the sack of Rome, for instance, is said to have been permitted because of men's misdeeds, but 'God showed his mercy to the Romans, when he allowed their misdeeds to be avenged so that nevertheless it was Alaric the Christian and very mild king who was responsible for this' (ed. Bately, p. 156). In the historical section, Scipio and Julius Caesar become examples of the ingratitude of states and the vanity of earthly success. A reference to resistance against odds by the Romans, under attack from all sides and attempting to repel an invasion by Hannibal, calls forth the comment that it was 'very clear that they were better thegns than they are now', in that they would not cease from the fight but stood firm in a tight corner and apparently hopeless situation (ed. Bately, p. 103).

In the first, geographical, chapter, the Old English author not only completely rewrites the section on northern and western Europe, drawing on contemporary information, but incorporates reports of life in Norway and of journeys to the White Sea and Baltic made to King Alfred by the Norwegian seafarer Ohthere along with a similar account by one Wulfstan, who travelled from Hedeby to the mouth of the Vistula.

Independence is also a feature of the prose of Ælfric and Wulfstan, although it takes a somewhat different form in each of these great writers. Obviously a careful and scrupulous teacher, Ælfric seems to have seen as his main task the provision not just of learning but of correct learning – true doctrine. His decision to compose the first series of *Catholic Homilies* was, he claims, taken because he saw and heard much heresy in many

English books, which ignorant men through their ignorance held to be great wisdom (ed. Thorpe I, 2). This concern for the ignorant led him also to place some restrictions on the use of the vernacular. So, for instance, to make parts of the Old Testament widely available was in his view very dangerous: as he says of the Book of Genesis, 'I fear that, if some foolish man either reads this book or hears it read, he will believe that he may live now under the new law just as the old fathers lived in that time, before the old law was established or as men lived under the law of Moses' (*Heptateuch*, ed. Crawford, p. 76). At the same time he is highly selective in what he includes in his saints' lives. Here his main purpose is moral teaching and his approach hagiographical. In retelling the Latin lives he rearranges and makes omissions in order to sharpen the moral structure. Those details in his sources that do not contribute to his immediate purpose – whether human interest or sensational story or doctrinal discussion – he tends carefully and scrupulously to excise, while he rejects altogether stories which he considers to be without proper authority (cf. below, p. 257).

In his homilies and sermons Ælfric is likewise both selective and critical, drawing on a wide range of Latin texts and – in the *Catholic Homilies* – providing a text for every Sunday and major feast throughout the church's year. Most of these homilies have as their main concern close analyses of biblical texts, often using complex allegorical methods of interpretation. Other sermons by Ælfric deal with catechetical matters or address themselves to questions of procedure – why turn east to pray, for example, or what are the reasons for fasting? However, Ælfric is concerned with far more than the elucidation of biblical texts or indeed the provision of information about religious observances. He touches on many other subjects and discusses a number of matters of contemporary relevance and importance, from the duties of bishops and abbots to admonish and advise, to the practice of divination and observance of superstition. He attacks lord-betrayers, false counsellors and corrupt judges and he wrestles with problems such as the apparent exclusion of women from the five thousand fed by Christ: 'if a woman is manly by nature and strong to God's will, she will be counted among the men who sit at the table of God' (*Catholic Homilies*, ed. Thorpe I, 188). 'No man may make himself a king, for the people have the option to choose that person for king who is agreeable to them; but after he has been hallowed as king, he has power over the people, and they may not shake his yoke from their necks' (*ibid.*, p. 212). At the same time, the king is justified in delegating authority and the laity must help to defend the realm. The English kings whom Ælfric commemorates are ones whose victories are related to their faith and who acquire sanctity after death in battle against their – and God's – enemies. Battle between kinsmen Ælfric sees as very wretched and bringing endless sorrow, but war is just when it is against 'the cruel seamen or against other nations who desire to destroy our homeland' (*Lives of Saints*, ed. Skeat II, 112–14). In his discussions of the existence of evil in a world created by God, Ælfric also addresses the questions of fatalism, suffering and disease. Foolish men, he claims, often say they must live according to destiny as if God compels them to evil deeds (*Catholic Homilies*, ed. Thorpe I, 111). However, nothing takes place by destiny, but all things are arranged by the judgement of God (*ibid.*, p. 114). In the case of God's chosen servants, persecution and affliction, permitted by God, will cleanse them from all sins, as gold is tried in fire. In the case of the wicked man sickness can be God's vengeance, though patience and prayers for mercy can cause him to be 'washed from his sins by that sickness as a foul garment by soap' (*ibid.*, pp. 4–6 and 470–2). This same subject of disease leads to a strong warning against unhallowed practices – a subject that Ælfric returns to on more than one occasion.

Any generalization about this prolific writer is dangerous; however, it is probably safe to describe as one of Ælfric's major achievements the way in which he has succeeded in distilling the wisdom of the church fathers to produce what are to all intents and purposes his own literary creations, while not departing from the 'sense' of his authorities (sometimes indeed giving close renderings of his Latin sources) nor forgetting that one of his aims is to write 'for the edification of the simple' (*Catholic Homilies*, ed. Thorpe I, 1).

In the case of Wulfstan, the debt to other writers is essentially a debt of ideas, though on occasion he actually reworks vernacular material by Ælfric, changing it so that it conforms to his personal style. His own special stamp is on everything he writes, whether he is attacking corruption, or warning of the terrors of the forthcoming end of the world, or calling for resistance to temptation. And whereas Ælfric's prime aim seems to have been the provision of instruction through orthodox book-learning – 'people need good instruction', he says, 'most particularly in this period which is the ending of the world' and 'everyone may the more easily withstand the tribulation to come, through God's help, if he is strengthened by book-learning' (*Catholic Homilies*, ed. Thorpe I, 2 and 4) – for Wulfstan there was no time at all to lose:

Beloved people, know the truth. This world is in haste and it is approaching its end, and so it is in the world ever the longer the worse, and so it must necessarily greatly worsen because of the people's sins, before the coming of Antichrist, and truly it will then be dreadful and terrible widely throughout the world.   (*Homilies*, ed. Bethurum, p. 267)

No quiet reflection for Wulfstan on the lives of God's saints, 'in whom he is wonderful'[6], no scholarly quest for 'wisdom' or 'true doctrine', only a concern for the essentials of the Christian religion, an acute awareness of sin and the consequences of sin, a passion for order and a burning zeal for reform. Wulfstan's homilies sometimes deal with subjects like the meaning of baptism, sometimes begin, like Ælfric's, with a gospel reading, the significance of which is then discussed, often show intimate knowledge of key patristic and Carolingian Latin texts, but over and over again the prelate reverts to his major theme. Like Isaiah his call is for repentance, and for repentance now before it is too late.

But Wulfstan was not just an eloquent preacher; he was also a statesman and law-giver with a concern for society, an administrator, working first for the Anglo-Saxon king Æthelred and then for his successor, the Danish king Cnut. As the author of legal codes for both rulers – written in English – he was well aware of the unjust laws and practices which needed changing and which he attacked with vehemence from the pulpit. As the spiritual head first of a bishopric and then of an archdiocese he was conscious of insufficiencies among the clergy; as a politician, he was concerned with the inter-relationship of Church and State and the maintenance of law and order. And for Wulfstan as for Ælfric no justification was needed for the use of the vernacular.

Byrhtferth, in contrast, had limited aims in writing his *Enchiridion* (or *Manual*, as it is often called). Although he covers a fairly wide range of subjects, from the differences between solar and lunar years and the significance of the intercalated day in leap-years to an account of Creation and a description of figures of speech, he is selective both in his choice of materials and in the language he provides them in. Like Ælfric he is very conscious of the limited capabilities of some of his audience: 'We could add many things here from the writings of wise men', he observes, 'but because we know that these things seem to clerks and country priests complex enough, we will now turn our speech to those young monks who have occupied their childhood with scientific books' (ed. Crawford, p. 132). The list of his sources is an impressive one, as is the skill with which he combines them. However, his major contribution to a history of Old English literary prose is arguably his style.

Old English prose style is as varied as its subject matter. Some writers are apparently inexperienced; others are highly sophisticated masters of the high, middle and low styles. There is no obvious correlation between the date of a composition and the degree of stylistic excellence it achieves. Many of the features admired in late Old English prose are already to be found in the early laws and charters and in the works of the Alfredian period, 'developments' being as much the result of changing fashions as of accumulated experience and expertise. Indeed, the two major sources of stylistic influence – Old English poetry and Latin prose – were both available to the literate Anglo-Saxon as models from the time of the conversion right up to the Norman Conquest, while the continuity of Old English prose is demonstrated by the fact that the translation of Gregory's *Dialogues* was revised a century or so later by someone using the language of the 'Winchester school', the early parts of the *Anglo-Saxon Chronicle* were rewritten and augmented to form what is traditionally known as the 'northern recension', Ælfric certainly knew and used works by Alfred and his contemporaries, and Wulfstan was apparently responsible for glosses in an early copy of the *Pastoral Care*. The rhythmical prose of Ælfric and Wulfstan was foreshadowed in earlier homilies in, for instance, the Vercelli Book, while Byrhtferth had as one of his sources Ælfric's *De temporibus anni*.

Even translations which closely follow their Latin originals often combine fidelity to their source with a sensitivity to the idioms of Old English. One example of stylistic excellence in works of this category is the passage in the Old English Bede in which the briefness of man's sojourn in this world is likened to the 'twinkling of an eye' that a sparrow takes to pass through a king's hall (the detail of the 'twinkling of an eye' is not found in the Latin):

Þyslic me is gesewen, þu cyning, þis andwearde lif manna on eorðan to wiðmetenesse þære tide, þe us uncuð is, swylc swa þu æt swæsendum sitte mid þinum ealdormannum and þegnum on wintertide, and sie fyr onælæd and þin heall gewyrmed, and hit rine and sniwe and styrme ute; cume an spearwa and hrædlice þæt hus þurhfleo, cume þurh oþre duru in, þurh oþre ut gewite. Hwæt he on þa tid, þe he inne bið, ne bið hrinen mid þy storme þæs wintres; ac þæt bið an eagan bryhtm and þæt læsste fæc, ac he sona of wintra on þone winter eft cymeð.   (ed. Miller, pp. 134–6)

O king, this present' life of men on earth, in comparison with the time that is unknown to us, seems to me as if you were sitting feasting with your ealdormen and thegns in wintertime and a fire was kindled and your hall warmed and it rained and it snowed and it stormed outside; and there came a sparrow and swiftly flew through the house, and it came in through one door and out through another. Now during the time that it is inside, it is not touched with the storm of winter, but that is for a twinkling of an eye and the smallest moment of time, but it immediately goes from winter into the winter again.

We may compare the no less effective colloquialisms of Werferth's account of the nun who was violently possessed by a devil when she started to eat a lettuce in the monastery vegetable garden without first making the sign of the cross. 'Hwæt dyde ic hire? hwæt dyde ic hire? ic me sæt on anum leahtrice, þa com heo and bat me' (*Dialogues*, ed. Hecht, pp. 30–1: 'What have I done to her? What have I done to her? I was sitting on a lettuce and she came along and bit me'), cries the demon on being driven out by the holy Equitius, who came running to help the woman.

The ornaments of style used by Anglo-Saxon prose writers were many, a significant proportion of them involving patterns of sound. Of these the favourite seems to have been alliteration, while verbal parallelisms, such as the repetition of a word-stem or word-ending and the use of balanced phrases or clauses, are also commonplace features, along with the use of word-pairs that are either synonymous or closely related in meaning. In the following (mainly independent) passage of the Old English Orosius, for instance, we find a variety of verbal repetitions including word-play, as well as alliteration, word-pairs, irony and apostrophe:

On the very night of the day on which Scipio said these words, the Romans thanked him for all his labour with a worse reward than he had earned of them, when they smothered and suffocated him (*hiene* . . . *asmorodon and aþrysmedon*) in his bed, so that he gave up his life. Ah, Romans, who may now have faith in you (*truwian*) when you gave such a reward to your most faithful (*getrywestan*) counsellor!

(ed. Bately, p. 119)

We may compare Ælfric's highly rhetorical passage on Herod's massacre of the innocents, where he explains that the flight to Egypt did not mean that Christ had abandoned his young warriors, but he sent them from this miserable life to his eternal kingdom. Blessed they were born, he says, that they might for his sake suffer death:

Eadig is heora yld, seoðe þa gyt ne mihte Crist andettan, and moste for Criste þrowian. Hi wæron þæs Hælendes gewitan, ðeah ðe hi hine ða gyt ne cuðon. Næron hi geripode to slege, ac hi gesæliglice þeah swulton to life. Gesælig wæs heora acennednys, forðan ðe hi gemetton þæt ece lif on instæpe þæs andweardan lifes. Hi wurdon gegripene fram moderlicum breostum, ac hi wurdon betæhte þærrihte engellicum bosmum. Ne mihte se manfulla ehtere mid nanre ðenunge þam lytlingum swa micclum fremian, swa micclum swa he him fremode mid ðære reðan ehtnysse hatunge. Hi sind gehatene martyra blostman, forðan ðe hi wæron swa swa upaspringende blostman on middeweardan cyle ungeleaffulnysse, swilce mid sumere ehtnysse forste forsodene.

(*Catholic Homilies*, ed. Thorpe I, 84)

Blessed is their youth, which could not yet confess Christ and might suffer for Christ. They were the Saviour's witnesses, although they did not yet know him. They were not ripened for slaughter, but nevertheless they blessedly died to life. Blessed was their birth, because they found the eternal life at the entrance to this present life. They were snatched from their mothers' breasts but they were immediately consigned to the bosoms of angels. The wicked persecutor could not by any service so benefit those little ones as he did by the fierce hate of persecution. They are called martyrs' blossoms, because they were like blossoms springing up in the midst of the chill of unbelief, withered as it were by the frost of persecution.

What is arguably the fullest exploitation of patterns of sound, however, is to be found in the later works of Ælfric and in Wulfstan's writings, which make extensive use of what is often known as rhythmical prose. Each of these writers evolved his own distinctive version from the precedents available to him, whether those of verse or prose, in the vernacular or in Latin. Ælfric's rhythmical prose is characterized by a consistent and regular use of two-stress units and a nearly constant use of phonetic correspondences, especially alliteration, which give it a superficial resemblance to verse: however, it differs from classical Old English verse in a number of ways, including the rejection of a distinctive poetic diction. The effects can only be seen from the original Old English:

Efne ða comon twegen seolas of sælicum grunde, / and hi mid heora flyse his fet drygdon / and mid heora blæde his leoma beðedon, / and siððan mid gebeacne his bletsunge bædon, / licgende æt his foton on fealwun ceosle.
                                    (*Catholic Homilies* II, ed. Godden, 83)

Lo, there came two seals from the sea-depths and they dried his feet with their fleece and warmed his limbs with their breath, and afterwards with a sign they asked for his blessing, lying at his feet on the fallow shingle.

As the passage shows, Ælfric is using alliteration to link two-stress units in pairs. In Wulfstan's writings, in contrast, alliteration generally operates internally within units in a series of two-stress phrases, which, somewhat like the classical half-line of verse, are severely restricted to certain rhythmical patterns. His mannerisms include a fondness for intensifying words such as 'ever', 'greatly', 'widely', 'all too frequently', and for parallelisms of word and clause. His usage may be illustrated from this passage:

Leofan men, beorgað eow georne wið deofles lara. Ne beon ge naðor ne to swicole ne to ficole, ne lease ne luðerfulle ne fule ne fracode, ne on ænige wisan to lehterfulle. Ne ge ahwar ne beon, þæs ðe ge betan magan, gewitan ne gewyrhtan æniges morðres oððon manslihtas, stala ne strudunga, ac strynað mid rihte. Scyldað eow wið gitsunga and wið gifornessa, and ðæt ge ahwar ne beon manswican ne mansworan, wedlogan ne wordlogan, ne on leasre gewitnesse ahwar standan.
                                    (*Homilies*, ed. Bethurum, p. 183)

Beloved people, defend yourselves vigorously against the teachings of the devil. Do not be either too deceitful nor too cunning, nor false nor vile, nor corrupt nor wicked, nor in any way too vicious, and do not be in any respect (in so far as you can emend it) witnesses or workers of murder or manslaughter, theft or robbery, but acquire wealth righteously. Defend yourselves against avarice and against greediness and do not in any way be deceivers or perjurers, violators of agreements or liars and do not stand in any respect in false witness.

In addition to figures of sound, Old English prose writers make considerable use of figures of thought. Of the frequent similes, some are derivative, like the comment in the *Old English Martyrology* that the firmament 'surrounds everything, sea and earth, just as the shell surrounds the egg, as scholars say' (ed. Herzfeld, p. 40). Others are the English author's own creation, like the simile embedded in a passage in the Old English Orosius on the sack of Rome by the Gauls, where the wretched survivors are described as creeping out of the holes that they had lurked in, as drenched in tears as if they had come from the other world (ed. Bately, p. 52). Imagery involving the sea or water is particularly common. We may compare Byrhtferth's extended metaphor:

We have stirred with our oars the waves of the deep pool; we have seen also the mountains around the salt sea-strand, and with stretched out sail and favourable winds have camped there on the borders of the fairest nation. The waves symbolize this deep art and the mountains also symbolise the magnitude of this art.   (ed. Crawford, p. 14)

and Werferth's simile (combined with metaphor) of the seaman caught up in a storm:

I am most like the person who is on a frail ship that is hard-pressed by the waves of a great sea: so I am now stirred up by the tribulations of this world, and I am struck with the storms of the strong tempest in the ship of my mind, and when I recall my former life which I spent previously in a monastery, then I sigh and murmur, like the person who approaches land in a frail ship and the whirlwind and storm then drive it so far on the sea that he finally can see no land.   (*Dialogues*, ed. Hecht, p. 5)

Such imagery extends into figurative interpretations of the sea in biblical texts, as in Ælfric's sermon for Midlent Sunday (*Catholic Homilies* I, ed. Thorpe, 182–4).

The most memorable imagery in Old English prose, however, is arguably that of King Alfred. One of his most remarkable characteristics is his ability to explain difficult points through the everyday and familiar image. So, for instance, in the *Pastoral Care* Gregory's reference to steps in his argument is transformed into a description of the discourse rising in the mind of the learner 'as on a ladder, step by step, nearer and nearer, until it firmly stands in the upper chamber (*solar*) of the mind which learns it' (ed. Sweet, p. 23). Other images include the different paths to the king's estate or to his assembly or to his army and the places different people have in a king's residence (*Soliloquies*, ed. Carnicelli, p. 77). We may compare Wulfstan's down-to-earth images of breaking and burning (*Homilies*, ed. Bethurum, pp. 267–8) – untypical images for him, since figures of thought such as simile and metaphor are almost entirely absent from his writings.

The master of the conceit, however, is Byrhtferth. His Latin shows a predilection for obscure, learned-sounding vocabulary and his Old

English is likewise erudite and at times even flamboyant. He delights in linking his discourses on scientific matters with patches of flowery prose:

I command to depart from me the mermaids who are called sirens, and also the Castalian nymphs, that is to say the mountain elves, who dwelt on mount Helicon, and I desire that Phoebus depart from me, whom Latona ... bore in Delos, as old and foolish triflers declared, and I hope that the glorious cherubin will be present and with his golden tongs bring to my tongue from off the heavenly altar a spark of the burning coal and touch the nerves of this dumb mouth, so that I therefore may *argute arguto meditamine fari*, that is, that I may wisely with wise deliberation turn this cycle into English   (ed. Crawford, p. 148).

His metaphors include the broody hen who, though grumbling, spreads out her wings to keep her chicks warm, the bee whose rough thighs become heavily burdened and who has to struggle with fierce winds in order to return home, and the builders, who begin by surveying the site, then hew the timber into shape before proceeding to construct their house (ed. Crawford, pp. 79 and 143). Such heightened passages are all the more surprising in view of Byrhtferth's own comments, apparently advocating the 'plain' style:

þeah we wace syn and þas þing leohtlice unwreon, hig magon fremian bet þonne þa þe beoð on leoðwisan fægre geglenged.   (ed. Crawford, p. 54)

Though we are weak and reveal these things lightly, they can be more helpful than those which are beautifully adorned in poetic manner.

(Note the repetition of the liquids and labials *w*, *l* and *f*.)
    Sometimes, however, even late Old English prose is of a deceptive simplicity. Ælfric himself provides the finest examples of this so-called plain style (a feature of his earlier works including most of the *Catholic Homilies*), which is founded on and often conceals a mastery of the art of rhetoric, whether it is being used obviously to arouse pity or fear, as in the homily for the Feast of the Holy Innocents quoted above, or unobtrusively to express deep truths in language that is simple and yet demonstrates the paradoxes inherent in them, as in the opening of his Creation homily:

An angin is ealra þinga, þæt is God ælmihtig. He is ordfruma and ende: he is ordfruma, forði þe he wæs æfre; he is ende butan ælcere geendunge forðan þe he bið æfre ungeendod. He is ealra cyninga cyning and ealra hlaforda hlaford. He hylt mid his mihte heofonas and eorðan and ealle gesceafta butan geswince, and he besceawað þa niwelnyssa þe under þyssere eorðan sind. He awecð ealle duna mid anre handa, and ne mæg nan ðing his willan wiðstandan.   (*Catholic Homilies*, ed. Thorpe I, 8–10)

There is one beginning of all things, that is God almighty. He is beginning and end; he is beginning, because he always has been; he is end without any ending, because he will be ever unended. He is king of all kings and lord of all lords. He holds with his might heavens and earth and all creation without effort, and he scans the depths that are under this earth. He raises up all mountains with one hand and nothing can withstand his will.

As Peter Clemoes has said of another passage by Ælfric, 'the sequence of his sentences, grammatically alike in form but skilfully varied, helps us to feel that all the paradoxes are parts of one great paradox, the central mystery of Christianity ... Here is writing ... in which style is consciously exploited by someone who understands the essential unity of thought and expression.'[7]

In the hands of educated and experienced writers, then, Old English prose was a sophisticated tool, capable of conveying complex arguments and expressing profound thoughts in a simple, direct and effective manner. King Alfred, in his preface to his Boethius, asked his readers not to blame him if they should understand the text better than he was able to, for 'every man must say what he says and do what he does according to the capacity of his intellect and the amount of time available to him'. The writers of Old English prose believed that the time available to them was short; the clarity of thought and the learning of the best of them ensured that it was not until many centuries after the Norman Conquest that their achievement in the use of the vernacular was to be matched.

1 See above, p. 72 and *Pastoral Care*, ed. Sweet, p. 6.
2 *Pastoral Care*, ed. Sweet, pp. 191, 220, 157 and 251, respectively.
3 References to early morning and to prayer are drawn from verse 2; the word *domine* has not been translated. I indicate Alfred's additions to the Latin source by means of italics.
4 Cf. *De consolatione* II, pr. vii: 'Then I spoke to [Philosophia] and said that she was well aware of how little I had been governed by worldly ambition. I had sought the means of engaging in politics so that virtue should not grow old unpraised' (Boethius, *The Consolation of Philosophy*, trans. V. E. Watts (Harmondsworth, 1969), p. 72).
5 *Ibid.*, p. 57.
6 *Catholic Homilies*, ed. Thorpe I, 446.
7 P. Clemoes, 'Ælfric', in *Continuations and Beginnings*, ed. E. G. Stanley (London, 1966), pp. 176–209, at 176–7.

5 Germanic legend in Old English literature

SCHOLARLY tradition wants us to speak well of the works we study; there would be little point in talking about something that was not beautiful and truthful, not 'interesting'. Germanic legend has interest, almost too much so, but its beauty is not in the usual places. The names of heroes and nations that the poets so endlessly roll off are not there for their euphony. It is a rare ear that lingers in delight over –

> Ðeodric ahte þritig wintra
> Mæringa burg; þæt wæs monegum cuþ.   (*Deor* 18–20)

Theodoric possessed for thirty years the stronghold of the Goths; that was known to many.

or

> Ætla weold Hunum, Eormanric Gotum . . .   (*Widsith* 18)

Attila ruled the Huns, Ermanaric the Goths . . .

As for uplifting plots, the poets seldom tell the stories they allude to, and their allusions are elliptical to the point of obscurity. When the tales are told, they turn out to be about sibling rivalry, kin murder, incest, shaky marriages, treachery and theft. Germanic legend seldom eulogizes the figures it condemns to historical action, and its themes are the stuff that fantasies of younger brothers are made of: an underdog's defiant resistance, the fall of a leader, the automaticity of revenge (called by Auden the earth's only perpetual motion machine). And as for truth, the poets prove by their inventiveness, their cavalier reorganization of chronology and geography, that the urge to create history out of next to nothing was not lost with the Greeks and Romans.

Nevertheless, Germanic legend matters to us: because it was somehow important to the Anglo-Saxons, who tried harder and harder with each passing century to establish a Germanic identity; and because an acquaintance with the stories enables us to follow what is going on in five Old English poems. But the lasting appeal of Germanic legend has little to do with utility, societal imperatives, or other practical considerations. Germanic legend holds our interest because it is extraordinary, a strange and enchanting offspring of the real and the dreamworld, of Clio and Morpheus.

Many have written much about a very few texts. The relevant Old English poems can be counted on the fingers of one hand: *The Finnsburh Fragment*, *Waldere*, *Beowulf*, *Widsith* and *Deor*, the first a single (now lost) leaf, the second two separate leaves, and the third charred around the edges. The first three poems are narratives, rich in action and dialogue; the last two are lyrical monologues that allude, in a sometimes riddling way, to the world of epic. Although Germanic legend in Old English literature is a small and much trampled cabbage-patch, the pre-1100 harvest from Scandinavia and the Continent is even sparser: the Old High German *Hildebrandslied* (about 68 lines, probably fragmentary, and written down *c.* 830 × 840); the Latin *Waltharius*, probably from the late Carolingian period, and a paraphrase of the same legend in an early eleventh-century Italian chronicle; perhaps 500 lines of Old Norse poetry, only a few verses of which survive in a contemporary inscription. Completing the corpus are a scattering of names in Anglo-Saxon royal genealogies, a reference to Hygelac the Geat in the *Liber monstrorum*, allusions to the legendary Ingeld and Ermanaric in Latin letters from the Continent, and an entry in two related German annals from *c.* 1000.[1]

Germanic legend as usually defined has to do with figures and events situated in a two-hundred-year period extending between the fourth and sixth centuries, from the incursions of the Huns and death of Ermanaric in 375 to the conquest of Italy by the *Langobardi* (Lombards) under Alboin in 568: the 'heroic' or founding age of a new Europe (see Fig. 1). When history becomes legend, events and circumstances change beyond recognition. Rulers from different centuries are represented as coexisting in some vague period 'before' our time, a past lacking all definition and substance. Ermanaric, mighty king of the Ostrogoths (d. 375), Guthhere (Gundaharius), the Burgundian ruler killed by the Huns around 437, Attila, the greatest and, as far as legend is concerned, only Hunnish king (d. 453), and Theodoric the Ostrogoth, ruler of Italy (d. 526), are portrayed as contemporaries and sometimes relatives. Within this fabulous time-span, it is absurd to ask whether Finn was killed before Weland raped Beadohild, or whether Sigemund slew his dragon before Heoden abducted Hild. Situated somewhere between history and fairy-tale, Germanic legend tells of a distant and largely imaginary past.

None of the stories takes place in the British Isles. The tales pay little attention to politics or religion. Architecture gets barely a sideways glance. The poets are concerned with one group in society – the king and his retainers – and with the aristocratic pastimes of this elite. Their heroes act out elaborate rituals of greeting, fighting and drinking, boasting and arming, gift-giving and parting, the generative grammar of life in the hall. The backdrop is painted in dramatic chiaroscuro: splashes of dark and light, deep shadows, glistening swords, night and fire, raven and dawn. The only primary colour mentioned is the yellow of shields.

National catastrophes are depicted as a series of personal and psychological conflicts. Ingeld loves his wife but, when reminded, his honour more; Ermanaric is a manic gift-giver but a depressed head-of-family who destroys his kin; Theodoric, a bad-luck Goth if ever there was one, is an exile and fugitive, harassed by monsters and bullied by his uncle; and Ongentheow, the fierce, grizzled ruler of the Swedes, brings an army to bay, cutting its king to pieces, just to get his old wife back. The poets convey meaning economically, through stark gestures and familiar motifs: the silent placing of a sword on Hengest's lap screams out vengeance; the wild circling of ravens in the skies over Finnsburh predicts slaughter. All the legends, at a certain distance, seem ingenious variations on a few formulae: courageous death, the good ruler and the grasping, the generous act and the cowardly, the loyal retainer and the treacherous. Despite, or perhaps because of, their focus on a masculine pride of life, the legends reveal a taste for stories in which women play a part. The *Beowulf*-poet's own penchant for women of legend, such as Hildeburh, is well known; he looks on, with a torturer's pity, as she suffers, guiltless, her world collapsing around her. Deor's six examples of legendary misfortunes name two Hilds (Beado- and Mæth-) and allude to a third. Widsith begins his far-travels by escorting a Hild (Ealh-) to the home of her future husband and slayer. And two of the three speeches in *Waldere* have been attributed to yet another Hild (*Hildegyth). Just as Fair Ellen or Fair Eleanor can be the heroine of almost any ballad, so the name 'hild' ('battle') seems favoured by Old English poets for the sorrowful princesses of Germanic legend.

The question of how legendary material reached the Anglo-Saxons has a traditional answer: song. Andreas Heusler, whose theories have dominated the study of ancient Germanic poetry in this century, accepted the unanimous opinion of scholars that short, narrative songs or 'lays' were the most important instrument for transmitting Germanic legend.[2] The key references to a singing *Germania* – in Tacitus, Ammianus, Ausonius, Priscus, Procopius, Gregory the Great, Bede, Altfrid, Einhard and Thegan – have been collected and discussed many times.[3] Yet no matter how memorable Julian the Apostate's comparison of the songs of the barbarians across the Rhine to the croaking of harsh-voiced birds, or Sidonius's complaint that he had to 'bear up under the weight of Germanic words' and to praise 'whatever the Burgundian, with his hair smeared with rancid butter, chooses to sing', or Venantius Fortunatus's dismay at the incessant humming of the harp that accompanied barbarian lays, their words tell us nothing about the kinds of poetry in question (work songs, drinking songs, satires, dirges or whatever). Nor do Tacitus's references to 'ancient songs' and to the enduring reputation of Arminius, Cassiodorus's allusion to the celebrated Gensimundus, Jordanes's statement about Goths singing of the deeds of their ancestors, or even the reference in Einhard to vernacular poetry, tell us more than that eulogistic poetry was widely known and practised.

The *Beowulf*-poet's depiction of two anonymous Danish scops reciting stories from Germanic legend (853–97, 1068–159) indicates only that one Englishman, in whatever century he lived, believed that sixth-century Danes were likely to behave that way, not that song was *his* medium of exchange. Curiously, none of the singers in the five Old English poems is an Angle, Saxon, Jute or Frisian. Paul the Deacon, the first 'German' historian with a sense of ethnic solidarity, notes around 790 that the bravery and success in war of the Lombard Alboin were still praised in the songs of the Bavarians, Saxons and other men of the same language. But it is not until 797 that we get our first unambiguous reference to narrative songs about a figure of Germanic legend, and this from a clergyman who was not amused.

St Paul's question to the Corinthians about light consorting with darkness, or Christ with Belial, was imitated first by Tertullian (What has Athens to do with Jerusalem?) and then by Jerome (What has Horace to do with the Psalter? Virgil with the Evangelists? Cicero with the Apostles?). Alcuin gave the formula new life when, in 797, he wrote to the head of an English community charging that his clerics delighted more in listening to certain songs than in reading the word of God:

Let the words of God be read when the clergy dine together. It is fitting on such occasions to listen to a reader, not a harper; to the sermons of the Fathers, not the songs of the heathen. What has Ingeld to do with Christ? The house is narrow; it cannot contain them both; the King of Heaven will have no part with so-called kings who are pagan and damned; for the One King reigns eternally in heaven, while the other, the heathen, is damned and groans in hell. In your houses the voices of readers should be heard, not the tumult of those making merry in the streets.[4]

Jerome's classical allusions are replaced with the name of a king from Danish legend, Ingeld, who is mentioned in both *Beowulf* and *Widsith*:

Hrothulf and Hrothgar, nephew and uncle,
kept kinship-bonds together for the longest time,
after they drove off the tribe of pirates,
crushed Ingeld's battle-force, cut down at Heorot
the might of the Heathobards.   (*Widsith* 45–9)

Alcuin may have thought it particularly distasteful for the monks to be listening not to just any old heathen tale but to one celebrating a great Danish victory, so soon after the monastery at Lindisfarne had been hit by Viking raiders. A fondness for Danish stories in the north of England seems to have gone hand-in-hand with a weakness for Scandinavian fashions in general. In a letter written a year or two earlier to King Æthelred of Northumbria (d. 796), Alcuin, writing with reference to the raid on Lindisfarne, scolded his countrymen for imitating the appearance of the Northmen:

Consider the dress, the way of wearing the hair, the luxurious habits of the princes and people. Look at your hairstyle, how you have wished to resemble the pagans in your beards and hair. Are you not terrified of those whose hairstyle you wanted to have?[5]

A more positive attitude towards the pagan past is visible a century later in translations of the Alfredian period. King Alfred himself seems to have believed that pagan Germanic legend had intellectual value and interest for his fellow Englishmen. At one point in his paraphrase of Boethius's *Consolation of Philosophy*, he abandons the world of classical paganism for a Germanic allusion, translating Boethius's question 'Where now are the bones of faithful Fabricius?' as 'Where now are the bones of the famous and wise goldsmith Weland?'[6]

Weland, who has no known historical prototype, is depicted on the Franks Casket and on several Gotlandic and Northern English stones; he is mentioned by the *Waltharius*-poet (*Wielandia fabrica*, 965), and by three Old English poets (*Beowulf* 455, *Deor* 1, *Waldere* I.2; II.9). (Only the Goths Ermanaric and Theodoric are named by as many.) In Old Norse, the smith appears in verse and in prose; and he is referred to in Middle English and Middle High German texts. Ingeld, like all the other North Sea/Baltic heroes with the exception of Hygelac (who gained the attention of two Frankish historians by raiding their kingdom), is not found outside Scandinavia or England.[7] Both Weland and Ingeld may be regarded as 'Germanic' on the grounds, familiar to us from modern comparative linguistics, that items labelled Gothic, Old Franconian, Old Saxon, Old Frisian, Old High German, Old English and Old Norse have something in common. But I would argue that this concept of 'Germanic' was not shared by the early Anglo-Saxons. The literary category we call 'Germanic legend' is ours, not theirs, and it is not so much a description as an explanation. Like the terms 'sunrise' and 'sunset', it is an interpretation of the evidence that has the potential to mislead.

W. P. Ker was clear about what he meant by Germanic legend, and it is different in at least two ways from what current scholarship means. He speaks movingly of the sense of kinship existing among all Germanic speakers in the fourth to sixth centuries, of how the legends of each group were from the beginning viewed as common to all:

In the wars of the great migration the spirit of each of the German families was quickened, and at the same time the spirit of the whole of Germany, so that each part sympathised with all the rest, and the fame of the heroes went abroad beyond the limits of their own kindred. Ermanaric, Attila, and Theodoric, Sigfred the Frank, and Gundahari the Burgundian, are heroes over all the region occupied by all forms of Teutonic language.[8]

It is true that the Anglo-Saxons never forgot that they had come over the water. (People who live on islands tend to remember such things.) And certainly Bede and the eighth-century English missionaries knew that Frisians, Danes and Saxons were *gens nostra*, 'our people'. But it was not until the Franks under Charlemagne had forged a new empire, stretching from Barcelona and Rome in the south up to Saxony and the frontiers of Denmark in the north, that Goths, Burgundians and Lombards were spoken of as part of that same group.

An Englishman in the age of Bede was unlikely to have heard of Ermanaric, let alone to have regarded him as kin. Goths were not seen as chic or German during the long period stretching from the death of Theodoric to the coronation of Charlemagne. Isidore writing in seventh-century Spain could see no family relationship between Goths and Franks; he believed that the former were descended from the Scythians. Fredegar, a Frank writing around 660, portrayed Theodoric the Ostrogoth as a Macedonian, reared in Constantinople; he, like the author of the *Liber historiae Francorum* (*c.* 727), honoured the Franks with Trojan, not Germanic, ancestry.

In history, the very appearance of movements for the defence, revival or recognition of common traditions usually indicates a break in continuity. 'Gothicism', the desire to forge ancestral links with the people of Ermanaric and Theodoric, suddenly became fashionable around 800. Jordanes's *Getica*, which traced the descent of the latter king back to the former, surfaced briefly in mid-seventh-century Lombard Italy, and was circulating by the late eighth century in Frankish territory. In 801, after his coronation in Rome, Charlemagne visited Ravenna. He took from there an equestrian statue which he believed was of Theodoric the Ostrogoth, and set it up before his palace at Aachen. Shortly afterwards, in the *Hildebrandslied*, we find for the first time a story of the exiled Theodoric; and somewhat later in the ninth century, in a verse in runes on the Rök stone in Östergotland (Sweden), the same Theodoric, brave lord of the Mærings, is said to sit on his steed, shield on his shoulder.

People with a professional interest in the past – historians, scholar-clerics, kings and vernacular poets – tend to talk to each other. A degree of literacy at some level in society is all that is needed to ensure a measure of influence for the written word. Between 805 and 860, we can trace, decade by decade, a growing interest in the Goths and their language: shortly before 800, in one early Carolingian text, the term *theodisca lingua* ('Germanic language': cf. modern German *Deutsch*) had expanded to include Old English and Langobardic as well as Frankish; by 805 Gothic had joined; by 830 all *nationes theotiscae* ('Germanic peoples'), Franks included, were, like Jordanes's Goths, given Scandinavian ancestry; and finally, around 860, a theologian could speak of a *gens teudisca*, a community of German-speaking *people*.[9] Stories about Ermanaric were recorded by scholars, and, on at least one occasion, used by a cleric to restrain a king. Towards the end of the century, Archbishop Fulk of Rheims (883–900) asked Arnolf of Carinthia, the East Frankish king and emperor (887–99), to show mercy to his kinsman Charles, exhorting him 'not to follow evil counsels, but to have pity on his people and strengthen a declining royal race, keeping in mind the example found in German books (*ex libris teutonicis*) of King Hermenricus [Ermanaric] who, through the wicked promptings of a certain counsellor, brought about the death of all his family'.[10]

Interest in Gothic language, legend and ancestry was something new, and almost certainly a response to the multicultural empire of Charles and his successors. Carolingian politics probably even influenced which fourth- to sixth-century 'German' kings made it into legend. The great Clovis, regarded by Gregory of Tours as establishing Frankish power throughout Gaul, and the remarkable Gaiseric, ever-victorious leader of the Vandals, are for some reason missing from the roll-call. The absence of Clovis may have something to do with the fact that he had set up residence in Paris, making northwest Gaul (the largely Latin-speaking Neustria) his power-base; if his son, the Frankish Theodoric I, was admitted into legend, it was because he had inherited what was, from a later perspective, the politically correct northeast portion of the kingdom (the largely Frankish-speaking Austrasia, where the Carolingians came from). The Vandals never in the Middle Ages became real 'Germans' or entered Germanic legend: they invaded Spain in 408 and crossed to Africa in 429, effectively detaching themselves from territory that would in the late eighth century become *Germania*.

Ker's list of heroes of Germanic legend includes none from the lands surrounding the North Sea and Baltic, probably because the fame of Ingeld, Onela, Hrothulf and a few score others never reached their continental cousins. His description treats as marginal the regions that provided Anglo-Saxon England with the bulk of its legendary material, and probably its trade as well. We call the legends of the Danes, Swedes, Geats and Frisians, 'Germanic' because, as Eric Stanley has vividly demonstrated, modern Anglo-Saxon scholarship was born of the Romantic movement, when Germany was the world centre of Germanic philology.[11] From the German perspective, Old English poetry was a temporarily alienated segment of German literature; and Scandinavia, needed storehouse of legend, was a kind of *Germania germanicissima*, preserving untarnished an antiquity that others rather carelessly lost. It is true that each of the three non-fragmentary Old English poems dealing with Germanic story treats its Scandinavian and Frankish material together. That they do so probably reflects their date and encyclopedic intention rather than a fourth- to sixth-century reality, a pan-Germanism that never was.

Even the most abstract and hypothetical notions can become commonplace if they are what people want to hear and what those in power want them to believe. In England, the devising of elaborate royal genealogies was a fairly late, antiquarian exercise.[12] The several backward expansions of the Anglo-Saxon king-lists testify to a growing, and constantly changing, need to establish legitimacy through illustrious continental ancestors. In the age of Bede, Woden was the stopping point. But the Anglian collection of royal pedigrees, compiled around 796, gives Woden a progenitor; and then – for the kingdoms of Lindsey and (in a narrative part of the *Historia Brittonum, c.* 830) Kent – additional ancestors going back several generations to Geat (Primitive Germanic *Gautaz*, probably the Gothic eponym). A pedigree going back to Geat apparently had propaganda value for English kings around 800, when the Carolingians were rediscovering their Gothic roots. The genealogy of King Alfred's father Æthelwulf, added around 892 to the *Anglo-Saxon Chronicle*, gives Geat a number of northern ancestors, among whom five – Scyld, Scef, Beaw, Heremod and Hwala – appear as legendary figures in Old English poetry. The expansion backwards to Scyld, eponymous ancestor of the Danish Scyldings, marks what looks like a new social reality, the integration of Dane and Englishman in one kingdom. Royal houses acquired not a little mythological depth and perhaps even some political legitimacy by claiming descent from the gods and rulers of the heartland of northern Europe. And what was of interest to kings was of practical and immediate interest to their subjects.

Attempting to date and place the five Old English poems dealing with Germanic legend is difficult and controversial. Distinguishing genres in a literature lacking, as far as we can tell, special terms for 'epic', 'elegy' or 'lay' can also be troublesome. The five poems are over and over again affirmed to be a very small, probably unrepresentative sample of what must have once existed. Yet so great is the desire to find an authentic 'lay', just one scrap of the kind of short song believed to have transmitted knowledge of the legends from generation to generation, that scholars have until recently made the *Finnsburh Fragment* one.[13] It has been thought that the forty-eight-line fragment is almost complete, missing only a few verses at the beginning and end, even though the loose (and now lost) leaf containing it may well be all that is left of a once sizeable poem. The extant portion deals in a vivid, close-up way with five days of the same battle at Finn's stronghold sung of by the *scop* (court poet) in Heorot (*Beowulf* 1063–162). At this pace, the Old English poet could have gone on for several thousand lines, from Hengest's birth to his betrayal of Vortigern and subsequent settlement of Kent, constructing a dark founding myth that undermines the foundation on which it rests. As it stands, the *Finnsburh Fragment* does not even exhibit the 'terseness' we require of a 'lay'. Surely there were quicker ways of announcing an enemy's approach, of explaining what that bright light flashing in the distance might be, than the one chosen by its first speaker:

> Ne ðis ne dagað eastan,   ne her draca ne fleogað,
> ne her ðisse healle   hornas ne byrnað.
> Ac her forþ berað;   fugelas singað,
> gylleð græghama,   guðwudu hlynneð,
> scyld scefte oncwyð.   Nu scyneð þes mona
> waðol under wolcnum   (3–8)

This is no dawn from the east, nor does a dragon fly here, nor are the gables of this hall burning here. Rather weapons are carried forward here; carrion birds sing, the grey-coated one [wolf] howls, war-wood resounds, shield answers shaft. Now the moon shines, wandering under the heavens.

Parallels to this stylistic device (the offering of alternative explanations before arriving at the correct one) have been located in Irish and Welsh literature, a useful reminder of the degree to which Old English 'Germanic' poetry was a part of contemporary society.[14]

If the two-leaf *Waldere* is not regarded as a 'lay', it is at least partly because a verse-epic treating the same legend survives in the 1456-hexameter *Waltharius*. The story of Walter – his escape from Attila's court with treasure and with Hildegyth (unnamed in the Old English fragment), and his great battle against Guthhere and Hagena (Old Norse Gunnarr and Hǫgni) – was popular over a wide area and for at least four centuries. The Old English text presents a number of problems: the original order of the leaves is uncertain; we cannot decide which of the four chief characters speaks the first ten lines of the (traditionally) second leaf; and the (probable) lack of a tragic ending bothers Germanists, who want Walter to end his days in battle, not marriage. Nevertheless, the poem is important for students of Germanic legend because its sixty-three lines provide vivid examples of, among other things, the tension between a heroic code and human affection, the lack of concern with chronology (the poet portrays Theodoric the Ostrogoth, Nithhad, Weland and Widia as older than Attila), weapons with a legendary past, stolen treasure, the hero's headlong drive for everlasting glory and the role of women in Old English poetry. Hildegyth does much of the talking in the two fragments, and manages to do it out of both sides of her mouth ('Fight, don't be a coward' and 'Be careful, you impetuous fool'), which must have annoyed Waldere if he were listening. After playing the valkyrie to perfection and inciting her hero to battle, she starts to worry and, anxiously, to repeat herself:

> ac ðu symle furðor   feohtan sohtest,
> mæl ofer mearce;   ðy ic ðe metod ondred,
> þæt ðu to fyrenlice   feohtan sohtest
> æt ðam ætstealle,   oðres monnes
> wigrædenne   (I, 18–22)

But you always sought the battle farther forward, an occasion beyond the limit; I feared for your fate, because you too rashly sought battle at that station(?) according to the war-plan of the other man.

The relationship between *Waldere* and *Waltharius*, or between them and the tenth-century poem by Ekkehard I of St Gallen and the Latin paraphrase in the early eleventh-century *Chronicon Novaliciense*, is unclear. Because literature in written form was not accessible to the vast majority of Anglo-Saxons, the latest fashions in Germanic legend had to come to them as oral narrative. But there was a continual interchange in early medieval Europe between written and oral modes of transmission, between the historical scholarship that recorded the presence of hostages among the Huns and the tall tales that told of their adventures. *Waldere*, like the other four Old English poems on Germanic subjects, did not exist in an enclosed 'oral' world.

In *Widsith*, *Deor* and *Beowulf*, knowledge of Germanic legend is taken for granted as belonging to both the poet and his public. Material is used in an allusive, referential way, not just thematically. It is true that, in *Beowulf*, the poet tells us as much as we need to know to follow the main story; in *Widsith*, the poet's opening and closing lines, and the scop's narrative insertions, give us a good idea of what is going on; and in *Deor*, acquaintance with the tales behind the allusions is not essential for understanding the general drift of the poem. But this minimalist inventory gives a wrong impression of the kind of enjoyment to be derived from the three poems. The pleasure of recognition, of sharing in an erudite game, seems to have been as important to the Anglo-Saxons as to readers of Ovid and Milton. Germanic legend was something people had to know, like chess, claret or cricket, if they wanted to be thought cultured. *Widsith* names some seventy kings and as many tribes in its 143 lines; *Deor*, in 42 lines, refers to five or six stories (depending on whether Weland and Beadohild count as one or two); and *Beowulf*, in 3182 lines, draws on about twenty legends. The audience's memory, like a frame, shapes and gives meaning to the poet's often fleeting allusions.

There was also the pleasure of surprise. All three poems introduce a fictive or new character into the known world of legend: Widsith, the far-travelled poet; Deor, the supplanted scop; and Beowulf, the Good Samaritan Geat. We follow each *novus homo* as he meets and mingles with the heroes of past times. The poet tends to use his titular character to explore the early stages, the *enfances*, of an established legend or hero, reconstructing what might have happened just before the main story starts. No-one had ever mentioned, for example, who took Ermanaric's bride-to-be, the legendary Svanhild, to the land of the Goths; it was Widsith. No story gave the name of Heoden's first court poet, the scop cast aside when his patron hired the golden-voiced Heorrenda; he was called Deor. Did anyone ever beat the legendary Breca ('breaker, wave') in a contest out on the ocean? The young Beowulf did. We can never be absolutely certain that the Anglo-Saxon poets knew the stories about Svanhild, Heoden and Breca that we think they knew. That they could have, however, is confirmed by the Old Norse *Ragnarsdrápa*, attributed to the ninth-century Bragi, a court poet thought to have British relatives. His famous *dróttkvætt* poem, probably the first in that metre to have come down to us, focuses on the climactic moments of the same three (or in the case of the mythological third, similar) legends: the death of Ermanaric at the hands of Svanhild's brothers; the abduction of Hild by Heoden; and Thor's famous rowing out with the giant Hýmir ('sea') to engage the monster on the ocean floor.[15]

The fictional scop, whom the *Widsith*-poet introduces and overhears, recites three supposedly traditional name-lists. The first is a catalogue of the kings of legend and the peoples they ruled, with the structure:

Þeodric weold Froncum,   Þyle Rondingum   (24)

Theodric ruled the Franks, Thyle the Rondings.

The second is a catalogue of tribes, mostly the North Sea and Baltic nations, with the structure:

Mid Seaxum ic wæs ond <mid> Sycgum   ond mid Sweordwerum
(62)

I was with the Saxons and with the Sycgan and with the Swordsmen.

The third is of heroes and rulers of legend, with the structure:

Emercan sohte ic ond Fridlan   ond Eastgotan   (113)

I sought Emerca and Fridla and Eastgota.

There is a tendency to think that this roll-call did not sound to Anglo-Saxon ears as it does to ours, but it probably sounded, if anything, more artificial and pedantic: a returned traveller's tedious enumeration of all the important people he saw on his last trip abroad, and how nice they were to him, how terribly generous. That is all Widsith tells us, for example, about two great heroes of legend: Guthhere, king of the Burgundians, and Ælfwine [Alboin], king of the Lombards. Many of the names in Widsith's catalogues are known to history (Theodoric the Frank) and legend (Ermanaric's nephews Emerca and Fridla); others are unknown but appear in another Old English poem (Sycgan = Secgan, Finnsburh 24); still others are 'speaking-names' (Thyle 'Spokesman', Sweordweras 'Swordsmen'), perhaps traditional, perhaps invented by the poet, perhaps a rationalization, a translation into recognizable elements, of an unfamiliar personal or tribal name. Some of the names are clustered in such a way as to suggest that the poet had a particular story in mind: lines 27–31, for example, mention three figures from the Finnsburh legend.

The three catalogues of Widsith are separated by short narrative episodes, which refer to major legendary events, such as the battle between the Goths and Huns. In contrast to the sometimes obscure names in the catalogues, all the stories alluded to in these 'epic' sections are well known. Several of the heroes named are mentioned in Beowulf: Offa establishing the southern boundary of his father's kingdom; Hrothulf and Hrothgar crushing at Heorot the attacking Heathobards under Ingeld; and the adventures of the legendary outlaw Hama. Widsith is, for no good reason, usually regarded as a very old poem, perhaps even older than Cædmon's Hymn. Whatever its age, it was probably not composed at any great remove, in time or place, from Beowulf.

The wit of Deor lies in part in the way it treats the legendary on an equal footing with everyday reality: the supplanted poet, as if to put his unhappiness into perspective, names famous figures of Germanic story who had (or gave others) a hard time. It is as if a jilted woman were to calm her nerves by reflecting that Medea, Clytemnestra, even Pasiphae, had boyfriend troubles too. Deor is divided by a repeated refrain into six stanzas, each one alluding to a situation from legend: Weland abused by Nithhad; Beadohild's pregnancy; the fatal love of Mæthhild and Geat (details unknown); the Gothic Theodoric's oppression of his subjects; Ermanaric's cruelty to his; and, finally, the abduction of Hild by Heoden. It is hard to find truly 'happy' endings among these Germanic tales; but the scop's refrain seems to turn each story into an exemplum of misery overcome:

Beadohilde ne wæs   hyre broþra deaþ
on sefan swa sar   swa hyre sylfre þing,
þæt heo gearolice   ongieten hæfde

þæt heo eacen wæs;   æfre ne meahte
þriste geþencan,   hu ymb þæt sceolde.
Þæs ofereode,   þisses swa mæg!   (8–13)

To Beadohild the death of her brothers was not so painful in her mind as her own affair, that she clearly had recognized that she was pregnant; she could never resolutely think how she should act about that. That passed over; so can this.

Beadohild, raped by Weland after he had killed her two young brothers, gave birth to Widia, a famous adventurer featured in *Waldere* and *Widsith*; so, Deor seems to be saying, everything turns out for the best in the end. (That need not have been Beadohild's view.) The scop explains his own miseries in the final stanza: he was forced into early retirement by the minstrel whose artistry (in the Middle High German *Kudrun*) so captivated Hild that she consented to elope with Heoden. In the Old Norse accounts, early and late, the result is not only tragic but permanent: an everlasting battle between father and husband over which Hild, true to her name, presides; at her command, the slain awaken each day at dawn to begin hostilities anew. A story of suffering destined to last until the end of the world was an odd choice for a scop wanting to console himself with the thought that sorrow, like joy, is transitory, or a poet to assure his audience that, man being mortal, his miseries must pass. This is not to suggest that Deor was fired for incompetence, just that an audience knowing the version of the legend that Bragi knew would find some irony, if not self-mockery, in the scop's concluding refrain.

Like Widsith and Deor, and like Aeneas, Troilus, Sir Galahad, Palamon and Arcite, Robin Hood and a host of others, Beowulf is a new hero in legend-land. The Old English poet endows him with a remarkable sense of the past and of the future. He can look back two generations, tracing the origins of the feud between the Swedes and Geats (2379–96, 2472–89, 2611–19 and 2922–98). He can also forecast the feuds of the next generation: on the basis of a piece of information picked up at the Danish court, he turns the Ingeld legend referred to by Alcuin into a political prophecy, a sequence of events likely to occur in the near future (2024–69). Earlier heroes of legend like Scyld, Heremod, Finn, Offa, Sigemund, Ermanaric and Hama are not made contemporaneous with the sixth-century events described, but are set in a distant mirror, conveying the illusion of a many-storied long ago. The poet's reconstruction for his protagonist of a northern heroic age presents such an internally consistent picture of Scandinavian society around AD 500 that his imitation of historical truth has been taken for the reality. Indeed, the one event in *Beowulf* recorded by the literate world – Hygelac's raid on the Merovingian kingdom – is referred to no less than four times (1202–14, 2354–66, 2501–8 and 2911–21), almost as a touchstone of authenticity.

Like a scholar, the *Beowulf*-poet imparts to things a unity they do not possess, and gets away with it: his interpretation is passed off as true. The legends in *Beowulf* seem to come in waves. Sometimes they function as an agreeable negative argument: a king should not behave like Heremod, or a queen, like Thryth. Sometimes they are used, indirectly, to praise. Pindar could think of no better way to honour a winning athlete than to tell him some old legend; the *Beowulf*-poet has an anonymous Dane celebrate Beowulf's victory by reciting the story of Sigemund's dragon-fight: in this way the new hero is raised to the level of the legendary world. When necessary, even myth becomes history: Beowulf's story of Hæthcyn's accidental slaying of Herebeald (2535–43) euhemerizes a fratricide in the Norse pantheon. Stories are told of Scyld, featured in the West Saxon royal genealogy; of Offa, in the Mercian; and of Hengest, in the Kentish. There is a high concentration of *hapax legomena*, particularly compounds, in the scop's story of Hengest at Finnsburh. These words are sometimes imagined as 'older', deriving from a pre-existing 'lay'; but they may well be, like Beowulf himself, newly coined, constructed on traditional (and thus 'old') patterns, claiming links to 'the past' and 'the ancestors'. The final scene of the Finnsburh episode shows Hengest boarding a ship and putting to sea, intending to sail to Denmark. Did a storm come up? Did the Danes fear to keep him? Was it boredom at home or long, sad evenings sipping tea with Hildeburh that led him to accept an invitation to England? Causal connections are never made. The poet's hearers are expected to be as sly and agile as he is, to serve as his accomplices, his conspirators in breaking and entering the past.

Each name or episode in *Widsith*, *Deor* and *Beowulf* may be regarded as an allusion to another poem. The lesson of recent critical theory, that no text is an island, that every work is a response to a conversation or dialogue that it presupposes but need not mention, was learned long ago by students of Germanic legend. The hard part is applying this wisdom to poems that are, indeed, islands, the preserved tips of icebergs that melted away long ago. We know how large a part ephemera – newspapers, children's literature, schoolbooks, cheap paperbacks, movies, television, pop music – play in our own lives, and can imagine equivalent 'oral' classes of material having a similar cultural importance in Anglo-Saxon England. But they have not come down to us; we shall never know what songs the cowherds sang the night Cædmon left the party early. To hear any part of the other side of the conversation, readers of the Old English poems have to tap material from a variety of foreign sources, many from the thirteenth century or later, in full awareness that the 'dialogue' changes dramatically over the years, that each poet makes the story again in his own way. Our ignorance means that we may expect to make mistakes.

It is, of course, safer, and more scientific, to say 'there is no positive evidence that the Anglo-Saxons knew the story of . . . ', for there rarely is. Explicitness was not a virtue in the poetry of Germanic legend; reticence was. But reading too much into this verse is probably less dangerous than reading too little. Poets give clues when they are responding to something outside their texts, when they want us to know that they mean more than they say. If we do not listen, it is not good manners but laziness: it is easier to believe that Old English verse is simpler, more innocent, less interesting to pry into than our own. Resentful at having to strain to hear, we deafen ourselves to the poet's voice.

A useful working principle for the student of Germanic legend is that all details in the text are capable of explanation, even at the cost of oversubtlety and error. Listen carefully to the poet, for example, as he tells us that Widsith escorted a certain young princess to her future husband:

Widsith spoke, unlocked his word-hoard, he who of men had travelled through most tribes and peoples over the earth; often he received on the floor of the hall a handsome treasure. His ancestors sprang from the Myrgings. He with Ealhhild, the good peace-weaver, first, from Angeln in the east, sought the home of the Gothic king Eormanric, the cruel oath-breaker.   (1–9)

It seems likely, as Chambers thought, that some specific evil deed accounts for the epithet 'cruel oath-breaker' at this point. Malone disagreed; he refused to see any allusion here to Ermanaric's future slaying of his lovely bride on trumped-up charges of adultery with her stepson, declaring that as far as we can tell the Ealhhild of the Old English poem was on the best of terms with her husband (this is like arguing that, because a friend of Caesar's said so, Brutus was an honourable man).[16] Old Norse verse evoking the same legend shows us just how devious early Germanic poetry can be. Bragi, at the very moment that Svanhild's brothers are poised to dispatch Ermanaric, refers to the Gothic king as 'joy, or love, of Foglhild' (= Svanhild); the poet also calls him 'chief kinsman of Randvér' (= his son). Both epithets are ironic reminders of what might have been, not assertions that Ermanaric was a devoted husband and father, and that the boys were wrong to want to kill him. When Widsith boasts that he sang the praises of Ermanaric's wife, spreading her fame through many a land (97–108), he is telling us, if we are listening, that she is a famous figure in Germanic legend, and that he alone, our self-regarding scop, was responsible. The Old English poet, no less than Hamlet, worked by indirections.

Different authors had different techniques. The *Widsith*-poet was partial to the half-said thing, distilling the complexity of legend into a single epithet or detail. Offa, he tells us, fixed the boundary of his kingdom *ane sweorde* 'with a solitary sword' (41), an emphatic phrase that suggests something more specific than 'in single combat'. The incident alluded to here may be related to the legend told by Sweyn Aageson and Saxo Grammaticus, in which Offa, wielding a famous sword, strove alone against two foes in order to wipe off the disgrace that earlier stained his people, when two warriors together killed one opponent.

The *Beowulf*-poet, on the other hand, is almost Chaucerian in his ability to make neutral or even mildly approving statements that suggest, despite the innocence of the speaker, that something is rotten in the state of Denmark. A scop, jubilant at Beowulf's victory, sings of Sigemund, relating how that hero would sometimes tell his adventures to Fitela, 'uncle to nephew' (881); but the Old English audience probably knew what even Sigemund did not yet realize, that Fitela was not only his sister's son but his own, through incest. (At least one event leading up to the incest story seems to be portrayed on a stone carving, perhaps from the early eleventh century, found at the Old Minster, Winchester.)

A single temporal adverb or adverbial phrase ('at that time, then still, for a while') can signal trouble. The *Widsith*-poet has his fictive scop declare that 'Hrothulf and Hrothgar kept for the longest time kinship-ties together, nephew and uncle' (45–6). And the *Beowulf*-poet, depicting the same pair, says in almost the same words 'at that time their kinship-bonds were still together, each true to the other' (1164–5), adding that both of them trusted Unferth. We can be pretty sure, even without consulting the late Scandinavian authorities that in part confirm our hunch, that Scylding family feelings will soon sour, and that Unferth might have something to do with the break. When Wealhtheow anxiously insists that Hrothulf will repay her and Hrothgar for their kindnesses to him, that he will be good to their boys when her aged husband is gone (1180–7), the poet is probably recalling a tradition that Hrothulf, an even more important figure in legend than Hrothgar, deposed and killed his cousins. And when Beowulf announces mysteriously that King Heorogar, who ruled the Danes for a long time, did not want to give his battle-equipment to his son, the bold Heoroweard (2155–62), we and the audience perhaps know, even if the Geat did not, that Heoroweard will eventually try to get his own back, attacking and killing Hrothulf, whose heroic last stand is probably the most famous episode of the entire Scylding cycle.

It is impossible to know how much more (or less) the Anglo-Saxons knew of Germanic legend than we do. Some conservative readings of the texts are based on the belief that our five poems are very old, that Germanic legend had only just begun to develop when they were composed. Even though the *Widsith*-poet names Emerca and Fridla immediately after mentioning the Herelingas (112–13), our scholarship is still unwilling to accept that the story of the two Harlung brothers,

Embrica and Fritla, found in the German *Quedlinburg Annals c.* 1000, formed a part of the Ermanaric cycle when the poem was new. Hama, a Gothic hero mentioned in *Widsith* (124), is described in *Beowulf* as having fled Ermanaric; he carried treasure to a 'bright stronghold' and chose 'eternal gain' (1198–201). This sounds like the story, known to us only from the thirteenth-century *Þiðreks saga,* that Hama, after running away from Ermanaric, entered a monastery, bringing with him weapons and gold. But we are told to reject this interpretation, for the penitential motif, so redolent of medieval romance, seems 'out of place' in an ancient Germanic work. To some extent we still share with Tacitus an idealized vision of the Germanic past, of a northern frontier brimming with simple, loyal, brave, proud and warlike pagans, men who were everything that materialistic, intellectual, cosmopolitan Romans were not.

The first certain use of Tacitus's *Germania* after 525, when it is cited in Cassiodorus's *Variae,* occurs in the *Translatio Sancti Alexandri* by the mid-ninth-century monk Rudolf of Fulda.[18] In both periods, the *Germania* appears, like a fairy godmother, to mark and legitimize the birth of a Germanic consciousness, conceived by kings and scholars in emulation of the Caesars. The imagination of the Anglo-Saxons was stirred by this tradition, vague and unformed, of something majestic out of the distant past, of a golden age in which men were taller, bolder, freer and more glorious. And Old English poets were moved to find and make some drama played by these great kings and heroes, cutting them loose from history and setting them free to perform their collective magic on a stage larger than their own lives or society. And if, despite their legendary courage, they meet, as most do, a tragic end, so much the better: a brave but defeated Ingeld becomes for centuries a symbol of the northern will to go down fighting; a charismatic but doomed Ermanaric or Theodoric provides for future generations an image of Germanic sovereignty. According to the poet of the *Vǫluspá,* the first thing gods do, when the new world rises out of the wreck of the old, is to sit on the ground and tell stories about their all-powerful past, sifting it for clues to the present:

> Þar muno eptir   undrsamligar
> gullnar tǫflor   í grasi finnaz,
> þærs í árdaga   áttar hǫfðo

There shall afterwards the wondrous golden chess-pieces be found in the grass, those which they had owned in days of old.[18]

Poets of Germanic legend, too, conjured up for their contemporaries a magnificent, aristocratic descent, a proud history embodying current hopes and fears, a pleasant dream transmuting the desert of daily existence into a landscape rare and strange.

1 For the major texts, see Further Reading below, esp. *Beowulf and its Analogues*, trans. Garmonsway and Simpson (1968), and Calder *et al.*, *Sources and Analogues* (1983), and also F. P. Magoun, Jr. and H. M. Smyser, *Walter of Aquitaine: Materials for the Study of his Legend*, Connecticut College Monographs 4 (New London, CT, 1950). On the pictorial monuments of Germanic legend, see R. N. Bailey, *Viking Age Sculpture in Northern England* (London, 1980), esp. ch. 6; J. Lang, 'Sigurd and Weland in Pre-Conquest Carving from Northern England', *Yorkshire Archaeological Journal* 48 (1976), 83–94; S. Margeson, 'The Vǫlsung Legend in Medieval Art', in *Medieval Iconography and Narrative: a Symposium*, ed. F. G. Andersen *et al.* (Odense, 1980), pp. 183–211. Important early studies in English include W. P. Ker, *Epic and Romance: Essays on Medieval Literature*, 2nd rev. ed. (London, 1908); H. M. Chadwick, *The Heroic Age* (Cambridge, 1912); and J. de Vries, *Heroic Song and Heroic Legend*, trans. B. J. Timmer (London, 1963). For cogent criticism of Chadwick's linking of Germanic heroic legend with 'heroic age' society, see R. Finnegan, *Oral Poetry: its Nature, Significance and Social Context* (Cambridge, 1977). On early attempts to find pagan remains in this literature, see E. G. Stanley, *The Search for Anglo-Saxon Paganism* (Cambridge and Totowa, NJ, 1975).

2 *Lied und Epos in germanischer Sagendichtung* (Dortmund, 1905), p. 4.

3 Examples are reviewed for English readers in J. Opland, *Anglo-Saxon Oral Poetry: a Study of the Traditions* (New Haven, CT, 1980), pp. 40–73, and T. M. Andersson, *A Preface to the Nibelungenlied* (Stanford, CA, 1987), pp. 3–16.

4 Letter no. 124, ed. E. Dümmler in Monumenta Germaniae Historica, Epistolae Karolini Aevi 4.2 (Berlin, 1895), 183; cf. also above, p. 21, n. 9.

5 *EHD*, p. 843.

6 *De consolatione philosophiae* II, met. 7; *King Alfred's Old English Version of Boethius' De Consolatione Philosophiae*, ed. W. J. Sedgefield (Oxford, 1900), p. 46, lines 16–17.

7 The *Beowulf*-poet's account of Hygelac's raid is not as close to the version in the sixth-century *History* of Gregory of Tours as it is to the abridgement of Gregory's narrative in the eighth-century *Liber Historiae Francorum*: see W. Goffart, '*Hetware* and *Hugas*: Datable Anachronisms in *Beowulf*', in *The Dating of Beowulf*, ed. C. Chase, Toronto Old English Series 6 (Toronto, 1981), 83–100. I must acknowledge here my profound debt to Walter Goffart for his comments and advice during the writing of his paper, for providing it with any stylistic niceties that it might have, and for the constant stimulation of his ideas and teaching.

8 Ker, *Epic and Romance*, pp. 21–2.

9 The key references are conveniently assembled in *Der Volksname Deutsch*, ed. H. Eggers, Wege der Forschung 156 (Darmstadt, 1970), 406–7.

10 Flodoard, *Historia Remensis Ecclesiae* IV.5, ed. J. Heller and G. Waitz, Monumenta Germaniae Historica, Scriptores 13 (Hanover, 1881), 564. *The Poetic Edda I*, ed. U. Dronke (Oxford, 1969), pp. 192–224, has a good account of the legendary Ermanaric.

11 *The Search for Anglo-Saxon Paganism.*

12 Major studies are K. Sisam, 'Anglo-Saxon Royal Genealogies', *Proceedings of the British Academy* 39 (1953), 287–346; D. Dumville, 'Kingship, Genealogies, and Regnal Lists', in *Early Medieval Kingship*, ed. P. H. Sawyer and I. N. Wood (Leeds, 1977), pp. 72–104; 'The Anglian Collection of Royal Genealogies and Regnal Lists', *ASE* 5 (1976), 23–50; H. Moisl, 'Anglo-Saxon Royal Genealogies and Germanic Oral Tradition', *Journal of Medieval History* 7 (1981), 215–48; and A. C. Murray, '*Beowulf*, the Danish Invasions, and Royal Genealogy', in *The Dating of Beowulf*, ed. Chase, pp. 101–12.

13 But see now E. G. Stanley, 'The Germanic "Heroic Lay" of Finnesburg', in his *A Collection of Papers with Emphasis on Old English*, Publications of the Dictionary of Old English 3 (Toronto, 1987), 281–97. Also *Finnsburh Fragment and Episode*, ed. D. K. Fry (London, 1974), pp. 25–6.

14 P. Sims-Williams, 'Is it Fog or Smoke or Warriors Fighting? Irish and Welsh Parallels to the *Finnsburg Fragment*', *Bulletin of the Board of Celtic Studies* 27 (1976–8), 505–14.

15 English translations of *Ragnarsdrápa* are in *The Poetic Edda I*, ed. Dronke, p. 206 (partial); E. O. G. Turville-Petre, *Scaldic Poetry* (Oxford, 1976), pp. 1–6 (partial); L. Hollander, *The Skalds* (New York, 1945), pp. 32–7 (full but incomprehensible); and A. Faulkes, *Snorri Sturluson: Edda* (London, 1987), pp. 7, 73–4, 106 and 123–4 (full but dispersed).

16 Chambers, *Widsith*, p. 24; Malone, *Widsith*, pp. 140–1.

17 Cassiodorus Senator, *Variae* V.2, ed. T. Mommsen, Monumenta Germaniae Historica, Auctores antiquissimi 12 (Berlin, 1894), 143–4; *Translatio Sancti Alexandri*, ed. B. Krusch, Nachrichten von der Gesellschaft der Wissenschaften zu Göttingen, phil.-hist. Klasse (1933), pp. 405–36.

18 *Edda: Die Lieder des Codex Regius nebst verwandten Denkmälern, I: Text*, ed. G. Neckel, 5th ed. rev. H. Kuhn (Heidelberg, 1983), p. 14 (str. 61).

6 Heroic values and Christian ethics

IN an image of compelling sadness, the Wanderer evokes the life of a lordless man. Cold and alone, he can do nothing but remember the joys of the past–companions in the hall, the giving of treasure and the favour of his lord. Not even sleep brings forgetfulness:

> Forþon wat se þe sceal his winedryhtnes
> leofes larcwidum longe forþolian,
> ðonne sorg ond slæp somod ætgædre
> earmne anhogan oft gebindað.
> Þinceð him on mode þæt he his mondryhten
> clyppe ond cysse, ond on cneo lecge
> honda ond heafod, swa he hwilum ær
> in geardagum giefstolas breac (*The Wanderer* 37–44)

Indeed, this he knows, who must long be deprived of the counsels of his beloved lord, when sorrow and sleep together often bind the wretched solitary one. It seems to him in his mind that he embraces and kisses his lord and lays hands and head on his knee, as he had previously, from time to time in days gone by, gained benefit from the throne.

Sleeping, the lordless man dreams of what he longs for most, the life of a retainer, here represented by synecdoche in the act of homage and the giving of treasure. To lack a lord is to lack place and role, friend and kin, help in need, and vengeance after death. The Wanderer's misery, having no remedy in this world, is balanced by the astringent comfort of the next. But even the Wanderer's final spiritual rejection of the world is figured in a lovingly detailed enumeration of its heroic joys: horse, kinsman, gift-giving, feasting, hall-joys, treasure, warriors and lord (*The Wanderer* 92–5).[1]

The ethos of heroic life pervades Old English literature, marking its conventions, imagery and values. The touchstone of that life – as represented in Old English literature at least – is the vital relationship between retainer and lord, whose binding virtue is loyalty. Continuing loyalty is ensured in the lord's giving of treasure. Through gifts of worth, a lord enhances both his own reputation and that of his retainer, and he lays

107

upon his man the obligation of future service. In the transaction of the gift, the object given – ring, armour, horse or weapon – becomes the material reminder of the retainer's reciprocal obligation when war service or vengeance is required. This certainly is the meaning of *Beowulf* 20–5, where Beow is praised for prudent munificence, because generosity is expected to ensure loyalty.[2] It is in the nature of a king, as *Maxims II* 28–9 observes, to distribute rings in the hall. Before the combats with Grendel and Grendel's mother, Hrothgar's last word to Beowulf is to assure him that he will be generously rewarded if he survives (*Beowulf* 660–1 and 1380–2). Upon his return home, Beowulf presents horses, armour and treasure to Hygelac and in turn receives golden armour, high rank and extensive land (2190–6). The economy of such generosity must be understood in the function of the exchange to enhance the reputation of both parties and confirm a continuing interdependence. It must also be understood (as the poetry clearly recognized) that the generosity of the lord was not necessarily effective when war came.

In the poetic articulation of the heroic ethos, a warrior's paramount goal is the achievement of a lasting reputation. *Dom biþ selast* ('Glory is best', *Maxims I* 80). In the world of *Beowulf*, a lasting reputation is a warrior's only hope for immortality:

> Ure æghwylc sceal   ende gebidan
> worolde lifes; wyrce se þe mote
> domes ær deaþe; þæt bið drihtguman
> unlifgendum   æfter selest   (*Beowulf* 1386–9)

Each of us must await the end of life in the world – let him who can achieve glory before death; that will be best afterwards for a warrior no longer living.

In his final words, Beowulf asks that his tomb be built on a coastal headland, so that seafarers, using the promontory as a landmark, will recall the barrow as *Biowulfes biorh* (2807). Both his desire for glory and his pursuit of it are thus appropriately memorialized in the last word of the poem, where Beowulf's men praise him as *lofgeornost* ('most eager for glory'). In a very different context, though once again connecting *deaþ* and *dom*, are Hildegyth's words of encouragement to Waldere in the fragmentary poem of that name:

> [. . .] is se dæg cumen
> þæt ðu scealt aninga oðer twega,
> lif forleosan   oððe l[. . .]gne dom
> agan mid eldum, Ælfheres sunu   (*Waldere* I, 8–11)

Son of Ælfhere, the day has come that you must necessarily do one of two things – lose your life or achieve among men a ?lasting glory.

Lasting glory is won only under conditions where one's life is in doubt. The good deeds (*godum dædum*, 23) by which Waldere will enhance his reputation are specifically acts of valour achieved with his sword, Mimming.[3] That achievement of such glory could be thought fitting praise for a contemporary king is suggested by the entry for 937 in the *Anglo-Saxon Chronicle*. This entry in verse memorializes the victory of Athelstan and Edmund, who achieved lifelong glory (*ealdorlangne tir*) in battle at an unidentified place called by the poet *Brunanburh*.[4] Put to flight, their enemies have no cause to boast of prowess in battle and have lost stature. The goal of heroic conduct is *dom*, or *lof*, or *mærðu*, which lives in the speech of those coming after. The medium for such lasting praise, *Widsið* suggests, is heroic verse. Even in poems whose focus is the world to come, rather than the present one, the concern for the after-life is, nonetheless, sometimes phrased in the language of heroic convention, as we see in *The Seafarer* lines 72–80 (see below, pp. 175–6).

If the ultimate heroic reputation may be gained by risking death in a glorious combat, the ordinary obligations of a retainer's life manifest themselves in the literature in less spectacular ways. As the Old English poem *Andreas* suggests, if the lord were to go into exile, his retainers were apparently expected to accompany him. When Andreas resolves to leave alone for treacherous Myrmedonia (where he will suffer for his faith), his companions protest that if they allow the saint to depart alone, they, being lordless (*hlafordlease*), would be welcome nowhere (*Andreas* 405–13).[5] The primary tasks of a retainer, however – at least as represented in Old English verse texts – were defence of the lord in battle and revenge for injuries.

What, precisely, was the nature of the loyalty which the hero owed his lord? The counterpart of the scenes of feasting and giving of treasure detailed in *Beowulf* and nostalgically evoked in *The Wanderer* and *Widsið* was warfare. *The Battle of Finnsburh* praises the five-day battle of Hnæf's men against the Frisians as a fitting repayment for their lord's 'white mead' (39). The retainers of the young Beowulf on the evening of Grendel's mother's attack are praised for their warlike readiness to support their lord (*Beowulf* 1246–50). And Wiglaf's first speech at the dragon's lair suggests that Beowulf's chosen men had formally undertaken to fight for the lord whenever he had need. His comment that death is better for a warrior than a life of disgrace (2890–1) should be understood in the context of the exile enforced as punishment on those who fled to save their own lives. The price of their cowardice was the loss of land rights for themselves and their kin.[6]

Those manifestations of loyalty which are praiseworthy in *Beowulf* – the killing of Dæghrefn (for the death of Hygelac), of Ongentheow (for the death of Hæthcyn), of Finn (for the death of Hnæf) and of Onela (for the death of Heardred) – are all acts of vengeance taken to repay the death of a lord. Not in every case was the vengeance immediate: Beowulf repaid Onela years later by supporting Eadgils, Hengest brooded for a winter as Finn's unwilling guest until the time when he could avenge Hnæf's killing. Such loyalty reflects the perceived importance of communal obligation as a way to protect the individual from isolation. The loneliness of a solitary life was greatly feared, and *Maxims I* (172–82) presents as axiomatic the observation that it is best for a man to have a brother for mutual comfort and protection.

The entry for 755 in the A-version of the *Anglo-Saxon Chronicle* uses the literary conventions of heroic life to shape its narrative of a struggle for power in Wessex (*c.* 757 × 786), and in so doing provides an unusually detailed representation of conflicts implicit in the heroic ethos.[7] It offers a story of loyalty (with an additional conflict between loyalty to lord and to kin), valour and vengeance, and its detail repays attention. According to the account, Cynewulf became king of the West Saxons after expelling Sigebryht, his kinsman, *for unryhtum dædum* ('for unjust deeds'). Some time later, Sigebryht confirmed the justice of this action by a further outrage – the killing of Cumbra, that nobleman who had been most loyal to him. This treachery earned Sigebryht an inglorious end, when a swineherd, most probably a dependent of Cumbra, avenged the murder by stabbing Sigebryht to death. The annal indicates that after thirty-one years had passed (correctly, twenty-nine), Cynewulf wished to expel Sigebryht's brother, Cyneheard, as well.

Having given this background, the account presents Cyneheard's response. Seizing the opportunity to attack the king when he is only minimally protected, Cyneheard rushes to Merton in Surrey to surprise the king while he is with his mistress. Unguarded and surrounded, the king mounts a valiant defence in the doorway of the woman's *bur* (her private chamber), wounding Cyneheard, though finally being overwhelmed by numbers. Cynewulf's guard, alerted too late, arrive to receive an offer from Cyneheard of *feoh ond feorh* ('property and life') as a settlement if they will agree to follow him. They refuse to serve their lord's *bana* ('slayer') and are slaughtered, save for a single British hostage who is gravely wounded.

The situation is reversed when the rest of the king's retinue arrive in Merton. Upon Cyneheard's offer of compensation, if they will follow him as king, the king's men decline settlement on the grounds that they could not follow the *bana* of their lord. They nonetheless offer safe conduct to any of their kinsmen in Cyneheard's company who wish to leave. Taking a heroic decision which mirrors that of the king's guard, however, Cyneheard's men refuse the offer, claiming that they could do no less than the king's guard who refused *feoh ond feorh*. In the ensuing fight,

Cyneheard's men are all slaughtered, save for the godson of Osric, Cynewulf's ealdorman. He too has been grievously wounded.

The extraordinarily lengthy account of Cynewulf and Cyneheard almost certainly owes its presence in the *Anglo-Saxon Chronicle* to its dramatic interplay of conflicting allegiance, absolute loyalty and valour against odds. That it would seem to be a textbook illustration of the themes of heroic conduct found in secular poetry should not be surprising. The appearance of these themes throughout Old English literature demonstrates their continuing appeal, and these heroic conventions offered familiar and satisfying narrative devices both for organizing the struggle between Cynewulf and Cyneheard and for conveying its moral point.

The symmetrical offers of compensation and safe conduct combined with the survival in each battle of only one man from the losing side suggests that the attraction of the account of Cynewulf and Cyneheard lies in the narrative creation and exploitation of balance. Narrative sympathy rests with Cynewulf, and the focal point of the story is on social order, which Sigebryht and Cyneheard both violate. The disturbance of order has a moral dimension as well which is reflected in the shifting balance of power between king's men and those of the usurper.[8] The king, weakened morally by his dalliance, is open to attack. Similarly, his band of select retainers pay for their lack of preparedness with their lives. The narrative focuses on the tensions created by the conflicting demands of kin and group, of king and usurper and of loyalty and self-interest. Order is seen to triumph as the attraction of life and compensation yields to the necessity for vengeance and as the demands of kinship, though pressing, give way to the demands of loyalty to lord.

In the poetry, feud and vengeance are more than practicalities; they are matters of honour and means to enhance a reputation or lose it. However, in contrast to the emphasis on kindred in the feuds of Icelandic literature, feud in Old English literature focuses primarily on conflict within the social group. In *Beowulf*, the grip of feud and vengeance is intimately connected to social order and is as inexorable as fate itself. Grendel's depredations necessitate vengeance, but the feud he engenders is beyond peaceful settlement, since

> sibbe ne wolde
> wið manna hwone   mægenes Deniga,
> feorhbealo feorran,   fea þingian,
> ne þær nænig witena   wenan þorfte
> beorhtre bote   to banan folmum   (*Beowulf* 154–8)

He did not wish peace with any of the men of the host of the Danes, to remove the deadly evil, compound with money, nor did any of the wise men there have reason to expect a noble compensation at the hands of the slayer.

Beyond the pale, Grendel is too savage to understand wergild or too monstrous to acknowledge its vital social function. While the imbalance created by Grendel's crimes requires redress, the inevitable price of Beowulf's victory over Grendel is further death, as Æschere's life is exacted by Grendel's mother, 'sunu deoð wrecan' (1278: 'to avenge the death of her son').

The Grendel kin are descendants of the fratricide, Cain, whose killing of Abel God himself avenged ('þone cwealm gewræc / ece Drihten', 107–8). But the monstrous progeny of Cain merely mirror behaviour in the civilized human world. Heorot is built only to await the destructive flames from the rekindled Heathobard feud (82–5). Finn and Hengest endure through the Frisian winter a fragile, unwilling peace until vengeance shatters their agreement (1127–53). The Franks and the Swedes nurse their enmity toward the Geats, and the sombre promise of their vengeance lends further poignancy to Beowulf's death (2910–27).

In its deadly necessity vengeance is more comprehensible and more predictable than fate, for it is the expected and praiseworthy duty of both kin and thegn. One of the classic expressions of the value and duty of vengeance is Beowulf's response to Hrothgar's grief at the death of his counsellor, Æschere:

> Ne sorga, snotor guma; selre bið æghwæm,
> þæt he his freond wrece, þonne he fela murne   (1384–5)

Do not grieve, wise man. It is better for each man that he avenge his friend than that he mourn much.

But the heroic and praiseworthy pursuit of vengeance has tragic consequences as well. Freawaru, promised in marriage to Ingeld to seal the settlement of a feud between the Heathobards and the Scyldings, would necessarily be unsuccessful (2029–31). Heorot itself would not survive this feud. Hildeburh, a Dane married to the Frisian Finn, having lost son, husband and brother in the feud at Finnsburg, must return to her people. So binding is the necessity for revenge that when Hrethel, as father to both men, is unable to avenge the presumably accidental killing of Herebeald by his brother, Hæthcyn (the poem calls it a 'feohleas gefeoht, fyrenum gesyngad', 2441: 'a fight without compensation, grievously undertaken'), he takes to his bed and dies.

To this point the discussion of kings, warriors and the ideals of their behaviour has been focused substantially on the literary conventions by which they are presented in Old English literature. However, assessing the congruence between the conventions of heroic literature and the 'reality' which called it forth is extraordinarily difficult. When H. M. Chadwick postulated a 'heroic' stage of society in Western cultures (for Germanic peoples, the period of Migrations, approximately the fourth to sixth centuries, AD), he did so in part to establish authority for 'historical' information possibly contained in national epics and lays written long after that 'heroic' stage.[9] (Old English heroic literature appears in manuscripts of the late tenth and early eleventh centuries.) Chadwick's hypothesis is, in fact, open to grave doubt and cannot be extended to recover a historical reality for the social customs of the migration. Still less does the literature provide reliable evidence of contemporary culture in Anglo-Saxon England, for literature does not mirror, in any straight-forward fashion, the society which produces it.

The features of early kingship in Anglo-Saxon England are insuf-ficiently documented to allow a specific portrait of the relationship of lord and retainer and the conduct expected of each. In the absence of con-temporary evidence, some have looked to Tacitus's *Germania* – a work of the late first century AD – where in chs. 14–15 is found a general outline of the behaviour and expectations of Germanic barbarian war-bands. Certainly, many of the traits which Tacitus describes in his account of the Germanic *comitatus* are consonant with features of heroic convention found in Old English literature. Tacitus speaks of generosity and feasting, feud and settlement, the valour expected of man and chief. In *Germania*, the chieftain leads in battle by example, not by authority, and wishes not to be surpassed in valour by his men. Further, Tacitus claims, the retainer's duty is to defend and protect the lord. It is a lasting shame for a retainer to survive his lord in battle. However, the virtues which Tacitus finds praiseworthy in the Germanic warriors were those virtues he found lacking in the Romans of his own day. Thus the *Germania* must be read as a work with a political and moral bias and is an unreliable guide to 'historic' details about either contemporary German barbarians or their post-migration descendants.

The divergence between the literary representations of warrior life and the social realities of both kingship and military life are usefully illustrated by the activities of Alfred the Great. The Anglo-Saxon king about whom we know the most, King Alfred (871–99), left behind both a military and an intellectual legacy. In a kingdom harried for forty years by Viking raiders, Alfred managed during his reign to contain the Vikings, limit their disruptions and secure Wessex. His military reforms, including the institution of a system of fortifications, paved the way for the territorial expansion of his son and grandson (see above, p. 13). Mindful as well of the importance of learning in the kingdom, Alfred set about translating Latin works he considered most needful – Gregory's *Pastoral Care*, Boethius's *Consolation of Philosophy*, Augustine's *Soliloquies* and the first fifty psalms. Other important Latin works were translated at his suggestion. Alfred seems to have viewed these two activities, warfare and scholarship, as integral to his kingship. In the prose Preface to his translation of the *Pastoral Care*, Alfred reflects nostalgically on an English past of heroic and righteous kings, marking how the kings who had power over the people in those days obeyed God and his messengers; and they held peace, morality and power within the country, and also extended their territory abroad; and how they succeeded both in war and in wisdom' (Sweet 3.5–9).[10] In this vision of kingship, the king occupies a middle position, exercising power (*onweald*) over his people but in turn being obedient to God and to the church. In this way the good king might keep peace, morality and power.

For Alfred, the external military affairs consisted in fighting the heathen Vikings, and a related domestic military concern lay in the deployment of defences and the organization of fighting forces. Of the three kingly pursuits which Alfred discusses (*sibbe, siodo* and *onweald*), *siodo* most sets Alfred and his ideal kings apart from the kings of literary heroic convention. In *Widsith* a king lives 'fittingly' (11, *þeawum lifgan*), and these words also praise Beowulf as an old king (*Beowulf* 2144). Nonetheless, the customs of the band of retainers which they lead are material and secular.[11] Alfred's use of *siodo* reveals his belief that in his internal affairs the king was responsible as well for the moral guardianship of his people. The translations of important instructional works which Alfred undertook or ordered reflect this commitment.

In one representative endeavour, the translation of Boethius's *Consolation of Philosophy* (chs. 18–19), Alfred calls into question and presents an unsparing corrective to the heroic pursuit of lasting praise. Wisdom renames such a goal 'idelan hlisan [ond] ðone unnyttan gilp' (Sedgefield 46.3: 'empty fame and idle boasting'). In his treatment of Boethius's argument on the vanity of pursuing fame, Alfred observes that in comparison to the universe, the earth is small, but a man's reputation cannot even extend very far on earth. Different languages and customs make the spread of reputation difficult, and death, finally, levels rich and poor alike. To Boethius's allusions to the Romans Brutus and Cato, Alfred adds from Germanic legend a reference to the smith, Weland. What little reputation is left for all of these can be written in a few letters (*mid feawum stafum awriten*: 46.25–6). By meditating on the vulnerability of writing, Alfred emphasizes how transitory a reputation preserved in this fashion must be. In Boethius, fame of the great lives in stone (II, pr. 7). In Alfred's translation of this passage of Boethius, writing is a fragile vehicle for fame, not only because (as in Boethius) histories may be lost, but also because of the shortcomings of the writers of those histories. Reputation may die out 'through the misconduct of those writers who for their sloth and carelessness and also negligence have left unwritten the deeds and the conduct of those men, who in their days were most illustrious and desirous of honour. And even though they have written down all their lives and deeds, just as they ought if they have done well, nevertheless, have their writings not grown old and perished as soon as they came into being, just as the writers did and also what they wrote about?' (Sedgefield 44.1–8). Reputation is not eternal; it is ended by death.

Moral stewardship can be seen as well in the laws Alfred promulgated and in those of his successors. For example, Æthelred's law code of 1008 (drafted under the supervision of Archbishop Wulfstan) begins, 'that we all shall love and honour one God and . . . will hold one Christian faith under the rule of one king' (*EHD*, p. 405). Alfred was not the first Christian English king to be concerned about the moral welfare of his subjects. But the modifications which Asser reports Alfred to have made in the service of his household retainers, by requiring their service in three shifts of one month each (presumably to allow them time to attend to their own estates), make the realities of royal service in the ninth century very distant from the service of the Germanic war band.

During the Viking depredations, warfare was a brutal reality, but the concept of war itself could be subject to analysis and question. A theory of the just war, with roots in late Christian antiquity, developed in the early Middle Ages by virtue of custom and necessity. Isidore of Seville distinguished between just and unjust wars, and Ælfric adapts this distinction to the realities of life in late tenth-century England. Of justifiable war (*iustum bellum*) Ælfric writes that it 'is rihtlic gefeoht wið ða reðan flotmenn oððe wið oðre þeoda þe eard willað fordon' (ed. Skeat II, 114: 'is a just war against the savage seamen or against other peoples who wish to destroy our land').[12]

There was, however, ample encouragement in the gospels for declining to kill at all, and according to literary tradition King Edmund of East Anglia gained a martyr's crown by his saintly refusal to fight the *flotmenn*. The *Anglo-Saxon Chronicle* entry for 870 simply records that Edmund had fought unsuccessfully against the Danes and was killed. Ælfric's life of Edmund, however, presents the king's death within the framework of the passion of a saint (see below, p. 252). Edmund, having consulted a bishop who advised flight or tribute, considers such counsel shameful. He refuses to bear arms and resolves on a martyrdom following Christ's example. In Ælfric's account, Edmund's reasons against flight are an interesting reversal of the loyalty of a thegn to his lord: '. . . ic gewilnige and gewisce mid mode, þæt ic ane ne belife æfter minum leofum þegnum, þe on heora bedde wurdon, mid bearnum and wifum, færlice ofslagene from þysum flotmannum' (ed. Skeat II, 318: 'I desire and wish heartily, that I alone do not live after my beloved retainers, who were, with their children and wives, suddenly slain by these pirates'). As admirable as

Edmund's piety was, secular and political order could not survive such royal self-sacrifice.

The pointed inversions of loyalty and vengeance in this account of Edmund's wish to die suggest another direction from which heroic values could be questioned. If the austere code of revenge which drives heroic behaviour in Old English verse made a satisfying hero, it also presented problematic ideals in an increasingly complex political order. The care which the narrative of Cynewulf and Cyneheard takes in representing appropriate loyalty and vengeance suggests how dangerous these forces, when unbridled, were perceived to be. The requirements of vengeance and loyalty to family and to group were powerful forces in Anglo-Saxon society, and royal law-codes both recognized and sought to control them.[13]

Vengeance could be exacted in one of two fashions – by blood or by wergild. Quite obviously, a routine indulgence in blood feud would embroil families in continual conflict, but a system of wergild (the establishment of a price for compensation depending on the act and on the station of the injured individual) had the attraction of providing an externally determined, honourable alternative to bloodshed. Both the law codes and the penitentials acknowledge the powerful obligation of vengeance, and secular payment for transgression was complemented by ecclesiastical penance. In the eighth-century penitentials attributed to Theodore and Bede, the penance assigned for murder was reduced if the murderer paid compensation. Such a reduction for the man who killed in warfare or under the orders of his lord suggests that the writers of these penitentials recognized war and loyal service as circumstances mitigating the gravity of the act.[14]

Despite the civil alternative of wergild, private vengeance in the form of blood feud seems to have been widely practised. In the blood feud the reciprocal relations of individual and kindred are most clear. By making good his obligation to pursue his kinsman's rights, the individual likewise ensured that his kin would look after him and exact vengeance or compensation if necessary.[15] The potential conflict between obligations to kin and to king exploited in the narrative of Cynewulf and Cyneheard appears elsewhere as a matter of royal concern. The laws of Alfred specify that in case of attack, a man and lord might fight on each other's behalf without incurring vendetta, but they further stipulate 'a man may fight on behalf of his born kinsman, if he is being wrongfully attacked, except against his lord; that we do not allow' (*EHD*, p. 415, nos. 42.5–6). Among the tenth-century regulations governing the payment of wergild is Edmund's code on the blood feud, limiting the liability of the kindred in the case of a murder. If the kinsmen of a man who has slain another formally abandon him and refuse to pay compensation, they are exempt from the feud and the slayer alone is liable (*EHD*, p. 428, nos. 1–1.3). Such an enactment made it possible for the kin in law and in honour to distance themselves from the originator of a feud. Financially and physically it was in the interest of the kinsmen to take advantage of such an opportunity.

The *Battle of Maldon* presents an opportunity to examine the points of intersection between the Old English literary conventions of the heroic ethos and the events of 'real life' in an occasional poem which is both a polished work of literature and a memorial of an historical event. At this intersection there is another meeting, this one between the language of heroic values and that of religious judgement. The poem is not datable precisely, and although several arguments have been made for composition after 1020, it is likely that the poem was composed not too long after the battle (which according to the *Anglo-Saxon Chronicle* took place in 991). The poem's precise place of origin is similarly unclear – it has been attributed both to Ramsey and to Ely. The latter foundation is slightly more likely, since Byrhtnoth's remains were interred there and the monastic community had received from him a generous endowment.

The *Battle of Maldon* commemorates the heroic resistance of an English army against a substantial force of Vikings in an engagement in August 991. The entry in the E-version of the *Anglo-Saxon Chronicle* merely records the death of Byrhtnoth and the subsequent payment of tribute to the Vikings: 'In this year Ipswich was ravaged, and very soon afterwards Ealdorman Brihtnoth was killed at Maldon. And in that year it was determined that tribute should first be paid to the Danish men because of the great terror they were causing along the coast. The first payment was 10,000 pounds. Archbishop Sigeric first advised that course' (*EHD*, p. 234). The contrast between the spareness of the *Chronicle* account and the rich heroic detail of the poem suggests that *The Battle of Maldon* was composed as praise for Byrhtnoth, a great secular magnate and religious benefactor. The only copy of the poem to have survived the Middle Ages was already a fragment, bound in a composite manuscript which was badly burned in the disastrous Cotton fire of 1731. The remains of the manuscript are now London, British Library, Cotton Otho A. xii, but that part containing the poem is burnt beyond use. That the poem is known to modern readers is due to a transcription made by one David Casley several years before the fire.[16] As we now have it, the poem lacks a beginning and an end, and its fragmentary condition must be kept in mind in any evaluation of the poem. The remaining fragment shows the English preparations for the battle, the decision to allow the Vikings safe passage to permit a fair fight, the death of Byrhtnoth, ealdorman of Essex, the flight of a portion of the English army, and the valour of the English who remained. The leader of the English forces, Byrhtnoth, is seen at the beginning of the fragment encouraging, arranging and advising his troops. These are composed of the *folc* and the *heorðwerod*, though the significance of this distinction ought not to be over-emphasized. The *folc* were the men of the *fyrd* (the levied army), though the size of the army at this battle is unclear, and the *heorðwerod* were presumably Byrhtnoth's personal retinue.[17] If he dismounted to fight amongst them in the expectation that they would be most loyal, he was greatly mistaken, for the Godric who flees from the battle was one of this *heorðwerod*. And Godric's flight on his slain lord's horse throws the English forces into disarray.

The impression of Byrhtnoth as a noble leader conveyed at the beginning of the poem is enhanced by his stirring and defiant reply to the Viking messenger's request for tribute to secure peace. Byrhtnoth flings back the messenger's own words, promising spear and sword as tribute. The only arbitration the English will accept is battle:

> Ne sceole ge swa softe   sinc gegangan;
> us sceal ord and ecg   ær geseman,
> grim guðplega,   ær we gofol syllon   (59–61)

Nor shall you get treasure so easily; point and edge [i.e. spear and sword] will arbitrate for us before that, grim battle, before we give tribute.

These are noble boasting words, and Byrhtnoth's courage, nobility and prowess have never been questioned. His subsequent action, however, in allowing the Vikings safe passage to permit a fair fight has been closely examined by modern students of the poem to determine both his motive for the decision and the judgement of the poet on his conduct.

Various suggestions have been made for the circumstances of the battle, but the most probable is that the Vikings had made a base on Northey island in the tidal estuary of the Blackwater river in Essex (near the modern town of Maldon). While it would be mistaken to take the details of the poem as historical 'fact', the situation which the poet outlines makes clear that the Vikings had to cross a tidal channel to get to the English. The English thus had a tactical advantage in protecting the mainland, but the situation was actually an impasse, since neither side could effectively attack the other. Even at low tide, the 'bridge' (probably a low-water ford) could be defended by just three men (*The Battle of Maldon* 74–83).

The lines which have caused the greatest interpretative controversy in the poem are those which describe the Vikings' request for safe passage and Byrhtnoth's response:

> þa hi þæt ongeaton   and georne gesawon
> þæt hi þær bricgweardas   bitere fundon,
> ongunnon lytegian þa   laðe gystas,

bædon þæt hi upgang   agan moston,
ofer þone ford faran,   feþan lædan.
Ða se eorl ongan   for his ofermode
alyfan landes to fela   laþere ðeode   (84–90)

When they recognized and perceived clearly that they had found the bridge-guardians fierce, the hated guests began to use cunning. They asked that they might have passage to cross over the ford, to lead the footsoldiers. Then the earl began, out of excessive courage, to allow too much land to the hated people.

The crucial terms in this passage are *lytegian* and *ofermode*. The Vikings (as much 'guests' in Essex as Grendel was in Heorot) request the chance to cross in safety to allow a decisive battle. *Lytegian* is a word unrecorded elsewhere in Old English, but it is related clearly enough to the adjective *lytig*, 'cunning' or 'wily'. Although attempts have been made to build a case for a relatively benign meaning for *lytegian*, it is difficult to avoid the conclusion that *lytegian* had an unfavourable sense: the Vikings 'used cunning' to secure their passage. One need not, however, draw the severe conclusion that Byrhtnoth was deceived or that his *ofermod* deluded him. The Vikings' 'cunning' may simply reflect a poetic judgement that the Vikings talked their way across the ford.

The second crucial term is *ofermode*. The philological evidence for *ofermod* meaning 'pride' or 'excessive courage' is substantial, although the noun occurs only infrequently. Most interestingly, *ofermod* occurs in an identical half-line in a collection of religious aphorisms, *Instructions for Christians* 130, where its meaning is clearly 'pride'. Similarly, Satan is described as the 'angel of pride' (*se engel ofermodes: Genesis A* 272). The religious context of both uses is apparent. However, the second possible Modern English gloss, 'excessive courage', may well be the more appropriate translation for a secular context.[18] It is difficult to reconcile a stinging judgement of sinful pride with a poem which is otherwise generous in its praise of a secular lord (and one well-known as a religious benefactor). Yet in isolation, even the gloss 'excessive courage' appears to be critical. Understanding the word, the passage, and the portrait of Byrhtnoth requires putting the comment in context. In other words, it is necessary to understand as much as possible the circumstances of the battle (and the way in which the text understands them), the context of leadership in late tenth-century England and the use of heroic conventions in the composition of the text.

There is no indication in the poem that the English were obviously outnumbered in the battle. Quite the contrary. Byrhtnoth's concluding words to the Vikings, 'god ana wat / hwa þære wælstowe   wealdan mote' (94–5: 'God alone knows who will control the place of slaughter') suggests a perception that the sides were even. Assuming that the Vikings were coming from an island, Byrhtnoth's tactical advantage extended only to the area which his men controlled on the mainland, but offered no opportunity to drive the Vikings out or to prevent their making a sortie elsewhere. Byrhtnoth's supposed tactical advantage is, upon examination, limited if not illusory, for its only advantage lay in protecting the lives of his men. In practical terms, using this 'advantage' would keep him from protecting the *folc and foldan* (54, 'the people and land') of Æthelred. In heroic terms, it was no advantage at all.

If Byrhtnoth was at all deceived, it was not by the Vikings but by the men on whom he had counted. Evidence from the Latin *Life* of St Oswald (a roughly contemporary account by Byrhtferth of Ramsey) suggests that the battle celebrated by the *Maldon*-poet was actually part of a continuing campaign and that the Viking raid of 991 was revenge for an encounter in Devon in 988 in which the English forces had been victorious. If the interpretation of this evidence is correct, then Byrhtnoth's decision to engage the Vikings was founded on two pieces of secure information: that England's defences had been adequate to ensure peace during the preceding fifty years and that the Vikings had been unsuccessful in their immediately previous encounter.[19]

Byrhtnoth's own valour as lord and leader is exemplary. He urges his men *dom gefeohtan* (129: 'to achieve glory by fighting') and his boast to the messenger is backed by deeds. When he is first wounded, Byrhtnoth kills his opponent and another warrior. Two other deadly strikes, a spear wound and a slashing blow to his sword arm, are required to disable the earl. Even then, before he drops to his knees, he encourages his *gode geferan* (170: 'good companions') to go forward. His last words are a prayer, after which 'heathen' warriors hew him down along with two companions. No such valour can be recorded of Godric (Odda's son) or of his brothers. In the context of the cowardly behaviour of these men, Byrhtnoth's courage and confidence were indeed too great.

Lines 185–201 of the poem highlight the enormity of the cowards' betrayal by twice alluding to Byrhtnoth's heroic munificence to them:

> and þone godan forlet
> þe him mænigne oft   mear gesealde;
> he gehleop þone eoh   þe ahte his hlaford   (187–9)

and he abandoned the good man who had often given him many a horse; he mounted the horse which his lord owned.

Others follow:

> and manna ma   þonne hit ænig mæð wære,
> gyf hi þa geearnunga   ealle gemundon
> þe he him to duguþe   gedon hæfde   (195–7)

and more men than was in any way fitting, if they had recalled all the favours which he had done for their advantage.

Godric's cowardly escape on Byrhtnoth's own horse is deliberately emphasized by the single named gift which defines Godric's failed heroic obligation to his lord. Similarly, the other cowards are condemned by mention of the gifts which Byrhtnoth is said to have given for their benefit. If the lord's munificence failed to secure the battlefield loyalty of his men, its memory would nonetheless serve to condemn them.

The reproof of the cowards in *The Battle of Maldon* is reminiscent of Wiglaf's exhortation to Beowulf's men during the dragon fight and his cold condemnation of their flight afterwards.

> Ic ðæt mæl geman,   þær we medu þegun,
> þonne we geheton   ussum hlaforde
> in biorsele,   ðe us ðas beagas geaf,
> þæt we him ða guðgetawa   gyldan woldon
> gif him þyslicu   þearf gelumpe,
> helmas ond heard sweord   (2633–8)

I recall the occasion when we partook of the mead, when we promised our lord in the beerhall, him who gave us there precious rings, that we would repay him for that battle equipment if such need befell him, repay the helmets and hard swords.

When the *comitatus* return from their flight into the woods, Wiglaf meets them with the bitter judgement that Beowulf had thrown away the battle equipment they were standing in. Their punishment of exile is a living death.

The actions of the cowards and the suicidally valiant behaviour of the remaining English army at Maldon are schematically opposed in terms of the values of the literary heroic code, and this opposition forms the second part of the picture of the relationship which the poem develops between lord and men. Upon perceiving that Byrhtnoth lay dead, his faithful *heorðgeneatas* urge each other to continue the fight to avenge their beloved lord or die ('lif forlætan   oððe leofne gewrecan', 208). Ælfwine, a young Mercian nobleman, is the first to speak. He claims a double obligation to Byrhtnoth, that the ealdorman was both his kinsman and his lord ('he was ægðer min mæg   ond min hlaford', 224). His resolve to fight to the death may be owing to his two-fold relationship to Byrhtnoth, but he states it in terms reminiscent of Tacitus's *Germania* – that thegns will not be able to reproach him that he left the field after his lord was dead. One after the other, the members of the dwindling English army vow to avenge their lord's death or die. Such loyalty is not the preserve of the aristocracy, and Dunnere, described as an *unorne ceorl* (256: 'a simple free man') urges that men fight without concern for their lives. The slaughter is terrible, and though the English take their toll on the Vikings, by the close of the fragment defeat seems inevitable. In the last speech of the poem, an old warrior, Byrhtwold, utters the words which have come to epitomize the heroic valour of the poem:

> Hige sceal þe heardra,   heorte þe cenre,
> mod sceal þe mare,   þe ure mægen lytlað   (312–13)

Courage shall be the fiercer, heart the bolder, spirit the greater, as our strength diminishes.

These ill-fated warriors portray their own resolve as if such behaviour were expected, and Ælfwine, especially, appears to suggest that disgrace follows the man who survives his lord (220–3). While there are instances recorded of men dying with their lord (for example, Bede reports in his prose *Life* of St Cuthbert, ch. 27, that Ecgfrith and most of his army were killed in 685 at *Nechtansmere*) and of suicidal loyalty (in the account of the retainers of Cynewulf and Cyneheard, discussed above), loyalty unto death seems not to have been the rule either in literature or in life. The Wanderer lives (albeit unhappily) without a lord, and the various heroes in *Beowulf* seek timely vengeance for their lords rather than death by their sides. It is possible that the stirring resolve in the battlefield speeches of Ælfwine, Offa and their companions was designed less as an expression of the norm than as a moral counterpart to the cowardice of the sons of Odda. Battlefield desertion may well have been a common occurrence, as Æthelred's law code of 1008 acknowledges.[20]

In *The Battle of Maldon*, as in the Chronicle entry on Cynewulf and Cyneheard, the principles of balance and symmetry are sources of heightened interest in the narrative. The English are arrayed against the Vikings, Byrhtnoth's speech of defiance hurls back the Viking's own words, the young Wulfmær pulls the spear out of Byrhtnoth's dying body and uses it to pierce Byrhtnoth's killer; slaughter inflicted is slaughter avenged. On a higher narrative level, balance plays off the cowardice of those who fled against the honour of the men who stayed. And at this level the focus of narrative interest is different in the two texts. In the story of Cynewulf and Cyneheard, doubt and resolution lie in the conflict between two routes to honour, the obligations of kin and group. In *The Battle of Maldon*, the struggle is of another sort, and the choice is not between forms of honour but whether to stand or to run.

There has always been a conflict between the individual heroic ethic (in the pursuit of valour and reputation whatever the cost) and the requirement for prudent aggression from an established army. The daring risk (for example, Beowulf's *beot* to fight Grendel without a sword) brings praise, reputation and treasure when made good, but is a problematic subject for verse when the hero is less obviously successful. The dramatic problem which the *Maldon*-poet had to treat was the simple and well-known fact that the English lost. Within the heroic tradition, the composer of a praise poem had limited options when his subject died in the middle of the battle and had part of his army run away in the process.

Virtue was found in the necessity when the *Maldon*-poet chose for his commemoration a heroic idiom pressed to its extreme. Its austerity and remoteness from the realities of tenth-century English military obligation provided a model of nobility in defeat, though there may be some irony for us in the poet's choice of idiom – the suicidal military virtues ascribed to the English may more nearly have been those of their opponents. The note of complaint which the text seems to make in lines 89–90 arises out of the nature of the code which it ascribes to Byrhtnoth and his loyal retainers. The realm of the heroic lies apart from the mundane, and the poem locates the nobility of the English precisely in their excess. For Byrhtnoth the measure of heroism lies in the excess defined by '*ofer*mode' and 'landes *to fela*'. Such excess must necessarily involve for us a paradox. His noble decision to engage the enemy ultimately led to his death, but it is his death, in part responsible for the following defeat, which ensures his glory. The heroic excess of Byrhtnoth's men lies in their choice of death in battle. For them too, death transforms the army's defeat into personal victory. *Dom* and *deað* are frequent companions. The heroic idiom of *The Battle of Maldon* is anything but naive. Its use suggests at once admiration, nostalgia and regret – admiration for the greatness of a secular magnate, nostalgia for the heroism of a brighter day, and regret that such heroism makes death its companion.

1 As he commits the treasure hoard of his now dead people to the earth, the so-called Last Survivor (though in a clearly secular context) similarly mourns the vanished pleasures of the retainer's life (*Beowulf* 2247–66).

2 Similarly, Hrothgar is praised for munificence in *Beowulf* 71–3 and 80–1. By explicit contrast, the avaricious king is liable to suffer exile and death (1709–22).

3 'Weorða ðe selfne / godum dædum, ðenden ðin god recce' (*Waldere* 22–3: 'Make yourself worthy by good deeds [i.e. bold action], while God guides you').

4 *The Battle of Brunanburh* 3. Similarly, a warlike and victorious Abraham, after his battle to free Lot, is described in *Genesis A* as *elne gewurðod / dome and sigore* (2137–8: 'made worthy by his courage, by glory and victory').

5 Aldhelm's letter to the abbots of Wilfrid similarly draws on the convention of the loyal retainer: 'Now then, if worldly men, exiles from divine teaching,

were to desert a devoted master, whom they embraced in prosperity, but once the opulence of the good times began to diminish and the adversity of bad fortune began its onslaught, they preferred the secure peace of their dear country to the burdens of a banished master, are they not deemed worthy of the scorn of scathing laughter and the noise of mockery from all?' See M. Lapidge and M. Herren, *Aldhelm: the Prose Works* (Cambridge, 1979), pp. 169–70 (Letter XII); see also P. F. Jones, 'Aldhelm and the Comitatus-Ideal', *Modern Language Notes* 47 (1932), 378.

6 R. Woolf, 'The Ideal of Men Dying with their Lord in the *Germania* and in *The Battle of Maldon*', *ASE* 5 (1976), 63–81, at 68–9, notes that the band of men which Wiglaf describes as Beowulf's retainers do not really constitute a *comitatus*, since the men have land rights which can be taken back.

7 For general discussion of this episode, see F. P. Magoun, 'Cynewulf, Cyneheard and Osric', *Anglia* 57 (1933), 361–76.

8 That Cynewulf might appear to be a usurper is smoothed over in the account by mention of the king's acting in conjunction with the West Saxon council and their justification for banishing Sigebryht because of wicked deeds.

9 H. M. Chadwick, *The Heroic Age* (Cambridge, 1912).

10 S. Keynes and M. Lapidge, *Alfred the Great: Asser's 'Life of King Alfred' and other Contemporary Sources* (Harmondsworth, 1983), p. 124, n. 2 suggest that this passage recalls *Historia ecclesiastica* IV.2, where Bede praises the times of Archbishop Theodore during which Christian kings terrified barbarian nations and when learning in sacred subjects was widely available.

11 For example, to the extent that Hrothgar embodies custom he acts with restraint, cares for his men, makes good his promises, shares treasures and distributes land (*Beowulf* 71–3 and 80–1).

12 For a discussion of war in Old English verse and its background in patristic commentary, see J. E. Cross, 'The Ethic of War in Old English', *England before the Conquest: Studies in Primary Sources presented to Dorothy Whitelock*, ed. P. Clemoes and K. Hughes (Cambridge, 1971), pp. 269–82.

13 See *EHD*, pp. 391–478, and discussion above, pp. 15–16. Many of the points raised here are usefully illustrated in the corpus of Anglo-Saxon laws. For example, the Laws of Ine extend wergild beyond blood relationship to spiritual relationship (god-father or -son) (*EHD*, p. 407, nos. 76 and 76.1). The Laws of Alfred set limits to vendetta in an effort to force civil settlement and specify that no vendetta would be incurred when fighting for one's lord or born kinsman or against an adulterer or fornicator (with one's wife, daughter or sister) (p. 415, nos. 42.5–7). The Laws of Athelstan set limits for payment for a slain man (p. 419, no. 11), and the Laws of Edmund specify the involvement of leading men and advocates in the civil settlement of a feud (p. 428, nos. 7–7.3).

14 See A. J. Frantzen, *The Literature of Penance in Anglo-Saxon England* (New Brunswick, NJ, 1983), pp. 76–7.

15 See H. R. Loyn, 'Kinship in Anglo-Saxon England', *ASE* 3 (1974), 197–209, at 203–4.

16 H. L. Rogers, '*The Battle of Maldon*: David Casley's Transcript', *Notes and Queries* 32 (1985), 147–55.

17 On the Anglo-Saxon use of the *fyrd*, see C. W. Hollister, *Anglo-Saxon Military Institutions* (Oxford, 1962), esp. pp. 59–102.
18 For a review of various strategies used to translate *ofermod*, see H. Gneuss, 'The Battle of Maldon 89: Byrhtnoth's *ofermod* Once Again', *Studies in Philology* 73 (1976), 117–37, at 119. For a sympathetic discussion of a neutral meaning for *ofermod*, see T. A. Shippey, 'Boar and Badger: An Old English Heroic Antithesis', *Leeds Studies in English* ns 16 (1985), 220–39, at 228.
19 E. John, 'War and Society in the Tenth Century: The Maldon Campaign', *Transactions of the Royal Historical Society* 5th ser. 27 (1977), 173–95, at 185 and 188.
20 *EHD*, pp. 445–6: 'And if anyone deserts from an army which the king himself is with, it is to be at the peril of his life and all his property. And he who otherwise deserts from the army is to forfeit 120 shillings.'

7 Pagan survivals and popular belief

BEDE tells the story of the conversion of the pagan English with lively detail and predictable bias in the first half of his *Ecclesiastical History*. For Bede, as for the sixth-century British historian Gildas, on whose writings he leans, the Angles and Saxons were invited to mid-fifth-century Britain as mercenaries who then turned against their Romano-British employers. Bede refers to them bluntly as 'pagans', 'heathen conquerors' and 'the enemy'. On the other hand, he is careful not to direct sympathy towards the Christian Britons, whose heart-wrenching miseries at the hands of the Saxons he paints with equanimity, assuring his readers that 'the fires kindled by the pagans proved to be God's just punishment on the sins of the nation'.[1] Having characterized the main parties in this warfare as equally corrupt, whether through rapacity or inner depravity, Bede proceeds to introduce the heroes of his tale. These are St Gregory's Roman missionaries, together with the enlightened English rulers who accepted their teachings.

According to Bede, the missionaries who landed in Kent in 597 had no interest in restoring the church to the status it had enjoyed during the late years of Roman Britain, nor did they much admire the forms of the faith that still flourished in Ireland and Wales. Instead, after a pagan hiatus of a hundred years or more, they set out to establish the true apostolic church in England once and for all. Their ecclesiastical model was the church of St Peter in Rome. Their spiritual models were Christ and the early saints and martyrs, in all their zeal and poverty:

As soon as they had occupied the house given to them [in Kent] they began to emulate the life of the apostles and the primitive Church. They were constantly at prayer; they fasted and kept vigils; they preached the word of life to whomsoever they could. They regarded worldly things as of little importance, and accepted only the necessities of life from those they taught. They practised what they preached, and were willing to endure any hardship, and even to die for the truth which they proclaimed.

(*HE* I.26)

In Bede's account, no arm-twisting was necessary to persuade the English kings to give up their pagan rites. All that was needed was the example of the missionaries' own devotion; and as with any good conversion stories, a strategic number of miracles helped the process along (see also above, pp. 4–7).

Like all things evil, if we are to believe Bede, paganism had an innate capacity to self-destruct. The story of the conversion reaches its climax in the scene in which Edwin, king of Northumbria and *bretwalda* or high king of the English, summons his chief noblemen to advise him on the wisdom of accepting the new faith (*HE* II.13). The most potent speech in favour of Christianity is made by Edwin's pagan priest, Coifi, who abruptly declares the old religion to be 'valueless and powerless' and who then, filled with joy at his new-found knowledge, proceeds to profane and then torch the old temple. Implausible as this scene might be if presented in isolation, it is given depth by a second speech that is framed by Coifi's two appearances. In it Bede gives an unnamed nobleman the part of a philosopher brooding about earthly transience. The nobleman likens the present life of man to the flight of a sparrow through a banquet-hall on a dark winter's night: 'While he is inside, he is safe from the winter storms; but after a few moments of comfort, he vanishes from sight into the wintry world from which he came' (cf. also above, pp. 6 and 82). The desire for a more secure shelter from the storm persuades this adviser to follow the new teachings, and the other elders follow suit.

Paganism in England, as opposed to English paganism, did not die out so easily. Within three or four generations after Bede's death and continuing until the Norman Conquest, it came to be reintroduced by wave after wave of Viking settlers. A scattering of Northumbrian place-names and picture stones, together with some dismissive references in Ælfric's tenth-century treatise *De falsis deis* to the cults of Odin, Thor and 'the shameless goddess' Frigg (alias Friya or Freya), confirm that the Vikings imported their mythology to England, though without much effect on Old English imaginative literature. The early eleventh-century laws of Cnut speak out strongly against heathenism as the practice of witchcraft, divination or idolatry; and they take idolatry to mean, 'if one worships heathen gods and the sun or the moon, fire or flood, wells or stones or any kind of forest trees'.[2] These proscriptions must chiefly have been directed not against the old Germanic paganism that Angles, Saxons, Jutes, Frisians and Franks had brought with them in their migrations from the Continent, but rather the pagan worship of Danes and Norwegians who had settled in England during the Viking Age.

Much as one is tempted to associate with the age of pre-Christian English heathendom the colourful stories that the Vikings later told about frost giants, Odin's eye and the final cataclysm of Ragnarǫk, there is no evidence that such tales had currency in England before the Viking Age. Anglo-Saxon paganism from the period before the Conversion remains fairly opaque to our eyes, chiefly because of the cloak of silence that the early clerics cast over the whole subject of cursed rites. The unconverted English revered the main gods of the Germanic pantheon.[3] We would not otherwise still name six of the days of the week after the sun, the moon, the war-god Tiw (Old Norse *Týr*), Woden the god of divination and the dead (Old Norse *Óðinn*), the storm-god Thunor (Old Norse *Þórr*) and the fertile Friya (Old Norse *Freyja*). But of how these gods were worshipped, with what attendant myths, we have little knowledge. The heathen English offered sacrifice at altars, but they had nothing resembling monasteries devoted to regular prayer. Lacking both a hierarchical church and the technology of book-making, they could have had no received body of theology. Whether or not they had professional priests is unclear. Bede and other monastic authors cannot be taken at face value on this point, as their writings are likely to be coloured by early Christian accounts of paganism in Mediterranean lands. The heathen English had healers, or shamans – men or women who specialized in cures and rites – but such people may have differed from their neighbours only in their degree of knowledge and self-assurance. As in later Iceland, some high-ranking men may have served as their own priests, as is suggested by the fact that several Anglo-Saxon holy places (such as Patchway, Sussex, from *Pæcces weoh* or 'Patch's shrine') were named after an owner rather than a god. It may be significant that when the first Roman missionaries in Kent wrote down a body of English laws, one of their first concerns was to devise a price for themselves within the Old Germanic system of wergild. No such step would have been necessary had there already been a specific wergild for priests.

The heathen English kept a great holiday at or near the midwinter solstice (Yule) and observed other festivals during the springtime months, of which we have echoes in the Easter and May Day celebrations, and at the time of harvest home. They practised a kind of baptism in the form of a naming ceremony for infants. They worshipped in groves, at wells and on hilltops, but their shrines are unmarked by any archaeological remains comparable to Roman temples or the great stone megaliths erected by pre-Celtic inhabitants of Britain. Only one site of a former temple has been plausibly identified, a modest wooden structure situated close by the former great hall at Yeavering, Northumbria, in the vicinity of a Bronze Age tumulus and ancient stone circle. A great heap of ox-skulls speaks to the number of sacrifices offered there, probably for the most part during *Blotmonaþ*, 'the month of sacrifice', corresponding to our November, when all cattle were killed except those which were to be fed over the winter.

Such pagan religious festivals as we know of matched the rhythms of the pastoral and agricultural year and featured cult figures rather than the high gods of the pantheon. One such cult figure, Nerthus, seems to have been worshipped widely among Germanic tribes dwelling in the region from which the continental Angles came to England. Tacitus (*Germania*, ch. 40) writes of her holy grove, chariot and rites and calls her *terra mater*, 'Earth Mother'. If this 'Nerthus' was the female consort of the Norse god Njörðr, as seems likely, then in her Scandinavian form she was thereby the mother of Freyr and Freyja. Little is known about specifically Anglo-Saxon cult figures. With some reticence, as fits a subject he would like to consign to oblivion, Bede mentions in his computistical work *De temporum ratione* that the name Easter, corresponding to Latin/Greek *pascha*, derives from the goddess Eostre, for whom the English named the fourth month *Eosturmonaþ*. Bede also states that the preceding month, *Hredmonaþ*, corresponding to our March, took its name from festivities honouring a goddess Hreda, while the eve of 25 December was celebrated as *Modranect*, or 'night of the Mothers'. One would give much to know who these mothers were and what connection their worship had to the Christian commemoration of the Nativity. Such scraps of information as these suggest that no matter how firmly patriarchal their social system was, the pagan English found room for honouring the female principle within the earthier reaches of their syncretistic religion.

Archaeological and onomastic evidence fills out this picture somewhat. The 'Harrow' names of England, like Harrow-on-the-Hill, indicate the site of a former place of worship (OE *hearh*). Some names like Wyham (Lancashire) and Weedon (Berkshire) derive their first element from Old English *wih* or *weoh*, 'shrine' or 'place of sacrifice'. Names alone, however, do not tell whether such shrines were of Anglo-Saxon or Romano-British origin. Place-names like Wednesbury and Wenslow indicate sites where Woden was once important, whether as a god or an ancestral hero. Names like Thunderfield and Thundridge speak of the former popularity of Thunor. From *draca*, an OE loanword from Latin *draco* meaning 'dragon', comes Drakelow ('dragon's hill') in both Derbyshire and Worcestershire. From *wyrm*, the native term for the same creature, comes Wormwood Hill in Cumberland. The Eildon Hills in the Borders, into which Thomas the Rhymer is said to have disappeared for seven years to become the consort of the Queen of Fairies, may derive their name from Old English *ylfe* 'elf' plus *dun* 'hill', as Eldon Hill, Derbyshire, more assuredly does. Puck of Pook's Hill, via Shakespeare's Puck, gets his name from Old English *puca* or *pucel*, 'evil spirit'. Many examples could be cited of similar names derived from the same pagan elements or from such other elements as *Tiw* 'the god Tiw', *þyrs* 'monster', *dweorh* 'dwarf', *scucca* 'demon' and *scinn* 'spectre or ghost'.[4]

St Gregory's policy of gently weaning the pagan English from their repugnant practices – 'whoever wishes to climb to a mountain top climbs gradually step by step, and not in one leap' (*HE* I.30) – permitted heathen shrines to be adapted to Christian use. The sacrifice of cattle could continue, as long as the bloodletting was rationalized by being linked to the sacrifice of the holy martyrs or some other clerical theme. Fountains or wells could be dedicated to the Virgin, though not to a pagan cult figure. The existence of a host of angels and demons compensated for the loss of pagan gods and elves. Thor's-hammer amulets were out; cruciform amulets were in. Grave-goods were prohibited, but not graveside gifts to the Church, which are well attested in Anglo-Saxon wills and were an attractive form of alms-giving. Exceptionally, even the provision of grave-goods could be rationalized within the framework of Christian belief: the tomb of St Cuthbert (d. 687), which was unearthed in 1104, 1539 and 1827, contained a comb and scissors, a paten, a golden chalice and a gold pectoral cross set with garnets.

The heathen grave-goods that were unearthed in 1939 at Sutton Hoo, Suffolk, where they were buried at the centre of a tumulus that covered an entire ship, provide striking evidence of Germanic funerary customs at a point when they had already been influenced by Christian beliefs.[5] Notably lacking among the objects are depictions of gods or scenes from mythological stories. The nearest thing to a pagan object included among the finds is an awe-inspiring ceremonial whetstone, thought to be a sceptre, whose ends are carved with the figures of eight human heads. The heads that ornament the two ends of the sceptre have been thought to relate to the veneration of ancestors and, possibly, to the idea of dynastic descent from Woden, who with Tiw and Thunor represented the upper realm and the martial and patriarchal powers in Germanic religion. Leaving this impressive object aside, the absence of overt pagan motifs from the Sutton Hoo burial can perhaps be attributed to the nature of this specific find.

The barrow unearthed in 1939 is generally believed to have commem-orated the death of Rædwald, king of the East Angles and *bretwalda* or high king of the English. Rædwald died in 624 or 625. According to Bede (*HE* II.15), he accepted baptism in Kent, but when he returned home his wife and advisers persuaded him to continue to honour the old religion. Bede condemns him for having tried to serve both Christ and the ancient gods. If the nobleman honoured by the Sutton Hoo ship burial was indeed Rædwald, then this form of funeral must attest to Rædwald's continuing ties to his old religion. On the other hand, the lack of heathen motifs and the absence of clear evidence that a body was ever deposited at the site may speak to his attachment to the new faith. In addition, some silver bowls with cruciform designs on them and, more significantly, two spoons inscribed 'Saulus' and 'Paulus' – christening spoons, it is believed – provide positive evidence of an interest in Christianity. What appears to be fence-straddling here may not have seemed so to Rædwald. Kings have always had both public and private selves. The Sutton Hoo burial may have been Rædwald's concession to his public self, which was bound to be a conservative one to be invoked on occasions of state.

Boar images figure prominently among the Sutton Hoo treasures, most strikingly in the form of two cunningly superimposed boars that ornament a pair of gold, garnet and enamel shoulder-clasps. In the verses known as *Maxims II*, which are included as part of the material prefacing the *Anglo-Saxon Chronicle* in one manuscript, the wild boar *toðmægnes trum*, 'strong in its mighty tusks', is mentioned in company with two other creatures admired for their fierce independence, the hawk trained for falconry and the wolf of the woods. Boars were sacred to Freyr, and their images were evidently talismanic. When the *Beowulf*-poet alludes to a helmet decorated with boar images so that 'no swords could cut through it' (1453–4), his remark suggests both literal and symbolic defence. The helmet unearthed at Benty Grange, Derbyshire, that is now in the Sheffield City Museum, provides striking confirmation of the prominence of the boar as a symbol of power among members of the warrior elite. Surmounting the helmet is a free-standing boar image with eyes of garnet, set in gold.

The absence of bear-motifs from Anglo-Saxon metalwork may reflect the veneration inspired by this animal dating from a very early period. The word *bera*, from which we have 'bear', originally meant simply 'the brown one'. The animal's true name was taboo. If the name 'Beowulf' derives from the two simplexes 'bee' and 'wolf', as some scholars think, it is surely a buried euphemism for 'bear', the bear being metaphorically the wolf of the bees whose honey it eats. Unlikely as this identification may seem, it is strengthened by the close parallel that has been established between the first two-thirds of *Beowulf* and the 'Bear's Son' type of folktale, a pan-European tale, especially popular in Scandinavian and Celtic lands, that tells of a young man born of a woman and a bear. From this paternity he derives his unusual strength.[6]

Two of the most expressive designs in early Germanic metalwork are the winged dragon that once decorated the Sutton Hoo shield and the pair of opposing dragons that formed the eyebrows and ridge of the Sutton Hoo helmet and carried on down to the nose and moustache of the facemask. This latter motif is particularly clear on the fine replica of the helmet that has been fashioned at the Royal Armoury in the Tower of London. Both figures show how Germanic artisans were able to play cunningly on the shape of the fearsome *wyrm*. Dragons were taken to be part of the natural world. Their chief vocation was to guard over treasures that had been ritually buried with the dead, thereby being 'killed' as far as the living were concerned. *Draca sceal on hlæwe, / frod, frætwum wlanc,* as the author of *Maxims II* succinctly remarks: 'Dragons live in barrows, aged, proud of their treasures' (26–7).

The fear inspired by dragons is amply evident from the last part of *Beowulf*, with its magnificent evocation of a dragon enraged by a fugitive's theft of a cup from its hoard. The destruction that ensues was surely meant to teach a lesson – not the same lesson, one might add, that some critics with only a mild interest in dragons have extracted from the text. To regard this scales-and-blood adversary as much like the dragons of fairy tale would be an error. As one critic has remarked, the *Beowulf* dragon is the *Beowulf* dragon. It is winged, fifty feet long, with a nearly impenetrable hide and a mean disposition. Add in poisonous teeth and a breath of literal fire, and the result is an awesome creature who is well up to its narrative task of providing the hero with a suitable death.

When one considers the dragons, serpents, giants, demons, elves, dwarfs and hags that are mentioned in Old English literature, it is both easy and condescending to dismiss the pagan Anglo-Saxons as 'frightened of all sorts of supernatural forces, like children lost in a forest'.[7] The heathen English believed in 'flying venom' and in invisible darts shot by elves with the same readiness as we believe in microbes.or traitors, without necessarily ever having seen either. In many cultures besides our own, a belief in the workings of unseen creatures helps to render the phenomena of life comprehensible, hence less threatening. A shaman can fight the evil eye or can ward off the darts of invisible enemies, but no-one can cure a patient of a disease of unknown nature or cause.

Rather than dismissing the pagan English as superstitious, we might consider them as possessed of animistic beliefs that in their essential features are well known among early and so-called primitive peoples of the world. The essence of animism is the belief that the world is alive in all its parts. To return to the passage from the laws of Cnut quoted earlier, it is the perception that 'the sun or the moon, fire or flood, wells or stones or any kind of forest trees' are parts of a single world endowed with spirit. Human beings are part of this animate world; they are not souls, exiled from God, who temporarily inhabit it or make use of it. For this reason, members of tribes generally called 'primitive' ask favour of the sun or moon before setting out on important undertakings, revere the spirit of fire that bursts out in the form of flame and avoid offending the spirits that inhabit mountains, woods and streams. In the words of the Native American author Paula Gunn Allen, the animistic philosophy that was taken for granted in North America before the coming of the whites, and that was deeply embedded in early European consciousness as well, embodies a principle of kinship that extends far beyond the human race: 'the supernaturals, spirit people, animal people of all varieties, the thunders, snows, rains, rivers, lakes, hills, mountains, fire, water, rock, and plants are perceived to be members of one's community'.[8]

Pagan burials were based on the widespread early European conviction that the soul is not annihilated at death, nor, as in Christian belief, is it released from this world. Rather, in association with the body, in a way that remains a mystery, it journeys to a new home in a land unknown to the living. For this reason, a place was often found for the burial or cremation of a real or symbolic horse, chariot, ship, or other vehicle, as well as for the provision of valuables and household objects that could be of use to the departed.

Particularly because they did not believe in a parting of the spirit and the flesh at death, the pagan English cared devotedly for the bodily remains of the dead. Tacitus, ever with an eye for heroic virtues, remarks that Germanic warriors of his day would bring back the bodies of the fallen 'even when a battle hangs in the balance' (Germania, ch. 6). There was no greater punishment than for the corpse of a criminal to be left exposed rather than being granted cremation or burial. Whether or not the poetic motif of the 'Birds and Beasts of Battle', present in eight Old English poems, derives from the respect that was once accorded the raven and wolf as creatures sacred to Woden, it gives grim expression to the idea of people being turned to meat. In Beowulf the motif sums up the desolate mood that ensues after the hero's death, when an unnamed messenger predicts future warfare and tribal dissolution facing the Geats:

> Forðon sceall gar wesan
> monig, morgenceald,   mundum bewunden,
> hæfen on handa,   nalles hearpan sweg
> wigend weccean,   ac se wonna hrefn
> fus ofer fægum   fela reordian,
> earne secgan   hu him æt æte speow,
> þenden he wið wulf   wæl reafode.   (Beowulf 3021–7)

Therefore the spear shall be raised in the hand and held aloft many a cold morning; no sound of the harp will wake the warriors, but the dark raven, eager over the slain, will have much to say, will tell the eagle how he fared at the feast when he strove with the wolf to strip the slain.

Although sometimes used exultantly, as at the end of the celebratory poem The Battle of Brunanburh, here, in a manner typical of this author, the motif of the carrion beasts gives ironic expression to the horror of warfare as seen from the side of the losers.

Three pagan funerals are described in Beowulf, and together they provide the pagan colouring of the poem with some of its sombre and majestic tints. They feature in turn a stately ship-funeral for the legendary Scyld Scefing, a pyre for the dead Hnæf and other warriors, and a pyre and tumulus for Beowulf himself. A look at Latin and Arabic ethnographic accounts of actual Germanic funerals confirms the basic verisimilitude of these poetic descriptions while raising the possibility that the *Beowulf*-poet deliberately played down the uglier aspects of paganism. According to Jordanes's account of the funeral of Attila the Hun, Attila's tribesmen not only buried weapons, insignia and precious treasures with him, but also sacrificed some of his human attendants. The tenth-century Arab merchant Ibn Fatlan, who wrote a detailed and fascinating account of a funeral among the Rus, a Swedish tribe that had settled along the Volga, also mentions human sacrifice. In this instance, consigned to the chieftain's pyre were his ship, his weapons, a quantity of food, a dog, a cock and hen, two horses, two cows, and a slave-girl who had previously volunteered for this duty and with whom some of the surviving noblemen first had ritual intercourse. Analogous practices may or may not have been known in pagan England. The *Beowulf*-poet's decorous accounts of funerals may have been part of a general effort to portray the old Germanic way of life in elevated tones, with the aim of integrating the best of pagan values into a Christian worldview.

Just as one can speak of competing mythologies and burial customs in early Anglo-Saxon England, there were competing bodies of folklore as well. In this realm, however, Germanic and Mediterranean traditions tended to reinforce one another. Beginning with Bede's *Historia ecclesiastica* and continuing on to Ælfric's lives of saints and other tenth- and eleventh-century texts, the Christian literature of Anglo-Saxon England abounds in dream-visions, miracles, portents, blessings, curses, magical cures and other expressions of folk belief. The Church had its own 'folk' narratives in the form of popular saints' lives. Adding miracles to miracles like beads on a string, these tales existed for the sake of their display of dramatic events proving both the human capacity for sanctity and God's willingness to intervene in human affairs (see also below, pp. 243–6).

One celebrated native saint was Guthlac, a reformed warrior who traded in his shield for Paul's breastplate of righteousness. Thus defended, he waged a successful campaign against demons in what was once the East Anglian wilderness. Just as dragons dwelt in pagan barrows, monsters lurked in pagan fens. From the fenland *þyrs*, or 'goblin', who is named matter-of-factly in *Maxims II*, to the diabolical fenland monsters of *Beowulf* – Grendel at one point is called a *þyrs* – is a short step. Of a kind with both these sorts of adversaries are the satanic minions who beset Guthlac. All the same, some of Guthlac's demons have a cartoon-like predictability that makes them seem like creatures who have stepped out of a homilist's fantasy rather than a real-life nightmare. At one point in the Old English prose *Life of St Guthlac*, in a scene that Bede would have enjoyed, the saint starts up from sleep and hears a throng of devils speaking Welsh with one another. They disappear from sight 'just like smoke' as soon as Guthlac intones a Latin psalm. There is nothing so wispy about the *Beowulf* monsters, which preserve the fearful corporeality of their antecedents in pagan belief.

When clerical authors did not negate pagan culture through silence, they reinvented it in their own terms. They made no attempt to deny the existence of the old gods. Instead, they euhemerized them: they identified them as real human beings, and thus they yoked them into history and into the Christian worldview. Woden is a prime example. In various parts of the *Anglo-Saxon Chronicle*, Woden is named as the ancestral figure from whom kings of the Kentish, Northumbrian, Mercian and West Saxon lines all claim descent. In the mid-ninth century, the West Saxon royal genealogy was dramatically expanded. Woden now appears as the son of a certain Frithuwald, and Frithuwald in turn, now going back fifteen generations, is made the son of Noah. Since Noah, with another nine generations, brings us back to Adam and thence to 'our father Christ', Woden is thereby made a lineal son of Christ, notwithstanding the shady past that the churchmen attributed to him. Still more importantly, the Germanic peoples as a group are thereby assimilated to the larger Judeo-Christian kin-group and are integrated into its history: in short, they are welcomed to the family.

The work known as *The Rune Poem* contains striking examples of Christian mediation of barbaric lore. Here, according to what seems to be an adaptation of an ancient formula, each of the letters of the Anglo-Saxon runic alphabet is written out next to a short set of alliterative lines that tells something about its name. The old rune ↑ (TIR), originally denoting the martial god Tir or Tiw, here means only 'heavenly sign' or 'constellation', in what must be a deliberate act of semantic reconstruction. The old rune ᛟ (OS), originally meaning 'god' (cf. the plural form *Æsir*), is reinterpreted as 'mouth', apparently thanks to the suggestive power of Latin *os*, 'mouth'. The rune ᛝ (ING) ought to denote a god equivalent to Old Norse Freyr, alias Yngvi-Freyr, the eponymous ancestor of the tribes whom Tactitus calls the Ingaevones, who dwelled near the coast in the region of the continental Angles (*Germania*, ch. 2). However, the Ing of *The Rune Poem* seems to be regarded as a hero rather than a god, or at any rate his identity is left mysterious. The rune ᛁ (SIGEL), originally denoting the sun as an object of reverence, is bereft of pagan associations and denotes simply the sun as a welcome sight to seafarers. The first rune in the list, ᚠ (FEOH, 'wealth'), keeps this meaning, but the poet adds a moralistic note concerning the dangers of hoarding money if one hopes for salvation. The last, ᛇ, does not appear in corresponding Old Norse rune lists. It is given a name, EAR or 'earthen grave', that allows the poet to end his work in a grimly homiletic fashion. *The Rune*

Poem may take its starting point from ancient Germanic tradition, but as it stands, it shows how deftly the author rehabilitated barbaric culture so as to render it innocent within the context of Christian faith.

Similar acts of appropriation abound in the several collections of Anglo-Saxon magical and medical texts that have come down to us.[9] What is interesting in these texts is that here and there, perhaps because of the desperate need that was felt for cures that worked, certain pagan elements slipped through. The wonderfully elaborate field blessing known as *Æcerbot*, for example (Storms, no. 8), includes among its four masses, its sixteen or more paternosters, its litany and its various other prayers, one heterodox invocation of a mysterious *Erce, eorðan modor* ('Erce, mother of earth'). Whoever this Erce is, she is integrated into the Christian universe, for the celebrant calls for the Almighty to bless her. Her consequent well-being, it is hoped, will make the field fertile again.

In an overtly pagan spell, *Wiþ færstice* (Storms, no. 2) – a title that seems to mean 'Against a Stabbing Pain' – the healer first tells of the loud ride of a host of creatures over a burial mound, then announces his intention to cast back the darts of 'mighty women' whom he later calls *hægtessan*, 'hags', who ride in the company of gods and elves, all of whom hurl spears. The stricken person has been hit by 'elf-shot', or invisible darts hurled by a hostile power. By means of this spell, plus a surgical operation whose exact nature one would perhaps not want to know, the healer intends to work a cure. Elsewhere among the Old English charms, 'elf-shot' is the name given to a disease afflicting horses. In recent years, as folklorists have discovered, some farmers in northern England as well as in Ireland and Scotland have spoken of 'elf-shot' as a cattle disease. Stricken cattle are believed to have been struck by projectiles that are identified with flintstones that can be seen lying in the fields.[10]

In another cure (Storms, no. 4), the healer attempts to remove a wen by banishing it to a nearby hill. A claim that the wen will shrink to nothing 'under the wolf's paw, under the eagle's feather, under the eagle's claw' probably alludes to tokens of power that the shaman wears or brandishes. In another (Storms, no. 7), the afflicted person seems to have been the victim of dwarf-riding. The dwarf has cast a *hama*, or animal pelt, over some poor person and has fastened reins on him so as to ride him like a horse. The concept of nightmare – originally, night-riding by a demon – is clearly operative here in a general sense. The result of this dwarf-riding seems to be a runaway fever that must be broken. Yet another cure (Storms, no. 20) is directed indiscriminately against the work of elves, 'night-striders', and people with whom the devil has had sexual intercourse. The same salve, suitably blessed at the altar, will do well against all three.

As this last example suggests, Anglo-Saxon cures and charms generally operated within a Christian context no matter how unsanctified their origin. They are the science of their day, and their ingredients make up a curious brew of herbalism, Mediterranean medical lore and Christian exorcism, with a dash of native shamanism thrown in. The wonderful thing about them is their unpredictability. One never knows what apotropaic powers or malevolent influences are going to be named next. Normally, if a mythological cure is attempted, the myths in question are Christian, as in a number of remedies against cattle theft. The usual logic of the cure is along the lines, 'Just as St Helena discovered the True Cross where it lay hidden, may I now find the cattle that have been stolen from me'. But in one charm (Storms, no. 9), when the healer specifies the power that nine herbs have against poison, infection and 'the hateful ones who rove through the land', he invokes the implied aid of both the Crucified Lord, who sent chervil and fennel to the seven worlds while He hung on the Cross, and Woden, who once smote a serpent into nine pieces.

Nowhere in Old English literature is the fusion of Germanic and Christian lore brought to more effective literary form than in *Beowulf*. Especially if this poem can be attributed to a Christian author composing not earlier than the first half of the tenth century, as has been argued recently,[11] then there is little reason to read it as a survival from the heathen age that came to be marred by monkish interpolations, as used to be the fashion.[12] Rather, it can be approached as a reinvention of the legendary Germanic past by a poet who was almost as distant from this age as living Americans are from Elizabethan England. Since this poem was linked to this past by an evolving oral tradition rather than the anchor of written history, we can look upon its making as a great act of historical imagination. By recreative acts such as this, the people of later Anglo-Saxon England refashioned their own spiritual identity, reflected as if in a distant mirror.

If this relatively new scholarly approach to the poem is justified, then the making of *Beowulf* (and, presumably, other poems like it, including the fragmentary *Waldere*) must have been a major assimilative act, analogous in its own way to the ascription of Woden to the line of Christ. *Beowulf* presents a vision of ancestral heroes and kings who, as pagans, were surely damned, according to orthodox theology. Somewhat amazingly, however, it presents them as noble souls who by their own intuition seem capable of discerning the one true God, and who – though only vaguely cognizant of the spiritual significance of what they are doing – are willing to war against God's enemies on earth. The great importance of *Beowulf* for its contemporary audience would have been its mediating role in relation to the early history and culture of the Germanic peoples, a subject about which Bede is silent.

Mention has already been made of the pervasive ways in which *Beowulf* draws on Germanic folk traditions and popular beliefs. What remains to be stressed is that by casting these elements with a new die, struck in the Christian faith, the poet endows them with a spiritual significance that they could not have had before. Beowulf is no muscled sword-slinger who has barged in from a saga. Rather, he moves through the narrative as a selfless thegn and dignified king whose dominant trait – power held in abeyance – recalls the character of the Christian Saviour. Significantly, he is given almost no role in the dynastic wars that are so frequently mentioned in the poem, and in the end he is praised for being the 'mildest of men, gentlest and most magnanimous to his people', rather than for any martial exploits.

Grendel and his mother, correspondingly, are given a home that is suggestive of hell mouth, and their evil is literally diabolic. The epithets the poet uses for them encompass practically everything unpleasant, whether from the earthly realm or the realm of spirits. They are like people, with a kind of rudimentary culture that encompasses fireplaces, swords and game-bags; at the same time, they have the size and appetite of giants or trolls. On one hand they recall the night-striders of Germanic folk-belief: the poet identifies them with *scuccum ond scinnum*, 'demons and spectres'. On the other, they are the devils of Christian belief: Grendel is referred to pointedly by the term *feond moncynnes*, 'the foe of humankind', as well as by other names usually reserved for Satan. The result of this unsettling mixture of elements is a terrifying uncertainty as to just what these creatures are. They show both real malice and real teeth. One suspects that neither a good coat of mail nor St Paul's breastplate of righteousness, taken by itself, would defend the hero against them. What he needs is an extraordinary synthesis of strengths, and this is what the poet gives him, in a creative act that must have had broad significance for members of the audience who were seeking to redeem their Germanic heritage and align it with their religious ideals.

By giving his monsters an ancestry that derives from Cain, the poet makes them a ghastly incarnation of the spirit of division in human affairs that, in the Augustinian view, has been present on earth from the time of the first siblings and that makes civil polity necessary. Like all beings of their kind, they are headed for hell. Their evil is absolute, unlike that of earthly trolls or dragons; and thus through one saviour's fortitude, in the more-than-faintly eschatological terms of this Christian poem, it can be completely purged. When Beowulf ascends through the waters of Grendel's mere after having put an end to both Grendel and his mother, the waters are miraculously *eal gefælsod*, 'entirely cleansed' (1620), as if by a successful exorcism.

As for the hero himself, in the end, he is released from this plane of existence. Despite all the pomp of the pagan ceremonies that are portrayed so majestically at the close, with the building of a pyre, the consignment of grave-goods to the earth, and the ritual circling of the dead king's barrow, the rites are appropriately empty. For Beowulf is a curious anomaly: he lives and dies by a heroic code of kinship-loyalty and vengeance, and yet he has an immortal soul. Long before his pyre is lit, his soul has left his corpse to seek out 'the judgement of the righteous' (2820), which one likes to think it finds.

In his gift of a spiritual dimension to the Grendel creatures, the *Beowulf*-poet transcended not only early Germanic monster-lore, but late antique pseudo-science as well. For at some remove or some stage of rumination, the poet's conception of monsters and dragons was surely influenced by the accounts of arcane races that figured in books of natural history deriving from the writings of Pliny and other classical authorities. This engaging science found specific expression in the *Liber monstrorum*, or 'Book of Monsters'; in the book of exotica known as *De rebus in oriente mirabilibus*, or 'Marvels of the East'; and in the so-called 'Letter of Alexander to Aristotle', which purports to be an eye-witness account of the oddities of India. Perhaps not by coincidence, copies of these last two works precede the unique copy of *Beowulf* that is preserved in London, British Library, Cotton Vitellius A.xv.[13]

Among the dragons, centaurs, griffins, camelopards, hermaphrodites, satyrs, Ethiopians, bearded Amazons and cannibalistic giants that are routinely featured in these works are such other creatures, less well known today, as the 'blemmyae', men whose eyes and mouth are in their chest; the 'cynocephali', or fire-breathing dog-headed men with boars' tusks and horses' manes; and the 'sciopods', with one giant foot which they use like a parasol. Examples like these confirm that from whatever source or sources the *Beowulf*-poet derived his conception of monstrous creatures, it was not chiefly from here. Monster-books make fascinating reading for their bric-a-brac of information bearing on early medieval popular belief, but in themselves, they could never inspire the vision of good and evil that is on display in this poem. This vision is something far more grand and chilling. In its dynamic portrait of a magnanimous hero's struggle against creatures that well from the very source of all ills, *Beowulf* evokes a grandeur and touches on depths of pain that have nothing to do with the trivial lore found in these compendia.

Much as one may like to think of 'pagan survivals' as having long since shrivelled away beneath the withering gaze of Reason, the study of folklore provides abundant evidence that old ideas die hard, if rooted in the rich soil of popular belief and custom. The burning of the Yule log and the hanging of mistletoe at Christmas; the maypoles, May queens and morris dancers of spring; the bonfires, the corn dolls and the harvest homes of autumn; the Jack-in-the-Green, the Hobby Horse, the horn dancers, the plough stots and the guisers and mummers of many a local festival – these are just a few examples of survivals that, for all we know, date back to pagan Anglo-Saxon times if not earlier. Relics of ancient belief, surviving in fossil form as thoughtless customs, are as banal in our world as every 'bless you' for a sneeze or every penny thrown into a wishing well, and their influence on popular attitudes can be at times profound. While the study of Anglo-Saxon paganism cannot account for all such beliefs and customs, it can improve one's understanding of more than a few of them.

As for Old English literature, one can scarcely hope to comprehend it without reference to both its Christian themes and forms and its pagan substrata of popular belief. Insofar as Anglo-Saxon paganism was not only a religion but also a major heritage encompassing the values, ethics, hopes, fears and collective memories of a people, it did not die with the Conversion, but rather lived on in the form of both odd pagan survivals and, more importantly, deep-set patterns of belief. The great challenge facing authors of this period was to find ways of integrating this Germanic heritage with the worship of Christ and with the whole intellectual order that derived from Mediterranean lands. Their success in this venture has had no small effect on how English-speaking peoples have thought and lived in subsequent centuries.

1 *HE* I.15, trans. Sherley-Price (from which I quote throughout), p. 57.
2 *EHD*, p. 455 (*II Cnut* 5.1).
3 Much information and speculation bearing on Anglo-Saxon paganism can be found in E. A. Philippson, *Germanisches Heidentum bei den Angelsachsen* (Leipzig, 1929); B. Branston, *The Lost Gods of England*, 2nd ed. (London, 1974); G. R. Owen, *Rites and Religions of the Anglo-Saxons* (London, 1981); and, more generally, H. R. Ellis Davidson, *Myths and Symbols in Pagan Europe* (Manchester, 1988).
4 See, for example, F. M. Stenton, 'The Historical Bearing of Place-Name Studies: Anglo-Saxon Heathenism', repr. in *Preparatory to "Anglo-Saxon England": Being the Collected Papers of Frank Merry Stenton*, ed. D. M. Stenton (Oxford, 1970), pp. 281–97, and K. Cameron, *English Place-Names* (London, 1961), pp. 119–25.
5 This stunning find has been the occasion for a precise set of descriptive volumes under the general editorship of R. Bruce-Mitford, *The Sutton Hoo Ship-Burial*, 3 vols. in 4 (London, 1975–83).
6 Tale type 301 ('The Three Stolen Princesses') in A. Aarne and S. Thompson, *The Types of the Folktale*, 2nd ed. (Helsinki, 1973). F. Panzer made the connection between *Beowulf* and the 'Bear's Son' tale in his *Studien zur germanischen Sagengeschichte, I: Beowulf* (Munich, 1910). Specific versions

of type 301 may or may not include princesses; regularly, however, they feature the hero's sequential struggle against two adversaries, one of which makes repeated attacks on a hall or farmhouse, while the other must be sought out in a nether world. The resemblance between *Beowulf* and certain episodes of *Grettir's Saga* and other Old Icelandic legendary narratives can perhaps be attributed to their common relation to this same folktale type.

7 R. Muir, *The National Trust Guide to Dark Age and Medieval Britain 400–1350* (London, 1985), p. 22.

8 P. G. Allen, *Spider Woman's Granddaughters: Traditional Tales and Contemporary Writing by Native American Women* (Boston, 1989), p. 9.

9 See G. Storms, *Anglo-Saxon Magic* (The Hague, 1948), and J. H. G. Grattan and C. Singer, *Anglo-Saxon Magic and Medicine* (London, 1952). Only the metrical charms – the charms incorporating *gealdor*, 'spells' – are included in ASPR 6, which thereby takes these pieces out of their best context for interpretation. K. L. Jolly, 'Anglo-Saxon Charms in the Context of a Christian World View', *Journal of Medieval History* 11 (1985), 279–93, provides a critical framework that can serve as a point of departure for understanding Old English magical texts.

10 For a modern Irish charm against fairy darts, with translation, see A. Carmichael, *Carmina Gadelica I* (Edinburgh, 1900), pp. 58–9, and cf. similar invocations on pp. 278–9 and 174–5.

11 A number of essays in *The Dating of Beowulf*, ed. C. Chase (Toronto, 1981), open up the possibility of a date for *Beowulf* considerably later than the eighth-century one that used to be accepted generally.

12 On the Romantic biases of much early Old English scholarship, see E. G. Stanley, *The Search for Anglo-Saxon Paganism* (Cambridge, 1975), first published as a set of essays in *Notes and Queries* 209–10 (1964–5).

13 On medieval monster-lore, see J. B. Friedman, *The Monstrous Races in Medieval Art and Thought* (Cambridge, MA, 1981), with remarks about *Beowulf* on pp. 103–7.

8   Beowulf

BEOWULF is generally held to be the first great narrative poem in the English language. This heroic tale, 3,182 lines in length, is about a man and his people in north European lands during the period when Germanic precursors of the English were still migrating to Britain. The poem is strongly linked to the Germanic roots of the English nation and displays the qualities of English before the language and literary tradition became quite intermingled with French, classical and other non-Germanic cultures. The style and metre of *Beowulf* is essentially that of other early Germanic poems like the Old High German *Hildebrandslied* and the Old Saxon *Heliand*, and many of the characters and incidents in the poem are referred to independently by early Germanic writers on the Continent. Indeed, although it is usually seen as the first great masterpiece of English literature, from another perspective it may be said that by virtue of its large scale, refined style and lofty theme *Beowulf* is also the chief glory of early Germanic poetry at large.

This poem in traditional style about Germanic heroes is told, however, by an Englishman with a local English outlook. Unlike the heroic-age figures described in *Beowulf*, the poet is a Christian whose intellectual horizons have been expanded to include not only biblical learning but the wider world of Christian-Latin culture in general. He probably had a nascent sense of an English nation or at least a *gens Anglorum*, as Bede had described the Germanic occupants of Britain. This English nation was a Germanic population which had just begun the process of assimilation with other cultures which, when completed, would make them English. The strivings and triumphs, the ceremonies and alliances of Beowulf and his people are presented by the poet from the point of view both of a brother German and of a person apart, separated from the events of the poem not only by the North Sea but also by a gulf of time and of intellectual change. His poem is a long meditation on the Germanic culture whence the English had taken their origins and to which they still felt closely related despite their incipient transformation into Englishmen.

It is important to keep in mind this perspective that the poet had on his subject matter, for the average reader of English literature often comes to

Beowulf with the naive expectation that reading this early poem will bring him face to face with the collective unconscious of English culture, will allow him to experience at first hand what is primordial, elemental and primitively powerful in it. But the experience is more complex than that, for the Anglo-Saxons who wrote and read *Beowulf* were themselves exploring the unconscious of their culture by returning to dark beginnings in an age long antecedent to theirs. If reading *Beowulf* is an exploration of our primal selves, we are led on that exploration by a refined, reflective, Christian Anglo-Saxon poet whose curiosity about the remote origins of his people is perhaps not unlike our own.

Like most Old English poems, *Beowulf* has no title in the unique manuscript in which it survives (British Library, Cotton Vitellius A.xv, which was copied round the year 1000 AD), but modern scholars agree in naming it after the hero whose life is its subject. The name of the poet who assembled from tradition the materials of his story and put them in their final form is not known to us, nor can we establish the date when he composed *Beowulf*. For most of this century there was agreement among most scholars that the poem was the product of the eighth century, a period of cultural florescence in England; but recent scholarly debate has shaken this consensus, and some scholars would assign to the poem a later date, although there is little agreement as to how late. Whenever the poet lived, it was centuries after the time of the events described in *Beowulf*. Extrapolating from what is firmly datable in the poem, we can deduce that the hero Beowulf would have been born near the end of the fifth century AD and died late in the sixth century. The poet, whenever he lived, was viewing the events of this life from a temporal perspective hundreds of years removed from the time of the poem's action.

The various peoples whose fortunes are described in the poem are all located in Scandinavia or northern Germany, the very regions from which the Angles, Saxons, Jutes and Frisians migrated to England in the fifth and sixth centuries. They include Danes, Swedes, Franks, Frisians and the *Geatas*, the last a group of people who inhabited what is today southern Sweden before their kingdom fell, apparently, and was absorbed into the larger Swedish nation. It is an irony that the great national 'epic' of England does not mention a single Englishman, but we may perhaps assume that to an Anglo-Saxon looking back on Scandinavia and northern Germany as it was in the sixth century, the peoples described in the poem would have seemed very near to the ancestors of the English, for Germania was the mother of nations, and England was one of her progeny. Although the poet's focus is on the *Geatas*, since this is the hero Beowulf's people, there is in the poem a fairly even-handed treatment of all the Germanic nations described, and all seem to share a more or less common culture.

The story opens not in Geatland, where Beowulf lives, but in the nearby kingdom of Denmark. The poet begins by emphasizing that the narrative takes place in *geardagum* 'in ancient days', and by assuring us that his story will be about noblemen (*æðelingas*). He then traces the mysterious origins of the Danish dynasty before settling on the poem's present time, which is the reign of the Danish King Hrothgar (a figure well-known to several early Scandinavian writers). We are told that Hrothgar had enjoyed a glorious reign, and he crowns his success by having a splendid hall erected, a building he names Heorot ('Hart'), which becomes the centre of government and royal ceremony for the realm. (From Scandinavian analogues we can deduce that the location of Heorot was the present-day town of Leire, some fifteen miles west of Copenhagen: see Fig. 1.) Every day Hrothgar entertains his retinue in the hall Heorot until a monstrous troll named Grendel, who dwells in a hidden watery cave not far from the royal hall, is enraged by the sounds of human concord and harmony and begins a series of nocturnal attacks. He breaks into the building after the king's men have retired in it and carries off and eats as many as thirty retainers at a time. The king is distraught. His retainers are helpless, for neither their efforts at defence nor their appeals to their pagan gods are of any avail against the enormously powerful troll. They are baffled as to who the monster is and whence he has come, but the poet informs us that the creature is in fact a misbegotten descendant of the primordial fratricide Cain, and like Cain he suffers the wrath of the Christian God.

After some years the young hero Beowulf hears of Hrothgar's distress and resolves to travel from Geatland with fourteen followers across the Kattegat to Hrothgar's realm, offering the king his services in the struggle against Grendel. Hrothgar welcomes Beowulf and his men with warmth and stately courtesy and gladly accepts his offer to do battle with Grendel. A mean-spirited courtier named Unferth, however, questions Beowulf's fitness for fighting with the monster and belittles him with a distorted account of a swimming feat that Beowulf had undertaken in his youth. With dignity and force Beowulf delivers a crushing rejoinder and cites earlier achievements which demonstrate his prowess in combat with hostile creatures, which Hrothgar and his men are delighted to hear. At the end of the evening's festivities, the Danish king and his retinue retire, leaving the *Geatas* to guard the hall. In due course Grendel emerges from the mist-covered moor and bursts through the door, attacking with such swiftness that he kills and eats a Geatish warrior before Beowulf can offer resistance. But the hero now swings into action, and the two fight tumultuously. Grendel realizes that the hero's grip is too much for him and tries to escape, but Beowulf manages to wrench off the creature's arm before he flees howling in pain.

There is rejoicing in Heorot after the victory, and some of the warriors follow the bloody track of Grendel to his watery habitat in order to satisfy themselves that the monster has died of his wound. They return to the hall to celebrate the victory. Both on the journey from the mere and in the hall a *scop* or royal minstrel celebrates Beowulf with songs in his honour, and after feasting Beowulf retires from the hall and goes to a separate building to sleep. During the night the Danes occupying the hall are surprised by another savage attack, this time from Grendel's mother, who carries off Hrothgar's chief counsellor in vengeance for her son's death. Hrothgar is despondent, but Beowulf vows to kill this monster as well or else die in the attempt. He goes to the eerie tarn where the trolls lived together and dives to the bottom of it, as the ogress swims out and seizes him and drags him out of the water into her cave behind a waterfall. The two fight savagely, and Beowulf is about to be killed when he sees on the wall a giant sword, with which he kills the ogress and then decapitates Grendel, whose corpse is lying in the cave. The gore from the decapitation runs into the water and churns up to the top of the mere, where the *Geatas* and Danes are waiting for Beowulf to return. They assume from the blood that Beowulf has been killed, but eventually the hero dives back under the waterfall and swims to the top of the mere, bringing with him the severed head of Grendel and the hilt of the giant sword, whose blade had melted away in the poisonous blood of Grendel.

There is again rejoicing, and Hrothgar bestows lavish gifts on Beowulf and his men and then, as a final gift, he addresses a long, wise speech to Beowulf, extolling his accomplishments and warning him against pride and avarice. Wealhtheow, Hrothgar's queen, bestows on Beowulf a magnificent torque or gold neck-piece, which we are told is fated to be lost in a disastrous Geatish campaign into Frankish lands in the future, when Beowulf's king (to whom Beowulf had presumably given the torque) will fall in battle wearing the treasure. This foreboding of disastrous events for the *Geatas* in the future is balanced by earlier statements that the Danish realm will also encounter disasters in the future, when internecine struggles will result in the burning of Heorot and further dynastic strife. The poet's undercutting of the hero's moment of supreme triumph by pointing out that misfortune and disaster will occur no matter how successfully men struggle against evil forces is characteristic of his narrative method and leaves one with a sense that even the most shining moments in the heroic world are darkened by the prospects of ineluctable tragedies to come and with a sense of fate implacable.

Beowulf and his men return to Geatland and to a warm welcome by his uncle, the Geatish King Hygelac. The young hero's exploits have brought glory to the Geatish name, and the sumptuous gifts which Hrothgar had given him and which he loyally gives in turn to his king and queen are palpable evidence of his high reputation. Now in a long monologue Beowulf gives Hygelac a detailed report of everything he had achieved in Denmark in his fights with Grendel and his ogress mother. This detailed recapitulation by the hero of what we have just been told by the narrator gives us our first insight into the mind and character of the hero, for his way of telling the story we have just witnessed, and the details he omits to tell his king (such as the strife with Unferth) and the details he adds (such as his prediction of the outcome of an alliance through marriage which he says Hrothgar is planning) reveal the hero's generosity, his perceptiveness and good judgement. Following his report there is a sumptuous banquet, and then the king bestows vast land holdings upon his heroic young nephew and elevates him to a position in the nation second only to his own.

At this point, about two-thirds of the way through the narrative, occurs the most extraordinary feature of narrative structure in the poem. In a single long sentence the poet says that Hygelac is later killed in battle, as is his son and successor, and that Beowulf ascends the throne and rules for fifty years until a fiery dragon begins to lay waste the kingdom of the *Geatas*. This sentence propels us with startling suddenness from the day of Beowulf's recognition for his first youthful triumph to almost the last day of his long life. This stark juxtaposition of beginning and end makes the poem seem like a diptych of the hero's rise and fall and suggests powerfully that even a long life like Beowulf's is a thing of fleeting brevity. But this impression that the poem gives access only to Beowulf's youthful beginnings and his final day is an artful illusion created by the poet's narrative method. In fact we are told many of the events of the hero's life in the period between his early ascent to renown and his last and fatal encounter with the dragon. This information is supplied in a network of digressions and flashbacks which permeates the final section of the poem. We learn that he was always a stalwart defender of the homeland in the battles his nation fights with various foreign powers under Hygelac and his successor as well as during Beowulf's own reign. We learn that Beowulf accompanied Hygelac on a wild and ill-advised piratical raid on Frankish lands, where the Geatish king fell in battle and lost his army, but was avenged by Beowulf, who saved the honour of the *Geatas* with his bravery. (This raid, which was alluded to when Beowulf received the torque from Hrothgar's queen, is documented and approximately dated by Gregory of Tours in his *Historia Francorum*, written in the late sixth century AD, and the other contemporary historians, but there is no mention by the historians of a hero like Beowulf, who seems to have been a fictional or legendary figure inserted into this historical setting by the poet.) We are also told of Beowulf's active role in wars with the powerful Swedish kingdom, of his service as a sort of regent and protector to the young King Heardred, who succeeded Hygelac, and of his eventual acceptance of the Geatish throne when it is clear that no one else has the strength to lead the nation successfully in the hostile and threatening world of the Germanic north.

Near the end of Beowulf's fifty-year reign as king, a fugitive in the Geatish realm antagonizes a dragon by stealing a golden cup from the hoard that the dragon is guarding. Enraged, the dragon flies through the air at night breathing fire. A large part of the kingdom, including the king's royal hall, is burned to the ground, and we are told that the dragon intends to leave nothing alive in the realm. News of the devastation is brought to Beowulf, and, knowing that he is the only one in the kingdom with experience in fighting supernatural monsters, he states that he alone will confront the dragon and try to kill it in order to save the kingdom. Accompanied by a young kinsman named Wiglaf and ten other Geatish warriors, Beowulf sets out to find the dragon's lair. Telling the others to stand aside, Beowulf challenges the dragon to come out of his barrow, and the fight ensues. The warriors flee in panic and Beowulf is on the brink of death when his kinsman Wiglaf returns to aid him. Between the two of them, they finally slay the dragon, but Beowulf has received his death-wound. He expresses hope that the hoard of treasure that the dragon had been guarding might be of help to his people after he is gone, and then he bids farewell to Wiglaf and the nation and dies. His soul, the poet says, departs for the judgement of those firm in truth, an ambiguous phrase which could mean anything from some kind of uncertain afterlife to simply the fame that heroes enjoy in the memories of truth-telling men. Wiglaf rebukes the ten cowardly retainers and predicts that once their cowardice becomes known abroad, the *Geatas'* surrounding enemies will not hesitate to attack, now that the mighty Beowulf is no longer there to protect the nation. Others too predict the impending fall of the Geatish nation, amid grim recollections of the many wars in which they have incurred the hatred of their neighbours. A pyre is prepared, and Beowulf's body is cremated in a typical heathen ceremony. An aged woman keens at the funeral fire and again predicts that Geatland will soon be conquered and the women led off into captivity. Ten days later a second ceremony is initiated. Beowulf's ashes are interred in a splendid tumulus which has been prepared for him on a high promontory visible to seamen far and wide and named 'Beowulf's Barrow'. All the treasure from the dragon's hoard is consigned to the tumulus with the hero, and twelve noblemen pace their horses around the shrine, chanting praises to the dead king. The mood at the end of the poem is a commingling of awe for the glorious hero, supremely triumphant in death, and of mystery and despair surrounding the nation whose inevitable doom has been predicted so insistently as the poem drew to its close.

This summary of the contents of *Beowulf* may suggest something of the poem's syncretic power, its awesome conflation of history and fantasy, of dignity and horror. For the most part the human characters seem to be taken from history, leading figures from some distant warrior aristocracy; the monstrous adversaries who threaten them, on the other hand, are the nightmarish products of the ancient demonology of the north. What we know of the sources of the poem confirms that this is in fact the case. Many of the human characters in the poem are well known to us in sources outside of *Beowulf*.[1] King Hrothgar, for example, is prominent in Old Icelandic saga, in the Latin *History of the Danes* by Saxo Grammaticus, in the list of Scandinavian kings called *Langfeðgatal*, and elsewhere. Hrothgar's ancestor Scyld Scefing is very well known in both Anglo-Saxon and Scandinavian royal genealogies, and his nephew Hrothulf has an entire saga devoted to him – the *Hrólfssaga Kraki*. Many characters in the poem are mentioned in the Anglo-Saxon poem *Widsith* as well, so that we assume that the *Beowulf*-poet's audience brought with them a knowledge of his characters even before they heard his poem. Beowulf's King Hygelac is well documented in Latin historical and semi-historical works, including one written, apparently, in England (the *Liber monstrorum*; see below). At times these sources outside of *Beowulf* help us to complete the sense of dark allusions in the poem. For example, Hrothgar's queen repeatedly expresses her anxieties over the future of her two sons and her troubled hopes that her nephew Hrothulf will be loyal to them and their succession when Hrothgar dies. From the surviving Scandinavian sources we can deduce that in fact Hrothulf deposed and killed Hrothgar's son and successor and seized the throne himself. Similarly, Beowulf's prediction, in his long speech to Hygelac on his return from Denmark, that Hrothgar's attempt to make peace with the Heathobards through an arranged marriage will fail is borne out by the continental chroniclers, who describe how the attempted alliance ends in assassination and war. These characters in *Beowulf* are indeed drawn from history and historical legend, and the poem actually interacts with some of that history in its narrative presentation. Beowulf himself, however, is not documented in sources outside the poem. As we have seen, he appears to be a fictional character inserted into the events of Danish and Geatish history that were familiar to the audience. The beginnings of such a mingling of fantasy with history may be detected in the description of King Hygelac's disastrous raid that is to be found in the probably English *Liber monstrorum* (whose date of composition has been variously placed from the mid-seventh century to the mid-eighth).[2] Here King Hygelac himself is said to have been of such amazing size that people come from great distances to view his huge bones on an island in the Rhine. In the later saga tradition of the Icelanders, Boðvarr Bjarki in the *Hrólfssaga* and

Grettir the strong in *Grettisaga* both have legendary features in common with Beowulf. But only in the Anglo-Saxon poem is the hero given epic proportions and dignity.

When we turn from the human characters to the Grendelkin, the dragon and other demonic elements in *Beowulf*, we find the poet drawing on a quite different kind of source. Many of the terms used to describe Grendel, such as *eoten*, *þyrs* and *ylfe*, come directly from pagan Germanic demonology (see above, pp. 134–9), but the poet also draws on Christian concepts of evil, associating the monster with hell and the devil. There seems to be a double perspective maintained in such characterization: to the pagan Germanic characters in the poem, Grendel is a monster out of pagan Germanic mythology; to the Christian poet and his Christian audience, the creature is known to be in truth a manifestation of evil as it is rightly understood by Christians. Two dragons are described in the poem. One is the dragon slain by Sigemund, whose exploit is narrated by the court minstrel in Denmark. This dragon is well-known in Germanic legend outside the poem. The dragon which kills Beowulf at the end of the poem seems to be much the same kind of creature. At least some Anglo-Saxons continued to believe in the existence of dragons well into the post-Christian period, for the *Anglo-Saxon Chronicle* states in the entry for the year 793 that 'fiery dragons were seen flying through the air' over Northumbria. But the majority of allusions to dragons are to be found in legendary literature, both pagan and Christian, and in lore – such as the Old English *Maxims II*, which state that 'a dragon is found in a cave, old and glorying in his treasure' (26–7).

The subject matter of *Beowulf*, then, suggests that a poet whose mind is well stocked with the imaginative literature of the early Germanic peoples and who has a fairly firm command of the history of Germania in the fifth and sixth centuries, has combined the two, giving a historical setting and weight to legends of preternatural creatures which are hostile to mankind and of a mighty hero who dares to challenge the evil monsters. The hero himself is not preternatural, although we are told repeatedly that he is the strongest man alive 'in that day of this life'. Because his physical strength is so great, swords tend to break under the force of his arm, and his most successful way of fighting is with his hands, as when he crushes the life out of Dæghrefn in vengeance for the death of Hygelac, or when he wrestles with Grendel and tears off his arm. But Beowulf's powers are limited. He complains that he wanted to hold Grendel in the hall for King Hrothgar to see, but the monster was too strong for him and got away. He is very nearly killed by the mother of Grendel in her watery cave, and when he prepares to face the dragon he apologetically explains that he must have special armour made because he cannot face such a dangerous creature without taking extraordinary measures to protect himself, and even then the outcome shows that he was unable to survive the wounds that the dragon gave to him. The poet seems to suggest that the very best of men might be very strong and awesomely courageous, but only the forces of evil in the world enjoy truly supernatural power.

In addition to the historical and legendary dimensions of *Beowulf* there is a third important ingredient in the narrative, and that is the religious atmosphere. How to portray the religious beliefs of his characters is a serious challenge to the poet because of his very boldness in choosing pagan Germanic heroes as his subject matter. The Anglo-Saxons themselves began to accept Christianity only from the late sixth century on, and throughout the Anglo-Saxon period paganism was a constant threat against which preachers railed and Christian kings and their retinues fought. When the *Beowulf*-poet sets out to show how admirable and at times even exemplary his people's non-Christian ancestors could be, he must be very careful not to appear to be encouraging a return to the dark ways of Germanic heathendom. He must celebrate the nobility of Beowulf and Hrothgar and Wiglaf without endorsing their religious beliefs, which any intelligent Anglo-Saxon would have known to be Germanic paganism. The poet achieves this resolution of conflicting imperatives with delicacy of selection and carefully controlled emphasis. First, he makes clear that his own faith is strongly Christian. He speaks of the true God and of the devil, and he alludes specifically to biblical events such as the Flood, the Last Judgement and Cain's slaying of Abel. The characters in the poem, on the other hand, never allude to Christian lore, for this information was not available to them. Instead they indulge in known pagan practices, such as cremation of the dead, the reading of omens, and the burial of lavish grave goods with their dead – all practices sternly and often forbidden by Christian Anglo-Saxon writers. In one passage near the beginning of the poem we are explicitly told that the Danes in Hrothgar's kingdom worshipped at heathen shrines, not knowing that the idols they venerated were the work of the (Christian) devil. Such an overt allusion to the paganism of the poem's characters could not be emphasized too much, however, for a Christian Anglo-Saxon audience would feel uncomfortable lending their sympathies to characters – even heroes – who are prominently portrayed as heathens. So, after this direct reference in lines 175–88 to their heathen rites, the poet mutes his allusions to the Germanic characters' religious beliefs. He does not deny their paganism; throughout the poem we hear of their heathen burial customs, of their belief in the power of totemic devices such as the boar images on helmets to protect warriors from injury, of their conviction that vengeance and fame are among the most desirable things for men to pursue. But the poem does not describe them addressing prayers to Woden and the thunder-god or performing other pagan rites which would have shocked the Christian

Anglo-Saxon audience of the poem. Rather he puts into their speeches allusions to 'the almighty' (*se ælmihtiga*), 'the ancient creator' (*ealdmetod*) or 'the ruler' (*wealdend*). At times they use the word 'god', but we have to remember that this word, then as now, was a generic term for any deity as well as a term which, in a specialized sense, could be used to refer to the Christian God. Editors and translators of *Beowulf* in the past have done a disservice to readers by capitalizing the first letter of these terms whenever they occur, implying that they always refer to the Christian God. Thus they make it appear as if heathens are alluding to a Christian Deity they could never have known. The original manuscript of *Beowulf* never capitalizes the initial letter of these terms; the custom of honouring the Christian Deity in this way was introduced much later than the Anglo-Saxon period. The modern reader of *Beowulf* is well advised to ignore the editors' capitalizations of the initial letters of words meaning 'god' and to allow the context to determine whether allusion is being made to the Christian Deity or to some vaguely conceived pagan god. The poet is clear in his mind as to the religious state of his heroic characters; they were as yet deprived of the revelation that missionaries in later centuries would bring to the English. When they speak of a deity, it can only be a deity such as their pre-Christian wits conceived it. The poet is not presenting them as Christians, a misrepresentation which would have seemed absurd to any intelligent Anglo-Saxon.

It is worth labouring this point, because it is central to what would seem to be a major purpose in the writing of the poem. The poet is living among a Christian people whose ancestors are known to have been pagan. Christian teachers among the Anglo-Saxons often urged that the fore-fathers of the nation should be forgotten precisely because they had been ignorant of Christian revelation and therefore were beyond salvation. But the Anglo-Saxons were also a people who took pride in their heritage and knew that their forebears had shown valour and achieved fame in heroic-age Europe. 'We have heard of the glory of the Spear-Danes', says the poet in the opening line of *Beowulf*, 'we have heard of how noblemen then showed courage'. And he sets out to celebrate the virtues and accomplishments of the men of olden times. Beowulf's victories over his adversaries both human and monstrous are praised by the poet and also by characters in the poem. In the narratives of the Swedish-Geatish wars in the latter part of *Beowulf* the valour of the kings and warriors on both sides of the conflict is extolled. Loyalty and generosity are praised, and at several points in the poem we are told that the behaviour of these heroic ancestors is exemplary even for the Christian audience of the poem: 'Thus must a young man do', says the poet in describing the munificence of the Danish prince; 'thus must a man do when he intends to achieve lasting fame at battle', says the poet as he recounts the valour and determination of Beowulf in his fight with Grendel's mother. 'He held to his high destiny', says Wiglaf of the dead hero, 'Of all men throughout the world he was the most glorious warrior.' And yet, despite the noble character and the mighty deeds of the kings and warriors in *Beowulf*, there is an underlying melancholy intermingled with the admiration of the heroes as well as a nostalgia for times past. Again and again throughout the narrative the poet undercuts the mood of exaltation with forecasts of disasters to come. As we noticed above, when Hrothgar's queen bestows the magnificent torque on Beowulf in recognition of his stupendous victory over the Grendelkin, the poet tells us in a sombre aside that this treasure would be lost when the Geatish army meets its nemesis in Frisia. Just after describing the building of the fair hall Heorot, the poet says that it will in time be consumed in the flames of internecine conflict, so that Beowulf's saving of the hall from Grendel, which is about to be narrated, is undercut before we are told about it. Beowulf takes pride in the lavish treasure he wins for his people when he gives his life to defeat the dragon, but in a final despairing gesture his subjects bury the treasure with his body, and we are told that the nation faces its demise at the hands of surrounding enemies. Aside from these narrative strategies of dark hints and sombre prophecies, there is a further sadness of a subtler kind that pervades the poem. Even as the great deeds of the heroic age are described, we are constantly aware that through no fault of their own these people are ignorant of the one thing needed for true hope – Christian revelation. What profits it a man if he gain the whole world but lose his immortal soul? Even the simplest Christian among the Anglo-Saxons would have been aware of this hard truth, which casts a rueful shadow over the triumphs and splendour of heroic age existence. In terms of their own culture Beowulf and his fellows persevered and prevailed: they fulfilled their destiny and won everlasting fame. But by a larger measure they fell short, through no fault of their own, of what is most important in life. Thus the poet artfully reminds his audience of their ancestors' shortfallings even as he urges them to take pride in these people. He lends dignity to his nation's ancestors without betraying contemporary Christian truth. At the same time, there may be a certain discreet questioning of the harsher side of Christian teaching. After having his sensibilities trained for 3,182 lines of poetry to revere the character and achievement of Beowulf, a reader must wonder a little at the justice of a creed that insists that such a paragon of heroic virtue, through no fault of his own, must be consigned to eternal damnation. Any such questionings as this are suggested with utmost subtlety and without any implication that the poet was anything but a devout Christian. But he was a Christian whose *pietas* before the deeds of the men of old could only lead him to ponder deeply and at times to wonder – perhaps a little dangerously.

Thus far we have dealt with the narrative content of the poem. We must also give attention to the organization and style of *Beowulf*, for in few poems is style so important, a fact which makes *Beowulf* a notoriously difficult challenge for the translator. First, the narrative is highly patterned. There is studied balance between the two parts of the poem, with the aged Hrothgar and the youthful Beowulf in the first part standing in poignant contrast with the aged Beowulf and the youthful Wiglaf in the closing episode. The contrast is underscored by the distribution of poetic formulae, with the epithets of the elderly which were applied to Hrothgar in the first part being used of the aged Beowulf in the second part, while young Beowulf's epithets fall to young Wiglaf. The pathos of inexorable ageing and decay is thus added to the hero's overthrow by time at the end of the poem. The same interplay of formulaic phrases heightens the poet's bold strategy of beginning and ending the poem with the obsequies of a hero, thus framing his poem with vivid tableaux of death and commemoration.

There is also verbal recurrence in certain set scenes in the poem. At banquets, whether in Denmark or Geatland, courteous invitations are extended, mead and wine are served, a royal lady comes forth and passes the cup, the king retires, and so forth. Speeches between king and retainer have a familiar ring, and the description of distribution of gifts involves a set vocabulary. The poet Richard Wilbur records the attentive reader's perception of such repetition in his poem '*Beowulf*':[3]

> The queen brought mead in a studded cup, the rest
> Were kind, but in all was a vagueness and a strain
> Because they lived in a land of daily harm.
> And they said the same things again and again.

But the recurrence of words and rituals in the poem serves an important purpose. In recurrence is order. The patterned lives of the ancestral heroes suggested by the patterned diction of the poem was something highly prized in an age when custom, order and ritual movement promised security while spontaneity and novelty were fraught with peril. Civilization in *Beowulf* is a precious and fragile achievement of a people surrounded by hostile forces both monstrous and human. Custom and order offer society some hope of control over a potentially chaotic world. 'He knew the custom of the retinue', the poet says approvingly of the retainer who addresses King Hrothgar with the proper forms. And as Hrothgar describes the ideal relations which will exist between the Danes and *Geatas*, he says they will be acting 'according to the ancient custom'. Repetitive accounts of customs and rituals are not inadvertent, but rather emphasize what would have been perceived as a positive good by the audience of *Beowulf*. Besides significant repetition, there are also patterns of climactic progression in the poem, and one such pattern knits the entire narrative in a firm design of ever-growing challenges to the hero. When he makes landfall in Denmark, Beowulf is challenged successively by the coast guard, by Hrothgar's retainer Wulfgar, and then, in a strident exchange, by Unferth. He meets each of these verbal challenges handily and emerges from them with his intelligence and diplomacy tested and proven. These encounters, however, are but prelusive to the hero's confrontation with Grendel, which results in victory after a short but hard-fought battle. The challenge to fight with Grendel's mother is made by Hrothgar following a horrifying description by the king of the menacing abode of the Grendel-kin. The hero's ringing acceptance of this challenge –

> Ure æghwylc sceal   ende gebidan
> worolde lifes;   wyrce se þe mote
> domes ær deaþe;   þæt bið drihtguman
> unlifgendum   æfter selest.
> Aris, rices weard,   uton raþe feran,
> Grendles magan   gang sceawigan.
> Ic hit þe gehate,   no he on helm losaþ,
> ne on foldan fæþm,   ne on fyrgenholt,
> ne on gyfenes grund,   ga þær he wille!   (1386–94)

Each of us must abide the end of earthly life; let him who can achieve fame before his death! That is the best there is for a dead warrior. Arise, lord of the realm; let us go swiftly to see the track of Grendel's kinswoman. I promise to you that she shall not escape to cover, neither into the earth's embrace nor into the mountain torrent, nor into the ocean's depth, go where she will.

is the single most eloquent statement of the Germanic heroic code in the poem, and it dignifies the hero's embarcation on a battle far more perilous than the one he had fought with Grendel. In this fight the monster is on her home ground, and she makes the most of it. Beowulf would have died, the poet says, had God not intervened, enabling him to find the giants' sword with which he dispatches the ogress. With the third and final monster-fight – that with the dragon near the end of the poem – the hero meets his most formidable enemy of all and is killed by the wounds the creature had given to him. This steady progression of increasingly dangerous challenges provides the basic structure and impetus of the narrative.

But other climactic patterns embellish and emphasize this central pattern of ever greater tests of the hero. The hero's preparation for each fight reflects the growing danger of his opponents; he removes his armour before the Grendel-fight and confronts the monster without weapons; he wears sword and armour to the fight with Grendel's mother and at one point we are told that his chain-linked byrnie saved his life; for the battle with the dragon he has a special 'all-iron' shield made for him since, he says, he doesn't know how else he would have a chance against the dreadful adversary. The speeches he delivers before each of these three fights also reflect the hero's increasing estimation of the danger he is facing. Most elaborate of all, the poet provides a dramatic audience for each of these fights, and the behaviour of the audience registers vividly the increasingly desperate odds in each encounter. The Danes who witness the fight with Grendel from their vantage point outside the hall are filled with fear and foreboding by the horrendous sounds of the struggle in Heorot, but they stand their ground and are there to rejoice at the monster's howling retreat. Later in the poem, when Danes and *Geatas* are waiting by the mere into which Beowulf had plunged to seek out Grendel's mother, they become so discouraged at the sight of blood churning up in the water that they despair of ever seeing Beowulf again, and the Danes abandon the watch and return despondently to Heorot. In the final fight with the dragon the men who are supposed to stand by the hero as he fights the fire-drake are so terrified by the creature's initial onslaught that they flee in panic, abandoning the King to his fate. (Wiglaf then returns to the side of Beowulf.) It has been suggested that this carefully calculated use of dramatic audiences in the description of the monster fights not only provides an objective measure of the mounting danger to the hero in his three encounters, but also affords a kind of secondary suspense which would compensate for the fact that the poet's audience knew the outcome of each monster-fight beforehand (the poet having announced the results of each fight before it begins, presumably because he was using traditional stories known to his audience) and would not be wondering excitedly how the battles ended.

The mounting sequences of the narrative structure are sometimes mirrored at the level of diction. In the sentence stating the unknown destination of Scyld's funeral ship the appositive expressions for 'men' emphasize the human incapacity for imagining the fate of the dead:

> Men ne cunnon
> secgan to soðe,   selerædende,
> hæleð under heofenum,   hwa þæm hlæste onfeng   (50–2)

Men do not know how to tell in truth, not counsellors in the royal hall, not heroes beneath the heavens, who would receive that cargo.

In the exchange between Beowulf and Hrothgar's deputy Wulfgar there is a courtly repetition of complimentary epithets for the king that skilfully suggests the dignity of the royal setting. Beowulf says,

> Wille ic asecgan   sunu Healfdenes,
> mærum þeodne   min ærende,
> aldre þinum,   gif he us geunnan wile,
> þæt we hine swa godne   gretan moton   (344–7)

I wish to give my message to the son of Healfdene, to the renowned prince, to your lord, if he will permit that we may greet his gracious self.

To which Wulfgar replies:

> Ic þæs wine Deniga,
> frean Scildinga,   frinan wille,
> beaga bryttan,   swa þu bena eart,
> þeoden mærne,   ymb þinne sið . . .   (350–3)

I shall ask the friend of the Danes, the Scylding lord, our dispenser of treasure, our renowned prince, about your matter, as you request.

Such leisurely naming of titles suggests effectively that this is a richly civilized society where men 'know the custom of the court'. And at the end of the poem the sombre succession of epithets for the dead King Beowulf gives ceremonial weight to the poet's closing verses:

> cwædon þæt he wære   wyruldcyninga
> manna mildust   ond monðwærust,
> leodum liðost   ond lofgeornost   (3180–2)

They said that he was of all worldly kings the kindest of men and the gentlest, and the most gracious to his people and the most zealous for fame.

Besides the various kinds of dictional ornament in *Beowulf* –. the building appositions, the weighty compounds, the kennings and formulae – there is the additional and important ornament of the verse form. The metre does more perhaps than anything else to give to *Beowulf* that aesthetic pleasure special to poetry, the sense of artistic control imposed on various, vivid, and at times turbulent subject matter. The poet's constant imposition of pattern and discipline on all that he says is expressive of a major theme of *Beowulf*, the continual struggle between what is natural, untamed, and chaotic in the world and human order and control. The reader (or listener) is probably affected more than he consciously realizes by the steady and elegant operation of the metrical restraints which discipline the poet's telling of the dragon's depredations, of Hrethel's grief over his son's death, of Grendel's eerie advance on Heorot, of Beowulf's indignant rejoinder to Unferth, or of the carefully cadenced account of the hero's funeral at the end of the poem. The traditional Germanic verse form is handled with classical perfection in *Beowulf*, and one of the lasting impressions one has after reading the poem is one of wild and colourful subject matter and of shifting moods of exultation, horror and sombre regret all being expressed through the masterly control of a craftsman's intellect. All in the poem is measured and carefully weighed, from the grandest speech or action to the smallest syllable.

The varied and interactive craftsmanship evident throughout the poem at levels of narrative structure and style has given rise to questions as to whether the poem is of oral or literate origin. In the middle of this century a school of oral-formulaic scholars began urging that *Beowulf* and most other Old English poetry had to be composed orally because there are many similar or identical expressions or 'formulae' (for example, 'grew up beneath the heavens', 'hither across the waves', and 'the expectation played him false') in the poetic texts, and the presence of these was taken to be unquestionable proof that the poems were orally improvised rather than composed with pen in hand.[4] Most scholars from the nineteenth century and before had assumed that formulae as well as other features of the style of Old English poetry (including the metre) were drawn ultimately from oral tradition, that the poetry of the Germanic peoples went through an oral stage (which left its permanent imprint on the style) before the advent of literacy, after which poets began to compose in writing. But to insist that the very texts we have from the Anglo-Saxons are all or virtually all oral improvisations is a broader claim than some are willing to concede. One effect of the assumption of oral origin is to devalue the artistry of the poem, since most people assume that poetry composed under pressure of improvisation could not have the careful planning and subtle artistry of poetry composed in writing, where the poet may pause long before phrasing a verse and may revise what he has written. One may find in the scholia of many editions and critiques the warning that not too much should be made of the precise meaning of a given phrase because 'it is merely formulaic', that is, a cliché utilized in oral composition. The logic underlying this assumption that any repetitive formula is bound to lack precise meaning is questionable. Nothing could be more formulaic than a judge's pronouncement, 'I hereby sentence you to hang by the neck until dead; and may God have mercy on your soul', but no person to whom that formula is addressed is likely to regard it as imprecise or 'mere'.

Those who insist that Old English verse, including *Beowulf*, must be orally improvised see little significance in the fact that all the Old English poetry that we have is known to us solely by virtue of written texts, and they show notably little interest in studying the manuscripts in which the poetry is preserved. Do the surviving manuscripts look like prompt notes for a wandering minstrel or like a hasty transcription of some oral improvisor's performance, or do they suggest something else? Perhaps it is time to return to the words of W. P. Ker, a scholar and critic deeply learned in both oral and written literature of the Middle Ages and one who *was* interested in familiarizing himself with the manuscripts in which that literature survives:

Beowulf and *Waldere* are the work of educated men, and they were intended, no doubt, as books to be read. They are not, like the *Elder Edda*, a collection of traditional oral poems. It may be accident that has made it so, but it is the case that the Anglo-Saxon books in their handwriting and their shape have the air of libraries and learning about them, of wealth and dignity. The handsome pages of the Junius MS. in the Bodleian (the *Cædmon* manuscript) belong to a learned world. The book of *Roland* lying near it is different – an unpretending cheap copy, not meant for patrons of learning to read, but more probably for the minstrel who chanted it. The *Beowulf* MS., though not so fine as the Junius one, is intended as a book to be read, and is got up with some care. From the look of it, one places it naturally in the library of a great house or a monastic school; and the contents of it have the same sort of association; they do not belong to the unlearned in their present form.[5]

Ker clearly thought that these 'books to be read' were composed in writing (he goes on to discuss the learned writings on which *Beowulf* is based), and if asked to explain the presence of formulae in the Old English poem, he might well have said that the written poetry of the English was modelled on a style evolved in oral poetry, just as Milton, in writing *Paradise Lost*, incorporated the formulae and invocations of the originally oral style of classical epic.

Probably there will never be sufficient evidence or arguments to persuade every scholar that *Beowulf* was of literate or oral origin, and perhaps the question is not of overriding importance if one's conviction as to the poem's origin does not blind one to its patent aesthetic qualities. Some oral traditions are capable of subtle and elaborate stylistic and narrative effects; if an adherent to the oral theory is willing to allow the *Beowulf*-poet such capacities for stylistic subtlety, then his theory of the poem's origin makes little difference. So long as we recognize the artful synthesis of style and subject matter to produce a coherent and moving effect, it little matters whether the process of creation was one of brilliant Mozartian spontaneity (itself the result of years of disciplined craftsmanship) or of long and laboured revision.

To modern readers *Beowulf* often seems at once profoundly native and profoundly strange. The story itself has universal appeal, and the voices of the characters have something unmistakably English in them with their combined eloquence and understatement, their melancholy and their firm resolve. But the narrator's telling of the story has much that is unfamiliar. The love of contrasts and digressions, the chronological leaps, and the failure to maintain a simple story line all remind us that the Germanic imagination was not conditioned by those precepts of the classical world which we have mistakenly come to think of as 'universals' (for example, Aristotle's 'beginning, middle and end' and the concept of decorum). In reading the poem we must be receptive to the aesthetic refinements of a barbaric sensitivity unconstricted by the rules of Greece and Rome. Dramatic contrast rather than linear plot lines seems to have special importance for the *Beowulf*-poet. His tale of glorious triumph and melancholy farewell, of splendour in the heathen world without hope, is like hearing only the first two movements of Beethoven's *Eroica* Symphony and no more – *allegro con brio* followed by a long funeral march. This sad and inspiring story is told with the intonations of a narrator who is speaking to an English-speaking audience that contemplates Beowulf, Hygelac, Hildeburh and Hrothgar with mingled feelings of kinship and regret. Anglo-Saxons must have been proud to hear of the courage, defiance and heroic resignation of their forebears, and they must have admired the steadfastness of people who bore up in a hopeless heathen world which required endurance of a kind which no Christian would ever have to display. The funeral march for Beowulf has a terrible finality which the Anglo-Saxon audience has been spared by its acceptance of Christian consolation. Readers of the poem today may not enjoy quite the same confidence of shared belief that united the original audience. The certainties which sustained scores of generations from Anglo-Saxon times to our own era have been shaken by scientific revelations, religious doubt and the traumas of modern history. It may be that we, more than the Anglo-Saxon audience for which *Beowulf* was originally created, can feel a close kinship with the desperate men of old – and can hope that we may learn from their heroic acceptance.

1 The relevant sources (mostly Scandinavian) are conveniently assembled and translated in *Beowulf and its Analogues*, trans. G. N. Garmonsway and J. Simpson (London, 1968).
2 The standard edition is *Liber monstrorum*, ed. F. Porsia (Bari, 1976). There is no English edition or translation of the work, though the relevant chapter is found in *Beowulf and its Analogues*, trans. Garmonsway and Simpson, p. 113. On the date and origin of the work, see M. Lapidge, '*Beowulf*, Aldhelm, the *Liber monstrorum* and Wessex', *Studi medievali* 3rd ser. 23 (1982), 151–92.
3 *Richard Wilbur: Poems 1943–1956*, 2nd ed. (London, 1964), p. 68 (from *Ceremony* (1950)).
4 The most frequently quoted works on the subject are F. P. Magoun, 'The Oral-Formulaic Character of Anglo-Saxon Narrative Poetry', *Speculum* 28 (1953), 446–67; A. B. Lord, *The Singer of Tales* (New York, 1960) and J. Opland, *Anglo-Saxon Oral Poetry* (New Haven, CT, 1980).
5 W. P. Ker, *The Dark Ages* (Edinburgh, 1904; repr. New York, 1958), pp. 162–3.

9 Fatalism and the millennium

AMONG the major concerns of the Anglo-Saxons, as the surviving Old English prose and poetry attest, were the questions of fate and free will, providence and individual responsibility. In the nineteenth and early twentieth centuries, a great deal of scholarly attention was given to a search for a common philosophical background for Germanic literature (distinct from the Latin learned tradition) to complement the readily identifiable shared elements in diction, style and verse form among Old English, Old Norse, Old Saxon and Old High German. One school of thought, once espoused widely and not without adherents today, holds that the belief in fate was a key feature of paganism, and that the degree to which humankind is seen to be controlled by fate in Old English literature shows the extent to which the inherent paganism of the text comes through untarnished or unalloyed. When fate is in competition with God, the text has been 'contaminated', usually by a 'pious interpolator', whose 'spurious' additions obscured the underlying Germanic heroic fatalism (never clearly defined or exemplified in any extant text). The key Old English word in these discussions is *wyrd*, which glosses Latin words as various as *fortuna*, 'fortune', *fatum*, 'fate', and mere *eventus*, 'event' or 'what happens'. Most modern scholars would probably agree with Morton Bloomfield that 'the widespread tendency to use the word "wyrd" as evidence of Germanic Paganism seems to be dangerously simplistic, for *wyrd* was soon given a Christian meaning', or with Dorothy Whitelock that,

the word used for fate can mean simply 'event,' 'what happens,' and though there are passages where some degree of personification is present, such as 'the creation of the fates changes the world under the heavens' or 'woven by the decree of fate,' I doubt if these are more than figures of speech by the time the poems were composed. If they are inherited from the heathen past, they may indicate that men then believed in a goddess who wove their destiny, but the poet who says 'to him the Lord granted the webs of victory' is unconscious of a heathen implication in his phrase.[1]

If this is the case, and given the fact that all surviving Old English literature is a product of the Christian era, we should be able to examine attitudes toward destiny in that literature without the attendant baggage of earlier scholarship which insisted on a fatalistic underlayer surviving from paganism which has no surviving texts to attest to its existence. We can view the literature, in short, as a body of writing which has no known antecedents in a pagan Germanic past but which occasionally addresses, as part of the subject matter of both its fiction and its philosophical, historical and homiletic prose, pagan times and pagan beliefs.

Let us begin with a glance at the subject of the previous chapter, *Beowulf*, a poem about a 'pagan' society by a poet with a clearly Christian perspective, and a poem in which from time to time the Christian God appears to be directing the events in the lives of men, even though they are ignorant of His existence and beyond His salvation. Robinson has recently demonstrated the effective use by the poet of words which we know refer to one thing in the Christian present but to other, darker things in the unenlightened past. He notes that when Beowulf says that the outcome of his battle with the dragon shall be,

'swa unc wyrd geteoð, / metod manna gehwæs' (2526–7): 'as wyrd, the measurer of each person, shall decree for us'. This surely is the meaning that the words have for Beowulf, and editors like von Schaubert who specify that *metod* here means 'fate' are clearly right. And yet Klaeber and others who insist that *metod* means '(Christian) God' are also right; they are simply viewing Beowulf's statement from the perspective of the narrating poet, for whom 'metod manna gehwæs' could only seem like an appositive gloss to 'wyrd', explaining providentially the true nature of *wyrd*, which, as Christians knew, was but the accomplishment of God's determinations. 'Metod eallum weold / gumena cynnes, swa he nu git deð.' ['*Metod* ruled all of the race of men, as he now still does'] says the poet (1057–8), but *metod* has undergone a momentous semantic change since the time when He was presiding over the noble heathens of the tale of Beowulf, and this, I believe, poet and audience fully understood.[2]

This is an especially important distinction for readers previously unfamiliar with Old English literature to understand as well, since it allows an inexperienced reader a more ready insight into a number of apparent ambiguities in both the verse and the prose than would be gained through extensive reading in inconclusive secondary discussions on genres and perspectives.

Other than *Beowulf*, the poems which concern themselves most with the inevitability of fate and its working on both men and on the things of the world are a group conveniently if not altogether convincingly classed as elegies and containing at least two masterpieces, *The Wanderer* and *The Seafarer. The Wanderer* begins,

Oft him anhaga   are gebideð,
metudes miltse,   þeah þe he modcearig
geond lagulade   longe sceolde
hreran mid hondum   hrimcealde sæ,
wadan wræclastas.   Wyrd bi∂ ful aræd!   (*The Wanderer* 1–5)

Often the solitary one awaits favour, the mercy of the Lord, although he,
sorrowful in mind, has had to stir, across the expanse of water, the frost-cold sea
with his hands, tread the paths of exile. Fate is fully inexorable.

Whatever the last line means (and my translation is the usual but by no
means the only one), it is uttered by the narrator as a prelude to a
catalogue of personal hardships involving the degeneration of societal
bonds, the loss of loved ones, lords and kinsmen, and the destruction of
what seems to have stood for civilization as the narrator knows it. As the
end of the poem approaches, there is a moving *ubi sunt* passage ('where
did horses, kinsmen, treasure-giver, banquet seats and hall-joys go?')
which seems to be answered in a rhetorically parallel catalogue, in which
many of the same objects fill the blank in the formula 'her bið____ læne':

Her bið feoh læne,   her bið freond læne,
her bið mon læne,   her bið mæg læne   (108–9)

Here (that is, in this world) are property, friends, men and kinsmen transitory.

But both the remedy and the end of the poem follow hard thereupon: the
are which the *anhaga* seeks in the opening lines is to be sought, according
to the closing line, 'to fæder in heofonum, þær us eal seo fæstnung
stondeð' ('from the father in heaven, where for us all stability stands').
Whatever connotations (if any) *wyrd* may possess beyond 'inescapable
event', the doctrinal context is clear – God laid waste the world; it is
inevitable that all earthly things perish; and what stability there is exists in
heaven. As we will note later when we consider the Anglo-Saxons'
conception of the approaching millennium, the earth in its youth was said
to have seduced mankind from the eternal, whereas in its last age, corrupt
and decaying, it brings man closer to the eternal things. If pagan and
Christian ethics are in contrast here, the evidence of the former seems
buried too deeply to make the distinction clear or relevant.

A glance at the concordance to Old English poetry or to Weber's list of
the occurrences of *wyrd* in Old English (see below, n. 1) will show that
roughly half of the occurrences in the verse are in the poems concerned
with Old Testament patriarchs or Christian saints, and that almost every
occurrence refers merely to 'events'. *Wyrd seo swiðe* (*Ruin* 24) like *wyrd
seo mære* in *The Wanderer*, discussed above, may hold some memory of a
past association with Fate, or it may be merely a dead epithet. Supporters

of a pagan interpretation of *wyrd*, even into recent times, took *wyrd bi∂ swi∂ost* in *Maxims II* as a clinching point in their arguments.[3] In fact, however, the half-line occurs in a catalogue of superlatives which appear to expand upon the statement *þrymmas syndan cristes myccle*, 'the glories of Christ are great'. Punctuation in Old English manuscripts (when it exists, though it does in this one) is metrical, and therefore of no help; but it appears that *wyrd bi∂ swi∂ost* is either a variation on 'the glories of Christ are great' or simply a continuation of the catalogue mentioned above: 'wind is swiftest . . . thunder is loudest . . . fate is strongest . . . winter is coldest . . . spring is frostiest . . . summer fairest'.

But what of an occasional use such as 'wyrd seo mære', '*wyrd* the famous' (*Wanderer* 100), which clearly hints at antiquity and which some scholars would view as a possible link to earlier destinal concepts while others view it as,

the linguistic remains of outmoded ideas [which] linger long after they have lost their full meaning: we 'thank our lucky stars' with little thought of medieval astrology. And in poetry, especially, older terms which have poetic associations are often felt to have more emotional and imaginative force because of those associations. When the poet of *The Wanderer* sees in the scene of ruin the work of *ælda scyppend* 'Creator of men', he sees it also as the work of *wyrd seo mære* 'Fate the mighty'. But God the omnipotent and fate the inexorable are equally regarded in the poem as the terrible force that destroys the work of man. *Wyrd* was not a sort of pagan god: it was a poetic term, often personified, for what is a timeless concept, pagan only in its associations, the concept of inescapable event.[4]

At the risk of sounding as simplistic as those who once insisted on equating *wyrd* with paganism, it is probably safe to say that a view which combines the attitudes noted above in the work of such scholars as Gordon, Whitelock, Bloomfield and Robinson, and amplified upon in far more detail in the exhaustive studies of Stanley and Weber on paganism and *wyrd*, respectively, is the prevalent one in contemporary Old English scholarship as well as the view of the author of this chapter. But a few nagging doubts remain. *Wyrd seo mære* and *ælda scyppend* may indeed have come by the time they appear in *The Wanderer* to be two aspects of the same force, but the former, as 'The Mighty *Wyrd*' still seems to echo a past personification which, whether once a Fate, a Norn or something quite different, may still seem to many to have held on to some earlier associations even as Christian matter has been added. And so may it in *Beowulf* 572–5 when *wyrd* 'often protects an undoomed earl', or when, in 1054–7, the poet tells us that Grendel would have killed more men 'nefne him witig God   wyrd forstode', 'except that wise God withstood *wyrd*'. It is admittedly difficult in cases of this sort to argue that the word is a clear personification of a kind of fate or destinal agent from either Germanic or classical antiquity, but it is equally difficult to say that the poet means 'God prevented the event' and no more.

In prose, the major discussion of the problem of fate comes in King Alfred's translation of the *Consolation of Philosophy* of Boethius. The *Consolation*, written in the early sixth century, became a key text in the history of Western humanistic thought and was translated and adapted again and again in England first by Alfred, then by Chaucer, and later by many others including Queen Elizabeth I. Although Boethius was unquestionably a Christian, his *Consolation* is not distinctively Christian in tone and is drawn almost entirely from the tradition of classical (especially Platonic) philosophy. For Boethius, the world was created by a divine and immutable reason which governs all things: when the governing is joined to the foresight of the divine mind, it is *providentia*; when it is viewed in relation to the things governed (that is, temporally), it is *fatum*. Boethius wrote for a world which believed in an all-powerful God and which viewed life as a pilgrimage through an alien land in which the true way to the eternal good would frequently be obscured. The *Consolation* became, therefore, a popular authority in later times for other societies which sought solutions to the same problems from relatively similar perspectives. And just as Boethius himself offered a synthesis of a number of popular philosophical and theological ideas, so his revisers and translators, in adapting the *Consolation*, both modified Boethius and introduced into his work aspects of other classical and medieval treatises. In the case of the Alfredian *Boethius*, neither the nature of the modifications nor the reasoning which dictated them is always clear.

Scholars have argued for years, for example, over the significance of King Alfred's use of the word *wyrd* in his translation and adaptation of Boethius's *Consolation of Philosophy*. On a simpler level, most handbooks and literary histories use Alfred's famous simile of the wheel of destiny, which replaces Boethius's intricate discussion of necessity through a simile involving orbiting spheres, to illustrate how Alfred modified the *Consolation of Philosophy*. More immediately interesting for our purposes, however, is the direct statement which precedes the introduction of the simile:

Sumu þing þonne on þisse weorulde sint underðied þære wyrde, sume hire nanwuht underðied ne sint; ac sio wyrd ond eall ða þing þe hire underðied sint, sint underðied ðæm godcundan foreþonce.

(ed. Sedgefield, p. 129)

Some things, then, in this world are subject to fate; some are not a whit subject to it; but fate and all things that are subject to it, are subject to divine forethought (i.e. providence).

In this instance, Alfred is using *wyrd* to gloss Latin *fatum*; sometimes, though not always, he uses it to gloss *fortuna* as well, though when he discusses the gifts associated with fortune he uses *sælða* and *woruldsælða*. One thing is clear, however; both here and in a passage immediately preceding (ed. Sedgefield, p. 128, 18–20) in which Alfred equates *wyrd* with 'God's work, which he does each day', God controls fate, just as in *Beowulf* (1056–8) he did in pagan Denmark and 'he now still does'. The complex and continuing scholarly debate over the nature of Alfred's alterations is beyond the scope of this introductory essay. The debate concerning *wyrd* in Alfred's Boethius, however, must be recognized as but one of a number of facets of a much larger issue which has at least three sides: the first (the proponents of which appear to be diminishing rapidly) holds that many of the differences between the Latin and Alfred's adaptation of it result from Alfred's (or his translator's) inability to make appropriate translations either due to the inadequacy of English as they knew it or the inadequacy of their grasp of the philosophical concepts. The second view is that Alfred's alterations were deliberate and purposeful, informed by Augustinian and Gregorian perspectives (and perhaps by a knowledge of commentaries on Boethius), and possessed of a Christian dogmatism which dealt both metaphorically and literally more with matters of this world than with speculative philosophy (and therefore more emotionally than rationally). A third view is that Alfred gave to his subjects a Boethius which had been filtered through not only commentaries but had been made almost into a source book for political ideas – what one scholar calls 'the only Boethius that late ninth-century Europe knew and hence virtually the only Boethius that anyone had known since the work was written'.[5] While Alfred could see *wyrd* as a force operating under the control of God, Ælfric saw the belief in fate as an act of folly. For him, God gives free choice to all, but in his divine foreknowledge knows how his people will behave through their own will. Unbelievers perish 'ðurh agenne cyre . . . na ðurh gewyrd, forðan ðe gewyrd nis nan ðing buton leas wena; ne nan ðing soðlice be gewyrde ne gewyrð, ac ealle ðing þurh Godes dom beoð geendebyrde' (*Catholic Homilies*, ed. Thorpe I, 114: 'through their own choice, not through fate, for fate is nothing but a false expectation, for nothing happens through fate, but all things are arranged through the judgement of God').

If one aspect of the Anglo-Saxon thought-world was fatalism, another of equal importance was the concept of a world in decline. Christians in the Anglo-Saxon period (those who wrote the texts under consideration here and the audience for whom they were written) apparently believed they were living in the last age of the world, that their sojourn through this life was a pilgrimage of sorts to the next, and that there was no permanence to be expected in the earthly existence. It is a thoroughly

Boethian perspective: 'Eala', Alfred translates, 'þæt nanwuht nis fæste stondendes weorces a wuniende on worulde' ('Alas, that there is nothing of firm standing work ever remaining in this world'). The weakness in the moral sense was the sort which for Augustine in *The City of God* led to the coming of the Goths to punish the Romans, just as for Ælfric and Wulfstan the Danes were sent by God to punish the degenerate English for their sins. In the later eschatological homilies it eventually leads to the coming of Antichrist and the appearance of the signs of Doomsday. But it is a perspective supplemented (and to a degree complicated) by another fascinating eschatological tradition – one which views the 'ages' of both the world and of man as directly related to one another.[6] A terse poetic example of the theme occurs in *The Seafarer* 87–90:

> wuniað þa wacran   ond þas woruld healdaþ,
> brucað þurh bisgo.   Blæd is gehnæged,
> eorþan indryhto   ealdað ond searað,
> swa nu monna gehwylc   geond middangeard.

Weaker ones live on and rule the world, enjoy it through their efforts. Glory is bowed down, the nobility of the earth ages and dries up, as does now every man throughout the world.

The idea goes back to Cyprian and is prominent both in Gregory and Augustine and continues through Bede. A similar manifestation of it occurs in *Guthlac A*:

> Woruld is onhrered,
> colaþ Cristes lufu,   sindan costinga
> geond middangeard   monge arisene,
> swa þæt geara iu   godes spelbodan
> wordum sægdon   ond þurh witedom
> eal anemdon,   swa hit nu gongeð.   (37–42)

The world is stirred up, the love of Christ grows cold, many troubles have arisen throughout the world, just as long ago God's messenger predicted in words and through prophecy, so now it has come to pass.

This is based on the Bible, Matt. XXIV.12, *quoniam abundauit iniquitas, refrigescet caritas multorum*, 'because iniquity abounds, charity cools', and concludes two lines later, 'Ealdað eorþan blæd', 'the joys of the earth grow old'.

The degree to which the concern with the decay of the world as a sign of its end was connected with the approach of the year 1000 has been the subject of considerable debate over the years. There can be little doubt that those who lived in England during the waning years of the first millennium of the Christian era had cause for concern. Early historians wrote of a tropical climate which attracted the Angles and the Saxons;

they told of bigger and stronger and healthier ancestors, and the Scandinavian invasions and ensuing political chaos seemed in accord with the signs of the end. But, as Gatch and others have noted,

it is now usually thought that there was no widespread alarm in Europe around the millennial year in anticipation of the coming of Antichrist and the end of the world. The end of the millennium did bring bad times, however. The Scandinavian invasions were suddenly and violently renewed and the political order, in England and on the Continent, appeared to be crumbling. It is not surprising that Christian writers expressed concern as to these portents. But it was probably no more than coincidence that the time was almost *anno Domini* 1000, the end – if one took the round number literally – of the sixth millennial age.[7]

Bernard McGinn agrees, noting that 'on the basis of a handful of texts, some nineteenth- and twentieth-century French historians created a picture of widespread terror in Christendom at the approach of the year 1000, the final year of the sixth and last millennium', but asserting that the tradition of 'the centuries since Augustine had been against the literalistic treatment of the final thousand-year period. That there were some preachers and writers of the time who expected the imminent End is a sign of the continuity of apocalyptic expectations rather than a mark of any special florescence.'[8]

One splendid example of that continuity which *does*, however, allude to the approaching end of an age is Blickling Homily XI, on Holy Thursday, which, after quoting Acts I.7 that only God knows the date of Doomsday, goes on to add that,

we witon þonne hweþre þæt hit nis no feor to þon; forþon þe ealle þa tacno ond þa forebeacno þa þe her ure Drihten ær toweard sægde, þæt ær domes dæge geweorþan sceoldan, ealle þa syndon agangen, buton þæm anum þæt se awerigda cuma Antecrist nuget hider on middangeard ne com. Nis þæt þonne feor toþon þæt þæt eac geweorþan sceal; forþon þes middangeard nede on ðas eldo endian sceal þe nu andweard is; forþon fife þara syndon agangen on þisse eldo. Þonne sceal þes middangeard endian and þisse is þonne se mæsta dæl agangen, efne nigon hund wintra and lxxi on þys geare.   (ed. Morris, pp. 117–18)

Nevertheless, we know that it is not far off, because all the signs and fore-tokens that our Lord previously said would come before Doomsday, are all gone by, except one alone, that is, the accursed stranger, Antichrist, who, as yet, has not come hither upon earth. Yet the time is not far distant when that shall also come to pass; because this earth must of necessity come to an end in this age which is now present, for five of the [fore-tokens] have come to pass in this age; wherefore this world must come to an end, and of this the greatest portion [already] has elapsed, even nine hundred and seventy-one years, in this [very] year.

The homilist goes on to say that the ages of the earth were not all equally long – in some three thousand years, in some less, in some more, but there is no doubt in his mind of the sentiment expressed more directly in the previous homily X, 'þisses middangeardes ende swiþe neah is'.

It appears clear enough that the two great prose writers of the late Old English period, Ælfric and Wulfstan, saw evidence of the last times in current events transpiring on either side of the year 1000.[9] Wulfstan's most famous sermon, the *Sermo Lupi ad Anglos*, which was written somewhere around 1014, opens with a tone not unlike those pre-1000 texts cited above from the Blickling homilies:

Leofan men, gecnawað þæt soð is: þeos worold is on ofste, and hit nealæcð þam ende, and þy hit is on worolde a swa leng swa wirse

(ed. Bethurum, p. 261)

Beloved men, know what is true: this world is in haste, and it approaches its end, and the longer it is, the worse.

Ælfric, moreover, in the Preface to his *Catholic Homilies*, announces the imminent end of the world as the context for his collection, because 'menn behofiað godre lare swiðost on þisum timan þe is geendung þyssere worulde' (ed. Thorpe I, 2): 'men need good instruction especially in this time, which is the ending of this world'.

There is, however, another attitude toward the permanence of the works of creation which asserts itself in the poetry – most prominently in a poem in the Exeter Book called *The Order of the World*. This poem invites its hearers to learn about the wonders of creation, cautioning them, however, that God permits only a limited insight into the subject, and it is ultimately our obedience which enables us to reach heaven. In this poem, however, everything in the world remains as stable as God made it at creation:

Forþon swa teofenede,   se þe teala cuþe,
dæg wiþ nihte,   deop wið hean,
lyft wið lagustream,   lond wiþ wæge,
flod wið flode,   fisc wið yþum.
Ne waciað þæs geweorc,   ac he hi wel healdeð;
stondað stiðlice   bestryþed fæste
miclum heahtlocum   in þam mægenþrymme
mid þam sy ahefed   heofon ond eorþe.   (82–9)

Therefore he joined together, he who well knew how, day with night, the deep with the high, the cloud with the water, the land with the wave, ocean with ocean, fish with water. That work weakens not, but it holds well, stands strong, fixed fastly by great powerful locks in the glorious majesty by which heaven and earth are raised up.

But while it has been given mankind to know of the order and stability of the universe, other mysteries remain – mysteries such as the sun's course when it sinks into the ocean at night, or who enjoys its light after it departs from the dwellers in the known world (76–81).

This seeming ambivalence concerning creation suggests not so much two conflicting Christian world views as two aspects of a larger issue. Both are on view, for example, in Alfred's *Boethius*. The prose adaptation of met. iii of bk II, quoted above in another context, chronicles the passing of the seasons and concludes wistfully: 'Eala, þæt nanwuht nis fæste stondendes weorces a wuniende on worulde' (ed. Sedgefield, p. 21, 8–9: 'Alas, that there is nothing of firmly standing work dwelling in the world'). By contrast, the adaptation of met. ii of bk III tells 'hu wunderlice Drihten welt eallra gesceafta mid þam bridlum his anwealdes, and mid hwilcere endebyrdnesse he gestaðolað and gemetgað ealle gesceafta; and hu he hi næfð geheaðorade and gehæfte mid his unanbindendlicum racentum' (ed. Sedgefield, p. 57, 3–6: 'how wonderfully God rules all creation with the bridle of his power, and with what fittingness he establishes and measures all creation, and how he controls and binds them with his unbreakable chains.')

J. E. Cross contends that the reference in *The Order of the World* is 'to the fixed order of the world and this belief is confirmed by other Old English writers', including Ælfric, whom he quotes on the fixed stars in the universe, not one of which 'shall fall from the fast firmament as long as this world shall remain thus whole'. The qualifying statement, Cross points out, reconciles the Boethian view of a stable creation with the sense that the stability was destined to last only until Doomsday, and that evidence of the decay of the present in comparison with the past was but one more sign of living the last days.[10] In like manner, Christian poets and homilists throughout the Old English period, whether writing salvation history, heroic verse, or didactic prose described a world created perfect but nearing its end, subject to fate, as are all things which are temporal, but to a fate which Old English writers from the *Beowulf*-poet through Alfred, Ælfric and Wulfstan would surely agree was subject, in turn, to an all-knowing and all-powerful God.

1 M. Bloomfield, 'Patristics and Old English Literature: Notes on Some Poems', in *Studies in Old English Literature in Honor of Arthur G. Brodeur*, ed. S. B. Greenfield (Eugene, OR, 1963), p. 37, n. 1; D. Whitelock, *The Beginnings of English Society* (Harmondsworth, 1952), pp. 27–8. For a history of scholarship on the subject, see E. G. Stanley, *The Search for Anglo-Saxon Paganism* (Cambridge and Totowa, NJ, 1975). For an exhaustive study of *wyrd* and of

the concept of fate in Old English and other early Germanic literatures, with a full bibliography, see G. W. Weber, *Wyrd: Studien zum Schicksalsbegriff der altenglischen und altnordischen Literatur*, Frankfurter Beiträge zur Germanistik 8 (Bad Homburg, Berlin and Zürich, 1969).

2 F. C. Robinson, *Beowulf and the Appositive Style* (Knoxville, TN, 1985), p. 48. The idea that God has ruled and helped even those who did not know him was widely known, and multiple levels of perception were recognized in both classical literature and in the interpretation of the scriptures. A brilliant, even when not altogether convincing, attempt to recover the 'heroic ethos' of *Beowulf* is G. V. Smithers, 'Destiny and the Heroic Warrior in *Beowulf*', in *Philological Essays: Studies in Old and Middle English Language and Literature in Honour of Herbert Dean Meritt*, ed. J. L. Rosier (Hague, 1970), pp. 65–81. Smithers contends that 'the terms in *Beowulf* that have to do with "fate" are nearly all matched in one or more of the cognate early Germanic tongues, in that sort of sense, and are thus ancient, at least as words' (p. 66); he then examines those words in their various concepts and attempts thereby to distinguish between the uses of *wyrd* as a destinal agent and its uses to mean merely 'what happens'.

3 For *wyrd* in the curious poem *Solomon and Saturn*, see Stanley, *The Search*, pp. 120–1.

4 I. L. Gordon, 'Traditional Themes in *The Wanderer* and *The Seafarer*', *Review of English Studies* ns 5 (1954), 1–13, at 4–5. See further the important surveys by B. J. Timmer, 'Wyrd in Anglo-Saxon Prose and Poetry', *Neophilologus* 26 (1940–1), 24–33 and 213–28, and 'Heathen and Christian Elements in Old English Poetry', *Neophilologus* 29 (1944), 180–5.

5 W. F. Bolton, 'How Boethian is Alfred's *Boethius*?', in *Studies in Earlier Old English Prose*, ed. P. E. Szarmach (Albany, NY, 1986), pp. 153–68, at 163. Two histories which offer overviews, which are both sensible and accessible to readers new to Old English culture, are M. McC. Gatch, *Loyalties and Traditions: Man and his World in Old English Literature* (New York, 1971), esp. pp. 103–15, and S. B. Greenfield and D. G. Calder, *A New Critical History of Old English Literature* (New York and London, 1986), pp. 46–51. The fullest treatment of the larger relationship of Alfred's version to the original of the *Consolation* is F. A. Payne, *King Alfred and Boethius: an Analysis of the Old English Version of the Consolation of Philosophy* (Madison, WI, and London, 1968). Her thesis – that Alfred shifted the Boethian emphasis on God's ordered control to that of man's almost frightening freedom of choice – has been sharply (and persuasively) criticized by, among others, K. Proppe, 'King Alfred's *Consolation of Philosophy*', *Neophilologische Mitteilungen* 74 (1973), 635–48, and W. F. Bolton, cited above. Bolton's point is that a large number of commentaries as well as Alcuin's substantial role in the medieval literary tradition of the *Consolatio* makes it pointless to view Alfred's work as an adaptation of Boethius's work of 524. He and others give Payne due credit, however, for putting to rest the theory of Alfredian ineptitude. J. S. Wittig, 'King Alfred's *Boethius* and its Latin Sources: a Reconsideration', *ASE* 11 (1983), 157–98, argues convincingly that the additions to the *Consolation* are not from commentaries but rather

from a variety of other texts in the Latin learned tradition available to Alfred and his translators.

6 The seminal essay on the subject, and one upon which this chapter draws heavily, is by J. E. Cross, 'Aspects of Microcosm and Macrocosm in Old English Literature', in *Studies in Old English Literature in Honor of Arthur G. Brodeur*, ed. Greenfield, pp. 1–22. Another important article is G. V. Smithers, 'The Meaning of *The Seafarer* and *The Wanderer*', *Medium Ævum* 26 (1957), 137–53 and 28 (1959), 1–22 and 99–104.

7 M. McC. Gatch, *Preaching and Theology in Anglo-Saxon England: Ælfric and Wulfstan* (Toronto and Buffalo, NY, 1977), pp. 78–9; see also below, pp. 190–205.

8 B. McGinn, *Visions of the End: Apocalyptic Traditions in the Middle Ages* (New York, 1979), p. 88. See also N. Cohn, *The Pursuit of the Millennium: Revolutionary Millennarians and Mystical Anarchists of the Middle Ages*, rev. ed. (New York, 1970).

9 See Gatch, *Preaching*, pp. 78–84 and 104–16.

10 Cross, 'Aspects', p. 20 (note that he refers to *The Order of the World* by Mackie's title *Wonders of Creation*).

10 Perceptions of transience

They say the Lion and the Lizard keep
The Courts where Jamshyd gloried and drank deep.

Rubaiyat of Omar Khayyam

PREOCCUPATION with transience is not found solely within Old English elegiac poetry, though students of the genre may be forgiven for gaining that impression. There can be no major literature of the world that does not number among its themes wonder at the demise of earlier civilisations and regret for the brevity of human life and human joy. In a literature such as that of the Anglo-Saxons, marked by a variety of influences and traditions, it is hard to attribute with certainty all manifestations of the transience motif. Earlier scholars drew our attention to parallels in other Germanic medieval literatures, notably in the prose and poetry of Scandinavia written down in Iceland. Old Icelandic poetry of the type called 'eddic' has obvious similarities with Old English in style, vocabulary and subject matter. Possible influence on Old English elegy from Celtic lament has also been explored. Recently scholarship has focused more on the Christian Latin background to Anglo-Saxon thought, and shown how many apparently native wood-notes wild are in fact straight translation from theological sources.

The Old English poems traditionally called 'elegiac' are all found in one manuscript, the late tenth-century Exeter Book. It is a disturbing thought that had that particular codex been lost or destroyed we should have had scarcely any evidence of this genre in Anglo-Saxon vernacular poetry. There would still be the 'elegiac' passages in poems of epic dimensions such as *Beowulf* and *Elene* as well as a considerable corpus of Latin poetry by seventh- and eighth-century Anglo-Saxons. Also the transience motif surfaces, of course, in other types of poem, not to mention appearing frequently in homiletic prose. But the vernacular 'elegiac' poems, so-called because no other covering adjective has yet been found for them, are a group with little in common except a preoccupation with loss, suffering and mortality. These poems include *The Seafarer, The Wanderer, The Wife's Lament, The Husband's Message, The Ruin, Deor, Wulf and Eadwacer* and *The Exile's Prayer* (sometimes called *Resignation*) – all stuck with these dreary titles imposed on them by early editors with more sense than sensibility. They are without titles of any kind in the manuscript.

There are practical difficulties in considering these poems as a group. For one thing they are not grouped in the manuscript. There is little to tell from the lay-out of the poems quite where one ends and another begins. Sometimes the change of subject matter is clear enough. But the scribe uses ornate initials when introducing sections of poems as well as new poems, and certainly in the case of the consecutive pieces *Riddle 60* and *The Husband's Message* it is not determinable whether we have two parts of one poem or two distinct poems with an overlap of subject matter. A more fundamental problem is that, though we can with precision date the manuscript, there are no linguistic tests that enable us to date the actual composition of the poems. The reading of them as a group is a matter of convenience determined by their similarities of tone and theme.

The Latin word from which 'transient' derives implied something that is passing, and the image therefore is one of a journey. The word however that the Anglo-Saxons use most often for the temporary nature of things of this world is *læne*, 'lent' or 'on loan', contrasted mostly with the *ece* 'eternal' nature of things of the next. 'Lent' and 'eternal' are not, for the modern reader, such a natural pair of opposites, and it is worth examining why they seemed so to the Anglo-Saxon mind. King Alfred provides the clearest answer:

Ac se þe me lærde . . . se mæg gedon þæt ic softor eardian (mæge) ægðerge on þisum *lænan* stoclife be þis wæge ða while þe ic on þisse weorulde beo, ge eac on þam *ecan* hame . . . Nis it nan wundor þeah man swilc ontimber gewirce, and eac on þa(re) lade and eac on þære bytlinge; ac ælcne man lyst, siððan he ænig cotlyf on his hlafordes *læne* myd his fultume getimbred hæfð, þæt he hine mote hwilum þar-on gerestan, and huntigan, and fuglian, and fiscian, and his on gehwilce wisan to þere *lænan* tilian, ægþær ge on se ge on lande, oð þone fyrst þe he *bocland* and *æce* yrfe þurh his hlafordes miltse geearnige. swa gedo se weliga gifola, se ðe egðer wilt ge þissa *lænena* stoclife ge þara *ecena* hama.[1]

But the one who taught me . . . may bring it about that I live more comfortably both in this temporary place on the road while I occupy this world, and also in that eternal home . . . It is no surprise that we work hard with such materials both in transporting them and building with them: it pleases everyone who has built a home, as his lord's tenant and with his help, to be there sometimes, and to hunt and hawk and fish and in every way to cultivate his rented property, sea and soil, until the time that he may acquire, through his lord's generosity, bookland and a permanent heritage: the rich benefactor can do this, since he has under his control temporary houses and eternal homes.

King Alfred, born teacher that he is, is using the terms *bocland*, land granted by written charter as an inheritance in perpetuity, and *lænland*, land granted for the duration of one or more lifetimes, as images for eternal life and mortal life. He could scarcely have used such images unless he were confident that they would be instantly understood, and it is arguable that it was precisely this practical distinction between two forms of land tenure that gave rise to the regular use of *læne* in poetic and homiletic antithesis to *ece*. Earth is *lænland*, heaven is *bocland*, the country guaranteed by no less a charter than the gospels. In Modern English, gospel and charter are not interchangeable words, but in Old English *boc* could be used equally for either. The gospels are *feower Cristes bec* 'the four books of Christ', but *boc* also regularly glosses Latin *cartula* 'charter'.

John Mitchell Kemble pointed out as early as 1849 the link between the concepts *lænland* and *læne*. In a discussion of *lænland* he adds the footnote:

The transitory possessions of this life were often so described, in reference to the Almighty: 'ða æhta ðe him God alæned hæfð'.[2]

The quotation is from the tenth-century will of Æthelric, who 'grants' to his widow 'those possessions which God has lent him' – though we may note that he 'grants' them for her lifetime only. Similarly, in the poem *Genesis*, what Adam forfeits is (consecutively) *læn godes, ælmihtiges gife* and *heofonrices geweald* 'the loan of God, the gift of the Almighty, possession of the kingdom of Heaven'. The last of these is transient in the sense that the right of access to it may be restricted or conditional. And clearly even Paradise was *lænland*.

It is this kind of background that allows us to make sense of the distinctions between *læne* and *ece* in a poem such as *The Seafarer*. The poet draws a careful distinction between life on earth (*læne*), life after death (*ece*), and the voyage or voyages of his persona which represent rejection of all secular pleasures and values of the one in search for the other. In savage paradox *lif on londe* 'life on land/life on earth' is not merely *læne* but *deade* 'dead'. The poet then tells us of his disbelief in the permanence of any *eorðwelan*, and it is clear from the context that 'the riches of earth' are a synonym for life itself. Three words which normally denote earthly well-being are wrenched into use for the eternal: *ecan lifes blæd / dream mid dugeþum* 'the splendour of eternal life, joy among heroes' (?'joy in the courts'). Seven lines later the same words reappear in their normal role to underline the abnormality of their use earlier:

> Gedroren is þeos duguð eal,   dreamas sind gewitene, . . .
> Blæd is gehnæged   (86–8)

All these heroes have gone, joys departed . . . Splendour declined.

The demonstrative here and in the intervening lines is stressed as a reminder to the reader of the distinction between transient and eternal *dream, duguð* and *blæd*.

The things that are *læne* are divisible into three: life itself, property and happiness. The first is a single entity, the other two composite. The poet of *The Wanderer* says:

Her bið feoh læne,   her bið freond læne,
her bið mon læne,   her bið mæg læne   (108–9)

which, summarized rather than translated, tells us that property, friend, man and kinsman are all 'on loan' or transient. The third, *mon*, probably refers to self, the implication being that one's own life is merely lent to one, while the necessarily impermanent nature of friendship and kinship ties is one theme of *The Wanderer* throughout. Since people may outlive all those they love, the only rational course of action is to transfer their affections to the undying, to seek *frofre to Fæder on heofonum* 'consolation from the Heavenly Father'. It is customary to cite in this context the parallel text from the Old Icelandic eddic poem *Hávamál*, which offers the same wisdom in a pagan and secular context:

Deyr fé,
deyja frændr,
deyr sjálfr it sama.[3]

It is somewhat simpler: 'cattle die, kin die, one's self dies', followed by the reminder that the one thing that does not die is one's reputation. It contrasts transient with permanent but both are human-centred, reputation being in the hands of the living. The Old English and Old Icelandic texts are linked by thought, vocabulary and alliteration and the motif may come from common Germanic stock, but in spite of superficial similarities there is a significant difference. The message of *The Wanderer* is God-centred, not only in the poem as a whole but also in this important use of the Christian oriented concept *læne* where *Hávamál* has the straightforward verb *deyja* 'to die'. On the other hand, in *The Seafarer* there is a passage which blends, in careful contrivance, human-centred and God-centred posthumous benefits:

Forþon þæt bið eorla gehwam   æftercweþendra
lof lifgendra   lastworda betst,
þæt he gewyrce,   ær he on weg scyle,
fremum on foldan   wið feonda niþ,
deorum dædum   deofle togeanes,
þæt hine ælda bearn   æfter hergen,
ond his lof siþþan   lifge mid englum   (72–8)

Therefore for every man the praise of the living, of those speaking afterwards, is the best of epitaphs, in that he should bring it about before dying, by actions on earth against the hostility of enemies, by valiant deeds against the devil, that the children of men should afterwards praise him and his glory live then with the angels.

The praise of the living clearly includes heavenly and earthly voices. The two lines which speak of actions on earth carefully balance human activity against human foe with spiritual battle against the infernal. The following two lines, equally impartially, balance rewards in reputation among the children of men and among angels. Anthropologists who tell us of shame cultures and guilt cultures might define the obsession with reputation among one's fellow-men as exemplifying the former, reliance on the judgement of God rather than one's peers as the latter. For the Anglo-Saxons, having inherited one set of values through secular Germanic thought and acquired another through Christian Latin teaching, the one does not preclude the other. Milton, some centuries later, had a similar experience. He also put the two side by side when he called the urge for earthly fame the 'last infirmity of noble mind' and tried instead to concentrate only on 'the perfect witness of all-judging Jove'. The poet of *The Seafarer*, in combining two traditions, the heroic – if we may so define it, preoccupation with survival of honour after loss of life – and the Christian hope for security of tenure in Heaven, is perceiving transience on two levels, or, at any rate, as contrasted with two types of permanence. The fighters in the tenth-century poem *The Battle of Maldon* by contrast, though Christian enough to call the Vikings 'heathens', express their thoughts mainly in terms of the human wavelength – what people will say about them. Their attitude to the nature of immortality has some justification in that a millennium later we are still reading the poem and accepting the poet's judgements on individual heroes and cowards, those who followed their leader's exhortation to achieve fame, *dom gefeohtan*, by fighting the enemy, who preferred death in battle to the long-lasting shame of riding home *hlafordleas* 'lordless', and those on the other hand who saved their lives at the expense of their name. The cheerful secular courage of the former is certainly closer to the teaching of *Hávamál* (as would doubtless have been that of their opponents) than of *The Wanderer*.

What we may loosely call the Germanic or heroic or secular perception of immortality in this period is the survival of personal reputation. It is narrowed to the individual. But Anglo-Saxon poets were demonstrably well-read in a range of literatures and they have a wider perspective. Elegiac poets could find plenty to muse on in the Bible alone, whether their thoughts on transience entailed not putting trust in treasures of earth 'where moth and rust doth corrupt', or comparing the life of man to the briefly blossoming flowers of the field. Some scholars have seen in certain elegiac poems direct borrowing from parts of the Bible. But our earliest known Anglo-Saxon poets were educated in classical as well as biblical traditions and it is clear that they enjoyed the intellectual challenge and the emotional and cultural riches which their reading brought them. We know that Bede could compose poetry in the vernacular but it was not a

skill which he himself valued and apart from his *Death-Song*, preserved
out of reverence for Bede rather than for composition in a barbarian
dialect, none survives. His hymns and epitaphs in Latin do, as does his *De
arte metrica*. Boniface and his circle, especially Lull and some of his
contemporaries, were eager in the practice and understanding of Latin
metres. Aldhelm and Alcuin probably felt undressed without a quill in their
hands. But among these it is Alcuin whose poems deal most directly and
gracefully with the theme of mortality, and who seems closest to the lyric
and elegiac poems of late antiquity. In his prose letters Alcuin advises the
love of eternal not perishable wealth: *Redemptio uiri proprie diuitie* and
amemus eterna et non peritura 'redemption is man's true wealth' and 'let us
love the eternal not the transient'.[4] Elsewhere he reminds his correspondents that we are stewards not owners of earthly goods, thoughts which
can easily be traced back to patristic theology and exposition.

For the influences on Alcuin's poetry we do not need to look far. He
himself tells us what manuscripts were in York's ecclesiastical library in
the eighth century and this must be considered a list of his own reading.
He names several poets, one of them being the sixth-century poet
Venantius Fortunatus, for whom Alcuin's own courteous epigram shows
particular affection. But there also were Virgil, Arator and Boethius, to
name obvious influences. And of course the library, in addition to the
works of poets and philosophers, held also the tomes of the great
theologians with their sights always on eternity and their rejection of the
world, the flesh and the devil.

Venantius, a Christian, was as happy to chant Virgil to himself for
recreation as the psalms. Other early Christian Latin poets could not rid
their minds of the words and cadences of their pagan predecessors
however much their Christian rationality urged them to do so. The
Anglo-Saxons similarly had a poetic and cultural inheritance which did
not disappear because of Christian-educated literary sensibilities. But
whether we are talking about poets writing in Latin or the vernaculars, in
England of the eighth century onwards or Europe in the sixth, one link
between them is the anguished affection with which a Christian poet
regards those lovely things of the world that the preacher tells him to
despise. Isidore is often cited as the source of the so-called *ubi sunt*
passages in Old English elegy. Certainly Isidore was known to the
Anglo-Saxons and certainly his heavyweight *Dic ubi sunt reges? ubi
principes? ubi imperatores?* 'where are the kings, the chieftains, the
emperors?' etc. etc. can be seen as one source for *The Seafarer*'s

> nearon nu cyningas   ne caseras
> ne goldgiefan   swylce iu wæron   (82–3)

There are now no kings nor cæsars, nor gold-givers such as there were.

But the poet goes on to recall their splendour with a sense of love and loss, which is far closer to the grieving tone of Venantius than the pompous one of Isidore.

Seventh-century English scholars such as Bede and Aldhelm were well-known to later generations of Anglo-Saxons, eighth-century writers perhaps less so. I do not know of any Old English translation of Alcuin's poetry, but still it is barely imaginable that it was unknown and without influence. In the elegiac vein his greatest tour de force is his lament over the Viking attack on Lindisfarne. It is his letters home rather than his poem on this event which are usually quoted by historians, but the poem *De clade Lindisfarnensis monasterii* deserves attention. It can be compared with Venantius's *De excidio Thoringiae* which Alcuin undoubtedly knew. Both poems are descriptions of destruction and as such are bound to have themes in common, but Alcuin is not using Venantius's poem as a model and there are no close verbal echoes. Venantius looks to Troy for comparison. Alcuin looks at Babylon, Rome and Jerusalem. Many of the themes that we find later in Old English vernacular poetry are signalled in Alcuin. The notion that since Adam's fall man is an exile on earth is the opening to Alcuin's poem, a theme we meet frequently in the literature of the period, and which may help our reading of *The Seafarer*. Alcuin begins:

> Postquam primus homo paradisi liquerat hortos
> Et miseras terras exul adibat inops . . .   (1–2)

Since first man left the gardens of Paradise and, a destitute exile, entered desolate lands . . .

The persona of *The Seafarer* is, similarly, always in exile, turning his back on loved but transient luxuries, hoping

> þæt ic feor heonan
> elþeodigra   eard gesece   (37–8)

that I, far from here, may search for the home of exiles.

Elþeodigra eard means literally 'land of foreigners', but in the context must refer to those who are foreigners on earth, citizens (at any rate *in spe*) of heaven. The poet then claims that there is no one living who 'will not always have sorrow because of his sea-journey', a statement that is manifestly nonsensical on a literal level and can only apply to the journey of the exile to his true home.

Alcuin continues with what might be termed the commonplaces of lament, that nothing earthly remains eternal, that no joy lasts. But Alcuin's poem is not commonplace. His grief for Rome is as poignant as his grief for Lindisfarne:

Roma, caput mundi, mundi decus, aurea Roma,
   Nunc remanet tantum saeva ruina tibi   (37–8)

Rome, capital of the world, glory of the world, golden Rome, now is left of you
only a wild ruin.

Having then sighed over Jerusalem he draws the expected but none the
less aching conclusion:

Sic fugit omne decus, hominis quod dextera fecit,
   Gloria seclorum sic velut umbra volat   (55–6)

So flies all wonder that man's hands have made, glory of ages flees like a shadow.

Venantius and Alcuin grieve over known places, even if not all the
victims of attack and slaughter can be identified. But one curious feature
of Old English elegiac poetry is that most of it mentions neither personal
nor place-names. (*Deor* is an exception.) These vernacular poems give the
reader no clues, or meagre ones at best, to help define the context that
produced them. *The Ruin* is unique among them in having no persona, no
'I' whose anonymous experiences are presented. It is a poem about a place
not a person, and we have no voice between us and the poet's direct
observation. Even so the absence of firm identification of this place has
caused much controversy. This used to be about whether the ruin was the
Roman city of Bath or some other Roman site. Now it is about whether
we are contemplating an actual place or an allegorical one, Bath, as one
critic has asked, or Babylon? In the following discussion I assume the
actual. It is a short poem, a mere 50 lines, and since the Exeter Book is
damaged at this point we do not even have a complete text. But more
clearly than any other of the elegies it focuses on the transient by focusing
on the past, and especially the contrast between past and present.

In the opening lines we have conflicting tenses and responses. The
masonry is both wonderful and decaying. Events have shattered it but it is
still *enta geweorc* 'the work of giants'. The roof is picked out as a
scurbeorg 'protection against storms' but that it is failing in its protective
function is signalled by the accompanying adjective *sceard* 'gaping'. The
poet moves from contemplation of the ruin to contemplation of the
builders, held in the grip of earth for a hundred generations. But the walls
themselves, lichen-covered, have known kingdom after kingdom.

We are much accustomed to see in Anglo-Saxon literature the influence
of other literatures. But we should also take into account visual reminders
of mortality. Anglo-Saxons mostly built in timber, and even when they
built in stone they did not rival Roman architecture. How fully any
Roman site was occupied in the days of early Anglo-Saxon settlement is
still under dispute by Romano-British historians, but even so there must

have been a fantastic number of ghost-towns or ghost-villas with no neat National Trust lawns surrounding them. Those of us who saw the Anglo-Saxon skeletons buried among the fallen pillars of Roman York under the present Minster were given a sharpened awareness of how the *enta geweorc* was perceived. But buildings are silent witnesses except for occasional memorial inscriptions or grafitti, and the poet of *The Ruin* can give no names to builders, rulers or citizens. He does, however, visualize these magnificent and nameless inhabitants:

> þær iu beorn monig
> glædmod and goldbeorht   gleoma gefrætwed,
> wlonc ond wingal   wighyrstum scan;
> seah on sinc, on sylfor,   on searogimmas,
> on ead, on æht,   on eorcanstan,
> on þas beorhtan burg   bradan rices   (32–7)

where once many a man bright in mood, bright with gold, glittering, proud, happy from wine-drinking, shone in his armour; he looked on treasure, on silver, on jewellery, on wealth, on property, on pearls, on this bright stronghold of the broad kingdom.

It is impossible in translation to get all the nuances of this description, but the general tenor is clear enough. The poet tries to parallel the evident splendour of the former city with equal imagined splendour of life within it. And in evoking past splendour he necessarily evokes too the passing of time between his vision and present reality.

As *The Ruin* is presented in the only surviving text there is no overt Christian comment. We are not formally invited to look at the transient in the light of the eternal. The 'ruined hall topos' may have been a commonplace, but this particular poet is as much impressed by achievement as musing on mortality and it is the tension between these two responses that differentiates *The Ruin* from either the lament of Venantius Fortunatus over the collapsed Thuringian roofs and palaces or that of Alcuin over Lindisfarne's altar. The impersonal quality of the poem must lie in the fact that as a traveller in an antique land the poet looks on an alien civilization. When we meet the 'ruined hall topos' in *Beowulf* and *The Wanderer*, it is drawn into the context of Germanic tribal loss.

The poet of *The Wanderer* may, like the poet of *The Ruin*, be contemplating Roman architecture. The *weal wundrum heah   wyrmlicum fah* 'a marvellous high wall decorated with serpent shapes', has certainly suggested Roman stone bas-relief to one editor. But ruins, for this poet, only serve to call up thoughts of death. His tenses move between past and implied future:

Ongietan sceal gleaw hæle   hu gæstlic bið,
þonne ealre þisse worulde wela   weste stondeð   (73–4)

The wise man naturally perceives how ghostly it will be when all the rich places of
this world lie deserted.

He looks at the buildings, not as the other poet did in order to imagine the
brilliance of life within them, but to catalogue modes of death:

> sumne se hara wulf
> deaðe gedælde,   sumne dreorighleor
> in eorðscræfe   eorl gehydde   (82–4)

The grey wolf tore one apart as he died; another by a grieving man was hidden in a
hole in the ground.

This is a universal, not a specific, description of death in battle. (From the
Anglo-Saxon viewpoint the lurking wolf is de rigueur.) But the poet moves
on to specify loss in terms which would naturally suggest to the Anglo-
Saxon audience their own culture. When he asks where is the treasure-
giver or where are the joys of the hall he is not inviting them to take a
historical perspective as the poet of *The Ruin* did. He uses the remnants of
a Roman past to focus on transience and mortality then shifts to emotive
rhetoric evoking the same themes within a local context. His purpose is to
demonstrate the inadequacy of the earthly in the light of the eternal. In this
he is much closer to Alcuin than the poet of *The Ruin*. Alcuin focused on
the eternal by describing the destruction of those named cities that had
been the pride of the known world. The vernacular poet names nothing,
but the effect is there:

> Yðde swa þisne eardgeard   ælda scyppend
> oþþæt burgwara   breahtma lease
> eald enta geweorc   idlu stodon   (85–7)

So the Creator of men destroyed this place until, empty of sounds and citizens, the
old works of the giants stood desolate.

With the same technique of oxymoron whereby the poet of *The Ruin*
focused on the non-roofly quality of the roofs, so this poet deliberately
calls God *scyppend* in the moment of describing his destructive powers.

Turning to the same topos in *Beowulf* we find it treated differently yet
again. There are two passages commonly called 'elegiac'. In the shorter
one the relevant lines end an account of a man mourning his son's death.
They are not entirely appropriate to the restricted context, suggesting loss
on a tribal rather than an individual scale. The poet is already anticipating
the destruction of the Geats, which, he implies, will follow his hero's
death:

Gesyhð sorhcearig   on his suna bure
winsele westne,   windge reste
reote berofene.   Ridend swefað,
hæleð in hoðman;   nis þær hearpan sweg,
gomen in geardum,   swylce ðær iu wæron   (2455–9)

He looks, bitterly sorrowful, on his son's home, the empty wine-hall, the
wind-swept resting-place robbed of delight. The riders sleep, the young men in
their graves; there is no music of the harp, no pleasure in the courts such as used to
be.

This is a rhetorical pattern we find often enough in Old English poetry,
description by negatives. Present misery is defined as absence of the joys of
the hall. Desolation is evoked by contrast. It is as far as it can be from the
triumphant note of *The Ruin* even though both poets are ostensibly
engaged in the same activity – contemplating deserted buildings and
contrasting their present with their past.

The other elegiac passage in *Beowulf* has, with the usual imaginative
brilliance of editors, been named 'The lay of the last survivor'. The action
that calls out the 'ruined hall topos' is the burial of a treasure-hoard by
one who believes himself to be the last of his tribe. General desolation is
therefore more appropriate in this context. The poet moves from the
specific thoughts associated with the treasure to the empty hall, from the
unpolished cups and unwielded swords to,

                         Næs hearpan wyn,
        gomen gleobeames,   ne god hafoc
        geond sæl swingeð,   ne se swifta mearh
        burhstede beateð   (2262–5)

There was no joy of the harp, pleasure of music, no good hawk winging through
the hall, no swift horse tramping the courtyard.

The similarity with the earlier quotation is obvious, and, equally obviously, there is not in either passage any immediate suggestion of eternal
benefit to be set against mortal loss. The poet of *The Wanderer* and Alcuin
are overt in their antitheses. For Alcuin the raid on Lindisfarne prompted
the exhortation:

        Quapropter potius caelestia semper amemus
        Et mansura polo, quam peritura solo   (119–20)

Therefore let us always love heavenly and abiding things rather than the dying
ones of earth.

The persona of *The Wanderer* similarly found no reason, in pondering
matters of this world, why his mind does not grow dark, and could only

lighten it by looking towards heaven. But if these thoughts are in the *Beowulf*-poet's mind (as indeed many readers would claim) they are less transparent. This is, of course, reasonable in one sense in that, however Christian the poet, his speakers in both elegiac passages are sited in the pagan past. However, since he allows his pagan king Hrothgar to speak of God, the absence of religious consolation here may well be deliberate.

The poet of *Deor* has, among vernacular poets, possibly the most philosophical approach to the temporary nature of earthly experience, which is one reason why scholars have read into so short a poem the influence of Boethius. Like the *Beowulf*-poet he sets his thoughts within the context of the Germanic past, a past, for both poets, in which legend and history merge. The lay-out of *Deor* in the manuscript gives the effect of a stanzaic poem (as opposed to the continuous alliterative long line elsewhere). The scribe divides it into six sections, beginning each with an ornamental initial and ending each with the statement *þæs ofer eode þisses swa mæg* 'that came to an end, perhaps this will too'. As this moral suggests, what we have here – in contrast to all the poems we have considered so far – is a meditation on the transient nature of earthly unhappiness. The consolation which the poet offers is not that of eternal bliss, but the fact of transience itself. In the first five sections he specifies well-known people, alludes to their misfortunes (or those of others in connection with them) in at most six lines, then offers his bleakly rational comfort. Nothing here about an everlasting future of song and banqueting!

Again, in contrast to the *Beowulf*-poet's technique of evoking desolation by describing lost pleasures, the *Deor*-poet accumulates the vocabulary of suffering. In the first four lines he alludes to Welund's *wræc*, *earfoð*, *sorg*, *longað*, *wea* and *wintercealdu wræce*: 'persecution', 'hardship', 'sorrow', 'longing', 'misery' and 'winter-cold suffering'. He then takes two lines to describe the actions that caused these, imprisonment and deliberate crippling. His language would be opaque to the modern reader if we did not know enough of Welund's story from elsewhere to feel fairly confident that the reference to Welund's enemy placing him in 'supple sinew-bonds' refers to the cutting of his sinews as an act of mutilation. The poet expects us to know enough about all his characters to fill in background for ourselves (cf. above, pp. 97–8). This may have been a valid assumption for his original audience. It is not always so for us and perhaps we miss many of his subtleties. The general progression is, however, clear. After four sections on the varied sufferings of individuals the poet moves to the reign of Eormanric (Ermanaric) and in a fine compression of ideas shows us the effects of a tyrant's rule. The standard half-line of praise for a good ruler – *þæt wæs god cyning* 'he was a good king' – is rewritten for the villain as *þæt wæs grim cyning*, the adjective 'savage' replacing 'good'. Instead of suitable ideas of government he had *wylfen geþoht* 'wolfish thought', the wolf, associated with outlawry, being the opposite of social order. Instead of inspiring proper loyalty in a society where the bond between lord and retainer was supreme,

> Sæt secg monig   sorgum gebunden,
> wean on wenan,   wyscte geneahhe
> þæt þæs cynerices   ofercumen wære   (24–6)

many a man sat, bound by suffering, expecting sorrow: he often wished for the overthrow of that kingdom.

The poet has moved from perception of transience in relation to the individual to analysis of wider effects. He and we know of the final outcome of battles between Goths and Huns and it follows that those who endured the tyranny had their wishes eventually fulfilled. The 'ruined hall topos' might here be replaced by the 'vanished empire topos' except that this poet leaves much to the educated imagination.

In his final section the poet moves to an overtly Christian perspective. The unhappy man – *sorgcearig* – finds, like the persona of *The Wanderer*, that his mind grows dark under the contemplation of earthly grief:

> sylfum þinceð
> þæt sy endeleas   earfoða dæl   (29–30)

it seems to him that his share of hardships is endless.

Yet the poet denies this explicit statement by juxtaposing the words *endeleas* and *dæl*. The mere fact of something being a 'division' or 'share' implies that it is finite and contained, and – as he has already demonstrated – everyone's share of misery, however harsh or prolonged, passes eventually. He reminds his *sorgcearig* man that all fate and change are under the control of a wise God, the distributor of fortune and misfortune alike.

As a consolation it is still bleak. But the comfort of the message must be that suffering (as well as being transient) is not random, a comfort that can only help those whose trust in the wisdom of God is secure. It is possible that the poet, as well as assuming knowledge of Germanic history and legend, assumes in his readers a similar grasp of Boethian philosophy to that of recent interpreters of *Deor*. But it is also possible that it would have seemed to him a simple truism of Christian thought that in a world created by a wise God suffering must have a purpose, and those who endure know, like the martyrs, that they are part of the divine pattern. As Alcuin said in honour of Lindisfarne's dead:

> Per gladios, mortes, pestes, per tela, per ignes,
> Martyrio sancti regna beata petunt   (223–4)

Through swords, deaths, plagues, through spears, through fires, the saints, in martyrdom, look for the blessed lands.

A passage in the *Anglo-Saxon Chronicle*, rhythmic enough in its antitheses to be sometimes printed as poetry, says of the martyrdom in AD 1011 of Ælfheah, archbishop of Canterbury,

Wæs ða ræpling se þe ær wæs Angelcynnes heafod ond Cristendomes. Þær man mihte þa geseon earmðe þær man ær geseah blisse on þære ærman byrig þanon us com ærest Cristendom ond blisse for Gode ond for worulde.[5]

He was then a prisoner, he who had been the head of England and of Christendom. There could be seen misery where once was seen joy in that sad city from which first came to us Christianity and joy in God and the world.

The writer of the *Chronicle*, a couple of hundred years later than Alcuin, still sees the ironic and subtle patterns in the alternation of earthly good and earthly ill and eventual eternal gain.

Finally, there are three 'elegiac' poems which deal with the transience of earthly happiness in the purely secular context of human relationships. They are *Wulf and Eadwacer*, *The Wife's Lament* and *The Husband's Message*. Though I treat these as secular, readers should be warned that other scholars have seen two of them as Christian allegories, and there are probably as many interpretations of *The Wife's Lament* as there are readers of it. Of all the poems discussed, *The Husband's Message* stands out as the only one with an apparently happy ending in human and earthly terms. The main protagonist, whether one calls him husband or lover, has been separated from the woman promised to him. Like the unhappy characters in *Deor* he has had his share of suffering. In *Deor* it is not always clear whether suffering ended only when life itself ended, or whether there was a recompense, a turn of Fortune's wheel, during life. It has been suggested that Welund's recompense was his revenge, that Beadohild's compensation for rape was to become mother of a hero. (Feminist critics might not see it that way.) But many of Eormanric's victims must have died before they could see their wishes fulfilled. We are told, however, that the protagonist of *The Husband's Message* has overcome suffering. The tone is jubilant. The reversal of fortune is largely attributed, in a somewhat sketchy plot, to his own efforts. We are given to understand that he was driven from home by feud, went into exile alone, but has in his new country established himself as a lord with all the good things that accompany such prosperity – gold, land, followers. His confidence does not seem to be shaken by any reflections on the transience of such. But the reader needs to be reflective. The man looks with equal confidence to the woman's arrival, reminding her of the vows that bind them. But in telling her to let no-one living hinder her from the journey, he alerts us to the possibility of hindrance and therefore failure. And though he does not thank the Almighty for his present achievements he recognizes, if his messenger reports him correctly, that their union is within god's gift:

> þonne inc geunne   alwaldend god,
> <þæt git> ætsomne   siþþan motan
> secgum ond gesiþum   <sinc brytnian>   (32–4)

Then Almighty God may grant to you both that the two of you together may share out treasure among men and comrades.

Without the background knowledge of Anglo-Saxon awareness of transience it would be easy to take this poem at face value. As it is, given a sentence which tells us that the man has all he wants if he may also obtain his bride, we inevitably respond to the conditional as a warning signal.

The Wife's Lament and Wulf and Eadwacer present the themes of loss, suffering and impermanence of human ties through a woman's voice. Both voices tell us of estrangement or separation from loved ones. Neither poem offers consolation in earthly or eternal terms. The implications of The Wife's Lament are that only death will end sorrow. She speaks of her wretchedness in woruldrice 'the earthly kingdom', tells us that,

>   ic æfre ne mæg
> þære modceare   minre gerestan,
> ne ealles þæs longaþes   þe mec on þissum life begeat   (39–41)

I can never rest from my sorrow, nor from all the longing that troubles me in this life.

Her final comment – that those are always unhappy who endure longing for a loved one – would be equally appropriate to the woman in Wulf and Eadwacer. In its stoicism it has some affinities with Deor, but it lacks any perspective beyond the immediacy of suffering. What these poems have in common with the ones considered earlier is the focus on transience. What they lack is the theological or philosophical dimension.

The preoccupation with transience is not one which the twentieth century comprehends very readily. The average undergraduate meeting Anglo-Saxon intimations of mortality is probably anticipating something like another seventy years of life in this world before facing the next. But one recent excavator of an Anglo-Saxon cemetery estimates the life expectancy of the Anglo-Saxon male as 32 years, of the female as 30.5 years. Recent statistics from a Kentish cemetery suggest a life expectancy into the late thirties, but demonstrate a peak mortality rate in the teens and early twenties. Infant mortality, less easy to demonstrate from the archaeological evidence, would be, inevitably, high. It is not surprising that Anglo-Saxon thinkers occupied themselves with meditations on that which might endure a little longer. They knew, with the poet of *The Seafarer*, that:

adl oþþe yldo   oþþe ecghete
fægum fromweardum   feorh oðþringeð   (70–1)

disease or age or violence crush life from the doomed

The poet of *The Fates of Men* has a more depressing list. People may die in the wolf's jaws, they may starve, be wrecked at sea, be killed by spear or sword in private quarrel or battle. They may fall from trees, be executed on the gallows or burned to death. The writers of Anglo-Saxon medical texts remind us of the appalling range of illness and accident that their contemporaries suffered. The students of excavated bones demonstrate the prevalence of arthritic complaints. For many their day-to-day existence must have been constant endurance of physical pain.

Yet physical suffering is not what the poems are about. The preoccupation is with emotional deprivation, the loss of those things which put joy into life, usually expressed in terms of human relationships. The poet of *The Dream of the Rood* waits with longing for heaven because,

Nah ic ricra feala
freonda on foldan,   ac hie forð heonon
gewiton of worulde dreamum,   sohton him wuldres cyning;
lifiað nu on heofenum   mid heahfædere   (131–4)

I have scarcely any powerful friends on earth: they went from here, left the joys of this world, sought the king of glory. They live now in heaven with the high father.

The friends that he has lost have found new and imperishable relationships. It is no accident that the poet chooses the words 'king' and 'father' for God. The closest bonds in Anglo-Saxon society were the ties of lordship and kinship. One of the commonest compounds for a lord places equal stress on the lordship and friendship elements of the relationship, *winedryhten* 'friend-lord'. One of the commonest compounds for a comrade in the hall is similarly dual in its emphasis, *winemæg* 'friend-kin'. When the poet tells us of his desire to join *Dryhtnes folc / geseted to symle* 'the people of the lord, sitting at the feast' it is clear that he visualizes heaven as a re-creation of the joys of the hall, the reciprocal love between lord, friends and kin established in an enduring context. The persona of *The Wanderer*, having lost the joys of the hall, foolishly attempted to find them again on earth:

sohte sele dreorig   sinces bryttan,
hwær ic feor oþþe neah   findan meahte
þone þe in meoduhealle   min mine wisse
oþþe mec freondleasne   frefran wolde . . .   (25–8)

Desolate without a hall, I sought a giver of treasure, where I could find, near or far, one who in the mead hall would show love for me, or would comfort me, friendless.

By the end of the poem he too finds the only security in the eternal. It should come as no surprise that the vision of the eternal is the re-creation and continuation of what has seemed to be the best of earth.

For the poet Cynewulf this life was a flickering torch. The common stock of poetic vocabulary reiterates the ephemeral nature of human existence. The body is only a *flæschama*, a 'flesh-garment', to be laid aside. The mind or heart or spirit is treasure locked in a *bancofa*, a 'box of bone'. The image links the physical reality of the rib-cage with the idea of carved and ornamented artifacts like the whale-bone Franks Casket. Such boxes intended for the safe-keeping of secular or spiritual treasure, jewellery or relics, were, however beautiful, of less value than their contents. But the image is sometimes less of safe-keeping than of imprisonment, the idea of a bone cage or prison, from which the spirit will be released into freedom. Hope of eternity often comes across as a longing for just such release. The poet of *The Seafarer* anticipates his voyage to Heaven in the following terms:

For þon nu min hyge hweorfeð   ofer hreþerlocan,
min modsefa   mid mereflode
ofer hwæles eþel   hweorfeð wide,
eorþan sceatas,   cymeð eft to me
gifre ond grædig   (58–62)

And so my thought now passes beyond the locked place of my breast, my soul with the sea-tide travels far over the whale's homeland, the surfaces of earth: it comes back to me eager and ready.

Eager and ready, as we shortly see, for *Dryhtnes dreamas*, 'the joys of the Lord'.

Bede's story of a pagan Northumbrian for whom this life was comparable with the flight of a sparrow through a warm and lighted room has been rehearsed often enough (e.g. above, pp. 6, 82 and 127). For him as for Bede the moral was that in pagan terms the contrast with this warmth and comfort was darkness, winter and storm from which the sparrow (or, by implication, the human soul) came and to which it returned. The promise of Christianity was, at any rate for the righteous, of a life after death that surpassed in brilliance anything experienced on earth. For the

Anglo-Saxons the hope of a heaven filled with everlasting joy, feasting and music must have been implicit in Christ's promise: *On mines Fæder huse synt manega eardungstowa* . . . *ic fare and wylle eow eardungstowe gearwian* – 'in my Father's house are many mansions. I go to prepare a place for you.'

1 *King Alfred's Version of St Augustine's 'Soliloquies'*, ed. T. A. Carnicelli (Cambridge, MA, 1969), pp. 47–8 [italics mine].
2 J. M. Kemble, *The Saxons in England*, 2 vols. (London, 1849) I, 310, n. 3. The will of Æthelric is ptd *Anglo-Saxon Wills*, ed. and trans. D. Whitelock (Cambridge, 1930), pp. 42–3.
3 *Hávamál*, ed. D. A. H. Evans (London, 1986), p. 54; trans. W. H. Auden and P. B. Taylor, *Norse Poems* (London, 1981), p. 156.
4 From Alcuin's letter to Bishop Higbald and an unknown community (see above, p. 21, n. 9), ptd *Two Alcuin Letter-Books*, ed. C. Chase (Toronto, 1975), p. 52; trans. S. Allott, *Alcuin of York* (York, 1974), p. 37. Alcuin's poems are ptd Monumenta Germaniae Historica, Poetae Latini Aevi Carolini I (Berlin, 1881); *De clade Lindisfarnensis monasterii* is trans. M. Allen and D. Calder, in *Sources & Analogues of Old English Poetry* (Cambridge, 1976), pp. 141–6.
5 *Two of the Saxon Chronicles Parallel*, ed. J. Earle and C. Plummer, 2 vols. (Oxford, 1892) I, 142; trans. D. Whitelock, *The Anglo-Saxon Chronicle* (London, 1961), p. 91.

11   Perceptions of eternity

IF in the literature of Anglo-Saxon England there are strong motifs of fatalism about life in this world and a sense of its transience, there is the equally persistent belief that this life prepares one for a more enduring life. At the end of *The Seafarer*, the speaker declares that *wyrd* ('what happens') and *meotud* (God as the ordainer of what happens) are more powerful than anyone's *gehygd* ('mind', 'thought') and concludes:

> Uton we hycgan   hwær we ham agen,
> ond þonne geþencan   hu we þider cumen,
> ond we þonne eac tilien,   þæt we to moten
> in þa ecan   eadignesse,
> þær is lif gelong   in lufan dryhtnes,
> hyht in heofonum.   Þæs sy þam halgan þonc,
> þæt he usic geweorþade,   wuldres ealdor,
> ece dryhten,   in ealle tid. Amen.   (*The Seafarer* 117–24)

Let us reflect where we may get a home and then consider how we might come to it, and then we ought also to strive so that we might come there, into the eternal blessedness, where life is dependent on the love of the Lord, hope in heaven. Thanks be to the holy one because he, the begetter of glory, honoured us, the eternal lord, throughout all time. Amen.

This present, worldly life is passing, but there is hope for a more stable and enduring life. The content of this hope and the forms it took are the subject of this chapter. We shall consider first the major thrust of early medieval eschatology, its focus upon the last judgement and the kingdom of God which the judgement will initiate. Then we may review the lesser motif of expectations concerning the state of the soul between the time of death and the day of judgement.

The theological term *eschatology* means in Greek the study of the 'last things', or the end of history as it is presently known.[1] It is, in its most fundamental sense, the expectation that God would intervene in a final and definitive way in the history of the Chosen People, perhaps by re-establishing the kingship of David, who had been anointed as Messiah. (The Greek word *christos* translates the Hebrew *messiah*, a person

190

anointed or set aside for some special role.) The early Christians recognized Jesus as the Messiah and believed that the resurrection and ascension certified the truth of this identification. In the gospels Jesus spoke of a coming time of cataclysm – of misrule by an Antichrist, of war and hardship, of cosmic disaster – that would presage the return or second coming of the Messiah and the resurrection of all the dead for judgement. Like messiahship, the resurrection of the dead was a notion that was current in Jewish circles at the time of Jesus. Because of the subjection of the Jews to foreign powers in the several centuries before and including the time of Jesus, expectation of divine intervention to re-establish the place of the Chosen People amongst the nations was politically seditious. A literature expressing these hopes of political and spiritual redemption came into being, but because espousing such ideas was so dangerous, the books tended to be both symbolic and cryptic. The prophet Ezechiel's vision of the valley of dry bones that rise and live again is both the most famous and one of the more accessible examples in the Hebrew canon of the genre, which is usually called apocalyptic literature.[2] Among the early Christian writings, eschatological notions are prominent in Paul (e.g. I Corinthians XV.35–54), in the so-called Synoptic Apocalypse (Mark XIII, Matthew XXIV–XXV, Luke XXI) and in the so-called New Testament Apocalypse or The Revelation of Saint John the Divine (to use the title it is given in the Authorized or 'King James' Version).

As time passed, expectations of an early *parousia* or return of the Christ were dashed, but not the basic hope itself. Christians saw the whole of history – 'salvation history', we have come to call it – as a piece, running from creation through the fall and the events recounted in Genesis and the other books of the Pentateuch whereby God elected and made covenants successively with such figures as Noah and Abraham and, most importantly and definitively, Moses at the time of the exodus from Egypt to the 'promised land'. Thereafter come the ages of kings and prophets, the troubled times after the fall of the kingdoms of Judah and Israel and finally the great pivotal moment, the resurrection of the Christ, which assured that God's promised victory for his people – now a new people, not simply Israel – would be effected. The Christ event gave new meaning to the events of scriptural history, which could now also be seen as presaging the events of the history of Christ. And the present time is the age of waiting for the final turning point or consummation (the *parousia*, resurrection and last judgement), sometimes spoken of as the millennium or the last of six thousand-year ages of history before the seventh and eternal age. (The 'thousand' years were taken, as an earlier essay has reported, to be round numbers signifying a long time, not as denoting literal, calendrical time (see above, pp. 166–8)). The ages, obviously, are analogous with the days of creation and the post-millennial era with the seventh-day rest. Eschatology (the term is a creation of modern theologians, although *ta eschata*, 'the last things', is of some antiquity) is the part of theology that deals with the ultimate hopes of the Christian community; and in the theology of the Early Middle Ages and (hence) Anglo-Saxon England it is a very central part of doctrine.

It is difficult to select just one or two sources to illustrate discussions of eschatology in Old English literature, for there are many interesting possibilities. The anonymous sermons of the Blickling and Vercelli manuscripts, for example, provide a number of interesting witnesses, some of them dependent on apocryphal writings (i.e. early Christian writings that were not accepted into the official canon of the New Testament but were often attributed to New Testament authors or other apostolic figures).[3] A thorough survey would of necessity touch on such exegetical treatments of apocalyptic passages in scripture as can be found in Bede's commentaries on the Gospel of Luke and the Apocalypse.[4] Here we must be contented with two samples in the verse literature, both Old English adaptations from Latin poems attributed to Bede, and references to important sermons of Abbot Ælfric of Eynsham. Although all of these texts were written in the form in which we now know them within a half century of the year 1000, the poems at least adapt sources about three centuries older.

The poem called *The Judgement Day II* (to distinguish it from another poem of similar subject in the Exeter Book), translates a rather shorter poem by Bede, *De die iudicii*.[5] The speaker in the poem is found in a sheltered grove with pleasant waterways. But a threatening sky belies his pleasant surroundings, reflecting or causing distress of mind. Fearful of the last judgement because of his sins, and also mindful of the contrasting futures of the blessed and the wretched, the speaker mournfully begins his speech, which continues the penitential mood of the opening passage and recalls the repentant thief on the cross next to Jesus's who quickly won salvation. Forgiveness is readily available now, but the day of judgement is coming when one will no longer be able to repent but must give an accounting for the manner of his or her life. A description of the events of the signs of the last times follows: earthquake and storm, falling stars and darkened sun and moon.

> Eac þonne cumað hider   ufon of heofone
> deaðbeacnigende tacn,   bregað þa earman;
> þonne cumað upplice   eoredheapas,
> stiþmægen astyred,   styllað embutan
> eal engla werod,   ecne behlænað,
> ðone mæran metod   mihte and þrymme.
> Sitt þonne sigelbeorht   swegles brytta

on heahsetle,   helme beweorðod.
We beoð færinga   him beforan brohte,
æghwanum cumene   to his ansyne
þæt gehwylc underfo
dom be his dædum   æt drihtne sylfum.   (111–22)

Then also from heaven on high will come hither signs indicating death; they will terrify the wretched; and then come the heavenly host, a strong, excited troop; they will leap about, the entire band of angels, surround the eternal one, the glorious creator with might and majesty. Then will the victorious author of the heavens sit on the throne, adorned with his crown. Woe be to those forthwith brought before him, coming from all quarters before his countenance so that each might receive judgement according to deeds from the Lord himself.

There is a description of the purging and punishing fire that surges throughout the creation. The punishment causes great suffering; all the solaces and joys of earthly life and company are gone. But for those judged worthy, now decked with flowers, there is bliss in the realm of heaven. There is no hardship in denial and right-doing in this world if one has in mind the state of the blessed in the kingdom.

The Judgement Day II is a reflection on the last judgement from the point of view of the penitent. It is consequently a fairly stark and foreboding picture of the last times with primary emphasis upon the depiction of the consequences of leading a less than upright life in the world, although it is clearly not from the point of view of a profligate person but of a human with deep moral sensitivity and great humility. Because of its purpose as a warning to those living this present life it tends to stress punishment and reward, not to describe the events of the last times.

More narrative is the Exeter Book poem known as *Christ III* or *Doomsday*,[6] which paraphrases and embellishes the gospel accounts of the last times in ways that were characteristic of the period. It greatly expands its principal source, an alphabetical verse of twenty-three couplets that is attributed to Bede. *Christ III* begins with no introductory ceremony, but with a simile drawn from the gospels and introduced almost as abruptly as the day of doom itself:

Ðonne mid fere   foldbuende
se micla dæg   meahtan dryhtnes
æt midre niht   mægne bihlæmeð,
scire gesceafte,   swa oft sceaða fæcne,
þeof þristlice,   þe on þystre fareð,
on sweartre niht,   sorglease hæleð
semninga forfehð   slæpe gebundne,
eorlas ungearwe   yfles genægeð.   (867–74)

Then with sudden calamity for earth-dwellers the great day of the mighty Lord at midnight will surprise with might the bright creation, as often the treacherous robber, bold thief, who travels in shadows, in the dark night, suddenly seizes carefree heroes sound asleep, accosts unready men with evil.

God's host assembles, the trumpet is sounded and the dead, raised for judgement, quake with fear. Christ (called both creator and Son of God) approaches Mount Sion with the splendour of the sun, a welcome sight to the blessed among those raised but dreadful to the sinful. Fire precedes the judge, with trumpets and a great din, as the world is consumed. As judge and host assemble on the mount, the poet once more stresses that for the blessed it is a glorious and welcome sight but for others quite the reverse.

> Daga egeslicast
> weorþeð in worulde,   þonne wuldorcyning
> þurh þrym þreað   þeoda gehwylce,
> hateð arisan   reordberende
> of foldgrafum   folc anra gehwylc,
> cuman to gemote   moncynnes gehwone.   (1021–6)

The most dreadful of days will come to pass in the world when the king of Glory through his power, will punish all nations, command human beings to arise from their earthen graves, [shall call] all people to come to the assembly, every one of humankind.

All of those raised will have bodies, will be young[7] and will bear the moral characteristics of their historical lives. 'Wel is þam þe motun / on þa grimman tide gode lician' (1079–80; 'Well is it for those who are able in that awful time to be pleasing to God').

The cross appears in the heavens; as in *The Dream of the Rood* it is seen as both the blood-stained instrument of torture and the radiant sign of victory. The multitude of raised humankind is divided, as in the gospel accounts, the good (sheep) on the right and the evil (goats) on the left. The judge addresses them separately in a long and elegant paraphrase of Matthew XXV.34–46. As the words of condemnation are spoken the accursed fall into the abyss of hell. Although theirs is a fate of non-being in which God no longer thinks of them, yet, too, they suffer eternally in heat, discomfort, torment and regret; and the audience of the poem is urged to mark this fact well. For the blessed, both angelic and human, in contrast, all is light and joy, as they sing eternally the praises of God.

And so, the poet concludes, it is a fair and joyful thing when the blessed person dies, for death fixes one's destiny once and for all time. For on doomsday such a one is admitted to the *eðel* or 'homeland' (1639), the goal for which all the righteous have yearned and laboured.

If one wants to follow the motifs of the last judgement and the kingdom of God in a more theological context, no better sources (after Bede's Latin exegetical commentaries on the relevant portions of Luke and the Apocalypse) can be recommended than two long sermons of Abbot Ælfric which have only fairly recently been published and have not yet found a prominent place in the literature.[8]

The first roughly parallels *The Judgement Day II*. It is a sermon entitled 'De die iudicii' ('Concerning the Day of Judgement') that comments on passages in Luke XVII.20–37, Matthew XXIV.15–31 and Mark XIII.14–27. The opening section is based on Jesus's answers to questions put to him concerning the coming of doomsday. His answers stress that the coming will be sudden and unexpected, whence it is important that one be in a constant state of preparedness. The flood of Noah and the destruction of Sodom are mentioned as biblical types or anticipations of the judgement, and it is said that it will be possible for pairs of humans (two in bed, grinding meal at a mill or ploughing in a field) at the moment of the coming to be found one just and the other damned. From line 227 the sermon paraphrases Matthew and Mark's descriptions of the signs of the last times. The distressing times of the Antichrist will be the first warning that the end is near, with their wars and apostasies from Christian faith. The time of trial and martyrdom will persist for three and a half years. Then there are to be the astronomical signs: darkening of sun and moon, the falling of heavenly bodies. These will presage the slaying of Antichrist and the *parousia* of the Christ in clouds and glory. The dead are raised at the sound of the trumpet and the judgement will take place. The evil are separated from the good and consigned to the eternal fire 'þær bið wop and wanung, and toða gristbindung' (line 433: 'where there will be weeping and wailing and grinding of teeth'). For the saved, however, there is 'unasecgendlicre blisse a butan ende' (line 439: 'indescribable joy for ever and ever').

The other piece by Ælfric is the most developed treatment of eschatological concerns in Old English, the so-called 'Sermo ad Populum, in Octavis Pentecosten Dicendus' or 'Sermon for the laity, for recitation on the octave of [or seventh day following] Pentecost'. Later in this essay there will be occasion to refer to its two earlier sections; here allusion must be made to the final passage (lines 273–574) in which the doomsday motifs are summarized. Using a Latin theological treatise, the *Prognosticon futuri saeculi* of Julian, bishop of Toledo (680–90), of which Ælfric had made a Latin summary for his own use,[9] as his source rather than scripture at first hand, as was primarily the case in 'De die iudicii', the sermon rehearses the narrative of doomsday once more. Among points that are emphasized more than would be the case in an explication, say, of Matthew XXV, is the description of the bodies in which those raised from the dead will be clothed:

Ælc man hæfð swaðeah his agene lenge,
on ðære mycelnysse þe he man wæs ær,
oððe he beon sceolde, gif he fulweoxe,
se ðe on cildhade oððe samweaxen gewat.   (308–11)

Each person will have nevertheless his proper height, in the size he had before or
would have had if (in the case of death in infancy or half-grown) he had been fully
grown.

The apostles will sit about the judge on thrones of their own, and they will
be joined by 'ealla ða halgan weras ðe ðas woruld forleton' (line 356: 'all
the holy ones who renounced this world'), for Ælfric characteristically
gives a place of preference to his fellow monastics in the kingdom. Four
groups are discerned: the specially blessed (apostles and monastics) who
join in the act of judgement, the redeemed, Christians who did not
persevere in the faith and the heathen peoples. There is emphasis on the
nature of the punishment of the damned after an extended paraphrase of
the speech of the judge from Matthew XXV, and there is a description of
the dwelling place of the elect, where thoughts are visible so that there is
no cloud on the unanimity of thought in that 'an ece dæg, ðe næfre
geendað' (line 568: 'one eternal day that will never end'). Although it is in
many ways a personal account of the doomsday strongly marked by the
personality, beliefs and style of its remarkable English author, this sermon
may serve as a benchmark of orthodox early medieval beliefs concerning
the last times with which to compare other accounts in the literature.

It cannot be stressed too strongly that the events of the last times, of the
last day with its resurrection and judgement, were at the very centre of
Christian eschatology in the earliest centuries of the Christian community
and in early medieval times. That is to say, the primary concern was with
the ultimate salvation of the world, or at least of the People of God. The
raising of women and men of all ages of human history to stand judgement
together and to join (if it had been their way of life within history) in the
full and eternal life of bliss was stressed in the picture of a general or
universal resurrection and in the insistence that the beings judged would
be not just spirit or soul but embodied creatures. Thus what happens to
the individual between the moment of death and the hour of the general
resurrection was a matter of comparative indifference. Individual salvation in isolation from the rest of mankind and notions of the continuing
existence of the soul in a state of freedom from the physical body were,
though present, not at the centre of the early medieval Christian's
conception of the afterlife. It must also be stated once more that life in the
kingdom was more important than life in history, but it would not take
place without life in the world and it gave the quality of life in the world a
very great urgency and importance: the way one lived affected one's own

future, indeed; but it was more important that the way one lived was a part of the history of salvation, of the great drama of which the resurrection was the pivotal point.

From the times of the New Testament writings, however, the fact that the *parousia* and the last day were to be deferred to the end of the millennium raised the question of the state of the faithful who had died before the last day. What was the nature of their being before their resurrection at the return of Christ to inaugurate the kingdom?

Occasionally, it was said or implied that being was suspended by death. Thus in *The Phoenix*, the poet speaks of life in the world as a period in which the blessed earn or merit (*earnað*, 484) 'ecan dreames, / heofona hames mid heahcyning' (482b–3: 'everlasting joy, a home in the heavens with the high king'),

> oþþæt ende cymeð
> dogorrimes,   þonne deað nimeð,
> wiga wælgifre,   wæpnum geþryþed,
> ealdor anra gehwæs,   ond in eorþan fæðm
> snude sendeð   sawlum binumene
> læne lichoman,   þær hi longe beoð
> oð fyres cyme   foldan biþeahte.   (484–90)

until the end of his days comes, when death, murderous and armed warrior, snatches the life of everyone and quickly sends transitory bodies deprived of souls into earth's bosom, where they will remain, covered by ground, until the coming of the fire.[10]

The view that humans awaited the resurrection in a state of suspension or of sleep would be the strictly orthodox position. Whether the poet of the Old English *Phoenix* took this position is not exactly clear. He is drawing an analogy with the mythical phoenix (which he believed to be historical), which dies on its funeral pyre and rises from the ashes. Thus he speaks in this context only of the body and its fate, which is of burial and natural decay until the resurrection when it will be somehow reconstituted.

Death is defined in the early Middle Ages with remarkable unanimity as the separation of the body and soul. There is universal agreement about the fate of the body between death and the last day: it is destroyed in the natural order of things. Concerning the soul, however, there is considerable ambiguity. On this subject, perhaps it will be most convenient to return to Ælfric's sermon 'In Octavis Pentecosten', which gives the most fully developed theological treatment of the subject in the literature of Anglo-Saxon England. Then we can glance at more imaginative and problematic accounts.

According to Ælfric's account, death, which can come at any stage of human life, is of two kinds, physical and spiritual (lines 118ff.). Everyone fears the former – which all, nevertheless, experience – but not enough take adequate account of spiritual death, which comes through sin and cannot claim righteous men and women. There is a great host awaiting us beyond the present life, and the prayers of the church (especially of the monastic order) and its sacraments are a great source of strength. At the death of good persons, God's angels are present to receive the soul and lead it to its reward. Similarly, the evil have their reward; but if a sinner wanted to repent his sins and do penance, the Judge

> him wolde mildsian, þæt he moste huru
> on Domes-dæge þam deofle ætwindan   (198–9)

will be gracious to him so that he can indeed escape the devil on Doomsday.

On some occasions the prayers of the church serve to alleviate the sufferings of those who have sinned.

It is generally agreed by historians that the doctrine of purgatory was not fully developed until at least a century after the time of Ælfric. When it came into being, it was inextricably associated with the sacrament of penance and the belief that one ought after death to complete penances that had been imposed by the church but not satisfied by the time of death.[11] Ælfric and his source, Julian of Toledo, came as close as any writers before the twelfth century to an expository description of purgatory, although they did not use the term or locate a specific place for purgation within the cosmic geography.

The following section of *In Octavis Pentecosten* (lines 216–72) speaks further of the soul between death and the day of doom and is the most closely related to the matter of purgatory. Books tell us, Ælfric says, that the soul has

> þæs lichaman gelicnysse on eallum hire limum,
> and heo gefret softnysse oððe sarnysse,
> swa hwæðer swa heo on bið, be þam ðe heo geearnode ær
>
> (217–19)

the likeness of the body in all its limbs, and it experiences comfort or pain, whichever it is in, according to what it earned before.

The souls of the wicked suffer in purging fire as long as necessary for the punishment of their sins, but sometimes intercessory prayers alleviate their situation. Meanwhile the blessed are in far better condition, although they are anxious for those still living and yearn for the double joy of the kingdom after the resurrection. But they must await the perfection of the number of the saints or citizens of the kingdom.

There are numerous reflections on the afterlife between death and the last judgement in Old English literature. Many of these are visionary, if only because they describe states of existence quite beyond the ordinary. Indeed, they have their source in a passage from the Apostle Paul:

I will go on to visions and revelations of the Lord. I know a man in Christ [i.e. Paul himself, in the opinion of most scholars and of the tradition] who fourteen years ago was caught up to the third heaven – whether in the body or out of the body I do not know, God knows. And I know that this man was caught up into Paradise – whether in the body or out of the body I do not know, God knows – and he heard things that cannot be told, which man may not utter. (II Corinthians XII.1–4)

Paul's refusal to speak here was an invitation for later writers to fill in the missing content of the vision, and an apocryphal tradition which originated as early as the third century survives, known as the *Visio Sancti Pauli* or Vision of St Paul.[12] Among other things, the *Visio* describes the going of good and evil souls, led by good and evil angels, from their bodies at the time of death, their judgement and the habitations of the good and the wicked. The *Visio*, in a variety of versions, was extremely influential in the production of visionary literature and of the language and geography of the afterlife to the time of Dante. It is noteworthy that motifs from the *Visio* were especially productive of literature in the European vernacular languages, including a prose adaptation in Old English: that is, they provided material not for theologians and professional churchmen, whose language was Latin, but for the instruction of folk who did not know the learned language of the church; they provided material for popular edification.

Among the vernacular materials that sprang from the *Visio Pauli* are a number of writings in which souls speak to their bodies at the time of death or (more characteristically) at the time of a periodic return to the body. There are two versions of a Soul and Body poem in Old English in the Vercelli and Exeter books. *Soul and Body I*, the Vercelli Book version, is the longer and more complete. It is also the more instructive for our purpose here, although the question of priority between these texts is vexed.[13] All should be mindful of the soul's *sið* (2: 'journey') when death comes and sunders the bond between body and soul. But weekly the soul will seek out its body, *geohðum hremig* (9: 'clamorous in its cares' – *hremig* ironically evokes the boasting of warriors and heroes) to berate it with the suffering it now endures. Unless Doomsday itself intervenes, it will come on these weekly visits for three hundred years.[14] Sorrowfully and coldly, 'spirit speaks to dust' ('cleopað . . . se gast to þam duste', 15–16). The body is berated for its lack of forethought. It did not consider that, although it must be food for worms, it also housed a soul. The soul claims to have longed for things spiritual but to have been denied by the body's greed and lust. Once adorned with gold and other ornaments, the body is now bone stripped bare. Happier by far had this body been born a bird or fish – or even one of the worms that now feasts on it – than that it was born a human and baptized so that the soul must suffer damnation. What will the judge say at the doom? Together again after the resurrection body and soul will suffer together eternally. The dust is dumb, cannot answer, and its decay is graphically described as a sharp-toothed worm called Greedy, making his feast. 'Be warned!' the poet is saying to the audience. The case is different for the holy soul, which consoles the body on its return visits. Though worms eat it as well as the wicked body, this body helped its soul to win salvation by fasting and despite poverty. But at the resurrection, reunited with the soul, it will partake in the life of joy. The poem breaks here, incomplete (and the Exeter version has only the speech of the wicked soul).

The soul–body address, here placed in the interim between death and doomsday, is in other contexts assigned to the hour of death and the last judgement itself. Wherever it is used, its purpose is not to spell out doctrine so much as to admonish the audience to live well in view of the eternal consequences of temporal behaviour. From the frequency with which it is used, it must have been thought effective; and however different modern sensitivities may be from Anglo-Saxon, the address of the soul of the wicked and the description of decay are as chilling and graphic passages on the ravages of the grave as one can imagine. One cannot but wince at such lines as:

Rib reafiað   reðe wyrmas,
beoð hira tungan totogenne   on tyn healfa
hungregum to frofre;   forþan hie ne magon huxlicum
wordum wrixlian   wið þone werian gast.
Gifer hatte se wyrm,   þe þa <g>eaglas beoð
nædle scearpran   (112–17)

Violent worms rob the rib, their tongues are torn in ten halves as compensation for the famished ones; therefore they cannot ignominiously mix word with the weary spirit. 'Glutton' is the name of that worm, whose jaws are sharper than a needle.

A large number of visions, many of them influenced in a general way by the *Visio Pauli*, take the form of visions recounted by persons who have apparently died and whose souls have been into the next world from which they return with cautionary messages for the living – and with a last chance in many cases to amend their own lives. It has been pointed out recently that these visions have much in common with a number of cases of near-death experience reported in modern times and sometimes taken as evidence of immortality. This is true to a remarkable extent, as the recent scholarly study of Carol Zaleski has demonstrated, but the modern near-death visions are almost always without content other than a general rosiness and sense of well being, whereas the medieval accounts invariably have much to teach about the destiny of the soul and the necessity of reform in the worldly lives of the audience. Despite striking resemblance to the medieval visions, the differences in the modern are very great: 'gone are the bad deaths, harsh judgement scenes, purgatorial torments, and infernal terrors of medieval visions; by comparison the modern other world is a congenial place, a democracy, a school for continuing education, and a garden of unearthly delights'.[15]

A remarkable number of the medieval otherworld visions have strong connections with Anglo-Saxon England. *The Vision of St Paul*, as we have already seen, was known in pre-Conquest England and translated into Old English as well as adapted in a number of ways to both verse and instructional prose. The visionary narratives in the *Dialogues* of Pope Gregory the Great (590–604) came from the pen of a pope greatly revered as the instigator of the conversion of the Anglo-Saxons. Bede has several important accounts in his *History*, which were also adapted by or known to writers of English. Boniface (d. 754), the Anglo-Saxon cleric who became the 'Apostle of Germany', included the influential account of the vision of the Monk of Wenlock in a letter.[16] In all of these cases (even though they may have been translated later into English) we are dealing with a learned literature in Latin. They themselves had a subsequent influence on such English poems as *Guthlac A*, one of two verse accounts of an Anglo-Saxon ascetic, but they were neither so popular nor so manifold in their influence as was the material derived from the *Visio Pauli*.

Of all the visionary accounts, by far the most famous and seminal is the account in Bede of the vision of Dryhthelm, a layman.[17] Bede, who says that he recounts the story 'in order to arouse the living from spiritual death', characterizes the story as one of a person who 'already dead came back to life and related many memorable things that he had seen'. He had, indeed, evidently died of an illness during the night; yet he sat up in the morning, terrifying those about his deathbed, and stating that he had been allowed to return from death to live very differently. Giving over his property to his family and the poor, he entered the monastery at Melrose and lived an exemplary life that gave witness to his remarkable experience.

With a resplendent guide, he recounted, he had passed through a great valley with fire, hail and snow on the left where souls leapt from heat to cold and back again. This was not hell, he was told. Passing into a region of darkness, he was left alone in fire and stench and met a great crowd of lamenting souls, harassed by laughing demons. Rescued by his guide, he was taken to a more welcoming region of flowers, light and happy inhabitants. The guide explains that the first area was one of purgation for those who had confessed but not completed their penance. The happier zone was for those who had lived well, even though they were not so perfect as to merit immediate admission to the kingdom.

The visionary is told that he will return to the land of the living and is admonished to live a better life than he had before. Pious persons – a monk, a king and a bishop are named – came to him for instruction. At his retreat he would often chastize his flesh by bathing in very cold water, praying and reciting the psalter as he did so. Leaving the water, he would never put on dry clothing, even though it was icy winter. To those who asked how he stood such torture, he replied 'Frigidiora ego uidi' ('I have seen colder things'). Bede contrasts this tale with another in the next chapter of the *History* (V.13), concerning a man who, refusing to repent, had died after having a vision that showed that the record of his bad deeds far outweighed the good. This person's vision was not for his own benefit, because it was too late for him; but it served for the benefit of others who heard of it and heeded its message.

Visions of the destiny of the soul in the interim between death and the resurrection of the last day are almost uniformly motivated, as were these accounts in Bede, by the desire to admonish individuals to live uprightly and to reform their lives. They are aimed more at the individual and her or his state of spiritual health than are accounts of the last judgement. They use language and imagery that are highly pictorial and vivid, that go beyond everyday life but follow recognized patterns and touch responsive chords in their audiences. Their utility as teaching devices and their popularity are undeniable. We would probably be better advised to emphasize their metaphoric appropriateness and communicative effectiveness than to regard them as literal pictures of the hereafter. Although they are not all among the great writings of European history, they descend not only from the Judeo-Christian tradition but also from the underworld voyages of the classical epic and they are part of the ancestry of Dante's *Divine Comedy*.

One report of a vision, however, is neither from the learned tradition nor a popularization based on an apocryphal writing like the Vision of St Paul. It is an account of several visionary experiences of a pious nobleman, Leofric, earl of Mercia; and it has the air of a contemporary record by someone close to Leofric, who was created earl by King Cnut (1016–35) and died in 1057 during the reign of Edward the Confessor. His wife, 'Godiva', is of legendary fame, and he was one of the great Saxon nobles of the eleventh century. A little manuscript written not many years after his death records Leofric's visions.[18] Three of the four visions have to do with appearances to the earl as he prayed late at night in the cathedral at

Canterbury or during a mass, also attended by the king, at Sandwich. The first vision reported in the document, however, is extremely interesting as an example of visions of the afterlife. In content, it resembles such near death reports from the other side of death as Bede's account of Dryhthelm, and it includes a number of the features of such visions that are outlined by Zaleski in her study. Yet the account states not that Leofric was taken off in death and restored to life but that he had the *gesihðe* ('vision') 'on healfslapendon lichaman' (line 2: 'in a state [body] of half sleep'), although he saw more clearly in this state than one normally does in dreams. Leofric must cross a very narrow bridge far above a raging river. A voice assures him that he will make the crossing safely. Across the bridge, he is taken to 'a very beautiful and fair field, filled with a sweet smell' (line 10). There is a great crowd, as on the Rogation days in England, wearing white (or baptismal) clothes like those of a deacon when he reads the gospel at mass. Leofric sees a man who is identified as St Paul, who has just celebrated the mass. Finally, residents of the place ask why Leofric, a sinful, living man, is among them. He is, it is said, 'baptized anew by repentance' (line 21) and will join the blessed in several years. The bridge, the explaining voice or guide and the sweet-smelling fair field with people all recall traditional elements of such visions; yet the absence of detail about the frightening place (and the lack of people in it) and the unusual reference to the Rogation days – a characteristically English liturgical detail – mark the account with strong individuality and freshness. The little report of Leofric's visions, then, has both strong connections with the tradition and departures from it that mark it as rooted in the nobleman's life and experience. It is very precious for that reason.

One might contrast with this the sense of the fundamental darkness of what lies beyond death as expressed by the unknown author of the poetic *Maxims II*:

> Meotod ana wat
> hwyder seo sawul sceal   syððan hweorfan,
> and ealle þa gastas   þe for gode hweorfað
> æfter deaðdæge,   domes bidað
> on fæder fæðme.   Is seo forðgesceaft
> digol and dyrne;   drihten ana wat,
> nergende fæder.   Næni eft cymeð
> hider under hrofas,   þe þæt her for soð
> mannum secge   hwylc sy meotodes gesceaft,
> sigefolca gesetu,   þær he sylfa wunað   (57–66)

God alone knows where the soul will go afterwards, and all the spirits which depart for God after the day of death and await judgement in the protection of the father. The future is dark and secret; the lord alone knows, the saving father. No one comes back here into the world who can tell people truly what kind of place is the ruler's creation, the dwellings of the victorious people, where he himself lives.

But for many Anglo-Saxons there was light and clarity about the future. They could describe in vivid detail an after-life in which the soul was separated from the body and journeyed to rest or torment. And beyond that they could depict the eventual return of Christ, the resurrection of all bodies to be reunited with their souls and the last judgement, inaugurating the eternal reign of God with the saints. The picture of eternity was one of a world transformed and redeemed. The picture of the afterlife was constructed to admonish those who heard or read of it to strive to win the final goal.

1 An extremely useful reference for matters of Christian history and doctrine, with extensive and reliable bibliographies and with a predilection for matters touching on the English church, is F. L. Cross and E. A. Livingstone, *The Oxford Dictionary of the Christian Church*, 2nd ed. (Oxford, 1974). For further bibliography, see M. McC. Gatch, *Preaching and Theology in Anglo-Saxon England: Ælfric and Wulfstan* (Toronto, 1977), esp. notes at pp. 212–13.

2 On apocalyptic themes (and especially the Antichrist) in early and medieval Christianity, see B. McGinn, *Visions of the End: Apocalyptic Traditions in the Middle Ages* (New York, 1979).

3 See M. McC. Gatch, 'The Eschatology in the Anonymous Old English Homilies', *Traditio* 21 (1965), 117–65, and 'Two Uses of Apocrypha in Anglo-Saxon Homilies', *Church History* 33 (1964), 379–91.

4 A modern edition of the commentary on Luke appears in Corpus Christianorum, Series Latina 120; the work on the Apocalypse is in *Patrologia Latina* 93, 129–206; translations of both have been announced for the Cistercian Studies Series (Kalamazoo, MI).

5 L. Whitbread, 'The Old English Poem *Judgement Day II* and its Latin Source', *Philological Quarterly* 45 (1966), 635–56. For further bibliography and comment, see S. B. Greenfield and D. G. Calder, *A New Critical History of Old English Literature* (New York and London, 1986), pp. 237–40.

6 Three poems on the Advent of Christ, the Ascension and Doomsday, grouped together at the beginning of the Exeter manuscript, were considered a tripartite 'epic' on the subject of the hero Christ by A. S. Cook and assigned to Cynewulf, whose signature clearly marks at least the Ascension poem as his (*The Christ of Cynewulf* (1900; repr. with Preface by J. C. Pope, Hamden, CT, 1964)). There is now a consensus that the three parts are separate poems. For bibliographical and critical details, see Greenfield and Calder, *New Criti-*

cal History, pp. 183 and 193–4. Lineation of the poem follows the convention, established by Cook, of continuous line numbering throughout the *Christ* group, in which *Doomsday* begins at line 867.

7 Sometimes it is said that, no matter the age at which they died or the manner of their dying, all will be the age of Christ at the time of his crucifixion. See, for example, the discussion of the resurrection of the body in Ælfric's homily, Pope XI, below.

8 Both are found in *Homilies of Ælfric: a Supplementary Collection*, ed. J. C. Pope, EETS os 259 and 260 (London, 1967–8), nos. XI ('Sermo ad populum, in octavis Pentecosten dicendus') and XVIII ('De die iudicii'). Both sermons are in Ælfric's rhythmical prose style and are printed in lines, which I cite. I have commented on both in *Preaching and Theology*, pp. 88–101.

9 Edited in Gatch, *Preaching and Theology*, pp. 129–46.

10 Translation adapted from my *Death: Meaning and Mortality in Christian Thought and Contemporary Culture* (New York, 1969), where *Phoenix* is discussed at pp. 81–7; see nn. 3–11 at pp. 200–1 for further bibliography.

11 A recent examination of the history of the doctrine is J. LeGoff, *The Birth of Purgatory*, trans. A. Goldhammer (Chicago, 1981). It is a very useful survey, although many critics agree that its view of the development (while chronologically quite accurate) is too mechanistic.

12 For bibliography and the text of the OE version, see A. DiPaolo Healy, *The Old English Vision of St. Paul*, Speculum Anniversary Monographs 2 (Cambridge, MA, 1978).

13 For discussion and bibliography, see Greenfield and Calder, *New Critical History*, pp. 235–7.

14 See Healey, *Old English Vision*, esp. pp. 45–50, on variant traditions in the Latin and OE texts. In some texts the return of the wicked soul to the body occurs on Sunday as a sabbatical respite from its sufferings.

15 C. Zaleski, *Otherworld Journeys: Accounts of Near-Death Experience in Medieval and Modern Times* (New York and Oxford, 1987), p. 7.

16 No. X; see *Briefe des Bonifatius, Willibalds Leben des Bonifatius*, ed. and trans. R. Rau (Darmstadt, 1968) or the English translation by E. Emerton, *The Letters of St. Boniface* (New York, 1940), pp. 25–31.

17 Bede, *HE* V.12. For further commentary, in addition to LeGoff and Zaleski, see J. M. Wallace-Hadrill, *Bede's Ecclesiastical History of the English People: A Historical Commentary* (Oxford, 1988).

18 Ed. by A. S. Napier in 'An Old English Vision of Leofric, Earl of Mercia', *Transactions of the Philological Society* 1907–10, pp. 180–8. On the rhetorical strategy of the piece, see P. Pulsiano, 'Hortatory Purpose in the OE *Visio Leofrici*', *Medium Ævum* 54 (1985), 109–16.

12 Biblical literature: the Old Testament

THE Old Testament captured the Anglo-Saxon imagination in some unexpected ways, as one of the poetic riddles in the Exeter Book testifies:

Wer sæt æt wine   mid his wifum twam
ond his twegen suno   ond his twa dohtor,
swase gesweostor,   ond hyra suno twegen,
freolico frumbearn;   fæder wæs þær inne
þara æþelinga   æghwæðres mid,
eam ond nefa.   Ealra wæron fife
eorla ond idesa   insittendra.   (*Riddle* 46)

A man sat at wine with his two wives and his two sons and his two daughters, beloved sisters, and their two sons, noble first-born; the father was in there of both of those princes, the uncle and the nephew. In all there were five lords and ladies sitting in there.

The conundrum by which twelve people turn out to be only five finds its explanation in the book of Genesis, where it is recorded that Lot's two daughters lay with him and each had a son by him. Yet if this poet found such episodes a gleefully unembarrassing source of wit, other Anglo-Saxon writers clearly found them a troubling challenge, finding it necessary to argue against taking the morals of the patriarchs as any sort of precedent for present practice.

In terms of quantity at least, the Old Testament was the major influence on Old English literature: it was the source for about a third of the extant poetry and for a large part of the prose, as well as influencing other writings. Some of that work is admittedly fairly unadventurous translation, but much of the writing shows how intensely and productively the Anglo-Saxons were engaged with the Old Testament. Poets, preachers, historians, even kings and generals found it an ever-useful storehouse of information and inspiration; its great collection of stories, poems, proverbs and prophecies provided a rich literary tradition for the Anglo-Saxons which both complemented and challenged the literary tradition of the Germanic inheritance.

The process of adapting and retelling Old Testament story in Old

English began early. The first religious poet, Cædmon, composed poems in the late seventh century using stories from Genesis and Exodus. Though these have not survived, a group of three probably early poems drawing on the books of Genesis, Exodus and Daniel appear in the late tenth-century Junius manuscript, together with *Christ and Satan*, a poem which is partly on the fall of the angels, while a poem on the story of Judith, perhaps composed in the tenth century, appears in the *Beowulf* manuscript. There are fourteen surviving copies of the psalter in Latin with an English gloss, and a complete translation survives in a Paris manuscript, known as the Paris Psalter: the first fifty psalms are in Old English prose, very probably by King Alfred, while the remaining hundred are in verse, probably taken from a verse translation of the whole book. At the end of the tenth century Ælfric translated part of the book of Genesis and composed a series of homiletic texts and narrative pieces using material from Joshua, Judges, Kings, Judith, Esther, Maccabees and Job. Around the year 1000 a prose version of the first five books of the Old Testament was compiled, using translations provided by Ælfric and another translator.[1] Both this version and the Junius poetic collection were provided with extensive illustrations. But the response to the Old Testament extended much further than this, through commentaries, sermons, discussions of military and political issues, and in poems such as the riddle of Lot. Indeed, in many ways the most imaginative response to the Old Testament is to be seen in *Beowulf*, which draws on biblical stories of creation, of Cain and the giants to form part of its mythic structure.

For the Anglo-Saxons the Old Testament was in the first place a history book, a record of events in antiquity. One major point of interest was that it offered an account of how the world and mankind began. When the bishop of Winchester wrote to the missionary Boniface around AD 730 to give advice about converting the heathen Saxons, he urged him to tease them with the absurdity of their beliefs about the beginning of things and to stress in contrast the clear account given by the Old Testament (*EHD*, p. 731). Bede's story of the conversion of the Northumbrians too suggests that one of the major advantages which Christianity appeared to offer the heathen Anglo-Saxons was a coherent account of the world's beginning. The same interest is evident in the genealogies, which trace the ancestry of the West Saxon kings back through the pagan god Woden to Noah and ultimately Adam. Despite the distance in time and space, the Anglo-Saxons could also see close parallels between themselves and the Hebrew tribes. At first it was perhaps the fact that the Hebrews of the early books were, like the Anglo-Saxons in the sixth and seventh centuries, invaders trying to establish themselves in a new and hostile land: that similarity seems to have struck Bede at least, who is thought to have modelled his *Ecclesiastical History* on the Book of Samuel.[2] Later, increasingly, the

Anglo-Saxons came to see the parallels between their own experiences at the hands of the Vikings and that of the Israelites who, though believing in the one true God, found themselves inexplicably oppressed and humiliated by the forces of the non-believers.

If the Anglo-Saxons found it fruitful to trace the similarities between Old Testament Hebrews and their own situation, there were also dangers. The Old Testament was the word of God, but too many of the practices which had been acceptable in the Old Testament world were perilously close to practices which the Anglo-Saxon church considered pagan or at least objectionable. Ælfric records the tendency of his contemporaries to cite Old Testament support for their own practices of taking concubines, and for their fondness for revenge, and he has to warn that sacrificial offerings, rituals concerning forbidden food, the marriage of priests and the involvement of the clergy in warfare were all Old Testament practices that were no longer acceptable in Christian times. One way of neutralizing these dangers was to insist that such biblical stories should be understood in a quite different, non-historical way, as allegories. Thus Abraham's attempted sacrifice of his son Isaac at God's command was not a precedent for human sacrifice but a figurative foreshadowing of God's sacrifice of his own son in the New Testament. The practice of interpreting Old Testament narratives as allegories probably goes back to pre-Christian Jewish tradition, but it was soon adopted by Christian theologians such as Origen and absorbed into the main stream of Christian tradition.[3] Allegory was used to make the Old Testament safe for Christian readers or to make it consonant with the New Testament by discovering Christian doctrines such as the Trinity hidden within it. But allegorical interpretation soon became a way of using the Old Testament, and the New Testament as well, as a vast store-book of imagery, a source of riddling metaphors and imaginative parallels. The impetus here is not to save the Old Testament for Christianity but to invite the reader to see imaginative parallels between moral truths and physical actuality, or between spiritual experience and historical events.

Such allegorical interpretation always attracted Anglo-Saxon writers, and was one of the important ways in which they perceived the relationship between the Old Testament and their own times. Perhaps this is clearest with Bede, who wrote a whole series of Latin commentaries on shrines and temples in the Old Testament – the tabernacle in Exodus, the building of Solomon's temple in Kings and the rebuilding of the temple after its destruction in I Ezra – and used allegory to relate these accounts to the spiritual qualities of the church and the priesthood in his own time. Just as he used the historical narratives as a literal model for his own account of the development of the English church, so he used allegory to make the Old Testament stories of temple-building into a potent symbol for the spiritual development of the church. His tour-de-force is the commentary on the Book of Tobias where the strange figure of Sara must have represented a disconcerting challenge to his powers (this female equivalent of Bluebeard marries seven times and each time her husband is found dead in the morning after the first night in her bed; but Tobias still insists on marrying her). Bede interprets her as an emblem of the Christian church. The tradition continued in the vernacular. King Alfred reproduces frequent examples in his *Pastoral Care*. Ælfric uses such allegorical interpretations of the Old Testament again and again in his homilies, and explains the theory of such allegory in his Preface to Genesis. There are further examples in Byrhtferth of Ramsey's *Enchiridion* and the anonymous homilies. It spilled over too into the interpretation of classical legend; thus King Alfred briefly tells the story of Orpheus and Eurydice, insisting that it is not true in the literal sense but that it carries an allegorical meaning, by which Orpheus looking back to hell symbolizes an individual returning to his old vices after reform. Allegory seems to have spread into the making of new narratives too (as in *The Seafarer*).

Old Testament reading invited an imaginative and individual response to literature. Allegory coexisted with literal or historical interpretations of the same stories, and allowed for multiple interpretations of the same episodes. One of the characteristic questions for modern readers of Old English versions of Old Testament story is how far allegorical meanings are implicit in the text, and what kinds of meaning.

The variety and richness of response can perhaps best be shown by looking at the ways in which different Anglo-Saxon writers handled particular books of the Old Testament. The book which the Anglo-Saxons knew best was probably Genesis. *Genesis A*, a long fairly faithful rendering of the book of Genesis into lively and often magniloquent verse, reflects many of the ways in which the Old Testament interested the Anglo-Saxons. Its structure is narrative and literal, following the sequence of the biblical book closely, but it often hints at particular points of interest and allegorical significance. One of the poet's particular concerns is the explanation of the origins of the human condition. It is evident in his treatment of the Adam and Eve story, and also in his account of Cain and Abel, where Cain's murder of his brother brought into the world evil and violence:

> Æfter wælswenge   wea wæs aræred,
> tregena tuddor.   Of ðam twige siððan
> ludon laðwende   leng swa swiðor
> reðe wæstme.   Ræhton wide
> geond werþeoda   wrohtes telgan   (*Genesis* 987–91)

After that bloody stroke evil was raised up, the fruit of misery. From that shoot sprang terrible things, worse and worse, cruel fruits. The branches of that crime reached widely over nations.

This idea of Cain's act giving birth to violence had a much more literal manifestation in the traditions about his descendants, discussed below. But it was the apparently unimportant incident of Abraham's conflict with four kings which seems most to have inspired this poet. Four kings lead their armies to attack the cities of Sodom and Gomorrah, and they carry off Lot and his family and possessions as part of their plunder; Abraham, hearing the news, collects his forces and defeats the four kings in battle to rescue his nephew Lot. The shift into dramatic detail and excited comment, using such traditional motifs of battle poetry as the raven circling in anticipation of corpses, probably owes something to the poet's recognition that here at last was an episode made for Anglo-Saxon poetry. But one can also see the poet's awareness of the story's relevance: for him it is a glorious victory over northern raiding armies, achieved by a force which was small but had God on its side:

> Næfre mon ealra
> lifigendra her   lytle werede
> þon wurðlicor   wigsið ateah,
> þara þe wið swa miclum   mægne geræsde   (2092–5)

No one, of all living creatures, has ever achieved a more glorious victory with a small army, fighting against so great a power.

The language here closely resembles the end of *The Battle of Brunanburh* when it celebrates the Anglo-Saxon defeat of the Vikings and Scots. Given the uncertainty of the poem's date it is not clear what resonance this passage had originally: if seventh- or eighth-century, it could recall the raids of Scots or Picts, Welsh or Mercians; if ninth-century, it could be prompted by Viking raids. Certainly when the poem was copied into the Junius manuscript around 1000 the reference to northern raiders could only have recalled the Vikings.

Ælfric calls Genesis the *gecyndboc* or 'book of beginnings', and it was indeed the story of origins that particularly appealed to Anglo-Saxon writers. The miracle which launched the first Anglo-Saxon religious poet Cædmon into poetry was, according to Bede's account, a visitation from an angel who compelled or inspired the peasant to sing a hymn of creation. This nine-line hymn, which survives in some copies of Bede's Latin account and was incorporated in the later translation of it, celebrates God's creation of heaven as a roof for mankind and then the earth itself. Such celebrations of creation seem to have been, or become, a literary theme. A similar poem is sung by the minstrel in *Beowulf* (see below) and there is a longer poem on the creation in the Exeter Book, known as *The Wonders of Creation* or *The Order of the World*. It emphasizes the sun as the greatest of the miracles of creation, and celebrates the mystery and wonder of the created world; no one, however wise, says the poet, can tell how the 'goldbright' sun moves under the earth or what land-dwellers may enjoy its light after it has dipped beneath the brim of the ocean.

Something of the same sense of wonder at the plenitude of creation is also to be found in prose, in Ælfric's *Hexameron*:

The birds which live on the water are webfooted by God's providence, so that they can swim and seek food. Some are longnecked, like swans, so that they can reach food on the bottom; and those which live on flesh are claw-footed and sharp-billed, so that they can bite, and with short necks, and swifter in flight . . . Not all kinds of birds live in England, nor in any country are all birds easily found, for they are many, and variable in size, and fly in various ways. (ed. Crawford, lines 250–81)

There is a striking contrast here to the elegiac poems which tell of decay and the world's old age.

If the creation story could be used to celebrate the goodness of the world, Anglo-Saxon writers also looked to the Bible to articulate their ideas about the origins of evil. One traditional explanation was the story of the fall of the angels. This story had been pieced together in Jewish and early Christian tradition from stray references later in the Bible, but for most Anglo-Saxon writers it was closely associated with the Genesis tradition of the creation of the world and the fall of man. Traditionally it was a story of pride and ambition, but Anglo-Saxon poets present a surprisingly dramatic and sympathetic picture of Lucifer's rebellion. *Christ and Satan* (a poem of 729 lines in the Junius MS) narrates the creation of the world and the fall of the angels, and then presents a plaintive series of speeches by Lucifer in which he evokes a sense of loss and grief very similar in mood to the Old English elegies:

> Hwær com engla ðrym,
> þe we on heofnum habban sceoldan?
> Þis is ðeostræ ham, ðearle gebunden
> fæstum fyrclommum; flor is on welme
> attre onæled . . .
> Hwæt, we for dryhtene iu dreamas hefdon,
> song on swegle selrum tidum,
> þær nu ymb ðone æcan æðele stondað,
> heleð ymb hehseld, herigað drihten
> wordum and wercum, and ic in wite sceal
> bidan in bendum, and me bættran ham
> for oferhygdum æfre ne wene
>   (*Christ and Satan* 36–40, 44–50)

Where has the glory of angels gone, which we were destined to have in heaven? This is a home of darkness, narrowly constrained by strong fetters of fire; the floor is in flame, burning with poison . . . Once we had joys in the presence of the lord, and song in heaven in better times, where now around the eternal one nobles stand, heroes around the high throne, praising the lord with words and works, and I in torment must endure in bonds, and never hope for a better home, because of my pride.

An even more dramatic account of the fall of the angels appears in what is known as *Genesis B*. Embedded within the Old English poem *Genesis* is a long sequence (lines 235–851) describing the fall of the angels (for the second time) and the fall of man, a sequence which derives from an Old Saxon poem composed on the Continent, perhaps in the ninth century. It seems that at some early stage, probably in the later ninth century, the leaves containing the account of the fall of man in the Old English *Genesis A* poem (in some earlier manuscript than Junius) were lost and the owner made good the damage by inserting the equivalent episode from the Old Saxon poem.[4] Whoever turned the latter into Old English verse was clearly skilled in Anglo-Saxon poetic tradition, whether an Englishman who had lived in Germany or a continental Saxon familiar with Anglo-Saxon literature, though it is uncertain whether he translated the whole poem or just what was needed to fill the gap. What clearly inspired the original poet, and presumably his translator, was the challenge of dramatizing the feelings and thoughts of the world's first sinner: the fallen angels and Adam and Eve are for him archetypes of rebels and sinners, whose experiences can tell us how evil came into the world. What marks this account is the quality of sympathetic understanding. Lucifer is driven by his passionate objection to being God's underling and his aspiration to higher things, dramatically expressed in soliloquy:

> 'Hwæt sceal ic winnan?' cwæð he. 'Nis me wihtæ þearf
> hearran to habbanne. Ic mæg mid handum swa fela
> wundra gewyrcean. Ic hæbbe geweald micel
> to gyrwanne   godlecran stol,
> hearran on heofne. Hwy sceal ic æfter his hyldo ðeowian,
> bugan him swilces geongordomes? Ic mæg wesan god swa he
> (278–83)

What shall I toil for? I have no need to have a superior. I can perform just as many wonders with my hands. I have great power, enough to make a more splendid throne, higher in heaven. Why must I serve for his favour, bow down to him with such subordination. I can be as good as. him.

When he rebels and is inevitably crushed by the omnipotence of God, he vividly describes the misery of failure, injustice and hell, and meditates revenge. The sense of a powerful, energetic spirit imprisoned by his pre-ordained place in the hierarchy is given substance by his literal chains in hell. From his fetters he conceives a plan for revenge, and invokes the claims of loyalty to persuade one of his followers to make the journey to earth.

The fall of the angels is one kind of tragedy. Lucifer is created stronger and brighter than all other angels but strives for still higher status, for freedom and independence. He is fully aware that he is rebelling against his lord, and the poet loads his account with references to Lucifer's pride. Yet the dramatization of his grief and resentment, together with the frequent echoes of a heroic society, strongly recall the sympathetic protagonists of the Old English elegiac poems, *The Wanderer* and *The Seafarer*. Lucifer becomes a kind of tragic figure like Prometheus or Macbeth, a powerful spirit fully aware of his act but also acutely sensitive to his failure, and still struggling to resist while chained in hell.

Equally important as an explanation for the world's evil was the story of the fall of man. This was one of the central themes for most writers on the first book of the Bible. Bede and Alcuin discuss it in detail in their commentaries on Genesis, and Ælfric deals with it in several of his Old English prose writings. For Ælfric it is an exemplary story of human free will. Because Adam and Eve's submission to the divine will would have had no value or meaning if they had no choice, God placed an arbitrary prohibition on one tree in Paradise:

Why would God forbid them so small a thing, when he had entrusted other great things to them? Truly, how could Adam know what he was, unless he was obedient in some thing to his Lord? . . . It was not shaped for him by God [that he should fall], nor was he compelled to break God's commandment, but God left him free and gave him his own choice.

(*Catholic Homilies*, ed. Thorpe I, 14–18)

The devil seduced Adam and Eve into disobeying God by appealing to their gluttony, their vainglory and their greed, telling them that they would be like angels, but it was through their own free choice that they fell, and God punishes them by making them mortal. But a rather different emphasis appears in *Genesis B*'s full and individual account of the fall of man. The sequence of events is very carefully constructed, and the poet's account is once again marked by a quality of sympathetic engagement. Here Eden contains two trees, one of good and the other of evil: to eat the fruit of the latter is irretrievably to bring sin and mortality and hell upon mankind. The devil, disguised as a serpent, first approaches Adam with his claim that he is a messenger from God who now wishes Adam to eat the forbidden fruit. The devil imaginatively suggests to Adam that God cannot face the rigours of the journey to earth and so has sent his subordinate with a message. Adam, more literal minded, refuses to budge from the explicit commands of God and complains that the tempter has brought no tokens of his divine authority. The devil then turns to Eve and persuades her to eat. With Eve the tempter appeals to her concern for Adam, suggesting that God will be angry with him for rejecting his messenger and that she can save her husband by accepting the fruit and persuading Adam to eat. She cajoles Adam into eating too, and the devil returns with a triumphant speech to hell.

What is striking in this account is the apparent innocence of the sinners. Eve is moved by her concern for Adam and believes that the tempter is from God; the vision of heaven which she receives on eating the fruit appears to confirm that she has acted rightly. The poet points out that God had given her a weaker mind than Adam, and that she persuaded Adam to eat out of a genuine loyalty to him, believing it was for his own good. Adam too accepts the fruit because he genuinely believes Eve's promise that it is God's will. We are facing here a failure in perception, an intellectual failure reflecting the limited powers of the mind which God gave them, not the overpowering of reason by greed or pride. Where Ælfric emphasizes the act of free will, the poet shifts the responsibility back to the devil and ultimately to God himself:

> Ne wearð wyrse dæd
> monnum gemearcod!   Þæt is micel wundor
> þæt hit ece god   æfre wolde
> þeoden þolian,   þæt wurde þegn swa monig
> forlædd be þam lygenum   þe for þam larum com   (594–8)

No worse action was ever marked out for men. It is a great wonder that the eternal God would ever permit it that so many a thegn should be led astray by lies, as came about through that advice.

Two kinds of tragic fall are thus dramatized in *Genesis B*: the angels act in full knowledge that they are in conflict with God, but are impelled by 'heroic' qualities of vengeance, loyalty, defiance, aspiration to freedom, rejection of a subordinate position; Adam and Eve, on the other hand, wish to serve the divine will but find themselves caught in a situation where that will is hard to discover. Elegiac laments invite our sympathy with both sets of fallen, while God becomes an almost impersonal figure of nemesis, the Almighty who by definition cannot have a rival and whose condemnation of Adam and Eve to mortality and exile is in a sense predetermined by the nature of the two trees.

It was not only the evil within human nature and the human situation for which explanations were sought in the book of Genesis; it was also the evil within the rest of creation. Ælfric reports a belief that some beings were created not by God but by the devil, and although he repudiates this doctrine it is clear that Anglo-Saxons were concerned about the origins of the darker creatures in the world and looked to the Bible for explanations. Genesis reports that the sons of God took wives from among the daughters of men, who gave birth to giants (ch. VI). Christian tradition interpreted this as marriage between the descendants of Cain and those of Seth, Adam's third son, and apocryphal legends developed about the giants and monsters who were descended from Cain and who, according to some versions, managed to survive the flood.[5] There is a fleeting reference to this myth in Felix's *Life of St Guthlac*, where the demons are called the seed of Cain, but it becomes a more central issue in *Beowulf*. The poet makes no overt reference to the Bible or the Christian religion but draws imaginatively on Old Testament story and themes to suggest the symbolic and mythic power of his creation, in the same way as he used Germanic legend. The way in which Cædmon and other poets drew on the opening of Genesis to celebrate the creation of the world has already been discussed above. The *Beowulf*-poet, showing his extraordinary talent in this as in all else he touched, turned the theme of the world's beginning into a challenge. When Hrothgar has finished his great golden hall for the Danes, he has his minstrel sing a song of God's creation of the world as if in celebration of the creative urge:

> cwæð þæt se ælmihtiga eorðan worhte,
> wlitebeorhtne wang, swa wæter bebugeð,
> gesette sigehreþig sunnan ond monan
> leoman to leohte landbuendum,
> ond gefrætwade foldan sceatas
> leomum ond leafum, lif eac gesceop
> cynna gehwylcum þara ðe cwice hwyrfaþ (*Beowulf* 92–8)

He said that the almighty made the earth, the beautifully bright land, with water surrounding it, the conqueror set the sun and the moon as lamps to bring light to landdwellers, and adorned the surfaces of the earth with branches and leaves; life too he created for all the kinds that live and move.

The Danish minstrel invites his audience, as the Anglo-Saxon poet invites his, to see a parallel between the building of Heorot and God's building of the world. But already the figure of evil, Grendel, is lurking threateningly in the darkness. As the minstrel concludes his song it merges with the narrative, so that we are not at first clear whether the enemy in the darkness threatening the creatures living in bliss is Satan threatening Adam and Eve or Grendel threatening the Danes. Old Testament allusion is here used to suggest the Satanic aspects of Grendel and the Edenic aspects of Heorot. Yet the parallel raises doubts not only about the hall's safety but also about the idea of creation: if the world was made by a wise, benevolent and all-powerful God, where do monster-figures like Grendel come from? The juxtaposition of the song and the monster impels the poet to go on to tell the story of Cain, who brought death and violence into the newly-created world and became the ancestor of all the evils – goblins, orcs, giants and others. The Cain story in turn introduces the concept of fratricide, invoking the archetypal example of that feuding between tribes and families which pervades the world of *Beowulf*. The Cain myth manages both to insist on the alien nature of Grendel and all he represents, and to hint at its origins in conflict between brothers. Old Testament allusion plays a complementary role when it returns once more after the death of Grendel and his mother. Beowulf brings back the hilt of the giants' sword with which he had killed them, and on it Hrothgar finds depicted the story of the Flood which destroyed the giants who lived in the old days. As Grendel is introduced by a reference to the Old Testament legend which described the origin of monsters, so his end is announced by an allusion to the biblical myth of their destruction.

For a rather different theory of the origins of giants, equally reliant on Genesis legend, one might turn again to Ælfric. He does not refer to the tradition about Cain's monstrous progeny, and his firm insistence that all his offspring were destroyed in the Flood suggests that he knew the story and gave it no credence. He prefers an alternative tradition, that the giants or *entas* were the descendants of Ham, one of Noah's sons. It is one of these 'ents', Nimrod, who in Ælfric's view was responsible for the building of the tower of Babel. Ælfric identifies this with the great city of Babylon and sees Nimrod as the first person who wished to make himelf a king.[6] (This tradition perhaps lies behind the reference in *The Wanderer* to the ruined city as *eald enta geweorc*, 'the old works of the ents'.) The Babel story is for him a myth explaining not only the origin of all the languages and nations of the world but also the origins of kingship and of cities, all associated with the 'ents'. For Ælfric the 'ents' were also the reality behind the stories of the pagan gods.

If Genesis was the most influential of the early books, the account of the Hebrews' departure from Egypt and their wanderings in the wilderness which forms the subject of the book of Exodus also interested the Anglo-Saxons, in several different ways. King Alfred began his legal code with a long excerpt from Exodus describing Moses promulgating his laws: he thus presents himself in a tradition of law-givers which began with Moses. Ælfric too presented Moses as the law-giver, in a homiletic account of the exodus focusing on the promulgation of the ten commandments. In another piece, called *On the People of Israhel*, he narrates their experiences in the desert, drawing attention to their murmurings against God and the clergy (*Homilies of Ælfric*, ed. Pope, pp. 638–66). Both allegorically and literally, the Anglo-Saxon church saw itself in continuity with the priesthood of the Hebrews, similarly faced with reconciling a rebellious people to God. Easily the most inventive and challenging response to this biblical book is the Old English poem called *Exodus*. Rather than tell the whole story of the book of Exodus the poet limits himself to a few central episodes: the Hebrews' escape from Egypt, their crossing of the Red Sea and the destruction of the Egyptians. The literal aspect of the narrative is not the poet's central concern and his method is highly oblique and allusive, almost in the manner of an extended riddle. Towards the end the poet seems to invite allegorical interpretation:

> Gif onlucan wile   lifes wealhstod,
> beorht in breostum,   banhuses weard,
> ginfæsten god   gæstes cægon,
> run bið gerecenod,   ræd forð gæð   (523–6, repunctuated)

If the interpreter of life, bright in the heart, the guardian of the body, will unlock the lavish good with the keys of the spirit, the mystery will be explained, counsel will come forth.

The allegorical meaning of these events was familiar to the Anglo-Saxons: Pharaoh stood for the devil, the Hebrews represented the Christians leaving the world (Egypt) for the next life (the Promised Land) and passing by way of baptism (the Red Sea) from servitude to the devil to the service of God. There are several possible allusions to such an interpretation (e.g. lines 40ff. and 532ff.) and yet much of the poetry seems to have little to do with such a way of reading the text; it is rather as if allegory is just one of a number of ways in which the poet invites us to read his poem. The most striking feature of the poem is its multi-valency: the way it throws off sparks of significance in all directions as the poet explores the story of the exodus. There are hints of symbolic parallels between the Hebrews' experience and man's journey to heaven and the harrowing of hell, which are never followed up; there are suggestions of great battles which do not actually occur; there are indications of an imaginary sea-voyage which takes place over a desert and a dry sea-bed. The whole is invested with a sense of drama and excitement as the Hebrews fight their way through sand and sea while the Egyptian army is destroyed by the descending waters.

The poem opens with praise of Moses as a law-giver (as Alfred and Ælfric had done), and presents him as the dominant figure throughout, both war-leader and speaker of wisdom; indeed, the dramatic climax of the story, the dividing of the waters of the Red Sea, takes place within his speech rather than in authorial narrative. The story of the escape from Egypt, the flight through the desert and the crossing of the Red Sea is presented in a strongly heroic and military light. Both fleeing Hebrews and pursuing Egyptians are seen as warriors, with repeated reference to their weapons, their armour and their courage. The biblical account has no battle, indeed much of the point of its story is that it was God who protected his people, and the battle never quite happens in the Old English version either, though it seems constantly threatened. Instead, the crossing of the Red Sea and the drowning of the Egyptians are treated as if it were a battle, with dramatic descriptions of blood and conflict, and the poem ends with the Hebrews collecting the plunder from their fallen enemies on the sea-shore. It is difficult to be sure how these scenes are to be read. Is the poet implying that, contrary to the Bible's emphasis on God's protecting hand, the Hebrews had to fight their way to the Red Sea? Or is he pointing to a figurative meaning, a reference to spiritual conflict with the devil? Or is it simply that the imagery of warfare, of blood and wounds and weapons, is his imaginative way of suggesting the grandeur of the conflict between Hebrews and Egyptians?

The questions are equally pressing in the case of the nautical imagery. The Hebrews are described as seamen, as sailors, as sea-vikings. The poet imagines them being protected from the heat of the sun by a God-sent cloud which he likens to a sail, though one, he says, without visible ropes or mast, so that the journey through the desert becomes a kind of sea-journey, which may in turn relate to the use of sea-voyage as an emblem of life in *The Seafarer*, *Christ II* and perhaps *The Wanderer*. Yet the cloud is also likened to a tent, and is somehow related to the pillars of cloud and fire, which not only guide the Hebrews through the desert, as in the Bible, but also protect them at night from the horrors of the wilderness and threaten them with punishment if they disobey Moses. The protecting cloud and the pillars seem almost to become emblematic of God himself, as guide, protector and stern judge. The theme of God's protecting role for his chosen people seems indeed to run through the poem, and prompts a digressive discussion of Noah and Abraham, to whom similar assurances of protection were given. The characteristic Anglo-Saxon interest in the Old Testament as a storehouse of examples of God defending his chosen people clearly plays a part here.

The historical books which follow Exodus and the associated books of law in the Old Testament struck Anglo-Saxon writers with a sense of the resemblance to their own time. Thus when Wulfstan adapted Ælfric's account of Old Testament history (around the year 1000) he added a passage on the Babylonian captivity in terms which inevitably remind us of his later account of the troubles of the English at the hands of the Danes:

At last the people became so estranged from God by their guilt that he let a heathen army (*here*) come and plunder that land; and the king Sedechias was taken prisoner and all the nobility who were in that country were killed or taken captive and brought away from that land, and for fully seventy years afterwards that nation was subjected to the power of their enemies, so completely were they estranged from God.

(*Homilies*, ed. Bethurum, pp. 149–50)

In the short treatise on the books of the Old and New Testament which he wrote for a landowner called Sigeweard, Ælfric indicates the purpose of his translation of the book of Judith:

Judith the widow, who overcame Holofernes the Syrian general, has her own book amongst the others, concerning her own victory; it is also set down in our manner in English, as an example to you people that you should defend your land with weapons against the invading army.

(*The Old English Heptateuch*, ed. Crawford, p. 48)

His comments a few lines later on the wars of the Maccabees against their oppressors are even more pointed and critical of his contemporaries:

They would not fight just with fair words, promising much but changing their minds afterwards, lest they should suffer the troubling saying which a prophet spoke about a certain nation: 'The Lord became angry with his people and shunned his inheritance and committed them into the hands of the heathens, and their enemies truly had power over them' ... I translated those books into English; read them if you wish as counsel for yourselves.

If one turns to his translation of the story of the Maccabees, one finds that it not only celebrates their heroic defence but ends with a discussion of the notion of the just war (the first in English) and of the three estates of society, those who pray, those who work and those who fight. The translation appears in a large collection by Ælfric now known, somewhat misleadingly, as the *Lives of Saints*, which also includes his version of the book of Kings and several accounts of soldier-saints. It is probably no coincidence that the collection was commissioned by Æthelweard, the ealdorman responsible for the military defence of the south-west against the Vikings; Æthelweard also commissioned the translation of the book of Joshua, another account of heroic battles against the heathens. It was presumably someone of the status of Æthelweard, or possibly King Æthelred himself, who prompted Ælfric to write a short piece setting out the Old Testament and classical precedents which justified a king deciding not to lead his armies in person (*Homilies of Ælfric*, ed. Pope, pp. 725–33).

Alongside this interest in military and political parallels at the literal level there was also an awareness of the figurative possibilities. Thus Ælfric offers a multiplicity of figurative interpretations of the story of

Judith, as an alternative to the literal and historical significance noted above:

In her was fulfilled the Saviour's words: 'Everyone who exalts himself will be humbled, and he who humbles himself shall be exalted.' She, humble and pure, overcame the proud one; small and weak, she cast down the mighty one, because she undoubtedly signified by her actions the holy assembly that believes now in God, that is Christ's church in all Christian people, his one clean bride, who with bold faith cut off the head of the old devil, always serving Christ in purity . . . She would not keep the cruel one's war-gear which the people gave her, as the narrative tells us, but cursed it with all his clothing, would not wear it but cast it from her, would not have any sin through his heathenness. There are some nuns who live shamefully and account it a small sin that they fornicate and think that they can easily make amends for something so small . . . Take example for yourselves from Judith, how cleanly she lived before Christ's incarnation.   (ed. Assmann, pp. 114–15)

Such interpretative possibilities provide a useful context for the anonymous poem on Judith. Only the last part of the poem survives but the poet's imaginative leanings are evident enough. The biblical version had been almost anti-heroic in its approach. When the Assyrian army under Holofernes invades Israel military resistance proves useless: it is God that destroys them, through the unlikely agency of the pious widow Judith, who seduces Holofernes by her ornaments and beauty and beheads him in his sleep, leaving the Assyrians to flee the country in dismay when they discover their leader's death. Judith seems to have been chosen, by God or the original story-teller, to emphasize that God has no need of man's military power: piety is enough. The Old English poet presents the story in a very different light, as a heroic conflict between opposing leaders and their armies. The beheading of Holofernes does not in itself bring victory: the head is only a sign of divine favour which the Hebrew warriors then need to convert into reality by taking up their weapons and marching in confidence against the Assyrians, for whom the headless body of Holofernes becomes a matching sign of divine disfavour and hopelessness. The climax is a lovingly described battle evoking all the traditional imagery and fervour of Anglo-Saxon battle poetry.

The poet is clearly skilled in handling the traditional themes and much of the art is expressed in the subtle undermining of the imagery of a heroic society. The Assyrians are presented as a version of the warrior society and Holofernes is a perversion of the traditional war-leader, using much of the old poetic formulae for a hero. The motif of a feast, so feelingly described in *Beowulf* and alluded to in *Maldon* and *The Wanderer*, is here perverted into an orgy at once comic and disastrous, at which

Holofernes screams and yells, forcing his men to drink to their own destruction:

> Ða wearð Holfernus,
> goldwine gumena,   on gytesalum,
> hloh and hlydde,   hlynede and dynede,
> þæt mihten fira bearn   feorran gehyran
> hu se stiðmoda   styrmde and gylede,
> modig and medugal,   manode geneahhe
> bencsittende   þæt hi gebærdon wel.
> Swa se inwidda   ofer ealne dæg
> dryhtguman sine   drencte mid wine,
> swiðmod sinces brytta,   oðþæt hi on swiman lagon,
> oferdrencte his duguðe ealle,   swylce hie wæron deaðe
>   geslegene,
> agotene goda gehwylces   (*Judith* 21–32)

Then was Holofernes, that gold-lord of men, in pouring joy, he laughed and shouted, called out and resounded so that people could hear that from afar, how that sternhearted one stormed and yelled, proud and merry with mead, he repeatedly urged the bench-sitters that they should feast well. So that evil one through all that day drenched his warriors with wine, that strong-hearted treasure-giver, until they lay in a swoon, utterly drowned all his warband, as if they were struck down by death, drained of all strength.

The usual loving relationship between warriors and war-leader (seen particularly in *The Wanderer*) is replaced by a relation of fear and distrust, symbolized best by the wonderful curtain or flynet surrounding Holofernes' bed, through which he can watch his men while they cannot see him. He commands arrogantly and his men hasten fearfully to obey. The theme comes to a climax in the semi-comic scene in the midst of battle when the Assyrians are destroyed by their own terrified reluctance to wake Holofernes and tell him of the Hebrew attack: thinking that he is still sleeping with the Hebrew maiden, though in fact he is dead, they stand distraught outside his tent, coughing nervously in an attempt to wake him, until one particularly bold warrior ventures in. On finding him dead the warriors then reverse the tradition of heroic loyalty and take to flight, leaving their leader alone and dead on the battlefield.

Against Holofernes is set Judith herself, not a pious widow as in the Bible, but a confident and beautiful virgin. She is a dominating figure who issues commands to her fellow-citizens, instructing them to guard the gates in her absence and commanding them to go to war when she returns. But she clearly exists in an affectionate relationship with them, marked by the account of the thronging of the ecstatic crowd around her when she returns. Her military status is emphasized by the fact that her prize at the end of the battle is not the bedcoverings and pots and pans of Holofernes, as in the biblical version, but his war-equipment, and there is no suggestion here, as there is in Ælfric, that she refuses to accept them. The poet underlines the point at the end when he remarks that God gave Judith both fame in the world and reward in heaven. Though the traditional vision of the heroic society seems to be mildly ironized or subverted in the picture of the Assyrian army, in the representation of Judith and the Hebrews there seems to be a full-hearted acceptance of heroic values within the context of a citizen army and the defence of the native land.

Yet just as Ælfric was able to read the Judith story both as a literal story of warfare paralleling Anglo-Saxon experience and as an allegorical narrative, so in the poem the figurative aspects seem to be at least faintly present. The emphasis on Judith's status as a virgin and the presentation of Holofernes as a diabolic figure intent to defile her hint at spiritual and religious symbolism. The imagery of light and darkness, purity and foulness, seems to lock together Judith herself, her city of Bethulia and the inviolate faith of the Hebrews (a faith which is marked as apparently Christian by Judith's prayer to the Trinity). Judith, the bright virgin who cannot be defiled by the foul Holofernes, is matched by the closely-guarded city under siege, with its vigilant watchmen guarding its gates, the city whose inviolate walls are seen shining bright through the darkness as Judith and her maid cross the no-man's land. It is perhaps at this level of symbol that literal or historical relevance and spiritual themes involving the conflict between devil and pure faith begin to merge.

Like other books of the Old Testament, the books of the prophets were read by the Anglo-Saxons in several ways. Within the context of the Old Testament the prophets are seen as intermediaries between God and his people, warning them of their crimes and of impending retribution. The Anglo-Saxon writer who responded to the prophets most on these terms was Wulfstan, who perhaps found himself more in tune with them than most Anglo-Saxons. His collection of excerpts from Isaiah and Jeremiah begins thus:

There are many things in books which can serve as an example, let him who will pay heed, for his own need. There was in olden days a man dear to God, the prophet Isaiah who foretold many things to the Jewish people, as it afterwards truly turned out, and that can be an example to every nation. Isaiah saw in a vision, as God granted it to him, what should happen to the people for their sins. He began then to sing and said thus: 'Hear now what God said in clear words. I have fed children and raised them up and they have left me and despised me. They mocked what they should have praised, and neglected what they should have followed, and took up foreign customs and changed all their ways; and therefore I tell you truly, your land shall be laid waste and your cities destroyed by fire. Foreigners shall harry you and when you pray and call to me, I will not hear you.'   (*Homilies*, ed. Bethurum, pp. 214–15)

Once again, the topical reference to the Viking invasions is difficult to miss. There follows a series of excerpts from the two prophets on robbery, pride, greed, gluttony, treachery and other vices of the time. Another Wulfstan piece lists excerpts from Ezekiel on negligent priests. It is difficult indeed to distinguish between the prophets' voices and Wulfstan's; Isaiah, Jeremiah and Ezekiel are clearly the model for his own writing. But Byrhtferth too, in his Latin *Life of St Oswald*, could appropriate the voice of the prophet Jeremiah as a warning to the English, quoting the prophet's warning that God would 'send and take all the kindreds of the north, and I will bring them against this land, and against the inhabitants thereof' (Jeremiah XXV.8–9).

More commonly, however, the Anglo-Saxons saw the prophets in a different light, as holy men who foretold or foreshadowed the coming of Christ. That was a role they had already begun to play in the New Testament references to them, and quotations from them therefore figure commonly in Anglo-Saxon writings on Christian themes. Bede's commentary on the song of Habbakuk (one of the minor prophets) thus interprets it as if spoken by Christ at the Passion. Ælfric lists a whole series of quotations from the prophets foretelling the coming of Christ and the Virgin Mary (see *Catholic Homilies*, ed. Thorpe I, xiii and II, i). This aspect is evident too in the references to Daniel, who was easily the most popular of the Old Testament prophets for the Anglo-Saxons: 'Daniel spoke clearly in his writings about the birth of Christ', says Ælfric. But the main interest for the Anglo-Saxons in the book of Daniel was neither its prophecies of Christ nor its examples of dream-interpretation, but its role as a historical book, a repository of dramatic stories about confrontations between God and a series of emperor-figures who represent the highest reach of man. Nebuchadnezzar in particular is an interestingly ambivalent figure. His conquest of Jerusalem is regularly presented as an act of divine retribution for the sins of the Hebrews, and Ælfric singled him out as one of the few pagans granted a perception of Christ before his coming. The account of him in the Book of Daniel shows him coming to recognize and acknowledge the true God. Yet he was also seen as a figure of grandiose pride, as we see for instance in Alfred's *Pastoral Care* (ed. Sweet, p. 38).

Both pride and divine retribution are important themes in the Old English poem called *Daniel*. The poem presents a series of falls, from prosperity and glory to pride and blasphemy, punished repeatedly by God. It begins with the Hebrews in Jerusalem, living in wealth and grandeur under the favour of God until they turn to devil-worship and neglect him, and passes on to the successive falls of Nebuchadnezzar and Balthasar (Belshazzar). In some ways this poem resembles *Genesis B* and *Christ and Satan*, using the biblical story as a framework for powerful and dramatic speeches of personal grief. Here it is particularly the speeches of the Hebrews in the fiery furnace that caught the poet's powers of imagination, as they lament their captivity and enslavement by the heathens but express their trust in God's power and call on him for help. Both the song of Azarias and the joint song of the three youths were frequently used in the liturgy, and their part in the religious life of Anglo-Saxon Christians surely contributes to the resonance these speeches have in the poem. Indeed, that part of the poem appears in expanded form as a separate poem or extract in the Exeter Book, no doubt prompted by the liturgical parallel. But one is also struck by the importance of the walled and secure city as a symbol in the poem: first Jerusalem, then Babylon under Nebuchadnezzar, and then Babylon under Balthasar are celebrated as powerful and safe citadels, only to be humbled by the destructive power of enemies. There is a pervading sense of human vulnerability in the poem: the poet dramatizes the human need to trust in the power of kings and the safety of walls, but articulates also an awareness that both can be crushed in a moment. The poem is of unknown date and one can only guess at the circumstances in which it developed. The lament over enslavement by heathens would have had a potent relevance when the poem was copied out at the end of the tenth century, but the sense of frailty and of the fleeting strengths of kings and city-walls would perhaps have had significance to the Anglo-Saxons at any time in the preceding centuries.

The psalms played an important role in the daily liturgy of the medieval church and it is to this that the many surviving copies of the psalms with an Old English gloss owe their existence. But it is striking that even the psalms could be read by the Anglo-Saxons with reference to their own times. Alfred's prose version is furnished with brief introductions which show how each psalm can be related to the situation of King David, their composer and speaker, but also to King Hezekiah and to Christ. Often the wording makes it impossible to miss the similarities not only to Alfred's lament over the decay of wisdom in the preface to the *Pastoral Care* but, more movingly, to the account in the *Chronicle* of his taking refuge in the marshes after escaping from the Vikings and the joy his supporters showed at his successful return:

David sang this tenth psalm when he was driven into the wilderness by King Saul, when his companions advised him to hide there . . . When David sang this eleventh psalm, he sighed that in his days righteousness and wisdom should be so diminished. And so does each righteous man when he sings this psalm . . . When David sang this thirteenth psalm, he lamented to the Lord that there should ever be so little fidelity in his days, and so little wisdom in the world . . . David sang this twenty-second psalm when he prophesied about his own return from exile . . . In this twenty-third psalm David prophesied concerning himself, how his ealdormen should rejoice at his returning from exile.[7]

Whether the psalm introductions influenced the way in which the chronicler and his source perceived Alfred's experiences, or whether the similarity to his own real experience led Alfred to the psalms and their prefaces, one is inevitably struck by the way in which situations are seen to repeat themselves over a gap of many centuries, between David and Alfred, Hebrews and Anglo-Saxons.

The sense of continuity is the characteristic note of Anglo-Saxon literary treatments of the Old Testament. For the Anglo-Saxons the Old Testament was a veiled way of talking about their own situation. Sometimes it was a matter of explaining how things came to be as they are in the world. Sometimes it provided a figurative framework for analysing the church and the clergy. But most often the Old Testament offered them a means of considering and articulating the ways in which kingship, politics and warfare related to the rule of God. Despite Ælfric's insistence that the old law had been replaced by the new, at least in its literal sense, in many ways the old retained its power for the Anglo-Saxons, and gave them a way of thinking about themselves as nations.

1 Ælfric's treatise on the Old and New Testaments, his preface to Genesis and the Old English prose versions of the first five books of the Bible are to be found in *The Old English Heptateuch*, ed. S. J. Crawford, EETS os 160 (London, 1922). His versions of Judith and Esther are in *Angelsächsische Homilien und Heiligenleben*, ed. B. Assmann, Bibliothek der angelsächsischen Prosa 13 (Kassel, 1889; repr. with a supplementary introduction by P. Clemoes, Darmstadt, 1964). Also relevant are 'Ælfric's Version of *Alcuini Interrogationes Sigeuulfi in Genesin*', ed. G. E. MacLean, *Anglia* 6 (1883), 425–73 and 7 (1884), 1–59; and his *Hexameron*, edited as *Exameron Anglice or the Old English Hexameron*, ed. S. J. Crawford, Bibliothek der angelsächsischen Prosa 10 (Hamburg, 1921; repr. Darmstadt, 1968). Ælfric's other renderings of Old Testament narrative and commentaries on it are to be found in the editions of his homilies and saints' lives by Thorpe, Skeat and Pope cited below (p. 291).
2 See J. McClure, 'Bede's Old Testament Kings', in *Ideal and Reality in Frankish and Anglo-Saxon Society*, ed. P. Wormald *et al.* (Oxford, 1983), pp. 76–98.
3 There is a lucid account of the development of allegorical interpretations of the Bible by J. Leclercq in *The Cambridge History of the Bible, II: The West from*

the Fathers to the Reformation, ed. G. W. H. Lampe (Cambridge, 1969), pp. 183–96.
4 See A. N. Doane, Genesis A: a New Edition (Madison, WN, 1978), pp. 22–3.
5 See R. Melinkoff, 'Cain's Monstrous Progeny in Beowulf', ASE 8 (1979), 143–62, and 9 (1980), 183–97.
6 See Ælfric's Interrogationes, ed. McLean, p. 40, and Catholic Homilies, ed. Thorpe I, 318.
7 Liber Psalmorum: the West Saxon Psalms, ed. J. W. Bright and R. L. Ramsay (Boston and London, 1907).

13 Biblical literature: the New Testament

UNLIKE the Old Testament poetry from the Anglo-Saxon period, Old English poems on New Testament themes were essentially non-narrative works. Anglo-Saxon poets ignored what one might consider to be the most attractive parts of the gospels, the stories of the nativity, the shepherds and the magi, the baptism of Christ, the turning of water into wine at the marriage at Cana, the raising of Lazarus, the moral teachings of the sermon on the mount and the accounts of miraculous healings, and chose instead to write about the great events of salvation history: the incarnation, the crucifixion, the harrowing of hell, the ascension and the last judgement. Moreover, in treating these subjects they did not draw primarily on the gospel texts: their main sources were the liturgy, apocryphal writings such as the *Gospel of Nicodemus*, Latin homilies and the traditions of the church.

This difference in approach results from a difference in the way in which God's plan for the world was thought to be revealed through the Old and New Testaments. The Old Testament showed the unrolling of God's plan through history: the creation of the world by God, man's fall from grace and the series of initiatives through which God tried to bring man back to himself. The New Testament showed God's revelation of himself through the incarnation of his Son. The Old Testament, then, was concerned with change; it constantly pressed forward towards the coming of Christ. The New Testament cut across this forward movement by showing the conjunction of history with eternity. In contrast to the narrative revelation of the Old Testament, the revelation of the gospels was static, a showing forth of the unchanging and eternal God, now seen in human form. In the words of the Epistle to the Hebrews,

At various times in the past and in various different ways, God spoke to our ancestors through the prophets; but in our own time, the last days, he has spoken to us through his Son, the Son that he has appointed to inherit everything and through whom he made everything there is. He is the radiant light of God's glory and the perfect copy of his nature, sustaining the universe by his powerful command.   (Heb. I.1–3)

The gospels, then, were not primarily the story of a human life; instead, they brought man face to face with eternity in the shape of God incarnate. Of course, they offered a narrative account of parts of Christ's life, but their significance lay in the relationship of that life to God's eternal plan.

This emphasis on God's plan of redemption can be seen in individual Old English poems and in the selection and arrangement of those poems in the manuscripts. The poem known as *The Dream of the Rood* places Christ's death on the cross at the centre of redemption history, from the tree in the garden of Eden to the tree of life by the river of life in the Apocalypse. In addition, it relates the theme of the cross as the tree of life very closely to the needs of the dreamer and to his future death and salvation. It is a meditation on the implications of Christ's death for man rather than a simple account of that death. The poem known as *Christ and Satan*, which forms the final item in a collection of biblical poetry in Junius 11 in the Bodleian Library, complements the manuscript's Old Testament poems, *Genesis* and *Exodus*, by showing Christ's reversal of man's fall. The first three poems in the Exeter Book, which are concerned with Christ's coming to earth, his ascension into heaven and his return as judge, and which are known collectively as the *Christ*, have been grouped together to illustrate a single theme: God's redemption of man. Christ's descent to earth is portrayed as something planned from the beginning of time, foretold by the prophets, long awaited by man; Christ's purpose is seen to be fulfilled only at the end of time, when he returns to judge those he has redeemed.

This way of looking at Christ's life derives from the church's liturgy, in particular, the liturgy for Advent and Lent. Each year the church relives the history of God's dealings with man. The main feasts of the church's year commemorate events from Christ's earthly life, especially those related to his birth and his death. At the same time, the church remembers the whole of salvation history, from the creation to the last judgement. These two time sequences were seen as strictly parallel to each other (cf. above, pp. 166 and 191). For example, God's creation of the world in six days was thought to be paralleled by his re-creation of it in six ages. The redemption of man by Christ's death on the tree of the cross was seen as a reversal of man's fall through eating the fruit of the tree of knowledge. Christ's transition from death to life at his resurrection, which took place at the Jewish feast of passover, was thought to be a re-enactment of the crossing of the Red Sea by the Israelites at the time of the first passover. Through the liturgy of the church, man was able to enter into these two series of events. During Advent he shared the longing of the patriarchs and prophets for Christ's coming. At the same time he knew that Christ had already been born, and he looked forward to his return as judge. During Lent the church prepared ,for the redemption by imitating Christ's forty-day fast while, at the same time, recalling the Old Testament events which led up to Christ's coming: God's creation of the world, the expulsion of Adam and Eve from the garden of Eden, the saving of Noah and his family in the ark, God's promises to Abraham and his covenant with Moses.

The way in which the Anglo-Saxon church understood Christ's birth is clearly expressed in the prayers and paintings in a tenth-century manuscript which belonged to Bishop Æthelwold of Winchester and which contained the solemn blessings given by the bishop during the mass. The blessings for the first Sunday in Advent link Christ's two comings in the words, 'that you who rejoice with devout mind at the coming of our redeemer according to the flesh, may receive the rewards of eternal life when he comes again in majesty'. The two paintings in the Advent section of the manuscript show the annunciation and the second coming. The first looks back to the Old Testament. It depicts Mary reading a book, recalling the belief, expressed among others by Bede, that she was familiar with Isaiah's prophecy of Christ's birth, 'The maiden is with child and will soon give birth to a son whom she will call Immanuel' (Isaiah VII.14). The second painting looks forward to the end of time and shows Christ returning to earth as judge, accompanied by angels carrying the symbols of his passion, the spear, the sponge and the cross. The association of ideas in these two paintings is close to that of the first and third parts of the Old English *Christ*, which present Christ's birth as the fulfilment of the prophecies and which depict the judgement as the time when man will be asked how he has responded to Christ's death on the cross.

The pictures in Æthelwold's Benedictional are concerned with abstract, intellectual relationships. The gospel story was seen to be true because it fulfilled the Old Testament prophecies; Christ's death would be recalled at the judgement and would provide the basis for that judgement. This kind of relationship played a major part in poems such as *The Dream of the Rood* and the first part of the *Christ*. Other poems, however, demanded an emotional response rather than an intellectual one. This response, too, derived from the liturgy. The Holy Week ceremonies, which involved a dramatic re-enactment of the events surrounding Christ's death, allowed the congregation to enter directly into the events they recalled. These ceremonies developed from the practice in fourth-century Jerusalem of recalling events such as Christ's entry to Jerusalem, his death on the cross, his resurrection from the dead or his ascension into heaven in the places where they originally happened. Accounts of the Jerusalem liturgy by early pilgrims to the Holy Land show how emotional these commemorations were; and the instructions for the Holy Week liturgy in the tenth-century English document known as the *Regularis concordia* make it clear that the purpose of, for example, the darkening of the church during the singing of the *Kyrie* on the last three days of Holy Week, was to evoke an emotional response. The Good Friday liturgy did not simply remind the congregation of Christ's death. The semi-dramatic reading of the Passion according to St John was followed, as it is today, by the solemn veneration of the cross, during which the following chants were sung:

Because I led you through the desert for forty years, and fed you with manna, and brought you into an exceedingly good land, you have prepared a cross for your Saviour.

What more should I have done for you, that I have not done? I planted you, indeed, as a most beautiful vineyard, and you have become very bitter to me, for in my thirst you gave me vinegar to drink and with a spear you have pierced the side of your Saviour.

In these chants, Christ is imagined addressing the congregation from the cross and reminding them of their ingratitude in the face of God's goodness. These reproaches formed the basis of a scene described in several Latin and Old English homilies, and in the third part of the *Christ*, in which Christ the judge reproaches man for failing to make some return for all that Christ had done for him. In tenth- and eleventh-century England, participation in the events surrounding Christ's death went further than this. The commemoration of the crucifixion was followed by a ceremony in which a cross, representing Christ, was buried in a curtained tomb placed near the high altar of the church. The monks took it in turn to watch over the tomb until Easter morning, when the cross was secretly removed. A further ceremony then took place in which a monk dressed in an alb went and sat by the tomb, impersonating the angel who announced Christ's resurrection to the women in the gospels, while three other monks approached the tomb, in imitation of the women coming to anoint Christ's body. The chants sung during this ritual are one of the earliest examples of church drama:

Whom do you seek in the sepulchre, O followers of Christ?
Jesus of Nazareth, who was crucified, O heavenly dweller.
He is not here, he is risen as he had foretold; go and announce that he is risen, saying: Alleluia, the Lord has risen today, the mighty lion, Christ the Son of God. Thanks be to God, eya.
Come and see the place where the Lord was laid, alleluia, alleluia. Go quickly and tell the disciples that the Lord is risen, alleluia, alleluia.
The Lord has risen from the grave, he who for us hung on the tree, alleluia.

In these ceremonies, the church did not merely recall past events; it re-created them in the present. Furthermore, it taught that man partici-pated in these events, not simply as an observer but as an actor. The Easter

Vigil service, which commemorated Christ's passover from death to life, was also the occasion when the font was blessed and the catechumens were baptized. Their baptism was a sharing in Christ's death and resurrection. As St Paul said in a passage from the Epistle to the Romans read during the Easter Vigil service: 'When we were baptized in Christ Jesus we were baptized in his death; in other words, when we were baptized we went into the tomb with him and joined him in death, so that as Christ was raised from the dead by the Father's glory, we too might live a new life' (Rom. VI.3–4). Moreover, Christ's death and resurrection – and man's sharing in Christ's death through baptism – were thought to be a recapitulation of the crossing of the Red Sea by the Israelites and of their entry into the promised land. Ælfric, for example, says in a homily for Quadragesima:

Seo Reade Sæ hæfde getacnunge ures fulluhtes, on ðære adranc Pharao and his here samod, swa eac on urum gastlicum fulluhte bið se deofol forsmorod fram us, and ealle ure synna beoð adylegode, and we ðonne sigefæste mid geleafan Godes lof singað, anbidigende mid geðylde þæs ecan eðeles.   (*Catholic Homilies II*, ed. Godden, p. 115)

The Red Sea, in which Pharoah and his army drowned together, is a symbol of our baptism. In the same way, in our spiritual baptism, the devil is stifled by us and all our sins are destroyed. Then, victorious, we sing God's praise with faith, patiently awaiting the eternal homeland.

It is ideas like these which lie behind the collection of poems in the eleventh-century manuscript, Junius 11, in the Bodleian Library, Oxford. The manuscript contains three Old Testament poems, *Genesis* (*A* and *B*), *Exodus* and *Daniel*, which provide parallels to much of the Old Testament material in the readings for Lent and for the Easter Vigil, together with a New Testament poem, *Christ and Satan*, which complements the Old Testament narratives by showing God's triumph over Satan through the death and resurrection of Christ. This last poem is a meditation on God's plan of salvation, established from the beginning of creation, a plan which, as the poet says, no one but God can fully understand:

                    Hwa is þæt ðe cunne
     orðonc clene   nymðe ece god?   (*Christ and Satan* 17–18)
     Who but eternal God understands the whole plan of salvation?

The Old English *Genesis* poem (*Genesis A*) and the extract translated from the Old Saxon *Genesis* and interpolated in it (*Genesis B*) had described the origin of Satan's feud with God and his success in seducing Adam and Eve from their allegiance to God (cf. above, pp. 212–14). *Christ and Satan* shows Christ's reversal of this apparent victory through a series of conflicts with Satan which culminate in the release of Adam and Eve from hell and their reinstatement as God's servants. As was the case in the two *Genesis* poems, the conflict between God and Satan is presented in heroic rather than religious terms. In other respects, however, the treatment of the theme of Satan's feud with God is very different. Whereas *Genesis A* and *Genesis B* presented the story of Satan's rebellion and fall and his temptation of Adam and Eve in a straightforward narrative way, in *Christ and Satan* the story has to be pieced together from a series of laments uttered by Satan and his followers after their fall into hell. In addition, Satan's adversary is not God the Father but Christ, creator and saviour of mankind and ruler of heaven and hell. Satan's fall is no longer seen as something which took place in the distant past; it becomes part of the ever-present conflict between good and evil in which the reader of the poem has to play his part.

The poem falls into three main sections: the laments by Satan and the other fallen angels about their folly in rebelling against God and losing their home in heaven, a brief narrative account of the harrowing of hell, the resurrection, the ascension and the last judgement and a final section on the temptation of Christ. Throughout the poem, Christ is shown as a figure of power who controls the order of the world (1–18), drives the rebellious angels out of heaven (67–8), breaks open the doors of hell (379–80) and leads the exiles back to their true home in heaven (502–7). Satan is no longer the proud figure described in the two *Genesis* poems but a weary and loquacious exile who ends his days measuring the pit of hell (698–709). These two opposing and contrasted figures are placed in a timeless setting which encompasses God's creation of the world at one extreme and the final judgement at the other. At the centre of this cosmic drama is man, trapped and imprisoned by Satan, rescued by Christ and now confronting his eternal destiny. Before him lies a choice: on the one hand, the misery of hell, presented in terms of exile from the joys of God's court in heaven – an image with powerful associations for a society of which the centre was the lord's hall – on the other, the bright city of God with its royal throne (285–97). Again and again the reader is reminded that he should learn from Satan's fate (193–208) and that he should thank Christ for freeing him from prison and leading him back to his true home (549–54). The moral, pressed home at intervals throughout the poem, is that man should realize the terrible end of those who rebel against God, and that he should accept what is so graciously offered to him by Christ.

The central figure in *Christ and Satan*, then, is man, and the time, the present. Like the figure of Mankind in the fourteenth-century morality play, *The Castle of Perseverance*, man is surrounded by the forces of good and evil and confronted by a choice between them. Satan's rebellion, the harrowing of hell and the last judgement are not events remembered from the past or anticipated in the future; they are experienced by man in the present and show him how he should act. This mingling of past, present and future time appears again in the other New Testament poems of the Anglo-Saxon period, *The Dream of the Rood* and the three poems known collectively as the *Christ*.

The first part of the *Christ* (*Christ I*) is based on a series of antiphons sung at the *Magnificat* during the days immediately before Christmas, though the material from these antiphons is enriched and expanded with a wealth of scriptural material and patristic commentary on it. In these antiphons the church associates herself with the longing of the prophets for the coming of the Messiah and, with them, calls on Christ to come and save his people. Most of the antiphons are addressed to Christ but some are addressed to his mother, to the city of Jerusalem or to Gabriel, the angel of the annunciation. The poem is usually printed as a series of twelve lyrics, each corresponding to one of the antiphons. In the manuscript, however, it is divided into five sections, each marked by a large capital, and that is how it will be considered here. The major theme of the poem is Christ's divine and human natures. To put it differently, it is not a poem about the birth of Christ but about the entry into historical time of the God who exists outside time with no beginning or end. The emphasis, then, is not on the human elements – the baby in the manger, the ox and ass, the shepherds and the kings – but on the significance of Christ's incarnation for the redemption of man.

The first part of the poem (1–70) is based on three antiphons:

O king whom all the peoples desire, you are the cornerstone which makes all one. O come and save man whom you made from clay.
O key of David and sceptre of Israel, what you open no one else can close again; what you close no one can open. O come to lead the captive from prison; free those who sit in darkness and in the shadow of death.
O Jerusalem, city of the great God; lift up your eyes round about and see your Lord who comes now to free you from your chains.

The themes of Christ's kingship and of his release of man from captivity are expanded through the use of biblical and theological ideas only hinted at in these antiphons. Christ is portrayed not only as the cornerstone which links together the Jews and Gentiles but as the craftsman and architect. He created man from the earth and now comes to restore the ruined house of man's body. The earthly city of Jerusalem, freed by Christ, is also a symbol of the heavenly Jerusalem, the reward given to man by Christ. The longing of the patriarchs and prophets for the coming of the Messiah is made one with the longing of the Christian for his home in heaven. Christ is both awaited and yet has already come. All depends on Christ: he chooses Mary as his mother; the initiative is his.

In the second part of the poem (71–163) the poet moves away from these large-scale themes to focus more sharply on the incarnation. This part of the poem begins with a dialogue between Mary and the sons and daughters of Jerusalem, based on the antiphon, 'O virgin of virgins, how can this be, for there is none like you either before or after? Daughters of Jerusalem, why do you wonder at me? What you see is a divine mystery.' The poet expands the theme of the antiphon by returning to the idea of the incarnation as the reversal of man's fall. Whereas in the first part of the poem this idea was expressed through the image of Christ renewing Adam's body, created from the earth (14–15), the emphasis here is on Mary as the one through whom the guilt of Eve is taken away (96–9). This address to Mary, and her reply, is followed by lines based on the antiphon, 'O rising sun, you are the splendour of eternal light and the sun of justice. O come and enlighten those who sit in darkness and in the shadow of death.' Christ is portrayed, as he was in the first section, as the light which enters the darkness of the world, but the poet also emphasizes the word 'eternal': Christ is the Word of God, eternally present with his Father, and now made flesh so that the Son of God and the Son of man are seen together in this world (120–6). This theme is taken up in the lines based on the third antiphon for this section, 'O Emmanuel, you are our king and judge, the One whom the peoples await and their Saviour. O come and save us, Lord, our God.' The word *Emmanuel* means 'God with us' and, in the closing lines of the section, the poet calls on Christ, the creator of the world, to come and lead those he created back with him to heaven where he lives eternally with his Father (149–63).

The third section of the poem (164–274) starts with a dialogue between Mary and Joseph which may be based on the antiphon, 'O Joseph, why did you believe what before you feared? Why indeed? The One whom Gabriel announced would be the coming Christ is begotten in her by the Holy Spirit.' The poem continues with lines based on the antiphon, 'O king of peace, born before all ages. Pass through the golden door, visit your redeemed and call them back to the place from which they fell through their fault.' At first sight this section of the poem seems concerned with the human dilemma of Joseph when confronted with his wife's pregnancy and the demands of the Jewish law, but this dialogue, like that with the daughters of Jerusalem earlier in the poem, is simply a prelude to a statement by Mary of theological truth: the divine origin of her son. The themes once again are that prophecy has been fulfilled (212), that Christ is both God and man, that Mary is the temple of God in which Christ rests (206). After the emphasis on the human birth of Christ in the dialogue with Joseph, the poet returns to the theme of Christ's eternal birth from the Father (218–23). Christ is the wisdom of God through whom he created all things (239).

The fourth part of the poem (275–377), like parts 2 and 3, starts with an address to Mary. This section is based on the antiphon, 'O queen of the world, born from royal stock, Christ proceeded from your womb like a bridegroom from his chamber; he who rules the stars lies here in the manger.' Mary is described in the Old English text as queen of heaven, earth and hell, she is the bride of Christ, fulfilling Isaiah's prophecy (mentioned in the antiphon, 'O king of peace', used in section 3) that God will pass through the golden gate and lock it after him. The section ends with a petition to Mary, as she holds the Christ Child, to plead with her Son to restore man to heaven. Here, the poet makes one of his sudden shifts in regard to time. In the earlier sections of the poem the audience imagined itself in the position of the patriarchs and prophets awaiting the coming of the Messiah; here they see Christ already born into this world. But, immediately, the poet returns to his broader theme of Christ's divine nature, in lines based on a North Italian antiphon, 'O Lord of the heavens, you who live eternally with the Father together with the Holy Spirit, hear your servants, come to save us, do not delay.' Once more he calls on Christ to come and save mankind, held captive by the devil. The themes of this section are those repeated throughout *Christ I*: man's helplessness, his imprisonment, his need of Christ, his desire for release. The tone is that of the chants for the fourth Sunday in Advent and the Magnificat antiphon for 19 December (not used in *Christ I*): *iam noli tardare*, 'do not delay'.

The fifth, and final, part of the poem (378–439) sums up the theme of Advent in a meditation on the mystery of Christ's incarnation, based on an antiphon sung at the end of the octave of Christmas, 'O admirable interchange: the Creator of mankind, assuming a human body, deigned to be born of a virgin: and becoming man without man's seed bestowed on us his divinity.' The poet then turns, once more, to man, who will receive God's favour, the reward of eternal life in heaven.

The second poem in the Exeter Book, known as *Christ II*, is concerned with Christ's ascension. It is by the poet Cynewulf, and his signature appears in runic letters at the end of the poem. The main source of the poem is a homily by Pope Gregory the Great, and the tone of the poem is much more homiletic than that of the essentially meditative *Christ I*, though many of the themes are the same. The substance of both poems is the theme of redemption through Christ's incarnation and the fact that this has enabled man to choose the life he will lead. In both, Christ is the powerful king who comes to save mankind. But whereas in *Christ I* the emphasis is largely on petition, and on the recognition of man's need, in *Christ II* there is a stress also on man's duty to take hold of the salvation offered to him, because the day of judgement will come. This theme is made explicit in the final passage of the poem where Cynewulf turns to his own needs. God is man's shield and no one who is under his protection need fear. The mighty God came humbly to earth. Yet the judgement will be terrible and man should take heed while he can. We must fix our hope on that harbour which Christ prepared for us when he returned to heaven and to which we will come after the sea journey of life. This homiletic element even affects the treatment of Old Testament prophecy in the poem. Cynewulf uses Gregory's expansion of a verse from the Song of Songs (II.8), 'I hear my beloved. See how he comes leaping on the mountains, bounding over the hills.' Gregory interpreted the passage as an allusion to the acts by which Christ redeemed mankind: the incarnation, the nativity, the crucifixion, the burial, the descent to hell and the ascension. Typically, Cynewulf draws a moral conclusion from the parallel: we must imitate Christ's leaps across the earth in our meditations so that we too can ascend to the heights of heaven.

Christ II provides a link between Christ I, with its celebration of the incarnation, and Christ III, which reminds man of the coming judgement. The opening lines of the poem contrast the appearance of white-robed angels at Christ's departure from this world with the angels who announced his birth. Christ's return to heaven marks the completion of his redemptive act, the moment when his human nature is taken up into heaven to God's throne. But it also prefigures his return as judge and therefore forms a fitting introduction to the description of the judgement in Christ III.

This third part of the Christ is based largely on a sermon by Caesarius of Arles and therefore shares the homiletic tone of Christ II. The message of both is similar: that man should repent while there is still time, and confess his sins to a priest so that he will not be shamed publicly at the judgement. But it also resembles Christ I in the way in which it transports the audience into a world where all history is present. Just as Christ I allowed the audience to move between the world of the prophets, the world of the gospels and the Anglo-Saxon world, so Christ III carries man forward to the day of judgement but, at the same time, transports him back to Golgotha and the death of Christ. Christ's blood-stained cross is raised up and Christ himself appears, still bearing the marks of the wounds in his hands, feet and side. Christ's sufferings are vividly brought before those awaiting judgement and they realize that it is they who have tortured him, not people in the distant past. The sense of immediacy is enhanced, as it is in the Good Friday ceremonies, by the reproaches addressed to men by Christ, by his reminders of how he created man, how he left his home in heaven in order to save him when he had fallen into the devil's power, how he suffered hardship and finally a cruel death for man's sake.

The way in which Christ himself is presented in these poems – and in some of the Old English homilies – shows the influence of two traditions, both stemming ultimately from the Bible and the liturgy. Christ's death on the cross is portrayed both as the culmination of the sufferings he endured for man and as a military victory. Descriptions of Christ's sufferings are associated primarily with literature on the last judgement, where they provide the basis for man's condemnation. In contrast, Christ's entry to Jerusalem, his harrowing of hell and his ascension are normally portrayed in Old English literature in a heroic, triumphal way. The Blickling homily for Palm Sunday, for example, compares Christ's entry to Jerusalem to the reception of a king returning from battle:

Þa bæron hie him togeanes blowende palmtwigu; forþon þe hit wæs Iudeisc þeaw, þonne heora ciningas hæfdon sige geworht on heora feondum, and hie wæron eft ham hweorfende, þonne eodan hie him togeanes mid blowendum palmtwigum, heora siges to wyorþmyndum. Wel þæt gedafenode þæt Drihten swa dyde on þa gelicnesse; forþon þe he wæs wuldres cyning.   (*Blickling Homilies*, ed. Morris, p. 67)

Then they carried waving palm-branches before him, because it was the Jewish custom, when their kings had won a victory over their enemies and they were returning home again, to go towards them with waving palm-branches in honour of their victory. It was very fitting that the Lord should act in the same way, because he was the king of glory.

In Cynewulf's ascension poem, Christ's arrival in heaven is described as the entry of a military ruler into his city:

Wile nu gesecan   sawla nergend
gæsta giefstol,   godes agen bearn,
æfter guðplegan.   Nu ge geare cunnon
hwæt se hlaford is   se þisne here lædeð,
nu ge fromlice   freondum togeanes
gongað glædmode.   Geatu, ontynað!
Wile in to eow   ealles waldend,
cyning on ceastre,   corðre ne lytle,
fyrnweorca fruma,   folc gelædan
in dreama dream,   ðe he on deoflum genom
þurh his sylfes sygor.   (*Christ* 571–81)

Now the Saviour of souls, God's own child, will seek the gift-throne of spirits after his war-play. Now you know for certain what the lord is who leads this army. Go now, quickly and gladly, towards your friends. Gates, open up! The ruler of all wishes to enter you, to go into his city with a great company; he who created all things long ago wishes to lead his people into the joy of joys, those whom he seized from the devil through his own victory.

The description of Christ the king demanding admittance through the gates of heaven is based on a passage from Psalm XXIII.7–10 which was sung when the Palm Sunday procession arrived at the locked doors of the church and which was commonly interpreted as a prophecy both of the harrowing of hell and of Christ's ascension. The most dramatic expression of this theme is that in Bede's description of the ascension:

Then an angel's voice came and said, 'Now open the gates and the Lord of everlasting peace, the King of glory, will enter in.' A voice from the inner ramparts of the bountiful city replied, 'Who is this King of glory who can enter heaven's gates?' . . . But a herald of the great Judge said, 'This is the powerful and mighty Lord who triumphantly overthrew the world's black prince in battle. Wherefore, be lifted up, you gates of eternal heaven, so the King of glory may enter, the King of virtue and grace.' Still amazed, the court of celestial citizens asks, 'Who is the King of glory, this King who is so praiseworthy?' Straightaway the Master's herald replied, 'He is the highest Author of all virtues; he shines forth as the King of glory.' At these words the King of glory, together with the shining host, entered into highest heaven, into his kingdom of glory.

(trans. Calder and Allen, *Sources and Analogues*, pp. 82–3)

In Cynewulf's poem these biblical images of triumph are extended through words and ideas which stem from the Anglo-Saxon world rather than from the world of the Bible. Christ is described as a prince (*æþeling*) with a band of thegns (*þegna gedryht*). He is a treasure-giver (*sincgiefa*) who offers rewards (*lean*) to those who follow him. He mounts a military attack on hell and returns to heaven with his booty, the souls he has rescued. And to celebrate his victory, like a true king, he gives gifts to his followers:

Ða us geweorðade   se þas world gescop,
godes gæstsunu,   ond us giefe sealde,
uppe mid englum   ece staþelas,
ond eac monigfealde   modes snyttru
seow ond sette   geond sefan monna.
Sumum wordlaþe   wise sendeð
on his modes gemynd   þurh his muþes gæst,
æðele ondgiet.   Se mæg eal fela
singan ond secgan   þam bið snyttru cræft
bifolen on ferðe.   Sum mæg fingrum wel
hlude fore hæleþum   hearpan stirgan,
gleobeam gretan.   Sum mæg godcunde
reccan ryhte æ.   Sum mæg ryne tungla
secgan, side gesceaft.   Sum mæg searolice
wordcwide writan.   Sumum wiges sped
giefeð æt guþe,   þonne gargetrum

ofer scildhreadan   sceotend sendað,
flacor flangeweorc.   Sum mæg fromlice
ofer sealtne sæ   sundwudu drifan,
hreran holmþræce.   Sum mæg heanne beam
stælgne gestigan.   Sum mæg styled sweord,
wæpen gewyrcan.   Sum con wonga bigong,
wegas widgielle.   Swa se waldend us,
godbearn on grundum,   his giefe bryttað.   (*Christ* 659–82)

Then he who created this world, God's spiritual son, honoured us and gave us gifts, a lasting place on high among the angels, and also sowed and set in the mind of men many kinds of wisdom of heart. One he allows to remember wise poems, sends him a noble understanding, through the spirit of his mouth. The man whose mind has been given the art of wisdom can sing and say all kinds of things. Another can with his fingers skilfully and loudly set the harp in motion before heroes, touch the joyful wood. One knows how to recite the divine law. One can describe the course of the stars, the broad creation. Another can skilfully write down language. To one he gives military success in battle, when the archers send arrows flying above the shields towards the armed men. One can swiftly steer the ship over the salt sea, stir up the restless ocean. One can climb the tall and upright tree. One knows how to make a weapon, a steely sword. One knows the expanse of the plains and the wide ways. So the ruler, God's Son, gives us his gifts on earth.

The idea that Christ gave gifts at his ascension comes from the Epistle to the Ephesians (IV.8), 'When he ascended on high he led a host of captives, and he gave gifts to men.' St Paul, however, is talking of spiritual gifts, whereas the gifts listed by Cynewulf also include talents such as playing the harp, climbing trees or steering a ship which are more appropriate to the secular, Germanic world. The theme is, in fact, a common one in Old English poetry, and forms the main part of the poems *The Gifts of Men* and *The Fates of Men*.

In *The Dream of the Rood* these two traditions are brought together. Christ is portrayed as the young hero, reigning from the cross, but, at the same time, he is described as cruelly stretched out, weary of limb, enduring severe torment. The combination is important for the argument of the poem, for here man is saved not, as he is in *Christ I* or *Christ and Satan*, by the intervention of a powerful king, but by participating in the suffering of Christ which ends in glory.

The Dream of the Rood has been preserved in two different versions. The first is found in a late tenth-century collection of religious prose and verse now in the Chapter Library at Vercelli in northern Italy; the second consists of extracts from the central part of this poem, or an earlier version of it, carved on the eighth-century Ruthwell Cross. The Vercelli text falls into four clearly defined sections: a descriptive vision of a strange sign which is eventually identified as a cross; a narrative vision in which the cross describes Christ's death and its own part in that death; an address by the cross to the dreamer, asking him to tell his vision to others; the reflections of the dreamer about the cross and the part devotion to it plays in his life. In form the poem is a dream vision and it contains the elements one would expect of such a vision including the figure of authority (the cross). The poem is also a meditation in correct form in that it involves recall and visualization of a scene from the gospels, reflection on the implications of the scene and moral decision arising from these reflections. No definite source has been found for the poem, and in this it differs from the three *Christ* poems with their identifiable homiletic and liturgical sources. Stylistically, however, it contains elements of the riddle form (a common literary form of the period: see below, p. 267) and many of the ideas in it can be paralleled in the art of the early Christian period, in the liturgy and in patristic commentaries on the Bible. The opening vision, which has all the ambiguities of the riddles, is also very visual and assumes familiarity with the jewelled crosses of the early Christian period and with a type of draped cross derived from the late classical military trophy. The picture of Christ willingly mounting the cross has all the heroic qualities of secular writing. The cross itself is portrayed as the retainer, forced to acquiesce in the death of its lord. Heaven is God's banqueting hall where the devout Christian will feast and receive treasure in the company of his friends. The dreamer participates in all this. In terms of time, he is like the Christian at the liturgy, where past and present merge and man can share in events from Christ's life as though he were really present. He also looks forward to his own death when he will receive his reward and meet once more the cross which is the object of his devotion. In this respect it is a true meditation, for prayer looks forward to the next world; its focus is not the present.

The heroic elements in *The Dream of the Rood* distinguish it from the treatment of Christ's death in *Christ III*. The most important difference between the two, however, concerns man's response to Christ's death. Emotionally, the last judgement poem is founded on guilt and fear. The poem presents the judgement as something to be feared rather than looked forward to, and when Christ speaks to man and recalls his death on the cross it is to reproach man with ingratitude. Man is made to feel that he was personally responsible for Christ's death on the cross, for that death was the result of man's sins. Man therefore views the crucifixion with a feeling of guilt: this is what he did. In *The Dream of the Rood* the whole atmosphere and approach is different. Death is something to be hoped for rather than feared. The reason for this is that man's role in Christ's death is viewed quite differently. The dreamer first sees a strange sign, which changes from a blood-stained cross to a jewelled one. At the start of the poem, he is contrasted with the shining cross of his vision, for he is full of sin. As he listens to the cross's account of Christ's death, however, his relationship to the cross changes. He gradually becomes assimilated to it, as the cross becomes assimilated to Christ. Like Christ, the cross suffers wounds which it retains in its glorified state; it is buried and raised from the grave; it shares the honour given to Christ. Through his devotion to the cross, the dreamer is able to share Christ's sufferings and, like the cross, he too can share Christ's glory. That is his hope, seen most vividly in the question asked by Christ at the judgement:

> Fríneð he for þære mænige   hwær se man sie,
> se ðe for dryhtnes naman   deaðes wolde
> biteres onbyrigan,   swa he ær on ðam beame dyde.
> *(Dream of the Rood* 112–14)

He will ask in front of the assembly where the man is who will taste bitter death for the Lord's name, as he did before on the cross.

The logic is subtle. The cross is the retainer of Christ. It is forced, against all the instincts of the retainer in the Germanic tradition, to assist at the death of its lord. Conventionally the retainer should avenge his lord but this the cross is forbidden to do. Yet, even though it has run counter to all that was demanded of the retainer, it is highly honoured. The reason is that the cross is seen as acting unwillingly. If man is like the cross he, too, can be seen in this way. He is forgiven as the soldiers were forgiven by Christ when he said, 'Father forgive them for they know not what they do.' Man, therefore, is relieved of the burden of guilt in Christ's death. He can see himself as the unwilling partner in Christ's death, as the cross was. If the cross can be forgiven, so can man. In this respect *The Dream of the Rood* is much closer to *Christ I* than to *Christ III*. In both, man is seen as helpless and dependent but as hoping in Christ's generosity. In both there is an emphasis on forgiveness, on gratitude and on reinstatement, on man's return to his home in heaven. Yet although both poems have this hope they are different in their manner, for *The Dream of the Rood* is concerned primarily with the individual, whereas *Christ I* is concerned with the group. In the first poem, man meditates on the mystery of the cross and its implications for him as an individual; in the second, man is one of a group, joined to the patriarchs and prophets, sharing in the redemption of the whole of mankind, a far more public matter.

The time scale of all these poems is divine, not human. All are concerned with salvation as something planned by God from the beginning. All portray Christ as the one in whom history intersects with eternity. All lift man from his time-bound existence into an immediate and direct experience of redemption. They are not imaginative reconstructions of the world of the Bible like those found in some late medieval works such as *The*

Book of Margery Kempe, and there is no place in them for the sentiment of the ox and ass at the manger or for the human details of the grief of Mary and John and Christ's forgiveness of the repentant thief. They are not stories about Christ's life, but meditations on salvation history, designed to show the significance of the gospel events for those who read or hear them.

14   The saintly life in Anglo-Saxon England

If a modern English traveller could suddenly be transported back a thousand years into an Anglo-Saxon church, he would be astonished at the differences between that and the churches with which he is familiar today: here, the atmosphere inside most churches is one of calm and beatific silence; there, the prevailing atmosphere would be one of tumult and squalor, the church packed day and night with crowds of diseased and penitent persons seeking release from their sufferings through the intercession of the saint whose shrine they were besieging. A memorable picture of such tumult is given by Lantfred, a foreign monk at Winchester in the 970s, who, describing the miracles performed through the agency of St Swithun – then recently discovered and recently translated – shows us the inside of the Old Minster crammed with persons afflicted with appalling physical deformities, festering wounds, blind, paralytic, deaf, dumb, mutilated indescribably by the just process of the law or by self-imposed penitential torture, all clustered around the shrine of St Swithun, lying there day and night moaning in pain and praying aloud for deliverance from their suffering. On occasion, Lantfred reports, the church's precincts were so plugged with diseased persons that they had periodically to be cleared to make way for the clergy. Whereas today such appalling sights of disease, deformity and suffering are hidden from sight in sanitized hospitals, a thousand years ago they were on full view, every day of the year, in every church which had a saint deemed to be capable of performing a miraculous cure.[1]

The focus of the people's attention in an Anglo-Saxon church, therefore, was the shrine of the saint who could intercede with God on behalf of the petitioning sufferer or sinner. We should not imagine that the saints were conceived abstractly as disembodied spirits. Theirs was a physical and palpable presence: that is to say, the saint was physically present in each shrine insofar as that shrine contained a relic of his/her body – a bone, a fingernail, a lock of hair, whatever.[2] And contact with the saint's miraculous power could be established by touching that relic. Accordingly, reliquaries were constructed so that the petitioner could have physical access to the saint – by reaching in and touching the relic, or at least by seeing it. Saints' relics were highly prized by their ecclesiastical owners, not only for their efficacy in curing illnesses, but also for their economic benefits, for it goes without saying that, if a rich man were to be cured by the saint, he would properly show gratitude by making a donation to the church which housed that saint's relics. Given this economic dimension, it is hardly surprising that trade in relics was big business. The market for relics was a lucrative one, with both royal and ecclesiastical collectors competing for the prizes. We know from Bede, for example, that Bishop Acca of Hexham acquired relics of apostles and martyrs from diverse sources, built altars to house them, and then assembled a collection of hagiographical books to explain their lives and passions (*HE* V.20). On the other hand, a famous royal collector was King Athelstan (d. 939), who is known to have amassed a huge collection of relics, and then distributed them to various churches. Exeter, for example, claimed to possess a long list of relics, the 'greatest part of which' was allegedly donated by Athelstan. These include the usual relics of Christ (parts of his manger, cross, sepulchre, soil from the Mount of Olives, etc.), of the apostles (bits of the hair and beard of St Peter), and of the martyrs (a stone that killed St Stephen, a coal that fried St Laurence), especially their bones. Indeed Exeter boasted relics of all the best known martyrs: Quirinus, Crisantus and Daria, Sebastian, Vitalis, Apollinaris, Quintinus, Cornelius, Marcellus, Vitus, Nicasius, Tiburtius, Ciriacus, Heresius, and so on and on (these are just the martyrs, by the way: Exeter possessed an even longer list of relics of confessors and virgins, but I omit them). From a relic-collector's point of view, it might be said that Exeter had, with King Athelstan's help, acquired a complete set. The same was true of Glaston-bury; and no doubt of many other English houses at that time. Given the market for relics, it is not surprising that unusual measures were some-times adopted to meet the demand. Simple theft, for example, was a frequent resort of those seeking to acquire relics.[3] Thus during the course of King Eadred's assault on the (Danish) kingdom of York in 948 the church at Ripon was burned, and the archbishop of Canterbury – Oda, who had accompanied the king on this expedition – took the opportunity of stealing the relics of St Wilfrid and taking them back to Canterbury, thereby sparking off a dispute which raged for centuries. Later in the tenth century a cleric of St Neot's in Cornwall stole the relics of his patron saint and headed east; once the theft was discovered he was hotly pursued by the rest of the clergy, but the thief threw himself on the protection of a powerful landowner in Huntingdonshire and, with the king's intervention as well, the stolen relics were allowed to remain in what became St Neots, Huntingdonshire. These are cases of theft of indubitable relics; but the hungry market and the prevalence of theft inevitably gave rise to frau-dulent practices and to phoney, itinerant relic-peddlars. The church was obliged to devise strict tests to verify the authenticity of relics offered for sale. Such a case occurred early in King Edgar's reign (959–75). Four relic salesmen from France came to the king claiming that they possessed the relics of St Audoenus (St Ouen). The king sent for his archbishop, Oda (he who had not balked at stealing the relics of St Wilfrid at Ripon!), who tested the relics by sending for a leper. When the archbishop, using the relics, made the sign of the cross over the leper, he was miraculously cured, and the relics were deemed authentic. How many fake relics failed to pass this or similar tests, the record does not allow us to say.[4]

The situation was aggravated by the fact that in the Anglo-Saxon period there were no controls on the process of canonization of a saint. It was not until the thirteenth century that canon law (in the 'Decretals' of Pope Gregory IX) stipulated a judicial process to assess the claims to sanctity of any alleged saint. Such control was the response of the church's central authority to local abuses. In our period, however, there were no such controls. The essential criterion for the creation of a new saint was the efficacy of his relics. If a man or woman were known to have lived a holy life (or better perhaps: not to have lived an evil life), and, after death, to have accomplished miraculous cures through his relics, the saint could be received straightway into the liturgical observance of the local church which first recognized the efficacy. There was frequently intense competition, especially in the late Anglo-Saxon period, between local churches to advance the claims of the saints whose relics they possessed; and this competition encouraged the creation of new saints. We can see the process at work in the case of St Swithun, the discovery of whose relics was narrated by Lantfred. Swithun was an utterly obscure ninth-century bishop of Winchester whose only claim to attention was that he was buried in a conspicuous tomb facing the west door of the Old Minster. In 969, Swithun appeared in a dream to a certain crippled smith, instructing him to go to his [Swithun's] tomb if he wished to receive his cure, and to report the dream vision to a local cleric, who in turn was requested to report the matter to Æthelwold, the bishop of Winchester: he did as instructed and was duly cured. In the same year a wretched, hunch-backed cleric was also visited in dreams by two angelic youths who instructed him to go to Swithun's tomb and pray there for his cure; he spent a night in prayer at the tomb and was overcome with sleep; when he awoke, he was miraculously cured of his deformity. After discussion with the monks it was determined that Swithun was indeed responsible for these miracles; accordingly, on 15 July 971, Bishop Æthelwold exhumed the remains of St Swithun and translated the relics to a shrine within the Old Minster. Miraculous cures followed in swift succession, and as the report of these cures spread, people came from farther and farther away: three blind women from the Isle of Wight, a blind woman from Bedfordshire, a paralytic from London, then sixteen blind people from London, then twenty-five people from all over England cured in one day, then thirty-six in the space of three days, then 124 in the space of a fortnight. Within a year or so, St Swithun's reputation as miracle-worker was firmly established, and Lantfred was set to work to record the translation (that is, the relocation and consecration of relics) and the miracles it had produced.[5] By this point, we may surmise, money was rolling into Winchester coffers in gratitude for all the cures. In any event, the translation of St Swithun in 971 established the pattern for future translations. Accordingly, twenty-five years later, in 996, when Bishop Æthelwold himself had been dead for twelve years, *he* appeared in a dream to a certain citizen of Wallingford, instructing the man to go to Winchester and report the vision. The man did so; Æthelwold's tomb was opened (by now, presumably, the flesh had decayed from the bones) and his relics translated; miracles followed; a local monk – Wulfstan, the precentor of the Old Minster – wrote them down; and so the pattern was repeated.[6] Thus were SS Swithun and Æthelwold installed as patron saints in Winchester. Once installed, their feast days would have been commemorated annually with masses and, on the vigil of these feasts, with prayers and readings during the Night Office, all suitably composed for the purpose. This is what the process of canonization entailed in Anglo-Saxon England; and we may surmise that the same process occurred at other English churches which claimed to possess the relics of a patron saint. That there were numerous such churches is clear from a document called 'Information concerning God's Saints who Rest in England' (*Secgan be þam Godes sanctum þe on Engla lande ærost reston*), which lists some fifty churches each of which possessed one or more English patron saints.[7]

As saints, Swithun and Æthelwold are relatively well known, above all because they found hagiographers to record their miracles. But there were numerous lesser-known Anglo-Saxon saints whose translations were not recorded, and who are often little more than names to us.[8] Furthermore, local (English) saints formed only a tiny proportion of the saints who were venerated at any one church. The total number of saints in question is not easily calculable. For the universal (western/Latin) church, the number must have run to thousands. For England it is possible to form a rough estimate of the numbers involved by looking at surviving litanies of the saints.[9] A litany is a particular form of prayer which consists of invocations to Christ the Lord ('Kyrie eleison'), asking him to pray for us, followed by invocations of individual saints, naming them and asking them in turn to pray for us. The number of saints named depended on the function for which the litany was intended: since they were chanted during processions (at, say, the dedication of a church), they might need to be extended indefinitely, and the extension was accomplished by inserting more names. Thus some fairly long litanies have come down to us. Usually the saints invoked are subdivided into patriarchs, apostles, martyrs, confessors and virgins, and the longest Anglo-Saxon litany (London, British Library, Harley 863, from Exeter) includes some 125 martyrs, 100 confessors and 70 virgins. From these figures – and bearing in mind that different litanies named different saints, even if they usually have a certain core in common – we may suppose that some 300 saints (not counting patriarchs and apostles) were culted in Anglo-Saxon England.

Who were all these saints? Who *were* Crispinus and Crispinianus, Vitus and Vitalis, Tiburtius and Tranquillinus, Narcissus and Nicasius, Eufemia and Eugenia, Potentiana and Emerentiana, and all the rest? Who indeed were the less strange sounding martyrs with which most litanies begin – Linus, Cletus and Clement? One may suspect that, of the countless Anglo-Saxons who recited the litany as an act of private devotion, few if any will have known the identity of all the saints whose aid was being implored. Nevertheless, it was the church's responsibility to control all these saints – to know when their feast days fell and how they achieved martyrdom or sanctity, for only with such knowledge could they be petitioned effectively for help. We gain direct insight into the religious observance of the Anglo-Saxon church by looking at the books pertaining to the cult of saints.[10]

The most simple and straightforward way of recording the feast days of individual saints was that of entering their names in a liturgical calendar. The calendar was set out according to the Julian year (i.e. beginning in January), with a separate manuscript page devoted to each month, and a separate line for each day of the month, in Roman reckoning (i.e. counting from ides, nones and kalends), with the days entered in the left-hand column. The name of the individual saint was then entered against his 'birthday' or *dies natalis* (not the day on which he was born into this world, but that on which he was 'born' into eternal life, i.e. died). So a typical entry consisted merely of date plus name (in the genitive). By consulting a calendar, one could see at a glance what saints' feast-days fell in any particular month, and so organize liturgical celebrations accordingly. Some twenty-five calendars survive from Anglo-Saxon England.[11] The earliest is of eighth-century date (the famous 'Calendar of St Willibrord'), but most date from the eleventh century. The 'Calendar of St Willibrord' is evidently a book that was used for the personal devotions of Willibrord (the Yorkshire saint who converted the Frisians, established the metropolitan see of Utrecht, founded the monastery of Echternach in present-day Luxembourg and died in 739) insofar as it records the feast-days of colleagues and friends alongside those of saints of the universal church; but the eleventh-century calendars are mostly institutional rather than personal, and reflect the practices of the individual churches to which they belonged. No two are alike in every detail, and from them we can get a clear notion of the diversity which obtained with respect to the cult of saints in late Anglo-Saxon England: while there was an agreed common core of the best-known saints, each church had its own patron saint and its own preferred commemorations. Only in comparatively recent times has the central authority of the church stipulated a universal practice in these matters.

In the early period the number of saints culted by any one church was considerably smaller, and hence more manageable, than was to be the case in the tenth and eleventh centuries. One could conceivably have committed the calendar of one's local church to memory, for ease of reference if for no other reason. However, a liturgical calendar will have been a fairly intractable object to memorize, and it is not surprising that someone should have hit upon the idea of reducing a church's calendar to the memorizable confines of a poem.[12] At York, sometime in the late eighth century, an anonymous poet attempted to versify his church's calendar in Latin hexameters. The resulting poem, called the 'Metrical Calendar of York', consisted of eighty-two lines; normally there is a line devoted to each saint, and each line contains both the saint's name and the date (in Roman reckoning) of his feast. Here, for example, are the lines for November:

> At its beginning November shines with a multi-faceted jewel:
> It gleams with the praise of All Saints.
> Martin of Tours ascends the stars on the ides.
> Thecla finished her life on the fifteenth kalends.
> But Cecilia worthily died with glory on the tenth kalends.
> On the ninth kalends we joyfully venerate the feast of Clement.
> On the eighth kalends Chrysogonus rejoices with his vital
>   weaponry.
> Andrew is rightly venerated by the world on the day before the
>   kalends.

As poetry, this is pretty turgid stuff; but its utility was obvious, and the York poem enjoyed enormously wide circulation on the Continent, where – with suitable additions and deletions – it was tailored to the needs of many churches. It also exercised considerable influence at home: in the early years of the tenth century an anonymous poet, using the 'Metrical Calendar of York' as his model, expanded the frame so that each of the 365 days of the year has a commemoration (often of saints so obscure as to defy identification); and a century later a poet at Ramsey used this and the York poem to produce a metrical calendar that is a valuable index of his monastery's observance in the eleventh century. Nor is it surprising that the idea of composing a metrical calendar should have occurred to a vernacular poet. There survives an Old English metrical calendar of 231 lines' length, copied in one of the manuscripts of the *Anglo-Saxon Chronicle*. The Old English Metrical Calendar records twenty-eight liturgical feasts, mostly those of the universal church (it also includes some non-liturgical dates, such as the beginning of summer and winter). The dates are set out serially, with an indication of the length of intervals, rather than by Roman reckoning. Here again is an example taken from November:

> Þæs ymb feower niht
> þætte Martinus   mære geleorde,
> wer womma leas   wealdend sohte,
> upengla weard.   Þænne embe eahta niht
> and feowerum   þætte fan gode
> besenctun on sægrund   sigefæstne wer,
> on brime haran,   þe iu beorna fela
> Clementes oft   clypiað to þearfe.   (207–14)

It was four nights on that glorious Martin died, the blameless man, sought the Almighty Ruler, the Lord of angels; and eight nights later, and four besides, that enemies of God drowned on the sea-floor, in the deep, the victorious white-haired man, the good Clement, to whom many people pray in times of need.

The seven feasts recorded for November in the 'Metrical Calendar of York' have been reduced to four in the Old English Metrical Calendar (in addition to the feasts of Martin and Clement it includes All Saints and St Andrew); moreover, the Old English poet has included a detail about St Clement's martyrdom – his drowning – from a source other than a calendar (we shall soon see what this source may have been). But the most striking aspect of the Old English poem is that the author has strictly excluded any feasts of purely local observance: it is as if he were trying to provide a list of the most important feasts that were observed nationally (thus St Augustine, apostle of the English is included, as is Pope Gregory the Great who sent him: but no other English saint). The fact that the poem is composed in English may indicate that it was intended for a layman; and the reference to the king in the final lines may suggest further that the layman in question was the king:

> Nu ge findan magon
> haligra tiida   þe man healdan sceal,
> swa bebugeð gebod   geond Brytenricu
> Sexna kyninges   on þas sylfan tiid.   (228–31)

Now you can find the feast days which should be observed, insofar as the stipulation of the Saxon king extends, at the present time, throughout Britain.

It would be a matter of great excitement if we could identify the king who concerned himself in this way with the liturgical calendar; but unfortunately no such identification is possible in the present state of our knowledge.

Calendars, then, provide the name of the saint and his feast day, but usually nothing more. Somewhat more information could be found in the martyrology.[13] In essence the martyrology was a reference book set out according to the calendar year: for each day it gave the date (in Roman reckoning) and the place of martyrdom (or in the case of confessors, the place where the tomb was located), and then the name of the saint, normally in the genitive. The martyrology had a specific liturgical function, at least in the later Anglo-Saxon period: as a result of the liturgical reforms of Carolingian churchmen (which were subsequently adopted by the tenth-century English Benedictine reformers), the martyrology was read daily when monks or canons assembled at chapter each morning, after Prime or morrow mass, in order to make clear what the daily devotions were to be. It goes almost without saying that the martyrology was therefore a text subject to continual revision designed to bring it into line with the observances of any particular monastic house or cathedral chapter; and therefore that no two martyrologies are the same. Nevertheless, the martyrology from which all later martyrologies ultimately descend is the 'Hieronymian' or 'Jeromian' Martyrology, so-called because it was falsely ascribed to St Jerome, but was in fact a work compiled first in Italy in the fifth century and then redacted in Gaul in the sixth century. The earliest surviving manuscript was written, probably at Echternach, under the direction of St Willibrord, and is now bound up with the 'Calendar of St Willibrord' which I mentioned earlier. The 'Jeromian' Martyrology has entries for every day of the year, beginning on 25 December. Its nature will be clear from one entry (I give that for 23 November, the feast of St Clement, which we have seen to be commemorated in the Old English Metrical Calendar):

The ninth kalends of November (= 23 November): at Rome, Clement the bishop; and in the cemetery (at Rome), Maximus (and) Felicity; and in Cappadocia, Niceanus, Chrysogonus (and) St Mark the bishop; in Caesarea in Cappadocia, Verocianus (and) Eutyches; at Alexandria, Peter the bishop; in Etruria, St Muscola . . . etc.

The information conveyed here is skeletal, telegraphic; and one can imagine that the need was soon felt for a somewhat more expansive treatment of the saints mentioned against each day. The scholar who first responded to this need was Bede who, by consulting various historical sources, was able to amplify many of the entries in the 'Jeromian' Martyrology, and thereby to create the first 'historical' or 'narrative' martyrology. Bede's Martyrology contained 114 entries, and began with 1 January (rather than with 25 December); its nature can be seen from the entry for 23 November:

23 November, at Rome, the feast of St Clement, the bishop who, at the Emperor Trajan's request, was sent into exile in the Pontus (= the Black Sea). While there, because he converted many to the faith through his miracles and teaching, he was cast into the sea with an anchor tied to his neck. But as his disciples prayed the sea receded three miles, and they found his body in a stone coffin within a marble oratory, and the anchor lying nearby.

Bede presumably started with the skeletal entry in the 'Jeromian Martyrology', which was available to him in a version very closely related to that in the Willibrord manuscript; but he amplified it by recourse to a *Passio S. Clementis*, which contained the anecdote concerning Clement's death and the discovery of his body. The result is that, through the addition of these anecdotal details, the feast of St Clement is made slightly more memorable (we have seen that the author of the Old English Metrical Calendar added an oblique allusion to the same anecdote in his entry for St Clement: perhaps he got it from Bede, or directly from the *passio*). It is not surprising, therefore, that Bede's Martyrology enjoyed enormously wide circulation. However, because he had provided entries for less than a third of the calendar year, it attracted so many additions and interpolations that – in the absence of a manuscript in Bede's own handwriting – it is never possible to be sure that an entry was actually written by Bede in the form in which it has come down to us. Nevertheless Bede's Martyrology stands at the head of all later 'narrative' martyrologies, and as such has influenced the form of the martyrology used by the present-day Roman Catholic church.

Another narrative martyrology, which for its range of learning bears comparison with Bede's, is the so-called Old English Martyrology.[14] This work was compiled probably in the later ninth century, perhaps in Mercia, by an anonymous author who was able to draw on the resources of a very substantial library. The Old English Martyrology consists of 238 entries, some of them fairly extensive. Unlike Bede, but like the 'Jeromian' Martyrology, the Old English martyrologist begins his work on 25 December; but in other respects it is clear that he was aware of Bede's work, even if he did not follow it in detail. The anonymous author was evidently a scholar with an independent cast of mind, for it would seem that he often used an entry in Bede as a point of departure, but consulted his sources afresh and was thereby able to construct a much more informative entry even than that found in Bede. Compare his entry for St Clement:

On the twenty-third day of the month is the feast of the pope, St Clement; St Peter himself consecrated him as pope and gave him the same power that Christ had given him, so that he had the key of the realms of heaven and power over hell. By his prayer this Clement caused water to come up from the earth where formerly no fountain had been. The Emperor Trajan sent his general, Aufidianus by name; he urged this Clement to forswear Christ, but was unable to turn his mind. Then he commanded an anchor to be fastened to his neck and to throw him into the sea. Christians stood weeping on the shore, and then the sea dried up over [three] miles. Then the Christians went into the sea, and there they found a stone house prepared by the Lord, where the body of Clement was placed in a stone coffin, and the anchor with which he had been thrown into the sea was put near it. Every year since, the sea offered a dry path for seven days to the people coming to his church. The church is in the sea three miles from the land, and it is to the east of the country of Italy. There a woman once forgot her child sleeping in the church, and the sea flowed around the church. When after the space of a year the people came there again on St Clement's day, they found the child alive and sleeping in the church; and it departed with its mother.

The Old English martyrologist has woven several sources together here. The notice that Clement was consecrated by St Peter is drawn from the *Liber pontificalis* (an annalistic history of the papacy), to which a biblical reference (from Matt. XVI.19) was added. The account of Clement's martyrdom was taken from the anonymous *Passio S. Clementis*, which Bede had previously used. The miracle of the sleeping child (not found in Bede) derives originally from Gregory of Tours's *Liber miraculorum*, but may have been taken by the martyrologist from an intermediate source. In some respects the Old English account is less detailed than Bede (the detail of Clement's exile in the Pontus is omitted, so that it is not clear where the miracle of the fountain occurred; and the vague reference to the land 'east of the country of Italy' is an imprecision which Bede would not have tolerated); but overall it allows a clearer picture of why St Clement was worthy of veneration. For this reason, the Old English Martyrology is one of the most original contributions to Anglo-Saxon hagiography.

By virtue of its extent, the Old English martyrologist's entry for St Clement verges on another genre of hagiography, namely the saint's life.[15] There are two broad categories of saint's life: the *passio* ('passion') and the *vita* ('life'). The *passio* was the literary form appropriate for a saint who had been martyred for his/her faith, whereas the *vita* properly pertained to a confessor (that is, a saint whose impeccable service to God constituted a metaphorical, not a real, martyrdom). By *passio* is meant an account in which the saint, usually of noble birth, adopts Christianity in days when the state government is pagan; the saint is brought before a local magistrate or governor and asked to recant his/her Christianity by sacrificing to the gods; the saint refuses to do so, even on the pain of innumerable tortures (normally described in excruciating detail), and is eventually killed, usually by beheading. By *vita* is understood a work which takes the following form: the saint is born of noble stock; his birth is accompanied by miraculous portents; as a youth he excels at learning and reveals that he is destined for saintly activity; he turns from secular to holy life (often forsaking his family) and so proceeds through the various ecclesiastical grades; he reveals his sanctity while still on earth by performing various miracles; eventually he sees his death approaching and, after instructing his disciples or followers, dies calmly; after his death many miracles occur at his tomb. Of course any number of variants is possible within these basic frameworks; but the framework itself is invariable. Accordingly, if a particular saint were deemed to be worthy of particular veneration, a *passio* or *vita* in the accepted form would be required so that it could be read out on the appropriate feast day, either in refectory while the monks or clerics dined in silence, or else during the Night Office on the vigil of the saint's day, when the *passio* or *vita* would be distributed in separate lections, each lection being punctuated by prayer and psalmody.

These are the institutional uses of saints' *vitae*; they could of course be read any time as an act of private devotion. We have seen that in the early Middle Ages the universal church culted an enormous number of saints, perhaps thousands, and it is not surprising that there should survive a substantial number of saints' lives from this period: C. W. Jones once estimated that some 600 survive from the period before 900. How many of these were known in England at any one time or place is difficult to say: Aldhelm used perhaps as many as thirty individual texts; Bede, perhaps a similar, or smaller, number; the Old English martyrologist likewise. Some of the texts were of course more widely read than others: important above all were Sulpicius Severus's *vita* of St Martin, a *vita* of St Anthony by Athanasius, and Jerome's three *vitae* of Malchus, Hilarion and the hermit Paul of Thebes. These works in particular were to prove immensely influential when, as soon happened, Anglo-Saxon authors began to compose *vitae* to commemorate their own native saints. In the early eighth century a number of English saints were thought of sufficient importance to merit Latin *vitae* of their own: Cuthbert, Guthlac, Ceolfrith and Wilfrid. English saints of the continental mission were similarly commemorated: one Willibald wrote a *vita* of Boniface, the Englishman known as the 'apostle' of Germany who was martyred by the Saxons in 754; an English nun at Heidenheim named Hygeburg wrote a *vita* of two brothers from Waltham who were active in the Bonifatian mission in Germany;

and Alcuin (d. 804) commemorated his ancestor Willibrord (who, as we saw, was instrumental in converting the Frisians) with a *vita*. Then in the tenth century, as cults of local English saints began to grow, a number of *vitae* were composed: we have already mentioned Lantfred's account of St Swithun and Wulfstan's of St Æthelwold. At the same time an Anglo-Saxon living abroad wrote a life of Archbishop Dunstan (d. 988), and the foreign scholar Abbo, living at Ramsey between 985 and 987, composed a *passio* of King Edmund of East Anglia who was martyred by the Danes in 869; in turn, Abbo's English pupil Byrhtferth composed *vitae* of Bishop Oswald of Worcester and York (d. 992) and St Ecgwine, an early eighth-century bishop of Worcester who was founder of Evesham Abbey. By the mid-eleventh century various anonymous *vitae* of other English saints were in existence (Neot, Rumwold, Birinus, Kenelm, Indract and Swithun yet again). Finally, the later eleventh century is characterized by the activities of professional hagiographers such as Goscelin and Folcard, both Flemish monks from Saint-Bertin, who went around England composing saints' lives on commission for various religious houses; a very substantial number of works by these two authors survives, but they have not yet been properly catalogued or edited.

It was the overall intention of any hagiographer to demonstrate that his saintly subject belonged indisputably to the universal community of saints, and this entailed modelling each *vita* closely on those of earlier authors, especially Sulpicius Severus, Athanasius and Jerome. Thus, for example, the anonymous Lindisfarne author derives his description of St Cuthbert verbatim from Sulpicius's *vita* of St Martin; many episodes in Felix's life of St Guthlac are based on the *vita* of Anthony and on Jerome's *vita* of Paul the hermit; in the tenth century Wulfstan bases many episodes of his *vita* of St Æthelwold on Sulpicius's life of Martin. The list of examples could be protracted indefinitely. But there are very good reasons for the dependence, sometimes verbatim, on earlier models. It is not so much a matter of plagiarism as of ensuring that the local saint is seen clearly to possess the attributes of, and to belong undoubtedly to, the universal community of saints.

In the first instance the saint's *vita* would have existed as a separate book or *libellus*. Often collections of material pertaining to one saint were gathered together to form such a book: a collection pertaining to St Martin, for example, was known as a *martinellus*, and such collections were very common. An early ninth-century *libellus* devoted to St Guthlac has come down to us as Cambridge, Corpus Christi College 307, and we have the fragmentary remains of another Guthlac *libellus* (London, British Library, Royal 4.A.XIV). A beautifully written manuscript devoted entirely to *vitae* of St Cuthbert was given by King Athelstan to St Cuthbert's community in the early tenth century (now Cambridge,

Corpus Christi College 183). From the late tenth century an equally lavish book survives which is devoted entirely to *vitae* of St Swithun (London, British Library, Royal 15.C.VII). No doubt there were once more. However, from the eighth century onwards it became increasingly more common to gather individual saints' lives into large collections, at first arranged randomly – as in the earliest known English example of such a collection, an early ninth-century manuscript now in Paris (Bibliothèque nationale, lat. 10861) – but later arranged according to the church year. Such a collection is called either a 'legendary' (implying that its contents were meant to be read, either institutionally or privately) or a 'passional' (originally implying a collection of *passiones* of martyrs, but later extended to include any sort of saint's *vita*).[16] The impulse to collect together saints' *vitae* into anthologies will no doubt have been initiated by the example of three immensely influential compilations: Gregory the Great's *Dialogi* – which at King Alfred's suggestion was translated into English by Werferth, bishop of Worcester, in the 890s – provides an anthology of miracle stories of local Italian saints, of whom the most important is St Benedict (whose life and works form the subject of bk II of the *Dialogi*); Gregory of Tours in his *Libri miraculorum* provides brief digests of the life and miracles of a large number of Gaulish saints (one book is devoted to martyrs, one to confessors, and four to the life and miracles of St Martin); and Aldhelm, who in his massive prose *De uirginitate* provided an anthology of nearly fifty saintly lives, some of them biblical, but many drawn from *passiones* of the martyrs and from early saints' *vitae*. There is good evidence that all these three works were widely studied in Anglo-Saxon England, even though they appear to have had little impact on the liturgy. By this I mean: excepting St Benedict, none of the Italian saints discussed in Gregory's *Dialogi* ever figures in an Anglo-Saxon calendar; very few of Gregory of Tours's Gaulish saints were actively venerated in England; and many of the saints treated by Aldhelm – such as Narcissus of Jerusalem or Ammon of Nitria – appear in no Anglo-Saxon calendar. In other words, these three works were extra-liturgical, intended as anthologies of edifying stories of sanctity.

However, unlike anthologies such as these, the impulse to compile a legendary or passional was primarily liturgical, in that the readings were normally set out according to the church year, so that they could be used in combination with a calendar or martyrology for any particular feast. The legendary which was to have the greatest influence on Anglo-Saxon observance was the so-called 'Cotton-Corpus Legendary', an enormous collection of some 165 saints' *vitae* arranged in order of the calendar year beginning on 1 January. The 'Cotton-Corpus Legendary' was apparently compiled in Northern France or Flanders in the late ninth century; but it is preserved uniquely in English manuscripts, and this is an indication of its importance for Anglo-Saxon hagiography. Above all, it was drawn on extensively by Ælfric, who is the most important hagiographer of the late Anglo-Saxon period.[17]

Before discussing Ælfric's hagiography, however, a few observations are necessary by way of clarification. The church year was made up of two great cycles of feasts, the *temporale* and the *sanctorale*. The *temporale* consists of the movable feasts, most of them keyed to Easter (which falls on a different Sunday every year), including Ascension, Pentecost (Whitsun), and so on. The *sanctorale* consists of the fixed feasts, celebrated on the very same date each year (no matter what the day of the week), including Christmas and all the saints' days. The two cycles were interleaved, as it were, but – given the mobility of Easter – the interleaving was different each year. As a matter of convenience, therefore, the *temporale* was usually kept separate from the *sanctorale* in sacramentaries and missals of the later Anglo-Saxon period. It will be clear from this that the legendary or passional belonged exclusively to the *sanctorale*. Now Ælfric composed three extensive collections of reading material for the church year: two series of *Catholic Homilies* (*sermones catholici*) and one series of so-called *Lives of Saints*. In spite of the names, all three collections contain both homilies (that is, extended explications of the *pericope*, or gospel lesson, for any feast) and saints' lives (in the sense I have defined them earlier). (Confusingly, some of the items, especially in the *Catholic Homilies*, consist of a homily followed by a saint's life, or vice versa.) Furthermore, all three collections contain material intended both for the *temporale* and for the *sanctorale* (those intended for the fixed feasts of the *sanctorale* are always prefixed with a Roman date reckoning): thus in *CH* I, 18 of 40 items are intended for the *sanctorale*; in *CH* II, 16 of 40; and in the *Lives of Saints*, all except five are for the *sanctorale*. If we also include the one stray saint's life (St Vincent), we have 62 items intended by Ælfric for the *sanctorale*. Some items are duplicated (St Stephen; St Martin) and Christmas day is triplicated, inasmuch as it stands at the head of each of the three collections. If we subtract these, the resulting 56 feasts are distributed evenly through the year, and it is possible to reconstruct the liturgical calendar which Ælfric must have been using; it would also be possible, in theory, to combine Ælfric's various lives so as to constitute a single passional. Although Ælfric himself apparently never did this, it is interesting to note that two later manuscript passionals (London, British Library, Cotton Vitellius D. xvii, of the mid-eleventh century, and Cambridge, University Library, Ii.1.33, of the twelfth) contain such combinations of Ælfrician saints' lives. In any event our reconstructed calendar permits several deductions about how Ælfric conceived the cult of saints. In the first place, the majority of the feasts commemorated by Ælfric are those of the universal church (in this respect, Ælfric resembles the poet of the Old English Metrical Calendar): there are no local or eccentric saints in Ælfric's *sanctorale*. Ælfric does include lives of six English saints (Cuthbert, Alban, King Oswald, King Edmund, Æthelthryth and Swithun); but by the time he was writing – in the last decade of the tenth century – all these were culted throughout England. Interestingly, Ælfric omits various French and Flemish saints who were evidently culted actively in tenth-century England (for example, Vedastus, Quintinus, Bertinus, Amandus and others), an omission which is curious in light of the prominence which these saints are accorded in the liturgical books associated with Bishop Æthelwold, Ælfric's mentor. He also omits Breton saints such as Iudoc and Machutus, who were culted at Winchester in his time. It would seem that Ælfric did not wish to venerate any saint in writing if there was the slightest doubt about that saint's universality. Minor and local saints had no place in Ælfric's *sanctorale*: he was concerned with the observance of the catholic church, as he conceived it.

Nevertheless, there are certain features of his *sanctorale* which strike one as peculiarities, especially if seen in the context of late Anglo-Saxon liturgical calendars. To take one example: Ælfric provides a life for St Eugenia, whose feast day he gives as 25 December; but there is no surviving Anglo-Saxon calendar with an entry for St Eugenia on that day. Why did Ælfric choose 25 December – of all days – for St Eugenia? The answer is that the Latin legendary which Ælfric was using as his source has a *vita* of St Eugenia on that day. The legendary in question was clearly the 'Cotton-Corpus Legendary', but in a form earlier than that which has come down to us in manuscript. In a very important study Patrick Zettel has shown that, both in the general question of Ælfric's choice of saints, and in the particular case of individual textual variants, Ælfric was following the 'Cotton-Corpus Legendary' in a form most closely related to that in a (now incomplete) twelfth-century manuscript in Hereford Cathedral Library (P.7.VI).[18] One text which Ælfric derived from this legendary is his life of St Clement, which is included in the first series of his *Catholic Homilies*. The *vita* included in the legendary for 23 November is the anonymous *Passio S. Clementis* which, as we have seen, was earlier used by the Old English martyrologist. It is therefore interesting to compare Ælfric's treatment of Clement with that of the martyrologist. Ælfric describes how Peter chose Clement as his successor; how (after increasing the Christian flock) he was denounced to the Emperor Trajan and exiled to labour in a stone quarry; how when he came to the quarry he miraculously discovered a fountain for the Christians imprisoned there; how through envy the pagans accused him and how Trajan sent one Aufidianus to punish him; how he was martyred by being cast into the sea with an anchor on his neck; how subsequently the sea retreated so his disciples could reach the place of martyrdom, where miraculously they found the martyr's body in a stone coffin; and finally, how once a child was miraculously preserved inside this coffin for a full year, after the sea had come in and caught the worshippers unawares. Ælfric ends his life of St Clement with a homiletic passage, explaining (by resort to Old and New Testament examples) why God should wish to kill his saints.

Ælfric's treatment is fuller and more coherent than that of the martyrologist. His account of the miracle of the fountain becomes comprehensible (in contrast to the martyrologist's telegraphic report), even though – like the martyrologist – he does not explain where Clement's exile was taking place. He follows the Latin text of the *passio* as he found it in the 'Cotton-Corpus Legendary', only departing from it on one occasion to add a cross-reference to a mention of Clement in another *vita* in the same legendary, namely in the *Passio S. Dionysii* (which Ælfric subsequently translated in his *Lives of Saints*). In the life of Clement, as in all his English writings, Ælfric shows himself as a meticulous and accurate translator, unprepared to embellish his source in any way. His intention was simply to provide for lay readers an abbreviated legendary containing readings for those saints' days which he judged to be most universal.[19]

After Ælfric there was not much left for other Old English hagiographers to do. Although Ælfric had composed two lives of St Martin (one of them extensive), an anonymous hagiographer produced yet another. An extensive version of the Seven Sleepers legend was also produced anonymously, even though Ælfric had treated this legend in his second series of *Catholic Homilies*. Lives were also composed for feasts in the *sanctorale* which Ælfric had treated: St Andrew, St Michael, SS Peter and Paul. Another translator, perhaps working in collaboration with Ælfric, produced a life of St Eustace drawn on the *passio* of that saint in the 'Cotton-Corpus Legendary'. Certain saints who were culted on the Continent, but who had been omitted by Ælfric, also found hagiographers, such as St Pantaleon and St Quintin (of whose Old English life a charred fragment survives). So, too, did several English saints omitted by Ælfric, such as Guthlac and Mildred, and the originally Breton saint, Machutus. In the very late eleventh century various saints, whose cults had only developed in England long after Ælfric's death, were commemorated with English lives (St Giles, St Nicholas). In all, there are some twenty Old English lives of saints in addition to those by Ælfric; but in sum they pale in contrast with Ælfric's achievement.

Thus far I have been speaking solely of lives of saints in prose. But there is also a substantial corpus of verse hagiography, both in Latin and English, from the Anglo-Saxon period. Bede composed a metrical life of Cuthbert (based on the anonymous Lindisfarne life) in addition to his prose life, and Alcuin wrote a metrical life of Willibrord to go alongside his prose life. The later tenth century witnessed a burgeoning of metrical Latin saints' lives: Frithegod of Canterbury produced a metrical version of Stephen's earlier life of Wilfrid, and Wulfstan of Winchester did the same with Lantfred's account of the miracles of Swithun; we also have anonymous metrical lives of Iudoc and Eustace from this period. One might well wonder why it was thought necessary to produce metrical lives in addition to prose lives. The answer is given by Alcuin in the preface to his *vita* of St Willibrord (which consisted of corresponding parts in prose and verse), where he explains that the prose is intended to be read out publicly to the members of an ecclesiastical community, but the verse is to be meditated upon in private by individual members of that community. It is clear that certain of the metrical lives in Latin – especially Bede's life of Cuthbert and Frithegod's life of Wilfrid – were written with this end in view, since the difficulty of their diction makes them unapproachable except through long, careful and meditative study.

A number of saints' lives in Old English verse has also come down to us, and it is interesting to ask whether these, too, might have been intended for private meditation by individual readers. But first it is necessary briefly to outline the corpus of Old English verse hagiography. Six poems are in question, of which three are by the enigmatic (and unidentifiable) poet who signs his poems with the runic signature 'Cyn(e)wulf' and who may have been writing in ninth-century Mercia: namely the poems called *Elene*, *Juliana* and *Fates of the Apostles*. Of the three remaining hagiographical poems, two are concerned with St Guthlac (*Guthlac A* and *Guthlac B*) and one with the apostles Matthew and Andrew (*Andreas*). Of these six, however, only one – namely Cynewulf's *Juliana* – could properly be described as a saint's life in the sense I have defined it. Of the others, *Elene* is an account of the search for and finding of the true cross in Jerusalem by Helena, the mother of the emperor Constantine (who in a vision had seen the cross as a sign of forthcoming victory), and the conversion to Christianity of Judas, the Jew who eventually helped Helena to find the cross and who took the name Cyriacus in religion. Cynewulf's poem, which is based on the Latin *Acts* of St Cyriacus, might arguably have been intended as a meditation on the feast of the 'Finding of the True Cross' (*Inuentio crucis*) which was celebrated universally on 3 May and which is commemorated in all Anglo-Saxon liturgical calendars and in the Old English Metrical Calendar; but it is only a saint's life insofar as it records the conversion of Judas/Cyriacus. Cynewulf's *Fates of the Apostles* is not properly speaking a saint's life either; it is an English version of a Latin text which circulated widely in the Middle Ages called the *Breuiarium apostolorum*, which gave a brief digest of where each of the twelve apostles conducted his apostolate, and how he died. Nor could the two anonymous Guthlac

poems be described as saints' lives. *Guthlac A* is a lengthy meditation on
Guthlac's saintly virtue, his victory over demons and his reception by
angels; but it has no narrative content and is in no sense a *vita*. It appears
unrelated to Felix's Latin life of Guthlac, except perhaps for the notice
that Guthlac was a saint who was aided by the apostle Bartholomew. To
judge from certain passages in the poem (lines 412–20, 488–90), its
intended audience was young monks who were in danger of being enticed
by the pleasures of the world. *Guthlac B* is more closely based on Felix's
life of Guthlac, but it, too, could not be described as a saint's life: it
concerns itself solely with Guthlac's death and his anticipation of it during
his last days, not with his life. But it could be read as a meditation – in the
sense intended by Alcuin – on Guthlac's sanctity, appropriate for his feast
on 11 April. The same cannot be said for *Andreas*, however. This lengthy
poem, based on the apocryphal (that is, pseudo-biblical, but rejected by
the Church as spurious) *Acts of Andrew and Matthew*, tells the story of
the apostle Matthew's capture by hideous cannibals in the land of the
Mermedonians, Andrew's divinely guided expedition to rescue Matthew,
and his eventual conversion of the Mermedonians. As a story it has its
merits, but it is non-liturgical (there is no feast for SS Matthew and
Andrew) and non-hagiographical, insofar as it does not follow the
conventional form of a saint's life; it is precisely the sort of text which
would have been rejected by Ælfric as heretical.

We are left, then, with only one Old English verse saint's life which
properly belongs to the genre, namely Cynewulf's *Juliana*. The poem
concerns St Juliana, who was martyred under the emperor Maximianus
(286–308). The story of her martyrdom is a conventional one: a wicked
governor, one Heliseus, lusts after the virgin Juliana and seeks her in
marriage; she, being devoted to Christ, spurns the marriage; she is
compelled through various tortures (including being hung up by her hair)
to make offerings to the gods, and is eventually executed. Although
Juliana is not included either by Aldhelm in his *On Virginity* or by Ælfric,
she was widely commemorated in Anglo-Saxon calendars on 16 February.
Cynewulf's poem is closely based on the Latin *Passio S. Iulianae*, which is
preserved in the Latin passional written at Canterbury in the early ninth
century and now preserved in Paris (Bibliothèque nationale, lat. 10861),
as well as in the 'Cotton-Corpus Legendary'. Why Cynewulf should have
chosen St Juliana as the subject for his poem is not immediately clear:
possibly she was especially venerated by the church which he served. In
any case we may suppose that the poem was intended for meditation –
again, in Alcuin's sense of the word – on her feast day.

In the preceding discussion I have been concerned principally with the
function of hagiography in general, rather than with the literary merits of
individual saints' lives. I would not wish to deny that individual lives may

have such merits: certainly Ælfric was the master of a terse and direct narrative style which, in his later saints' lives at least, often approached poetry in his use of alliteration and rhythm. But if we assume that, because of these literary features, Ælfric's or Cynewulf's saints' lives can be treated and enjoyed in isolation as we would enjoy, say, a life from Dr Johnson's *Lives of the Poets*, then we do great violation to their hagiographical intentions. Certainly Ælfric regarded himself as the apologist of the universal church: and it would have been no compliment to tell him that his hagiography imparted individual characteristics to individual saints. On the contrary, Ælfric would wish his saints to be seen merely as vessels of God's divine design on earth, indistinguishable as such one from the other, all worthy of our veneration and all able to intercede for us with the unapproachable deity. The saint's power of intercession was the hagiographer's uppermost concern: and hence it did not matter whether the saint was tall or short, fair or bald, fat or thin, blonde or brunette. In a sense, it probably did not matter whether he was named Cletus or Clement, Narcissus or Nicasius. The saints were distinguished – if at all – by the glory of their martyrdoms (a visible token of their acceptance to God) and by their efficacy in dealing with various human suffering. Saints were therefore a much more prominent aspect of Anglo-Saxon spirituality than they could conceivably be in a modern, mechanized society. The cumbersome apparatus for knowing them and appealing to them – calendars, martyrologies and saints' lives – was an urgent necessity in an age when other kinds of spiritual comfort were few. If we would understand the spiritual universe of the Anglo-Saxons, therefore, we must learn to understand that apparatus.

1 There is no comprehensive study of the cult of saints in Anglo-Saxon England; for a recent study of one aspect of the subject, see S. J. Ridyard, *The Royal Saints of Anglo-Saxon England: a Study of West Saxon and East Anglian Cults* (Cambridge, 1988). Bibliographical orientation in medieval hagiography in general is available in *Saints and their Cults: Studies in Religious Sociology, Folklore and History*, ed. S. Wilson (Cambridge, 1983), pp. 309–417. On the nature of English shrines in the post-Conquest period (which is better documented than the pre-Conquest), see R. C. Finucane, *Miracles and Pilgrims: Popular Beliefs in Medieval England* (London, 1977). On Lantfred, see below, n. 5.

2 See D. Rollason, *Saints and Relics in Anglo-Saxon England* (Oxford, 1989); on the Exeter list, see pp. 159–60, and on Athelstan as a relic collector, pp. 160–3. There is still much of use in the earlier study by M. Förster, *Zur Geschichte des Reliquienkultus in Altengland* (Munich, 1943).

3 See P. J. Geary, *Furta Sacra: Thefts of Relics in the Central Middle Ages* (Princeton, NJ, 1978), esp. pp. 59–63 on Anglo-Saxon England (which, however, omits any mention of the cases of Wilfrid, Neot and Audoenus discussed here).

4 There is (to my knowledge) no study of the authentication of relics in Anglo-Saxon England; for the continental dimension, see two studies by K. Schreiner, 'Zum Wahrheitsverständnis im Heiligen- und Reliquienwesen des Mittelalters', *Saeculum* 17 (1966), 139–69, and '"Discrimen veri ac falsi": Ansätze und Formen der Kritik in der Heiligen- und Reliquienverehrung des Mittelalters', *Archiv für Kulturgeschichte* 48 (1966), 1–53.

5 Lantfred's *Translatio et miracula S. Swithuni* (from which the preceding details are drawn) is among the texts ptd M. Lapidge, *The Cult of St Swithun*, Winchester Studies 4.2 (Oxford, forthcoming); an incomplete edition is in *Analecta Bollandiana* 4 (1885), 367–410.

6 See *Wulfstan of Winchester: the Life of St Æthelwold*, ed. M. Lapidge and M. Winterbottom (Oxford, 1991). For bibliographical details concerning the various Anglo-Latin *vitae* referred to throughout the present article, see M. Lapidge, 'The Anglo-Latin Background', in S. B. Greenfield and D. G. Calder, *A New Critical History of Old English Literature* (New York, 1986), pp. 5–37.

7 See D. Rollason, 'Lists of Saints' Resting-Places in Anglo-Saxon England', *ASE* 7 (1978), 61–93.

8 Some guidance is given by D. H. Farmer, *The Oxford Book of Saints* (Oxford, 1978), though it omits many of the saints named in Anglo-Saxon litanies, among them some of those which I quote here by way of example. Still useful is F. G. Holweck, *A Biographical Dictionary of the Saints* (London, 1924).

9 See M. Lapidge, *Anglo-Saxon Litanies of the Saints*, Henry Bradshaw Society 106 (London, 1991).

10 There is no reliable or comprehensive study in English of the liturgical books used in the cult of saints; see instead the excellent guide by R. Grégoire, *Manuale di agiologia: Introduzione alla letteratura agiografica*, Bibliotheca Montisfani 12 (Fabriano, 1987), and the earlier work by R. Aigrain, *L'hagiographie: ses sources, ses méthodes, son histoire* (Paris, 1953), pp. 11–192. Latin hagiographical texts are controlled by means of the Bollandists' great *Bibliotheca Hagiographica Latina*, 2 vols. (Brussels, 1899–1901), with *Supplementum* by H. Fros (Brussels, 1986).

11 *The Calendar of St Willibrord*, ed. H. A. Wilson, Henry Bradshaw Society 55 (London, 1918); *English Kalendars before A.D. 1100*, ed. F. Wormald, Henry Bradshaw Society 72 (London, 1934; repr. 1988).

12 On Latin metrical calendars from Anglo-Saxon England, see A. Wilmart, 'Un témoin anglo-saxon du calendrier métrique d'York', *Revue Bénédictine* 46 (1934), 41–69; M. Lapidge, 'A Tenth-Century Metrical Calendar from Ramsey', *Revue Bénédictine* 94 (1984), 326–69, and P. McGurk, 'The Metrical Calendar of Hampson', *Analecta Bollandiana* 104 (1986), 79–125. The Old English Metrical Calendar is ptd ASPR 6, 49–55 (note that this poem normally passes under the utterly inappropriate title 'Menologium': a *menologium* is a Greek liturgical book containing lives of saints, corresponding to the

Western Church's *martyrologium* or martyrology, on which see below); it is trans. K. Malone, in *Studies in Language, Literature and Culture of the Middle Ages and Later*, ed. E. B. Atwood and A. A. Hill (Austin, TX, 1969), pp. 193–9.

13 On martyrologies, see H. Quentin, *Les martyrologes historiques du moyen âge* (Paris, 1908), and J. Dubois, *Les martyrologes du moyen âge latin*, Typologie des sources du moyen âge occidental 26 (Turnhout, 1978). The 'Hieronymian' or 'Jeromian' Martyrology is ed. G. B. de Rossi and L. Duchesne in *Acta Sanctorum, Novembr.* 2.1 (Brussels, 1894), with commentary by H. Quentin and H. Delehaye, *Commentarius perpetuus in Martyrologium Hieronymianum*, in *Acta Sanctorum, Novembr.* 2.2 (Brussels, 1931). There is as yet no reliable edition of Bede's Martyrology; for the present one uses J. Dubois and G. Renaud, *Edition pratique des martyrologes de Bède, de l'Anonyme lyonnais et de Florus* (Paris, 1976); the entry for St Clement is on p. 212.

14 *Das altenglische Martyrologium*, ed. G. Kotzor, Abhandlungen der bayrischen Akademie der Wissenschaften, phil.-hist. Klasse 88 (Munich, 1981); a more accessible – but less complete and accurate – edition with accompanying translation is by G. Herzfeld, *An Old English Martyrology*, EETS os 116 (London, 1900). On the sources of the entry for St Clement, see J. E. Cross, 'Popes of Rome in the Old English Martyrology', *Papers of the Liverpool Latin Seminar Second Volume*, ARCA 3 (Liverpool, 1979), 191–211.

15 The best account of the literary forms of hagiography is W. Berschin, *Biographie und Epochenstil im lateinischen Mittelalter*, 2 vols. (Stuttgart, 1986–8; in progress); there is nothing comparable in English. On *passiones* in particular, see H. Delehaye, *Les passions des martyrs et les genres littéraires* (Brussels, 1921). The older study by C. W. Jones, *Saints' Lives and Chronicles in Early England* (Ithaca, NY, 1947), contains much of value.

16 On legendaries, see G. Philippart, *Les légendiers latins et autres manuscrits hagiographiques*, Typologie des sources du moyen âge occidental 24–5 (Turnhout, 1977).

17 The Cotton-Corpus Legendary is so named because it is preserved in its fullest (and earliest surviving) form in a manuscript written at Worcester in the third quarter of the eleventh century, now broken up and preserved in London, British Library, Cotton Nero E. i and Cambridge, Corpus Christi College 9; for the constitution of the original manuscript, see N. R. Ker, 'Membra Disiecta, Second Series', *British Museum Quarterly* 14 (1939–40), 82–3.

18 P. H. Zettel, 'Saints' Lives in Old English: Latin Manuscripts and Vernacular Accounts: Ælfric', *Peritia* 1 (1982), 17–37.

19 On Ælfric as hagiographer, see *inter alia* R. Woolf, 'Saints' Lives', in *Continuations and Beginnings: Studies in Old English Literature*, ed. E. G. Stanley (London, 1966), pp. 37–66; J. Gaites, 'Ælfric's Longer Life of St Martin and its Latin Sources: a Study in Narrative Technique', *Leeds Studies in English* 13 (1982), 23–41; and P. Szarmach, 'Ælfric's Women Saints: Eugenia', in *New Readings on Women in Old English Literature*, ed. H. Damico and A. H. Olsen (Bloomington, IN, 1990), pp. 146–57.

15   The world of Anglo-Saxon learning

D U R I N G·the Anglo-Saxon period, English schools were among the finest in Europe.[1] From English schools came the great masters whose writings instructed generations, centuries even, of Insular and continental students alike: one has only to think of the works of Aldhelm, Bede and Alcuin, which were copied and studied intensively up to the twelfth century and beyond. This achievement is all the more remarkable when one considers that the Anglo-Saxons were among the first peoples in Europe who were obliged to learn Latin as a foreign language if Christianity – a religion of the book *par excellence* – was to flourish. Throughout the Anglo-Saxon period, English schools benefited from the instruction of foreign masters domiciled there: the Roman monks who came with the Gregorian mission; Aidan and his fellow Irishmen who established a school at Lindisfarne in the mid-seventh century; Archbishop Theodore (d. 690) and Abbot Hadrian who taught at Canterbury in the late seventh century; John the Archchanter from St Peter's in Rome who taught at Wearmouth-Jarrow at roughly the same time; Grimbald of Saint-Bertin, John the Old Saxon and Asser of St David's in Wales, all of whom were invited by King Alfred in the late ninth century to assist him in the establishment of English schools; then men such as Lantfred and Abbo, both from Fleury, who in the later tenth century spent brief periods at the schools of Winchester and Ramsey respectively; and finally scholars such as Goscelin and Folcard, both from Saint-Bertin, who resided in England in the later eleventh century. The list could be extended considerably. But although Anglo-Saxon schools were indebted to foreign masters throughout the period of their existence, the native Anglo-Saxon aptitude for learning also asserted itself – as, pre-eminently, in the cases of Aldhelm, Bede and Alcuin; but there were many more. It is not possible in the compass of a short essay to survey all the achievements of Anglo-Saxon schools; rather, I shall try to convey some notion of how these schools functioned and, where possible, to identify what characterizes the Anglo-Saxon achievement in the domain of learning.

A principal source of our knowledge of Anglo-Saxon learning is the manuscripts which the Anglo-Saxons wrote and which have come down

264

to us. There are about a thousand of these, which vary in date from the late seventh century until the time of the Norman Conquest.[2] Many of them are still preserved in English libraries (principally the British Library in London, the Bodleian Library in Oxford, and Corpus Christi College in Cambridge); others migrated to the Continent at various times in various circumstances (for example, the famous Codex Amiatinus, a lavish manuscript of the Bible which was written at Wearmouth-Jarrow in the early eighth century and taken to Rome as a gift for the pope, or the later Vercelli Book, which somehow ended up in the cathedral library of Vercelli, perhaps taken there by an English pilgrim on the way to Rome). Furthermore, the thousand or so manuscripts which have survived must represent a small proportion of the books which once existed, since so many books have been destroyed in the course of centuries by men, fire and neglect. We can begin our investigation of Anglo-Saxon learning by considering the writing in these manuscripts and the scribes who wrote them.

The Anglo-Saxons had two types of alphabet: the Roman alphabet, learned from the earliest missionaries, and the runic alphabet, which was shared with other Germanic peoples and no doubt brought to England at the time of the Anglo-Saxon invasions. These two types of alphabet were entirely discrete, and had differing functions and significance, though they experienced some mutual influence (see above, p. 27, for runic letters borrowed into the Roman alphabet to represent English sounds). Runic letters were designed to be engraved on stone, wood, metal or bone (they mostly consist, therefore, of intersecting straight lines) and are not entirely suitable for writing in manuscripts. Nevertheless, the Anglo-Saxons treasured the runic alphabet more than did other Germanic peoples, and continued to copy the runic alphabet into manuscripts – through a sort of antiquarian interest – during the Anglo-Saxon period.[3] Rune-masters must be credited with a certain degree of learning. For example, the Franks Casket, a rectangular bone box of eighth-century date and Northumbrian origin, is engraved with inscriptions both in runic and Roman script. The craftsman who made the Franks Casket is probably to be credited with designing its entire lay-out and with transcribing and engraving the inscriptions. In this respect it is noteworthy that the panels on the Casket reproduce scenes from the gospels, such as the adoration of the magi, alongside a scene from the story of Weland, the legendary Germanic smith. In the same way the craftsmen, who engraved the numerous stone crosses which are found in many parts of England, often drew on Germanic legends and Christian symbols and could use the runic alphabet alongside the Roman: a splendid example here is the Ruthwell Cross, where both alphabets are used. Such craftsmen enjoyed a high reputation in Anglo-Saxon society, and their skills were sung in poems such as *The Gifts of Men*, where the individual 'talents' allotted to men are listed (similar lists are found in *Christ* 659–95 and *The Fortunes of Men* 64–98). The learning of these craftsmen is not properly 'book learning', but it is learning nonetheless.

The Roman alphabet was introduced by the Roman missionaries who came with Augustine in 597. These early missionaries also brought books, as Bede tells us, and the books served in turn as models for English scribes once they had been taught how to write. From about 700 onwards, we have manuscripts written in both Latin and English, in a wide variety of scripts, ranging from the very formal uncial and half-uncial scripts used principally for biblical and liturgical books, to the informal minuscule scripts used for scholarly books and documents. It is not possible here to survey the varieties of Anglo-Saxon script; but suffice it to say that during the Anglo-Saxon period books written in England were as elegant and accomplished as any written anywhere in Europe.[4]

Manuscripts were produced by highly trained scribes in ecclesiastical *scriptoria* ('writing offices'), normally housed either in monasteries or cathedral churches. However, in addition to ecclesiastical *scriptoria*, we now know that Anglo-Saxon kings from Athelstan (d. 939) onwards maintained a body of professional scribes – what later would be called a chancery – for royal business such as the drafting and copying of charters.[5] In any case the skill of a professional scribe had to be acquired through long training. One Old English poem, *The Gifts of Men*, characterizes the scribe as *listhendig* ('deft of hand', 95) and contrasts him with the scholar, who is said to be *larum leoþufæst* ('limber in learning', *ibid.*). From this contrast it is clear that the scribe was not regarded as the possessor of learning, but only as its transmitter; like the rune-master, the scribe was a kind of craftsman whose skill was highly prized.

Skills such as engraving and writing existed alongside, but independently of, literacy in Latin. Among laymen literacy in Latin was rare, and was restricted to the court and to a few noblemen such as Ælfric's patron, the ealdorman Æthelweard. Yet many laymen must have possessed many kinds of specialized learning. For example, medical treatises reveal that Anglo-Saxon 'leeches' (or physicians: OE *læce*) practised medicine to a standard as high as any in Europe, and evidently drew their knowledge not only from books but from first-hand experience with the dozens and dozens of plants mentioned in Old English charms and recipes.[6] The story told by Bede (*HE* V.2) of the dumb and leprous boy cured by John of Hexham shows that there was a clear-cut distinction between fields of specialized knowledge, for John dealt simply with the boy's speech problems, leaving the dermatological problems to a physician. Observation of the natural world accounted for another sort of specialized knowledge: *The Seafarer* displays some considerable knowledge of ornithology, and knowledge of falconry is implied by various passages in the poetry (*Gifts of Men*, 80–1; *Beowulf* 2263–4; *Maldon* 7–8). No Anglo-Saxon manual of falconry has come down to us, but such manuals no doubt once existed (King Harold, for example, is known to have owned or written a book on hunting, which presumably included falconry). Music was another skill possessed by laymen, and *The Gifts of Men* specifies that the harper required training in music as well as in verse-craft (49–50; cf. *Beowulf* 2105–10). Skill in warfare was another traditional field where training and experience were necessary, and although no manual of warfare survives, it is worth noting that *The Gifts of Men* once again distinguishes between those who have skill in combat (39–40) and those who are suitable to command (76–7). Estate management also required skill and experience, and the treatise entitled *Gerefa* ('The Reeve') reveals how the competent reeve must know what is to be done in each season, what tools are necessary for each job, and so on. One could easily point to many more fields where traditional knowledge was acquired and transmitted by the Anglo-Saxon laity but, because such knowledge was not the concern of the learned classes who knew Latin and wrote books, it was seldom recorded and has rarely come down to us.

Nevertheless, it is at times possible to glimpse something of what was embodied in traditional knowledge by considering the various kinds of wisdom poetry – gnomes, riddles, charms, catalogue poems – which have been preserved.[7] Let us consider, for example, the collection of riddles preserved in the Exeter Book. None of these riddles can be treated simply as a pure folk-riddle, yet many of them contain what are obviously popular elements. I quote no. 42:

Ic seah wyhte   wrætlice twa
undearnunga   ute plegan
hæmedlaces;   hwitloc anfeng
wlanc under wædum,   gif þæs weorces speow,
fæmne fyllo.   Ic on flette mæg
þurh runstafas   rincum secgan,
þam þe bec witan,   bega ætsomne
naman þara wihta.   Þær sceal Nyd wesan
twega oþer   ond se torhta Æsc
an an linan,   Acas twegen,
Hægelas swa some.   Hwylc þæs hordgates
cægan cræfte   þa clamme onleac
þe þa rædellan   wið rynemenn
hygefæste heold   heortan bewrigene
orþoncbendum?   Nu is undyrne
werum æt wine   hu þa wihte mid us,
heanmode twa,   hatne sindon.

I saw two wondrous creatures openly enjoy sexual intercourse, out of doors; if the deed was successful, the fair-haired, haughty woman received fulfilment beneath her clothes. By means of runic letters upon the floor I can tell the names of those creatures to the men who know books. There shall be Need (N), two of these, and the bright Ash (Æ), only one on the line, two Oaks (A), and Hail (H) in the same quantity. Who has unlocked, with the craft of a key, the fetters of the treasure-door, that held against men skilled in mysteries the riddle, fast in mind, its heart wrapped up by bonds of cunning? Now it is clear to people at their wine how those two low-minded creatures are called among us.

The solution of a riddle required mental exercise, insofar as each descriptive element could be applied to many subjects, but in their totality could apply to only one: in this case, 'Cock and Hen'. No Latin source has ever been found for it and, because the cock is a typical character in the popular riddles of many countries, we may have here some vestige of a folk-riddle. Nevertheless, the riddle has been recast for a bookish audience, as is clear from the use of runes to indicate the solution (the runes must be rearranged and spelled out to yield their secret): the words which contain two N's, one Æ, two A's and two H's are *hana* ('cock') and *hæn* ('hen'). The example of Riddle 42 may serve to make the general point, that although there may be popular (or even pagan) elements in surviving Old English literature, we must never forget that it has all been transmitted to us through the filter of literate (which means, in effect, Latinate) Christianity.

That some vestiges of popular learning are still visible, however, is suggested by the fact that many features of Old English literature, especially the wisdom literature, have close counterparts in other Germanic literatures (especially Old Norse), which may indicate a Germanic origin earlier than the advent of Christianity and book-learning in Anglo-Saxon England. One traditional way of transmitting ancient lore concerning the legendary past, for example, was by means of genealogical catalogues. Such catalogues apparently provided the substance of the OE poem *Widsith*. Another type of mnemonic verse which has Icelandic and Norwegian analogues is found in *The Rune Poem*, in which each stanza is devoted to a single rune and was intended to help in the memorization of their names. Thus the poem's first line says, 'Feoh biþ frofur fira gehwylcum' – '*Feoh* ('wealth', but also a rune-name) is a comfort to every man' – so expressing in a sententious way a piece of commonplace wisdom, no doubt a popular expression. Other expressions of traditional knowledge are found in poems such as *Precepts* or *Maxims*, which consist of strings of commonplaces. Thus in *Maxims I* we find statements such as 'Cyning sceal mid ceape cwene gebicgan, / bunum ond beagum' (81–2: 'A king shall acquire a queen by purchase, with goblets and rings'), or again, 'Forst sceal freosan, fyr wudu meltan' (71: 'Frost shall freeze, fire destroy wood'). Gnomic statements such as these are found elsewhere in Old English verse (e.g. *Seafarer* 106 = *Maxims I* 35), and are occasionally quoted by Ælfric in his homilies. Indeed, some gnomic statements of obviously popular origin have even been interpolated into the *Dicts of Cato*, an Old English prose translation of the Latin *Disticha Catonis*, a famous collection of Latin proverbs which was used as a school-text in Anglo-Saxon England (see below, p. 276). Another kind of wisdom literature which is apparently didactic in function but which may also preserve elements of traditional lore is the 'flyting' or 'contest', which takes the form of a dialogue between two contestants each trying to out-do the other in knowledge. The best-known examples are *Solomon and Saturn* (both the prose and poetic versions) and *Adrian and Ritheus*, both of which are clerical productions but which contain traditional proverbs alongside scriptural lore.[8] Most of their questions can be paralleled in Latin (especially Hiberno-Latin) sources, but a few are arguably of native, popular origin, such as those on the reasons for the redness of the rising and setting sun (*Solomon and Saturn* 55–6; *Adrian and Ritheus* 7–8).

Various evidence, therefore, can give us a glimpse – it is no more than that – of popular learning in Anglo-Saxon England. But it was in the domain of Latin learning that Anglo-Saxon schools achieved their great reputation in the early Middle Ages, and to them we must now turn. When Augustine and the Roman missionaries arrived in England in 597, there were no schools and no trace of the educational system which had flourished under the Roman empire. In order to assure the spread of Latin Christianity among the English, the missionaries' first task will have been the establishment of schools for the training of native clergy. Latin was the language of the church, and had to be learned by priests and monks in order for them to perform their ecclesiastical services. Knowledge of Latin was indispensable for understanding the Scriptures, but also for reading most kinds of text, for Latin was the first language of Anglo-Saxon scholarship: in Latin were written poetry, formal and private letters, pedagogical treatises on matters such as metrics and grammar, legislation, scriptural commentary and much else.[9] And because such works were written in Latin, they stood a much better chance of survival than works composed in the vernacular: note, for example, that virtually all the Latin writings of Aldhelm and Bede have come down to us, whereas their (well attested) compositions in Old English have been lost. Above all, Latin was the language of instruction; the vernacular had no place in ecclesiastical schools. Thus the students in Ælfric's *Colloquy* implore their master: 'We beseech you, master, to teach us how to speak "Latinately" (i.e. in Latin: *latialiter*), for we are idiots and can only speak corruptly.'

The earliest schools will have been set up on the pattern of Gaulish ones, and their aim will have been the severely functional one of teaching the future clergy how to read and understand the Bible and how to perform the liturgy. Such schools were evidently successful, for we learn from Bede (*HE* III.18) that by about 630 the schools in Kent could supply teachers for a new school founded in East Anglia by King Sigebert. Within a generation or two these schools supplied the first native bishop (one Ithamar of Rochester, consecrated in 644), and, shortly thereafter, the first native archbishop of Canterbury (Deusdedit, consecrated in 655).

Augustine and his Roman colleagues were monks, and the establishment of monasticism in England also dates from the period of their mission. Throughout the entire Anglo-Saxon period, it was monastic schools which were the principal seats of learning; and it was these schools which transmitted ancient learning to the Middle Ages. However, it is important not to exaggerate the monks' interest in this ancient learning. Their principal concern was not with classical literature, nor with educating laymen: their sole work was God's work, the *opus Dei*, that is, the performance of the Divine Office at regular intervals during each day; and in order to understand the Office, Latin was essential. At those times when a monk was not performing the Office, he could most profitably be engaged in reading, as the *Rule of St Benedict* tells us (ch. 48), or, during meal-times, in listening to others read edifying works aloud (ch. 38). In other words, the concern of monasteries was not with Latin learning as an end in itself, but as a means of serving God. For this purpose, most Anglo-Saxon monasteries (at least those of any substantial size) will have had a school, the principal function of which will have been the instruction of the oblates and novices in their care. By the same token cathedral clergy, which from at least the late eighth century followed its own rule modelled on that of Benedict (namely the *Regula canonicorum* of Chrodegang of Metz), will have needed to train future ministers, and will in many cases have done so by establishing schools.

In respect of schooling, women seem to have had the same opportunities as men. From the earliest period of Anglo-Saxon Christianity we have evidence of 'double houses' or monasteries for both men and women; and it is clear that many of these double houses were under the rule of an abbess (a well-known example is Whitby, which for many years in the seventh century was ruled by the Abbess Hild who figures so prominently in Bede's *Ecclesiastical History*: *HE* IV.23). Only in the later Anglo-Saxon period do we find nunneries proper. In any event, nuns apparently followed the same curriculum as monks. The parity of the sexes in this regard is reflected in the pair of OE words *rædere* and *rædistre* ('male reader' and 'female reader', respectively). Women composed letters and verse in Latin, as we learn from the example of Boniface's female correspondents Eadburg and Leobgyth, as well as from the writings of

Burginda (writing perhaps at Bath Abbey, *c.* 700) or Hygeburg, an English nun at Heidenheim in Germany who in the late eighth century commemorated the saintly lives of her two brothers (Wynnebald and Willibald) in a long saint's *vita* (see above, p. 253). That women were proficient in Latin is clear too from Aldhelm's massive treatise *De virginitate*, which was dedicated to Abbess Hildelith and her nuns at Barking Abbey, Essex. Women may also have been the dedicatees of Latin writings such as Boniface's *Enigmata*, which is concerned in part with the subject of virginity. Recall, too, that it was under the patronage of Abbess Hild of Whitby (d. 680) that the poet Cædmon composed his religious verse. No Anglo-Saxon woman achieved the scholarly status of an Aldhelm or a Bede, but in this respect England was no different from the rest of Europe.

Unfortunately, it is not possible to form a comprehensive impression of how Anglo-Saxon schools functioned and what subjects were taught. We have a small number of witnesses who throw some light on the subject. For example, Bede tells us (*HE* IV.2) that Theodore and Hadrian in their school at Canterbury 'gave their hearers instruction not only in the books of holy Scripture but also in the art of metre, astronomy and ecclesiastical computation'. In one of his letters Aldhelm, who had been a student of Theodore and Hadrian, mentions the difficulty of these same subjects (and adds the information that Roman law was studied there as well). In his long poem on the saints of York, Alcuin describes the curriculum taught at York by his master Ælberht:[10]

There he [Ælberht] watered parched hearts with diverse
     streams
of learning and the varied dew of knowledge:
skilfully training some in the arts and rules of grammar
and pouring upon others a flood of rhetorical eloquence.
Some he polished with the whetstone of true speech,
teaching others to sing in Aonian strain,
training some to blow on the Castalian pipe,
and run with lyric step over the peaks of Parnassus.
To others this master taught the harmony of the spheres,
the labours of the sun and the moon,
the five zones of heaven, the seven planets,
the regular motions of the stars, their rising and setting,
the movements of the air, the tremors of earth and sea,
the natures of men and cattle, of birds and wild beasts,
the diverse forms and shapes of numbers.
He regulated the time for Easter's celebration,
revealing the great mysteries of holy Scripture.

Here, apparently, we have a thorough account of the curriculum in one influential English school: grammar, rhetoric, metre, astronomy, geography, arithmetic (or numerology?) and computus. Yet it is not possible to corroborate each of Alcuin's statements by means of external evidence, and for some at least of the subjects he lists (astronomy, for example: see below, p. 279) there are grounds for doubt about the profundity of Ælberht's teaching. In other words, we must at every point attempt to corroborate the evidence of witnesses such as Bede, Aldhelm and Alcuin with that of indirect witnesses of various kinds (letters from disciples to former masters, hints in hagiographies) to reconstruct the way in which teaching was conducted. The atmosphere of the schoolroom can often be glimpsed from the so-called scholastic colloquies, cast as dialogues between master and pupils and apparently composed by the masters as exercises in speaking Latin.[11] Although the sentences in these colloquies are marked by some degree of artificiality, the descriptions of daily affairs – particularly in the colloquies composed in the early eleventh century by Ælfric Bata (a former student of the better known Ælfric) – give us a glimpse of classroom life. In Ælfric Bata's colloquies students of varying degrees of ability are portrayed reading, writing, chanting or learning by heart the set-texts which were assigned daily; it is also quite clear from Ælfric Bata that failure to master these set-texts was punished by whipping.

One of the first tasks of the young oblates was to commit to memory certain daily prayers (the Lord's Prayer and the Creed), followed by the entire psalter – the psalter formed the basis of the Divine Office, and was recited in its entirety once every week at the various offices – and the series of hymns which formed part of the Office. The stress throughout was on memorization: Latin texts needed to be learned by heart, because parchment was expensive and books were in short supply (a monastery would be lucky to have one copy of a curriculum text: there was no chance that each student could be supplied with a copy!). Instead students were required to copy the day's given passage of set-text from dictation onto a wax tablet; when the text had been memorized, the tablet could be erased, ready to receive the following day's passage. The passages were explained word by word (perhaps even syllable by syllable) by the master. In the case of the more difficult poetic texts, a prose version was supplied. Thus we have prose versions of the Office hymns and of the Monastic Canticles, as well as of a poem which was one of the hardest set-texts studied in Anglo-Saxon schools, namely the third book of the *Bella Parisiacae urbis* by Abbo of Saint-Germain-des-Prés (see below, p. 276). The prose versions were designed to elucidate the (often complex) syntax of the verse; thus an elliptic line of Abbo such as 'Burra, probum fateor buteonem, qui arua bidentat' (III.96) was clarified by the prose version provided by an

Anglo-Saxon master: 'Fateor probum buteonem, qui bidentat burra arua' ('I confess that he is a good lad who digs the red fields'). This pedagogical technique of rendering Latin verse as prose and vice versa may well lie behind the Anglo-Saxon fondness for what Bede called *opera geminata* or 'twinned works', which consisted of a verse text and a corresponding prose counterpart.[12] The best known examples are Aldhelm's *De virginitate* and Bede's *Vita S. Cuthberti*; but there are many less well known examples of the form from later Anglo-Saxon England, a fact which suggests that the scholastic technique of paraphrase was a popular one with English masters.

Another index to the way set-texts were studied in Anglo-Saxon schools is provided by glosses in surviving manuscripts.[13] Very frequently the most difficult or interesting words of a Latin text are accompanied by explanations (which may vary in length from a one-word synonym to a two- or three-sentence exposition). These explanations or glosses apparently represent the responses of masters to difficulties in the set-texts; they may be copied above the words they explain (interlinear glosses) or be added in the margins of the manuscript (marginal glosses); they may be written in ink or be scratched on the parchment with the stylus (drypoint glosses); they may be in Latin or Old English; and they may vary in frequency from scattered or isolated glosses to the word-for-word gloss. Sometimes a manuscript of a popular classroom text may preserve the annotations of different generations of masters. Study of glossed manuscripts, therefore, can help us to understand the way that curriculum texts were understood and interpreted by Anglo-Saxon masters, and this information, in turn, is a useful index to the quality of Anglo-Saxon learning.

The process of interpreting texts by means of glosses and annotations was taken a step further in the compilation of glossaries. In the simplest form of glossary, the words which were glossed (called *lemmata*) and their accompanying glosses were copied out in the order in which they occur in the text; the glosses collected together in this way to form an elementary glossary are referred to as *glossae collectae*. A list of *glossae collectae* could be used as an aid to the interpretation of the text in question, but would be cumbersome to use for someone who was searching for the meaning of an individual word. Accordingly, the *lemmata* with their glosses were often arranged in alphabetical order. The process of alphabetization could be based simply on the first letter of each *lemma*; this arrangement is referred to as A-order, and is found, for example, in the first three entries of the so-called Epinal-Erfurt Glossary, compiled *c.* 700: *Apodixen: fantasia*; *Amineae: sine rubore*; *Amites: loergae*, and so on. A more complex arrangement, known as AB-order, was based on the first two letters of each *lemma*, as in the well-known Corpus Glossary, compiled probably at Canterbury sometime in the eighth century; its first three entries are *ABminiculum*: *adiutorium*; *ABelena*: *haeselhnutu*; *ABiecit*: *proiecit*, and so on. On rare occasions, as in the case of the tenth-century Harley Glossary, the alphabetization was based on the first three letters of each *lemma* (called ABC-order).

From the point of view of an Anglo-Saxon schoolmaster, the alphabetized glossaries were the easiest to use, for difficult words could be searched for as in a modern dictionary. It is not surprising that a substantial number of glossaries – some with Latin *lemmata* and Latin glosses, some with Latin *lemmata* and English glosses – have survived from the Anglo-Saxon period. For modern scholars, however, whose task is to determine what texts were studied in Anglo-Saxon schools, *glossae collectae* are far more useful, for the occurrence of *lemmata* in sequence often makes it possible to identify the text from which the *lemmata* are drawn, whereas identification becomes much more difficult when the original sequence is destroyed in the process of alphabetization. Sometimes, indeed, batches of *glossae collectae* are supplied with rubrics indicating the source of the *lemmata*. This is the case with one of the most important Anglo-Saxon glossaries, the so-called Leiden Glossary, a manuscript now in Leiden but which was copied at St Gallen *c*. 800 from a collection of English materials. This same collection of English materials was copied elsewhere on the Continent as well, with the result that a number of continental glossaries related to the Leiden Glossary have been preserved. It is clear from many of the explanations in these glossaries that they originated in the school of Theodore and Hadrian in late seventh-century Canterbury.[14] They are thus a precious testimony to the school which Bede praised (*HE* IV.2) in such glowing terms. Since both Theodore and Hadrian were Greeks of Mediterranean origin (Theodore from Tarsus in Asia Minor, Hadrian from Africa), it is not surprising that the explanations which they gave for difficult words reflect on occasion their reading in Greek sources and their Mediterranean background. For example, in explaining the list of impure birds in Leviticus (XI.13–19), they explained what the ibis was by noting that it 'mittit aquam de ore suo in culum suum ut possit degerere; indeque medici ipsam artem dedicerunt' ('it sends water from its beak up its anus so that it can digest its food; and from this physicians learned the same technique'). The ibis is an Egyptian bird, and its alleged medical practice is referred to in various Greek medical sources such as Galen. Theodore – whose interest in medicine is mentioned by Bede – was simply trying to convey some notion of a very peculiar bird to an audience who had never seen an ibis; but what the Anglo-Saxon students made of Theodore's explanation is impossible to imagine. Throughout the glosses of the Canterbury school there is an acute awareness of the difference between the Mediterranean and Anglo-

Saxon worlds; and perhaps at certain points a sense of longing for a distant land. Thus in the explanation of the *porphyrio* or purple gallinule, an African bird said by the glossator to have beautiful plumage and be kept in cages by Libyan kings, we find the added comment: 'porphirio non fit in brittania' ('there is no purple gallinule in Britain'). Certainly no such bird was to be found in the English marshes and fens, nor in the royal halls of Kent.

Glossaries, then, are one kind of scholarly tool which could be used by Anglo-Saxon masters and which can throw some light on the Anglo-Saxon classroom. It is unlikely, however, that glossaries were used in the classroom itself for teaching purposes; they are rather a sort of reference-work, to be consulted by the master at points of difficulty. But there is one type of glossary which could be employed more easily for didactic purpose, namely the so-called class-glossary, where entries are arranged according to subject and consist of lists of names of birds, trees, plants, fish, animals, household implements and so on. An example of a class-glossary of this sort is Ælfric's *Glossary*. The lists of words in such glossaries could easily be memorized (recall that, in Benedictine monasteries at least, the monks were expected to communicate in Latin, and they accordingly will have needed to know the Latin vocabulary for everyday objects); and, to aid memorization, the same vocabulary-lists could be employed in scholastic colloquies, which were designed to give students practice in speaking Latin. The close relationship between colloquy and class-glossary may be seen in the expanded version of Ælfric's *Colloquy* made by his student, Ælfric Bata; here the hunter, for example, is asked to describe his daily prey: 'Capio utique ceruos et ceruas et uulpes et uulpiculos et muricipes et lupos et ursos et simias et fibros et lutrios et feruncos, taxones et lepores atque erinacios et aliquando apros et dammas et capreos et aliquando lepores' ('I catch stags and deer and foxes and dog-foxes and wildcats and wolves and bears and apes and beavers and otters and ferrets (?) and badgers and hares and hedgehogs and sometimes boars and antelope and wild goats and sometimes hares'). The words in this list were evidently taken in a batch from a class-glossary, and are not in any sense an accurate record of what an Anglo-Saxon hunter might have been able to catch in a day's outing.

Once students had acquired an elementary knowledge of Latin – from memorizing the Psalter and other prayers, from memorizing word-lists and scholastic colloquies – they were able to proceed to the study of the school-texts themselves. The texts studied in Anglo-Saxon schools were more or less those which were studied in continental schools, as can be seen from surviving manuscripts. One manuscript in particular, which seems to be a compendium of Anglo-Saxon curriculum texts, gives us an impression of what texts were being studied at the time it was written:

Cambridge, University Library, Gg. 5.35, a manuscript written at St Augustine's, Canterbury, in the mid-eleventh century.[15] The first (and easiest) part of this book includes various Christian Latin poetry such as the *Evangelia* of Juvencus, the *Carmen paschale* of Caelius Sedulius, the *De actibus apostolorum* of Arator, the *Epigrammata* of Prosper of Aquitaine, the *Psychomachia* of Prudentius, the *De ave phoenice* attributed to Lactantius (the OE poem *The Phoenix* is based on this); these are followed by the *De consolatione Philosophiae* of Boethius, a text which was added to the Anglo-Saxon curriculum some centuries after the other texts had been well established (the earliest English use of this text dates from the period of King Alfred's educational reform: see above, p. 17). The second part of Gg. 5.35 comprises texts of much greater difficulty, such as Aldhelm's *Carmen de virginitate* and the third book of the *Bella Parisiacae urbis* by Abbo of Saint-Germain-des-Prés,[16] as well as various Carolingian Latin poets. The third part contains texts less difficult than the second; most of the texts in this part are concerned with wisdom and the acquisition of wisdom, such as the *Disticha Catonis* and the various riddle collections of Symphosius, Aldhelm, Tatwine, Eusebius and Boniface.

Of these various curriculum texts, those in the first part of the manuscript were commonly studied in schools all over Europe in the early Middle Ages. Those in the second and third parts, however, were unique to the Anglo-Saxon curriculum, and gave Anglo-Saxon learning – in Latin as well as in the vernacular – an individual and characteristic stamp. The difficult texts such as Aldhelm and Abbo were studied intensively for the arcane vocabulary which they contained: archaisms, neologisms, grecisms. Concern with the display of this arcane vocabulary (which is often referred to as 'hermeneutic' because much of it derived originally from Greek-Latin word-lists or *hermeneumata*) is found in nearly all Anglo-Latin literature of the tenth and eleventh centuries,[17] but it also is reflected in various works in English. An example in verse is the brief Old English poem known as *Aldhelm*, where words of Greek and Latin origin are carefully but ostentatiously woven into the fabric of the poem's alliteration. Among prose writers, it is clear that Byrhtferth in his *Enchiridion* attempted to embellish his prose style by the use of obscure English words as well as by the use of Latin expressions (see above, p. 86). Nor is it surprising that Byrhtferth's Old English prose should take this form: the Latin prose of his saints' lives (*Vita S. Ecgwini* and *Vita S. Oswaldi*) and chronicle (*Historia regum*) abounds in obscure, hermeneutic vocabulary.

Also characteristically Anglo-Saxon is the use of riddles or *enigmata* for teaching purposes. Aldhelm's collection of one hundred *enigmata* is intended (as he states) to exemplify the metrical features he had discussed in his metrical treatises (see below, p. 278).[18] The forty *enigmata* composed by Tatwine are similarly didactic in intent (the subject of one of them, no. xvi, is 'Prepositions governing two cases'). The *enigmata* of Eusebius, which were added to Tatwine's forty in order to make up the canonical number of 100, show a pervasive interest in grammar (nos. ix, xix, xxxix and xlii) and chronology (nos. xxvi and xxix). Boniface composed twenty *enigmata* on the virtues and vices, and various Latin riddles are attributed, doubtfully, to Bede, including the so-called *Flores* and *Iocoseria* in Gg. 5.35. Alcuin, too, in his *Disputatio regalis iuuenis Pippini cum Albino scholastico* paraphrases the riddles of Symphosius for elementary didactic purposes. The nature of these Anglo-Latin *enigmata*, however, is quite different from that of the vernacular riddles. Consider, for example, one of Aldhelm's *enigmata* (no. xxxv):

My nature appropriately reproduces my name in two aspects, for the 'shadows' have part of me, and the 'birds' the other part. Only rarely does anyone see me in the clear light, particularly since at night-time I frequent hiding-places beneath the stars. It is my custom to chatter in mid-air in a harsh voice. I am recorded in Romulean books, although my name is Greek, while I inhabit nocturnal shadows through my name.

This riddle is not designed to puzzle the reader, merely to impress him. The reader of the Exeter Book riddles was obliged to guess the solution (see above, p. 268) – a difficult, and sometimes impossible, task; here, however, the solution is given at the outset – *nycticorax* – and the problem is simply the etymological one of explaining the word given as the title.[19] The riddle plays on the two parts of the name: *nyks/nyktos* ('night') and *korax* ('raven'); the name of the creature is thus 'night-raven', apparently a kind of owl. The riddling exercise has become an exercise in etymology: a clear reflection of the author's didactic intentions.

In the study of these various curriculum texts, it is evident that the emphasis throughout is linguistic, what was understood by the term 'grammar' in the early Middle Ages. Grammar in this sense seems to have dominated the Anglo-Saxon curriculum, to the virtual exclusion of other disciplines. As far as the sources permit us to tell, Anglo-Saxon schools did not pursue the full range of subjects defined – by late antique authorities such as Cassiodorus and Martianus Capella – as the *trivium* (that is, grammar, rhetoric and dialectic) and *quadrivium* (geometry, arithmetic, astronomy and harmony). In the early Middle Ages, study of these various *artes* was regarded as preparatory to the study of the Scriptures; and for understanding the Scripture, the most necessary discipline was grammar, with the others being more or less superfluous (only at a later time, from the ninth century onwards, did the subjects of the *quadrivium* receive attention). As I have said, grammar was understood in the wider sense, not only of understanding Latin, but of interpreting literary texts, above all the Bible.[20] For this purpose, rhetoric and dialectic were less essential, though it should be mentioned that Bede was sympathetic to the techniques of classical rhetoric (he composed a treatise on the rhetorical devices used in Scripture) and Alcuin composed a treatise on rhetoric and dialectic.

Perhaps because they were among the first peoples of Europe converted to Christianity who were not native speakers of Latin, the Anglo-Saxons devoted particular attention to grammar, above all to aspects of Latin which were taken for granted by the grammarians of late antiquity, such as the declension of nouns and conjugation of verbs. Grammatical treatises were written by Boniface, Tatwine, Alcuin, Ælfric and various anonymous authors. Abbo of Fleury, after he had returned to the Continent, composed a treatise entitled *Quaestiones grammaticales* which he dedicated and sent to his former students at Ramsey. Orthography was another persistent Anglo-Saxon concern. Bede wrote a treatise *De orthographia*, and a work with the same title was compiled by Alcuin. Reflection on the alphabet is pervasive in the Anglo-Latin *enigmata*: Tatwine, for example, composed a riddle entitled 'Versus de nominibus litterarum' ('Verses on the names of the letters'). The same concern may lie behind the Anglo-Saxon penchant for acrostics (used by Aldhelm, Tatwine and Boniface) and for cryptography, where vowels are replaced either by punctuation marks or by other letters so as to constitute a sort of secret script; and it would appear that it was Boniface who introduced cryptography to the Continent. Yet another aspect of the same linguistic awareness is seen in the Anglo-Saxons' devoted study of Latin metrics: Aldhelm's massive *Epistola ad Acircium* contains two distinct treatises on metre (*De metris* and *De pedum regulis*), and Boniface and Bede also wrote works on the subject. In all these domains – grammar, orthography, metre – the Anglo-Saxons were the undisputed schoolmasters of medieval Europe, and some of their treatises, especially those of Bede, survive in hundreds of copies and were used as textbooks up to the time of the Renaissance.

In other respects, however, English schools lagged far behind those on the Continent. This is particularly so in the case of the scientific subjects which made up the ancient *quadrivium*. We know from Bede (*HE* IV.2) that astronomy had been studied at the Canterbury school of Theodore and Hadrian, but no Anglo-Saxon writer shows any expert knowledge of the subject. Bede wrote an elementary handbook on cosmology and related matters (the *De natura rerum*). Ecclesiastical computus – the complicated means of calculating the dates of the movable feasts of the liturgical year – was of course studied in England as elsewhere, and Bede's explanatory treatises on the subject (*De temporibus*, *De temporum ratione*) were widely studied in medieval schools and even today represent the most helpful introduction to the subject. Abbo of Fleury taught computus during his stay at Ramsey, and his teaching is reflected in Byrhtferth's *Enchiridion*. But computus was a separate, practical discipline, and had little to do with the complex mathematics which constituted the study of arithmetic, astronomy and harmony as it was pursued in continental schools from the ninth century onwards. Only in the eleventh century do the textbooks of the *quadrivium* (Macrobius, Martianus Capella, Hyginus), which had been the staple of the scientific curriculum in continental schools, appear in English libraries. No Anglo-Saxon author shows more than a superficial familiarity with such scientific texts: Byrhtferth, for example, who certainly had studied Macrobius, seems to have used him more as a stylistic model and a source of Greek words than as a source of scientific information.

Anglo-Saxon learning presents a curious paradox, therefore. In some respects, Anglo-Saxons were in the vanguard of European learning – this is particularly true in the field of grammar and related disciplines – but in others were an undistinguished backwater. The most characteristic feature of their learning, however, is their fascination with linguistic detail, and this fascination is reflected in countless ways: in the use of runic and cryptographic alphabets in manuscripts, in the pursuit of obscure, hermeneutic vocabulary, in the use of etymology as a pedagogical device, in the pervasive fondness for riddles and riddling, to name only a few. And it is, finally, this same fascination which speaks directly to us as we study the literature of Anglo-Saxon England.

1 No reliable study of Anglo-Saxon schools exists. As general background (with some discussion of England) see, for the earlier period, P. Riché, *Education and Culture in the Barbarian West, Sixth through Eighth Centuries*, trans. J. J. Contreni (Columbia, SC, 1976), and for the later period the same author's *Les écoles et l'enseignement dans l'Occident chrétien de la fin du Ve siècle au milieu du XIe siècle* (Paris, 1979).

2 H. Gneuss, 'A Preliminary List of Manuscripts written or owned in England up to 1100', *ASE* 9 (1981), 1–60.

3 R. I. Page, *An Introduction to English Runes* (London, 1973); for the Franks Casket, see pp. 174–82, and for the Ruthwell Cross, pp. 148–53. For runes in manuscripts, see R. Derolez, *Runica Manuscripta* (Bruges, 1954).

4 The script found in English (and other) manuscripts up to 800 is studied by means of E. A. Lowe, *Codices Latini Antiquiores*, 11 vols. and suppl. (Oxford, 1934–72); see also his *English Uncial* (Oxford, 1960). For the later period see T. A. M. Bishop, *English Caroline Minuscule* (Oxford, 1971), and for manuscripts containing Old English, N. R. Ker, *Catalogue of Manuscripts containing Anglo-Saxon* (Oxford, 1957). There is a brilliant overview of early

medieval palaeography (including England's contribution) by B. Bischoff, *Latin Palaeography*, trans. D. Ganz and D. Ó Cróinín (Cambridge, 1990).

5 S. D. Keynes, *The Diplomas of King Æthelred 'the Unready'* 978–1016 (Cambridge, 1980), pp. 134–53.

6 M. L. Cameron, 'The Sources of Medical Knowledge in Anglo-Saxon England', *ASE* 11 (1983), 135–55; 'Bald's Leechbook: its Sources and their Use in its Compilation', *ASE* 12 (1983), 153–82; 'Anglo-Saxon Medicine and Magic', *ASE* 17 (1988), 191–215.

7 T. A. Shippey, *Poems of Wisdom and Learning in Old English* (Cambridge, 1976); N. Howe, *The Old English Catalogue Poems*, Anglistica 23 (Copenhagen, 1985).

8 J. E. Cross and T. D. Hill, *The Prose 'Solomon and Saturn' and 'Adrian and Ritheus'* (Toronto, 1982).

9 There is a convenient survey of Anglo-Latin literature by M. Lapidge in S. B. Greenfield and D. G. Calder, *A New Critical History of Old English Literature* (New York, 1986), pp. 5–37; since this essay gives full bibliographical references to Anglo-Latin writings discussed in the present article, they are not repeated here.

10 *Alcuin: the Bishops, Kings and Saints of York*, ed. P. Godman (Oxford, 1982), pp. 112–15.

11 W. H. Stevenson, *Early Scholastic Colloquies* (Oxford, 1929); *Ælfric's Colloquy*, ed. G. N. Garmonsway, 2nd ed. (London, 1947); and G. N. Garmonsway, 'The Development of the Colloquy', in *The Anglo-Saxons: Studies in some Aspects of their History and Culture presented to Bruce Dickins*, ed. P. Clemoes (London, 1959), pp. 248–61.

12 P. Godman, 'The Anglo-Latin *opus geminatum*: from Aldhelm to Alcuin', *Medium Ævum* 50 (1981), 215–29; G. R. Wieland, '*Geminus stilus*: Studies in Anglo-Latin Hagiography', in *Insular Latin Studies*, ed. M. W. Herren (Toronto, 1981), pp. 113–33.

13 See M. Lapidge, 'The Study of Latin Texts in late Anglo-Saxon England, I: the Evidence of Latin Glosses', and R. I. Page, 'The Study of Latin Texts in late Anglo-Saxon England, II: the Evidence of English Glosses', both in *Latin and the Vernacular Languages in Early Medieval Britain*, ed. N. Brooks (Leicester, 1982), pp. 99–140 and 141–65, respectively.

14 M. Lapidge, 'The School of Theodore and Hadrian', *ASE* 15 (1986), 45–72; the 'Leiden Glossary' is ed. J. H. Hessels, *A Late Eighth-Century Latin-Anglo-Saxon Glossary preserved in the Library of the Leiden University* (Cambridge, 1906).

15 A. G. Rigg and G. R. Wieland, 'A Canterbury Classbook of the Mid-Eleventh Century (the "Cambridge Songs" Manuscript)', *ASE* 4 (1975), 113–30; see also Lapidge, 'The Study of Latin Texts in late Anglo-Saxon England', and G. R. Wieland, 'The Glossed Manuscript: Classbook or Library Book?', *ASE* 14 (1985), 153–73.

16 P. Lendinara, 'The Third Book of the *Bella Parisiacae Urbis* by Abbo of Saint-Germain-des-Prés and its Old English Gloss', *ASE* 15 (1986), 73–89.

17 M. Lapidge, 'The Hermeneutic Style in Tenth-Century Anglo-Latin Literature', *ASE* 4 (1975), 67–111.

18 M. Lapidge and J. L. Rosier, *Aldhelm: the Poetic Works* (Cambridge, 1985), pp. 61–9; the translation of the 'Night-Raven' riddle is taken from p. 77.

19 N. Howe, 'Aldhelm's *Enigmata* and Isidorian Etymology', *ASE* 14 (1985), 37–59.

20 V. Law, *The Insular Latin Grammarians* (Woodbridge, 1982), and M. Irvine, 'Bede the Grammarian and the Scope of Grammatical Studies in Eighth-Century Northumbria', *ASE* 15 (1986), 15–44.

Further reading

The reading list which follows is intended to provide simple and swift bibliographical orientation for the uninitiated reader in any of the specified areas of interest. It will be realized that, in many fields of Old English scholarship, the bibliography is practically inexhaustible. With respect to individual texts, therefore, we have simply attempted to cite some of the classic interpretative studies (with no attempt at comprehensiveness), in the hope that the enterprising student will derive from such studies a preliminary orientation, and will thereafter be able to pursue particular interests by consulting the more comprehensive works of reference listed throughout.

1 Bibliography

A complete list of all surviving Old English texts, with references to standard editions, is given in *A Plan for the Dictionary of Old English*, ed. R. Frank and A. Cameron (Toronto, 1973). For secondary literature on the subject there is the truly comprehensive work by S. B. Greenfield and F. C. Robinson, *A Bibliography of Publications on Old English Literature to the End of 1972* (Toronto and Manchester, 1980); more recent work is listed in the annual bibliographies in *ASE* (from 1972 on) and in the *Old English Newsletter* (from 1967 on).

2 Historical and cultural background

An excellent bibliographical guide is S. D. Keynes, *Anglo-Saxon History: a Select Bibliography*, Old English Newsletter Subsidia 13 (Binghamton, NY, 1987); see also J. T. Rosenthal, *Anglo-Saxon History: an Annotated Bibliography 450–1066* (New York, 1985). General studies include: F. M. Stenton, *Anglo-Saxon England*, 3rd ed. (Oxford, 1971); D. Whitelock, *The Beginnings of English Society* (Harmondsworth, 1952); P. Hunter Blair, *An Introduction to Anglo-Saxon England*, 2nd ed. (Cambridge, 1977); H. Mayr-Harting, *The Coming of Christianity to Anglo-Saxon England*, 3rd ed. (London, 1990); D. Hill, *An Atlas of Anglo-Saxon England* (Oxford, 1981); J. Campbell, E. John and P. Wormald, *The Anglo-Saxons* (Oxford, 1982), a book which is richly illustrated; and C. E. Fell, *Women in Anglo-Saxon England* (London, 1984; repr. Oxford, 1986).

An invaluable compendium of sources in translation is *EHD*, to be supplemented by various translations, including: M. Lapidge and M. Herren, *Aldhelm: the Prose Works* (Cambridge, 1979); M. Lapidge and J. L. Rosier,

282

Aldhelm: the Poetic Works (Cambridge, 1985); *The Letters of Saint Boniface*, trans. E. Emerton (New York, 1940); *Bede's Ecclesiastical History of the English People*, ed. and trans. B. Colgrave and R. A. B. Mynors (Oxford, 1969); *Alcuin: the Bishops, Kings, and Saints of York*, ed. and trans. P. Godman (Oxford, 1982); S. Allott, *Alcuin of York* (York, 1974), a collection of Alcuin's letters in translation; and S. Keynes and M. Lapidge, *Alfred the Great* (Harmondsworth, 1983). A collection of some relevant Norse poems, which provide significant background to Anglo-Saxon culture, is *The Poetic Edda, I: Heroic Poems*, ed. U. Dronke (Oxford, 1969).

A survey of Anglo-Latin literature is given by M. Lapidge in S. B. Greenfield and D. G. Calder, *A New Critical History of Old English Literature* (New York, 1986), pp. 5–37. The most authoritative studies of (aspects of) Anglo-Latin culture are W. Levison, *England and the Continent in the Eighth Century* (Oxford, 1946) and P. Sims-Williams, *Religion and Literature in Western England, 600–800*, Cambridge Studies in Anglo-Saxon England 3 (Cambridge, 1990). There is also much of relevance to our understanding of the cultural background of Old English literature in two collaborative volumes: *England before the Conquest: Studies in Primary Sources presented to Dorothy Whitelock*, ed. P. Clemoes and K. Hughes (Cambridge, 1971), and *Learning and Literature in Anglo-Saxon England: Studies presented to Peter Clemoes*, ed. M. Lapidge and H. Gneuss (Cambridge, 1985).

3 Manuscripts

The indispensable guide for students of Old English literature wishing to explore the manuscript context of the literature they study is N. R. Ker, *Catalogue of Manuscripts containing Anglo-Saxon* (Oxford, 1957), with supplement in *ASE 5* (1976), 121–31. All manuscripts – Latin and Old English – which survive are listed helpfully by H. Gneuss, 'A Preliminary List of Manuscripts written or owned in England up to 1100', *ASE 9* (1981), 1–60. For English manuscripts of the earlier period (up to 800), see the relevant entries in E. A. Lowe, *Codices Latini Antiquiores*, 11 vols. and suppl. (Oxford, 1934–71; 2nd ed. of vol. 2, 1972) and *English Uncial* (Oxford, 1960). For manuscripts of the later period, see T. A. M. Bishop, *English Caroline Minuscule* (Oxford, 1971), and D. N. Dumville, 'English Square Minuscule Script: the Background and Earliest Phases', *ASE 16* (1987), 147–79. The best general introduction to the palaeography of medieval manuscripts is now B. Bischoff, *Latin Palaeography: Antiquity and the Middle Ages*, trans. D. Ó Cróinín and D. Ganz (Cambridge, 1990). A useful collection of plates illustrating the development of script (including various kinds of Anglo-Saxon script) is found in M. P. Brown, *A Guide to Western Historical Scripts from Antiquity to 1600* (London, 1990); some vernacular manuscripts are usefully illustrated and discussed in R. L. Collins, *Anglo-Saxon Vernacular Manuscripts in America* (New York, 1976). There is a brilliant demonstration of how knowledge of the manuscripts in which Old English poetry is preserved is fundamental to any attempt at interpretation by J. C. Pope, 'Palaeography and Poetry: Some Solved and Unsolved Problems of the Exeter Book', in *Medieval Scribes, Manuscripts and Libraries: Essays presented to N. R. Ker*, ed. M. B. Parkes and A. G. Watson

(London, 1978), pp. 25–65; also essential for any of the biblical verse preserved in the Junius manuscript is B. C. Raw, 'The Construction of Oxford, Bodleian Library, Junius 11', *ASE* 13 (1984), 187–207. Many of the best known surviving manuscripts of Old English literature are available in facsimile editions in the series Early English Manuscripts in Facsimile (Copenhagen). For an introductory study of English runes, see R. I. Page, *An Introduction to English Runes* (London, 1973).

4 Old English language

For the history of the English language (including Old English), see A. C. Baugh, *A History of the English Language*, 3rd ed. rev. T. Cable (London, 1978), esp. chs. 3 and 4. There are two comprehensive and complementary bibliographies by A. G. Kennedy, *A Bibliography of Writings on the English Language from the Beginning of Printing to the End of 1922* (Cambridge, MA, 1927) and M. Tajima, *Old and Middle English Language Studies: a Classified Bibliography 1923–85* (Amsterdam, 1988).

Dictionaries   The fullest dictionary currently available is J. Bosworth and T. N. Toller, *An Anglo-Saxon Dictionary* (Oxford, 1898) with *Supplement* by T. N. Toller (Oxford, 1921) and *Revised and Enlarged Addenda* by A. Campbell (Oxford, 1972). A convenient single-volume dictionary is J. R. Clark Hall and H. Meritt, *A Concise Anglo-Saxon Dictionary*, 4th ed. (Cambridge, 1969). These dictionaries will eventually be superseded by the Toronto *Dictionary of Old English*, ed. A. Cameron, A. C. Amos, A. diP. Healey *et al.* (Toronto, 1986–), of which two fascicules (*C* and *D*, in microfiche) have so far appeared.

Concordances   Especially useful for the study of Old English poetry are J. B. Bessinger and P. H. Smith, *A Concordance to Beowulf* (Ithaca, NY, 1969), and *A Concordance to the Anglo-Saxon Poetic Records* (Ithaca, NY, and London, 1978). A. diP. Healey and R. L. Venezky, *A Microfiche Concordance to Old English* (Toronto, 1980) is now the indispensable tool for any serious study of the Old English lexicon; it is to be used in combination with A. Cameron, A. Kingsmill and A. C. Amos, *Old English Word Studies: a Preliminary Author and Word Index* (Toronto, 1983).

Grammars   The standard reference work in English is A. Campbell, *Old English Grammar* (Oxford, 1959); more comprehensive, but available only in German, is K. Brunner, *Altenglische Grammatik*, 3rd ed. (Tübingen, 1965). For syntax there is the monumental work of B. Mitchell, *Old English Syntax*, 2 vols. (Oxford, 1985); it is provided with comprehensive indices, and the serious student of Old English should develop the habit of consulting these indices for any line of prose or verse requiring elucidation. Introductory guides include: R. Quirk and C. L. Wrenn, *An Old English Grammar*, 2nd ed. (London, 1957); G. L. Brook, *An Introduction to Old English*, 2nd ed. (Manchester, 1962); and B. Mitchell and F. C. Robinson, *A Guide to Old English*, 4th ed. (Oxford, 1986), which is written in an admirably clear way that is easily approachable by those studying the language without the benefit of formal instruction.

5 Literary history

Because most Old English poetry cannot be dated, it is not possible to write a chronological account of Old English literature (on the problems involved in dating, see the excellent study by A. C. Amos, *Linguistic Means of Determining the Dates of Old English Literary Texts* (Cambridge, MA, 1980)), though there is a commendable – but necessarily outdated – attempt to treat the subject chronologically by C. L. Wrenn, *A Study of Old English Literature* (London, 1967). Old English literary history is normally organized in terms of particular themes or genres. The fullest coverage is given by S. B. Greenfield and D. G. Calder, *A New Critical History of Old English Literature* (New York and London, 1986), but there are many interesting perspectives in M. McC. Gatch, *Loyalties and Traditions: Man and the World in Anglo-Saxon Literature* (New York, 1971). Immensely valuable, above all for its treatment of the manuscript bases of the literature, is K. Sisam, *Studies in the History of Old English Literature* (Oxford, 1953). On the growth of our conception of Old English literary history, there are two interesting studies by E. G. Stanley: *The Search for Anglo-Saxon Paganism* (Cambridge and Totowa, NJ, 1975) and 'The Scholarly Recovery of the Significance of Anglo-Saxon Records in Prose and Verse: a New Bibliography', *ASE* 9 (1981), 223–62. Finally, the literary historian should always bear in mind what has been lost to us: see especially R. M. Wilson, *The Lost Literature of Medieval England*, 2nd ed. (London, 1970).

6 General literary criticism

Various volumes of collected essays provide a general introduction to Old English literature. One such volume (now inevitably outdated in some respects) is *Continuations and Beginnings: Studies in Old English Literature*, ed. E. G. Stanley (London, 1966). Useful too is *Old English Literature in Context*, ed. J. D. Niles (Cambridge and Totowa, NJ, 1980). Two recent books range widely over the corpus of Old English prose and verse: B. C. Raw, *Anglo-Saxon Crucifixion Iconography and the Art of the Monastic Revival*, Cambridge Studies in Anglo-Saxon England 1 (Cambridge: 1990), and M. Clayton, *The Cult of the Virgin Mary in Anglo-Saxon England*, Cambridge Studies in Anglo-Saxon England 2 (Cambridge: 1990). For a study of the role of women in Old English literature, see J. Chance, *Woman as Hero in Old English Literature* (Syracuse, NY, 1986).

7 Poetry

Sources and analogues   M. J. B. Allen and D. G. Calder, *Sources and Analogues of Old English Poetry: the Major Latin Texts in Translation* (Cambridge and Totowa, NJ, 1976); D. G. Calder *et al.*, *Sources and Analogues of Old English Poetry, II: the Major Germanic and Celtic Texts in Translation* (Cambridge and Totowa, NJ, 1983).

General Essential Articles for the Study of Old English Poetry, ed. J. B. Bessinger and S. J. Kahrl (Hamden, CT, 1968); S. B. Greenfield, *The Interpreation of Old English Poems* (London and Boston, 1972); T. A. Shippey, *Old English Verse* (London, 1972); *Anglo-Saxon Poetry: Essays in Appreciation*, ed. L. E. Nicholson and D. W. Frese (Notre Dame, IN, 1975); B. Raw, *The Art and Background of Old English Poetry* (London, 1978); *Old English Poetry: Essays in Style*, ed. D. G. Calder (Berkeley, CA, 1979); K. O'B. O'Keeffe, *Visible Song: Transitional Literacy in Old English Verse*, Cambridge Studies in Anglo-Saxon England 4 (Cambridge, 1990). On rhetorical devices in Old English poetry, see J. J. Campbell, 'Knowledge of Rhetorical Figures in Anglo-Saxon Poetry', *Journal of English and Germanic Philology* 66 (1967), 1–20, and for onomastic wordplay in Old English there is a fundamental article by F. C. Robinson, 'The Significance of Names in Old English Literature', *Anglia* 86 (1968), 14–58. Two valuable studies of the language of Old English poetry are D. Donoghue, *Style in Old English Poetry: the Test of the Auxiliary* (New Haven, CT, 1987), and P. Clemoes, *Symbolic Action: Interactions between Thought and Language in Old English Poetry*, Cambridge Studies in Anglo-Saxon England (Cambridge, forthcoming).

Oral formulaic theory   F. P. Magoun, 'The Oral-Formulaic Character of Anglo-Saxon Narrative Poetry', *Speculum* 28 (1953), 446–67; A. B. Lord, *The Singer of Tales* (New York, 1960); L. D. Benson, 'The Literary Character of Anglo-Saxon Formulaic Poetry', *Proceedings of the Modern Language Association* 81 (1966), 334–41; J. Opland, *Anglo-Saxon Oral Poetry* (New Haven, CT, 1980); J. M. Foley, 'The Oral Theory in Context', in *Oral Traditional Literature: a Festschrift for Albert Bates Lord*, ed. J. M. Foley (Columbus, OH, 1981), pp. 27–122, and 'Literary Art and Oral Tradition in Old English and Serbian Poetry', *ASE* 12 (1983), 183–214.

Metre   The classic studies of Old English metre include E. Sievers, 'Old Germanic and Old English Metrics', trans. G. D. Luster, in *Essential Articles*, ed. Bessinger and Kahrl, pp. 267–88; J. C. Pope, *The Rhythm of Beowulf* (New Haven, CT, 1942); A. J. Bliss, *The Metre of 'Beowulf'* (Oxford, 1958) and *An Introduction to Old English Metre* (Oxford, 1962); and T. Cable, *The Metre and Melody of 'Beowulf'* (Urbana, IL, 1974). In recent years, however, there has been an explosion of interest in Old English metre, resulting in some important new studies: D. L. Hoover, *A New Theory of Old English Meter* (New York, 1985); G. Russom, *Old English Meter and Linguistic Theory* (Cambridge, MA, 1987); and C. B. Kendall, *The Metrical Grammar of Beowulf*, Cambridge Studies in Anglo-Saxon England 5 (Cambridge, 1991).

Collected editions and translations   The standard collected edition is ASPR, though this is hardly suitable for beginners. Various introductory guides (such as that by Mitchell and Robinson, listed above) contain editions of the most popular Old English poems; and an excellent introduction and edition of some of these is J. C. Pope, *Seven Old English Poems* (New York, 1966). There is a useful and fairly complete collection of Old English poetry in translation by S. A. J. Bradley, *Anglo-Saxon Poetry* (London, 1982). R. F. Hamer, *A Choice of Anglo-Saxon Verse* (London, 1960) contains texts with facing translations.

Individual Poems
(a) *Beowulf* The standard scholarly edition (which includes a vast assemblage
of notes and ancillary material) is *Beowulf and the Fight at Finnsburg*, ed. F.
Klaeber, 3rd ed. (Boston, 1950); a usable student edition is *Beowulf*, ed. C. L.
Wrenn, rev. W. F. Bolton (London, 1973). G. N. Garmonsway and J. Simpson,
Beowulf and its Analogues (London, 1968), provides translations of the major
historical and legendary texts relevant to the poem; as does R. W. Chambers,
Beowulf: an Introduction to the Study of the Poem, 3rd ed. rev. C. L. Wrenn
(Cambridge, 1959), though much of its discussion, particularly that on archae-
ology and genealogy, is now thoroughly out of date and must be used with
caution. For a bibliographical guide to studies of *Beowulf* up to 1969, see D. K.
Fry, *Beowulf and the Fight at Finnsburh: a Bibliography* (Charlottesville, VA,
1969). There is a useful anthology of essays on *Beowulf* ed. L. E. Nicholson, *An
Anthology of Beowulf Criticism* (Notre Dame, IN, 1963). Of the legion book-
length studies on *Beowulf*, the following deserve mention: D. Whitelock, *The
Audience of Beowulf* (Oxford, 1951); A. G. Brodeur, *The Art of Beowulf*
(Berkeley, CA, 1959); K. Sisam, *The Structure of Beowulf* (Oxford, 1965); E. B.
Irving, *A Reading of Beowulf* (New Haven, CT, 1968) and *Rereading Beowulf*
(Philadelphia, PA, 1989); J. D. Niles, *Beowulf: the Poem and its Tradition*
(Cambridge, MA, 1983); and F. C. Robinson, *Beowulf and the Appositive Style*
(Knoxville, TN, 1985). On the question of the date of *Beowulf*, which has been
vigorously debated in recent years, see *The Dating of Beowulf*, ed. C. Chase
(Toronto, 1981).

(b) *Other heroic poetry* There is a useful collection of the heroic poems by J.
Hill, *Old English Minor Poems* (Durham, 1983). Individual editions include
Deor, ed. K. Malone (London, 1933); *Finnsburh: Fragment and Episode*, ed.
D. K. Fry (London, 1974); *Waldere*, ed. A. Zettersten (Manchester and New
York, 1979); *Widsith*, ed. K. Malone, Anglistica 13 (Copenhagen, 1962), and see
also R. W. Chambers, *Widsith: a Study of Old English Heroic Legend* (Cam-
bridge, 1912); and *The Battle of Brunanburh*, ed. A. Campbell (London, 1938).

(c) *The Battle of Maldon* The text most widely in use is that by D. G. Scragg
(Manchester, 1981); valuable commentary is also found in E. D. Laborde,
Byrhtnoth and Maldon (London, 1936). A new text, with full apparatus of
scholarship by many hands, is *The Battle of Maldon A.D. 991*, ed. D. G. Scragg
and M. Deegan (Oxford, 1991). There is again a host of articles on the poem,
among which the following are perhaps most stimulating: M. J. Swanton, 'The
Battle of Maldon: a Literary Caveat', *Journal of English and Germanic Philology*
67 (1968), 441–50; J. E. Cross, 'Oswald and Byrhtnoth: a Christian Saint and a
Hero who is a Christian', *English Studies* 46 (1965), 93–109; H. Gneuss, *Die
'Battle of Maldon' als historisches und literarisches Zeugnis* (Munich, 1976) and
'The Battle of Maldon 89: Byrhtnod's *ofermod* Once Again', *Studies in Philology*
73 (1976), 117–37; R. Woolf, 'The Ideal of Men Dying with their Lord in the
Germania and in the *Battle of Maldon*', *ASE* 5 (1976), 63–81; and F. C.
Robinson, 'God, Death and Loyalty in *The Battle of Maldon*', in *J. R. R. Tolkien:*

Scholar and Storyteller, ed. M. Salu and R. T. Farrell (Ithaca, NY, and London, 1979), pp. 76–98.

(d) *Elegies*   There are editions of *The Wanderer* by R. F. Leslie (Manchester, 1966) and by T. P. Dunning and A. J. Bliss (London, 1969), of *The Seafarer* by I. L. Gordon (London, 1960), and of *The Wife's Lament, The Husband's Message* and *The Ruin* in *Three Old English Elegies*, ed. R. F. Leslie (Manchester, 1961). See D. Whitelock, 'The Interpretation of *The Seafarer*', in *The Early Cultures of Northwest Europe*, ed. B. Dickins and C. Fox (Cambridge, 1950), pp. 259–72; S. B. Greenfield, 'The Formulaic Expression of the Theme of Exile in Anglo-Saxon Poetry', *Speculum* 30 (1955), 200–6; E. G. Stanley, 'Old English Poetic Diction and the Interpretation of *The Wanderer, The Seafarer* and *The Penitent's Prayer*', *Anglia* 73 (1955), 413–66; G. V. Smithers, 'The Meaning of *The Seafarer* and *The Wanderer*', *Medium Ævum* 26 (1957), 137–53 and 28 (1959), 1–22 and 99–104; J. E. Cross, 'On the Genre of the *Wanderer*', *Neophilologus* 45 (1961), 63–75; P. A. M. Clemoes, '*Mens absentia cogitans* in *The Seafarer* and *The Wanderer*', in *Medieval Literature and Civilization: Studies in Memory of G. N. Garmonsway*, ed. D. Pearsall and R. A. Waldron (London, 1969), pp. 62–77; P. L. Henry, *The Early English and Celtic Lyric* (London, 1966); K. P. Wentersdorf, 'The Situation of the Narrator's Lord in *The Wife's Lament*', *Neuphilologische Mitteilungen* 71 (1970), 604–10; J. C. Pope, 'Second Thoughts on the Interpretation of *The Seafarer*', *ASE* 3 (1974), 75–86, and *The Old English Elegies: New Essays in Criticism and Research*, ed. M. Green (London and Toronto, 1983).

(e) *Biblical poetry*   There are separate editions of *Genesis A* by A. N. Doane (Madison, WI, 1978); of *Genesis B* by B. J. Timmer, *The Later Genesis* (Oxford, 1948); of *Exodus* by P. J. Lucas (London, 1977) and E. B. Irving (New Haven, CT, 1953); of *Daniel and Azarias* by R. T. Farrell (London, 1974); of *Judith* by B. J. Timmer, 2nd ed. (London, 1961); and of *Christ I* as *The Advent Lyrics of the Exeter Book*, ed. J. J. Campbell (Princeton, NJ, 1959). On scriptural poetry in general, see G. Shepherd, 'Scriptural Poetry', in *Continuations and Beginnings*, ed. Stanley, pp. 1–36, and R. Frank, 'Some Uses of Paronomasia in Old English Scriptural Verse', *Speculum* 47 (1972), 207–26. For individual poems, see F. C. Robinson, 'Notes on the Old English *Exodus*', *Anglia* 80 (1962), 373–8; R. Woolf, 'The Fall of Man in Genesis B and the Mystère d'Adam', in *Studies in Old English Literature in Honor of Arthur G. Brodeur*, ed. S. B. Greenfield (Eugene, OR, 1963), pp. 187–99; J. W. Earl, 'Christian Traditions in the Old English *Exodus*', *Neuphilologische Mitteilungen* 71 (1970), 541–70; J. F. Vickrey, '*Exodus* and the Battle in the Sea', *Traditio* 28 (1972), 119–40; R. T. Farrell, 'The Unity of the Old English *Daniel*', *Review of English Studies* 18 (1967), 117–35 and 'The Structure of Old English *Daniel*', *Neuphilologische Mitteilungen* 69 (1968), 533–59; A. W. Astell, 'Holofernes' Head: *tacen* and Teaching in the Old English *Judith*', *ASE* 18 (1989), 117–33; R. B. Burlin, *The Old English Advent: a Typological Commentary* (New Haven, CT, 1968); J. R. Hall, 'The Old English Epic of Redemption: the Theological Unity of Junius 11', *Traditio* 32 (1976), 185–208.

(f) *The Dream of the Rood*   There is a useful edition of *The Dream of the Rood* by M. Swanton (Manchester and New York, 1970). Individual studies include: R. Woolf, 'Doctrinal Influences on *The Dream of the Rood*', *Medium Ævum* 27 (1958), 137–53; J. A. Burrow, 'An Approach to *The Dream of the Rood*', *Neophilologus* 43 (1959), 122–33; M. Swanton, 'Ambiguity and Anticipation in *The Dream of the Rood*', *Neuphilologische Mitteilungen* 70 (1969), 407–25; E. Ó Carragáin, 'Crucifixion as Annunciation and the Relation of *The Dream of the Rood* to the Liturgy Reconsidered', *English Studies* 63 (1982), 487–505; C. B. Pasternack, 'Stylistic Disjunction in the *Dream of the Rood*', *ASE* 13 (1984), 167–86; E. B. Irving, 'Crucifixion Witnessed in *The Dream of the Rood*', in *Modes of Interpretation in Old English Literature: Essays in Honour of Stanley B. Greenfield*, ed. P. R. Brown, G. R. Crampton and F. C. Robinson (Toronto, 1986), pp. 101–13.

(g) *Cædmon*   C. L. Wrenn, 'The Poetry of Cædmon', *Proceedings of the British Academy* 32 (1946), 277–95; G. Shepherd, 'The Prophetic Cædmon', *Review of English Studies* 5 (1954), 113–22; K. Malone, 'Cædmon and English Poetry', *Modern Language Notes* 76 (1961), 193–5; F. P. Magoun, 'Bede's Story of Cædmon: the Case History of an Anglo-Saxon Oral Singer', *Speculum* 30 (1955), 49–63.

(h) *Cynewulf*   Editions include A. S. Cook, *The Christ of Cynewulf* (Boston, 1909); *Juliana*, ed. R. Woolf (London, 1965); *Elene*, ed. P. O. E. Gradon (London, 1958); and K. R. Brooks, *Andreas and the Fates of the Apostles* (Oxford, 1961). For studies of the poet, see D. G. Calder, *Cynewulf* (Boston, 1981) and E. Anderson, *Cynewulf: Structure, Style and Theme in his Poetry* (Rutherford, NJ, and Toronto, 1983).

(i) *Wisdom poetry*   Wisdom poetry is helpfully collected by T. A. Shippey, *Poems of Wisdom and Learning in Old English* (Cambridge and Totowa, NJ, 1976); see also R. J. Menner, *The Poetical Dialogues of Solomon and Saturn* (New York, 1941); C. Williamson, *The Old English Riddles of the Exeter Book* (Chapel Hill, NC, 1977); and M. Halsall, *The Old English Rune Poem: a Critical Edition* (Toronto, Buffalo and London, 1981).

7 Prose

A few standard pieces of Old English prose will appear in most introductory guides, but otherwise the student is obliged to consult standard scholarly editions, and it is to these that reference is made here. A brief but useful selection of Old English prose in translation is M. Swanton, *Anglo-Saxon Prose* (London, 1975). Some parts of the *Anglo-Saxon Chronicle* are trans. in *EHD*, and extracts from a number of Alfred's writings are trans. Keynes and Lapidge, *Alfred the Great*. For bibliography, see K. J. and K. P. Quinn, *A Manual of Old English Prose* (New York and London, 1990).

(a) *Alfredian and other ninth-century prose*   *King Alfred's West-Saxon Version of Gregory's Pastoral Care*, ed. H. Sweet, EETS os 45 and 50 (London, 1871);

King Alfred's Old English Version of Boethius De Consolatione Philosophiae, ed. W. J. Sedgefield (Oxford, 1899), of which there is a separate translation by Sedgefield, *King Alfred's Version of the Consolation of Philosophy done into Modern English* (Oxford, 1900); *King Alfred's Version of St Augustine's Soliloquies*, ed. T. A. Carnicelli (Cambridge, MA, 1969); *Liber Psalmorum: The West Saxon Psalms*, ed. J. W. Bright and R. L. Ramsay (Boston and London, 1907); *Bischofs Wærferth von Worcester Ubersetzung der Dialoge Gregors des Grossen*, ed. H. Hecht, Bibliothek der angelsächsischen Prosa 5 (Leipzig, 1900); *The Old English Version of Bede's Ecclesiastical History of the English People*, ed. T. Miller, EETS os 95 and 96 (London, 1890–1); *The Old English Orosius*, ed. J. Bately, EETS ss 6 (London, 1980); *An Old English Martyrology*, ed. G. Herzfeld, EETS os 116 (London, 1900). Studies include: F. A. Payne, *King Alfred and Boethius* (Madison, WI, 1968); W. H. Brown, 'Method and Style in the OE *Pastoral Care*', *Journal of English and Germanic Philology* 68 (1969), 666–84; K. Proppe, 'King Alfred's Consolation of Philosophy', *Neuphilologische Mitteilungen* 74 (1973), 635–48; J. M. Bately, *The Literary Prose of Alfred's Reign: Translation or Transformation* (London, 1980); J. M. Bately, 'Lexical Evidence for the Authorship of the Prose Psalms in the Paris Psalter', *ASE* 10 (1982), 69–95; J. S. Wittig, 'King Alfred's Boethius and its Latin Sources', *ASE* 11 (1983), 157–98; A. J. Frantzen, *King Alfred* (Boston, 1986); *Studies in Earlier Old English Prose*, ed. P. E. Szarmach (Albany, NY, 1986); J. M. Bately, 'Old English Prose before and during the Reign of King Alfred', *ASE* 17 (1988), 93–138 and E. G. Stanley, 'King Alfred's Prefaces', *Review of English Studies* 39 (1988), 349–64.

(b) *The Anglo-Saxon Chronicle*   The most widely quoted text of the *Anglo-Saxon Chronicle* is C. Plummer and J. Earle, *Two of the Saxon Chronicles Parallel*, 2 vols. (Oxford, 1892–9). This edition is slowly being replaced by the multi-volume edition *The Anglo-Saxon Chronicle: a Collaborative Edition*, ed. D. Dumville and S. Keynes; of this series two relevant volumes have appeared: *The Anglo-Saxon Chronicle MS A*, ed. J. Bately (Woodbridge, 1986) and *The Anglo-Saxon Chronicle MS B*, ed. S. Taylor (Woodbridge, 1983). There is a facsimile edition of MS A, ed. R. Flower and H. Smith, *The Parker Chronicle and Laws*, EETS os 208 (London, 1941). For studies of the prose of the *Chronicle*, see C. Clark, 'The Narrative Mode of the *Anglo-Saxon Chronicle*', in *England before the Conquest*, ed. Clemoes and Hughes, pp. 215–35; S. D. White, 'Kinship and Lordship in Early Medieval England: the Story of Sigeberht, Cynewulf and Cyneheard', *Viator* 20 (1980), 1–18.

(c) *Ælfric*   There is a useful bibliography on Ælfric by L. M. Reimsma, *Ælfric: an Annotated Bibliography* (New York and London, 1987). For individual works, see *The Homilies of the Anglo-Saxon Church: the First Part, containing the Sermones Catholici or Homilies of Ælfric*, ed. B. Thorpe, 2 vols. (London, 1844–6): contains the work usually known as Ælfric's *Catholic Homilies*, in two series; includes a facing translation. For the Second Series, a more recent edition is *Ælfric's Catholic Homilies: the Second Series, Text*, ed. M. Godden, EETS ss 5 (London, 1979). *Ælfric's Lives of Saints*, ed. W. W. Skeat, EETS os 76, 82, 94 and 114 (London, 1881–1900; repr. as two vols. 1966), with facing translation. *Homilies of Ælfric: a Supplementary Collection*, ed. J. C. Pope, EETS os 259 and

260 (London, 1967–8). The Old English translation of the Hexateuch which is partly by Ælfric and partly anonymous is ed. S. J. Crawford, *The Old English Version of the Heptateuch*, EETS os 160 (London, 1922), rev. N. R. Ker (London, 1969). On Ælfric, see D. Bethurum, 'The Form of Ælfric's Lives of Saints', *Studies in Philology* 29 (1932), 515–33; P. A. M. Clemoes, 'Ælfric', in *Continuations and Beginnings*, ed. Stanley, pp. 176–209; C. Clark, 'Ælfric and Abbo', *English Studies* 49 (1968), 30–6; J. Hurt, *Ælfric* (Boston, 1974); M. McC. Gatch, *Preaching and Theology in Anglo-Saxon England* (Toronto, 1977); *The Old English Homily and its Backgrounds*, ed. P. Szarmach and B. Huppe (Albany, NY, 1978); M. R. Godden, 'Ælfric's Saints' Lives and the Problem of Miracles', *Leeds Studies in English* 16 (1985), 83–100. On the form and sources of Ælfric's homily collections, see C. L. Smetana, 'Ælfric and the Early Medieval Homiliary', *Traditio* 15 (1959), 163–204, and 'Ælfric and the Homiliary of Haymo of Halberstadt', *Traditio* 17 (1961), 457–69.

(d) *Byrhtferth* *Byrhtferth's Manual*, ed. S. J. Crawford, EETS os 177 (London, 1929), with translation. See especially P. S. Baker, 'The OE Canon of Byrhtferth of Ramsey', *Speculum* 55 (1980), 22–37 and 'Byrhtferth's *Enchiridion* and the Computus in Oxford, St John's College 17', *ASE* 10 (1982), 123–42.

(e) *Wulfstan* The standard edition is *The Homilies of Wulfstan*, ed. D. Bethurum (Oxford, 1957), still to be supplemented by A. S. Napier, *Wulfstan: Sammlung der ihm zugeschriebenen Homilien nebst Untersuchungen über ihre Echtheit* (Berlin, 1883); the best known of Wulfstan's homilies is ed. separately by D. Whitelock as *Sermo Lupi ad Anglos* (London, 1939). On Wulfstan, see D. Whitelock, 'Archbishop Wulfstan, Homilist and Statesman', *Transactions of the Royal Historical Society* 24 (1942), 24–45; D. Bethurum, 'Wulfstan', in *Continuations and Beginnings*, ed. Stanley, pp. 210–46; A. McIntosh, 'Wulfstan's Prose', *Proceedings of the British Academy* 35 (1949), 109–42; O. Funke, 'Some Remarks on Wulfstan's Prose Rhythm', *English Studies* 43 (1962), 311–18; S. Hollis, 'The Thematic Structure of the *Sermo Lupi*', *ASE* 6 (1977), 175–95; and Gatch, *Preaching and Theology in Anglo-Saxon England*.

(f) *Anonymous prose* There is a substantial body of anonymous Old English prose; see in general D. G. Scragg, 'The Corpus of Vernacular Homilies and Prose Saints' Lives before Ælfric', *ASE* 8 (1979), 223–77. For the Vercelli Book homilies, see the complementary editions of M. Förster, *Die Vercelli-Homilien, I: I–VIII. Homilie* (Hamburg, 1932) and P. E. Szarmach, *Vercelli Homilies IX–XXIII* (Toronto, 1981), with the studies of D. G. Scragg, 'The Compilation of the Vercelli Book', *ASE* 2 (1973), 189–207, and R. E. Boenig, 'Andreas, the Eucharist and Vercelli', *Journal of English and Germanic Philology* 79 (1980), 313–31. For the Blickling Homilies, see the edition of R. Morris, *The Blickling Homilies of the Tenth Century* (London, 1874–80), with discussion by D. G. Scragg, 'The Homilies of the Blickling Manuscript', in *Learning and Literature in Anglo-Saxon England*, ed. Lapidge and Gneuss, pp. 299–316. The anonymous late Old English translation of the Latin romance *Apollonius* is ed. P. Goolden, *The Old English Apollonius of Tyre* (Oxford, 1958).

Index